THE RETRIEVAL OF THE BEAUTIFUL

Northwestern University

Studies in Phenomenology

and

Existential Philosophy

THE RETRIEVAL OF THE BEAUTIFUL

Thinking Through Merleau-Ponty's Aesthetics

Galen A. Johnson

Northwestern University Press
Evanston, Illinois

Northwestern University Press
www.nupress.northwestern.edu

Printed in the United States of America

10 9 8 7 6 5 4 3 2 1

Library of Congress Cataloging-in-Publication Data

Johnson, Galen A., 1948–

The retrieval of the beautiful : thinking through Merleau-Ponty's aesthetics / Galen A. Johnson.

p. cm. — (Northwestern University studies in phenomenology and existential philosophy)

Includes bibliographical references and index.

ISBN 978-0-8101-2564-3 (cloth : alk. paper) — ISBN 978-0-8101-2566-7 (pbk. : alk. paper)

1. Merleau-Ponty, Maurice, 1908–1961—Aesthetics. I. Title. II. Series: Northwestern University studies in phenomenology & existential philosophy.

B2430.M3764J64 2010

111'.85092—dc22

2009027736

∞ The paper used in this publication meets the minimum requirements of the American National Standard for Information Sciences—Permanence of Paper for Printed Library Materials, ANSI Z39.48–1992.

For my wife, Jean M. Johnson

Contents

Illustrations

Abbreviations

Works by Merleau-Ponty

AD	*Adventures of the Dialectic,* trans. Joseph Bien (Evanston, Ill.: Northwestern University Press, 1973)
AvD	*Les aventures de la dialectique* (Paris: Éditions Gallimard, 1955)
C	*Causeries, 1948,* text established and annotated by Stéphanie Ménasé (Paris: Éditions du Seuil, 2002)
"CD"	"Cézanne's Doubt," trans. Michael B. Smith, in *The Merleau-Ponty Aesthetics Reader: Philosophy and Painting,* ed. Galen A. Johnson (Evanston, Ill.: Northwestern University Press, 1993, 1998), 59–75
"DC"	"Le doute de Cézanne," in *Sens et non-sens* (Paris: Les Éditions Nagel, 1948, 1966), 15–44
"EM"	"Eye and Mind," trans. Michael B. Smith, in *The Merleau-Ponty Aesthetics Reader,* 121–49
EP	*Éloge de la philosophie* (Paris: Éditions Gallimard, 1953, 1960)
"ILVS"	"Indirect Language and the Voices of Silence," trans. Michael B. Smith, in *The Merleau-Ponty Aesthetics Reader,* 76–120
IP	*L'Institution, la passivité: Notes de cours au Collège de France (1954–1955),* text established by Dominique Darmaillacq, Claude Lefort, and Stéphanie Ménasé (Paris: Éditions Belin, 2003)
IPP	*In Praise of Philosophy and Other Essays,* trans. John Wild, James Edie, and John O'Neill (Evanston, Ill.: Northwestern University Press, 1963); includes *Themes from the Lectures at the Collège de France, 1952–1960*
N	*Nature: Course Notes from the Collège de France,* compiled and with notes by Dominique Séglard, trans. Robert Vallier (Evanston, Ill.: Northwestern University Press, 2003)

NC	*Notes de cours au Collège de France, 1959–1961,* preface by Claude Lefort, text established by Stéphanie Ménasé (Paris: Éditions Gallimard, 1996)
NN	*La Nature: Notes, cours du Collège de France* (Paris: Éditions Gallimard, 1995)
OE	*L'Oeil et l'esprit* (Paris: Éditions Gallimard, 1964)
PhP	*Phénoménologie de la perception* (Paris: Éditions Gallimard, 1945)
PM	*La prose du monde* (Paris: Éditions Gallimard, 1969)
"PNP"	"Philosophy and Non-Philosophy Since Hegel," trans. Hugh J. Silverman, in *Continental Philosophy I: Philosophy and Non-Philosophy Since Merleau-Ponty,* ed. Hugh J. Silverman (New York: Routledge, 1988), 9–83
PP	*Phenomenology of Perception,* trans. Colin Smith (London: Routledge and Kegan Paul, 1962)
PW	*The Prose of the World,* trans. John O'Neill (Evanston, Ill.: Northwestern University Press, 1973)
RC	*Résumés de cours (Collège de France, 1952–1960)* (Paris: Éditions Gallimard, 1968)
S	*Signs,* trans. Richard C. McCleary (Evanston, Ill.: Northwestern University Press, 1964)
SB	*The Structure of Behavior,* trans. Alden L. Fisher (Boston: Beacon, 1963)
SC	*La structure du comportement* (Paris: Presses Universitaires de France, 1942; 3rd ed. 1953)
SeNS	*Sens et non-sens* (Paris: Les Éditions Nagel, 1948; 5th ed. 1966)
Si	*Signes* (Paris: Éditions Gallimard, 1960)
SNS	*Sense and Non-Sense,* trans. Hubert L. Dreyfus and Patricia Allen Dreyfus (Evanston, Ill.: Northwestern University Press, 1964)
VI	*The Visible and the Invisible,* trans. Alphonso Lingis (Evanston, Ill.: Northwestern University Press, 1968)
VIn	*Le visible et l'invisible,* ed. Claude Lefort (Paris: Éditions Gallimard, 1964)
WP	*The World of Perception,* trans. Oliver Davis (London: Routledge, 2004); English translation of *Causeries, 1948*

ABBREVIATIONS

Works by Others

CJ — Immanuel Kant, *Critique of Judgment,* trans. Werner S. Pluhar (Indianapolis, Ind.: Hackett, 1987). Kant's *Critique of Judgment* will be cited in the text and notes as *CJ,* with the section number first and the page number following it, separated by a slash.

DPK — Paul Klee, *The Diaries of Paul Klee, 1898–1918,* ed. Felix Klee, trans. from the German authorized by Felix Klee (Berkeley: University of California Press, 1964); originally published as *Tagebücher von Paul Klee 1898–1918* (Cologne: Verlag M. DuMont Schauberg, 1957). Citations of Klee's *Diaries* will be cited in the text and notes as *DPK,* with the page number first and the entry number following it, separated by a slash.

Preface

Maurice Merleau-Ponty seldom spoke of beauty, yet his philosophy is about the beautiful. It is also about the sublime. That is the fundamental argument of this book. The beautiful is the depth, rhythm, and radiance of Being itself. The ontology of Flesh as element and the ontology of the Beautiful as elemental are folded together, for Desire, Love, and Beauty are part of the fabric of the world's element, Flesh itself, the term at which Merleau-Ponty arrived to replace Substance, Matter, or Life as the name of Being. Merleau-Ponty's philosophy extends the aesthetic realm, which since the time of Kant has meant a limited domain, over the entire realm of *aisthesis,* and the beautiful is enlarged as the entire realm of the sensible. Moreover, since aesthetic experience and the experience of love are interwoven in so many important ways, a certain sense of aesthetic desire is also part and parcel of the meaning of the Flesh-Beauty pairing. In a founding passage from *The Visible and the Invisible,* Merleau-Ponty wrote that "henceforth movement, touch, vision, applying themselves to the other and to themselves, return toward their source and, in the patient and silent labor of desire, begin the paradox of expression" (*VI* 144; *VIn* 189).

We are making this argument and developing its terms in a philosophical and artistic climate in which the beautiful has been pronounced useless, irrelevant, embarrassing, or dead. This has been said by the philosophers—Collingwood, Dewey, Dufrenne—and by the artists—Duchamp, Warhol, Newman. In an interview in 1968, Barnett Newman said: "About twenty-five years ago, for me painting was dead. There was the kind of painting that was trying to make the world look beautiful. . . . People were painting a beautiful world, and at that time we realized that the world wasn't beautiful."[1] Newman spoke for most in the art world when he wrote a short essay, "The Sublime Is Now," in which he argued that a contemporary concept of the sublime focused on experimentation and the event, rather than beauty, was the driving inspiration of contemporary artwork. Yet an examination of the reasons given for bifurcating the beautiful from the sublime—reasons given by Kant, Newman, and Lyotard—do not seem to hold up, and we must also speak of a beauty-sublime intertwining. That is another argument and conclusion at which we will arrive near the end of this study.

The word "retrieval" in our book's title is not to be taken to mean merely to repeat a history of philosophy and certain aesthetic tradition, but to repeat, review, and revise.[2] The English term "reenactment" may better capture this sense, or the marvelously complex French term *reprise,* for it also has the flavor of recapturing, retaking, or literally "grasping again" in the sense of renewal or revival—*prise, reprise, surprise.* The question that matters is therefore what beauty means now, if it means anything of import, in this place, at this time, at the onset of the twenty-first century. It is a question of the reworking, reenactment, or *reprise* of the tradition. The argument of this book is that it is a serious loss for philosophical thought, our lives with others, and our openness to the world and nature that throughout the twentieth century beauty has been a nearly completely neglected idea. Nevertheless, this very philosophical trope must itself be reworked and reconfigured in an altered cultural climate. Every culture owes it to itself to rethink and rework its tradition and fundamental philosophical ideas, discarding the chaff from the wheat, the skin from the grapes, and inventing new bread and wine.

Much of the trouble about beauty has been that its greatest philosophical spokespersons—Plato, Kant, Hegel, Santayana—developed its meaning in terms of purity, perfection, and permanence of form, devoid of desire and the expanse of emotions to which the experiences of beauty open us. Of these four, only Plato grasped the link between desire and the beautiful, but he construed the meaning of desire negatively as a lack or neediness, thus rendering beauty vulnerable to its critics. The judgment "this is beautiful" came to be seen as the effort to possess or grasp, if not a literal possession, then at least possession by the objectifying "gaze," thus demeaning and harming the aesthetic object. Merleau-Ponty's reflections on desire and the "paradox of expression" afford us the opportunity to think desire otherwise than negatively in terms of an *aisthesis* that is a surplus and opening to others, nature, and the world, a plentitude given in vision, touch, hearing, and the other sensory modalities that connects us with a kind of time that is not only our own personal past but a more originary, archaic, and mythical past and future that are our common humanity and heritage. This kind of aesthetic desire and perception is overlaid by the power of a material imaginary that is a "repetition without an original" in our own experience as we enjoy the attractions of wood, water, fire, clouds and sky, faces, bodies, children, and the patterns of nature. The sensible is our "element," and this is about depth and a fold in time in which past, present, and future are "simultaneous." Merleau-Ponty ended the third, last, and greatest of his aesthetic essays, titled "Eye and Mind," by saying that "we are never in a position to take stock of everything objectively or to think of progress in itself; and the whole of human history is, in a certain sense, stationary: . . . the very first painting in some sense went to the farthest reach of the future" ("EM" 149; *OE* 92). Speaking of the works of Rodin, Rilke began: "I come before you to remind you of your childhood. No, not of yours, but rather of all that ever was childhood. For it should be possible to awaken memories that are not yours, memories that are older than you."[3] *Aisthesis,* aesthetic desire, and material imaginary result in a kind of "clairvoyance," Merleau-Ponty tells us, that is the true meaning of the unconscious: "I did not know and I have always known it." This paradoxical yet true double formula sums up our experiences of the beautiful—and our experiences of love, too, for in the words of Merleau-Ponty, "love is a clairvoyance" (*IP* 75).

The first part of our book presents the dilemma about the "eclipse of beauty" in our times and then enters into a detailed and systematic study of Merleau-Ponty's aesthetic writings, especially "Eye and Mind." The second part argues that there are resources for developing the themes of a reconfigured notion of the beautiful in the writing and artwork of Paul Cézanne, Auguste Rodin, and Paul Klee. These are the three artists whose thought and work are stitched into the structure of "Eye and Mind" and who most influenced Merleau-Ponty's aesthetic thinking. Thus, we devote a chapter to each of them, seeking to explicate the leading ideas of their varying aesthetic thinking. Rainer Maria Rilke is important for us throughout, for it was Rilke who wrote two lengthy essays on Rodin, engaged in a correspondence with his wife, Clara, about Paul Cézanne's paintings published as *Letters on Cézanne,* and visited with Paul Klee (*DPK* 317/959). From these varied aesthetics emerge the fundamental themes of the retrieval of the beautiful: desire, repetition, difference, radiance, rhythm, and the sublime. The third part of our book takes each of these up in turn, steadily hewing our thinking closer to the lines and the colors of thought and writing that are the flesh and bones of Merleau-Ponty's ontology of the Flesh. We conclude in our final chapter with a direct dialogue of Kant with Merleau-Ponty, and also with Lyotard, on the subject of the beautiful and the sublime. As we experience with Rodin's *Balzac,* beauty and the sublime blend into one another when the beautiful grows powerful, majestic, mysterious, and transcendent. Merleau-Ponty concluded the important ontological part 4 of "Eye and Mind" with a phrase from Klee's *Diaries* that came to be inscribed as the epitaph on Klee's tomb:

"Diesseitig bin ich gar nicht fassbar." Merleau-Ponty gave the epitaph his own uniquely turned philosophical translation: "I cannot be grasped in immanence" ("Je suis insaisissable dans l'immanence"). The entire epitaph reads: "I cannot be grasped in the here and now. For I live just as well with the dead as with the unborn, somewhat closer to the heart of creation than usual, but far from close enough" (*DPK* p. 419).[4]

Acknowledgments

This work has been supported by many individuals and institutions to whom I am deeply grateful, and I wish to acknowledge them here all too inadequately and briefly. My study and research have been supported financially by a sabbatical leave awarded by the University of Rhode Island (URI) as well as a Summer Stipend from the National Endowment for the Humanities and a Franklin Research Grant from the American Philosophical Society, all in 2005. I am most grateful for their belief in this project. I thank Stephen Noble for my gracious introduction at the Bibliothéque Nationale–Site Richelieu and the *salle des manuscrits* to work with Merleau-Ponty's *inédits,* and his own deep scholarship on Merleau-Ponty, Husserl, and questions of expression. The Richard Beaupre Research Grant awarded from the University of Rhode Island Center for Humanities enabled travel and research at the Stiftung Zentrum Paul Klee in Bern, Switzerland. At the Paul Klee Zentrum archive, Dr. Christine Hopfengart has been extraordinarily welcoming and helpful, and I acknowledge her support here. Travel grants have also been received from the URI provost, M. Beverly Swan, the dean of the College of Arts and Sciences, Winifred Brownell, and the URI Alumni Association. I express my thanks to all of them.

Members of the International Merleau-Ponty Circle as well as the International Association for Philosophy and Literature, where portions of my text have been presented, have been most encouraging, supportive, and creatively critical. In particular, I single out Larry Hass, Edward S. Casey, Gail Weiss, Leonard Lawlor, Stephen Watson, Mauro Carbone, Hugh J. Silverman, Wayne Froman, William Hamrick, Randall Johnson, Helen Fielding, Véronique Fóti, Glen Mazis, Duane Davis, Ted Toadvine, James Morley, Ernie Sherman, Gary Madison, and Martin C. Dillon. I am honored by the memory that Mike Dillon (1939–2005) was present at my first presentation of some of these ideas at the conference of the Merleau-Ponty Circle held at Muhlenberg College in 2004. I thank Ed Casey for inviting me to share early stages of this project in his graduate seminar at Stony Brook University. I also thank colleagues in Europe for their invitations to present parts of this work at their Merleau-

Ponty centenary conferences in 2008: Gabrielle Hiltmann (University of Basel, Switzerland), Emmanuel de Saint Aubert (CNRS, École Normale Supérieure, Archives Husserl, Paris), and Etienne Bimbenet (Université Jean Moulin, Lyon, France). Their generosity and hospitality has been extraordinary.

It was a great privilege to teach a senior seminar at the University of Rhode Island on the theme of this book in spring 2006, and many of the eighteen members of that seminar made important and specific contributions. I thank all of them and want to single out in particular Michaela McCaughey, Erin Vachon, Dean Bond, Meredith Rathbun, Cortnee Connor, Laura Killingbeck, Keeghan Gilheeny, Dan Cummings, Robert Sutphen, Keely Barr, Micah Daigle, Robert Fryklund, and Kirk Benttinen. I am deeply grateful to Hugh J. Silverman, Vesela Sretenovic, and Bill Hochhausen, all of whom were special guest presenters in the seminar and shared their thinking and enthusiasm for the aesthetics of Merleau-Ponty. I thank Vesela Sretenovic, formerly curator of the David Winton Bell Gallery at Brown University and now at the Phillips Collection in Washington, D.C., for her insight into the contemporary art world, especially installation, and particularly for her Bell Gallery exhibition, "InVisible Silence," dedicated to Merleau-Ponty. Bill Hochhausen deserves my deep gratitude for his invitations for me to speak on these themes at the Pratt Art Institute and for our many conversations sharing his profound insight into the art of Cézanne, schooled not only by his reading and study of Cézanne and Merleau-Ponty, but also by his own artistic work as a sculptor, painter, and draftsman. I owe a debt of gratitude to my former philosophy student at the University of Rhode Island, now a professor of philosophy in his own right, Bryan Bannon, who helped me launch this project as my research assistant in summer 2004 and shared in many of its earliest bibliographic and textual discoveries. I also thank my faculty colleagues at the University of Rhode Island who have supported this project through discussion and listening to its presentation; I thank, in particular, Richard McIntyre, Cheryl Foster, Lynn Pasquerella, Stephen Barber, Jennifer Jones, Alain-Philippe Durand, Naomi Mandel, Ryan Trimm, and Donald Zeyl. Don Zeyl has assisted me with some points of Greek grammar and translation. At URI, I also thank Judith Tolnick, former director of the Fine Art Center Galleries, and Linda Mugica, curator of the Fine Arts Slide Collection, for their detective work in securing art images and permissions. To my friends at Northwestern University Press who have lent their expertise and support to make this project a reality, a thousand thanks: Tony Steinbock, Henry Carrigan, Jenny Gavacs, Marianne Jankowski, Paul Mendelson, Rudy Faust, and Paul Fermin.

I thank those nearest my heart, my family and close friends. Among five brothers, all of whom have been encouraging, I have had the good luck that my brother Tim is a professor of classics at the University of Florida and has been helpful on this project on some of the points where it intersects with classical languages, literature, and mythology. I thank my good friend, Albert Silverstein, for team-teaching seminars in which some of these ideas were worked out and for our many philosophical conversations on these themes. I thank my good colleague and friend, Michael Smith, for his expert assistance with French translation and his own deep understanding of Merleau-Ponty's aesthetics. My deepest thanks is for my wife, Jean, and my children, Renee, Toby, and Marjorie, all of whom have given me their encouragement and shared their ideas. For Renee, she will find memories of the beauty of African desert landscapes and sunsets we have shared, and for Toby, memories of the art and sites of Paris we experienced together. To Marjorie, I have had the uncanny double experience of being both father and professor, which is an unexpected blessing and joy. She has shared in the excitement of discovery as this work has unfolded, and her interest in it as well as in philosophy and art history has provided much inspiration. My wife, Jean, has traveled with me to France, Germany, and Switzerland to do this research, has listened to my talks and presentations in Allentown, Helsinki, Strasbourg, Washington, D.C., Chicago, Basel, and Paris, and has given me wise feedback and guidance as the book was under way. She is not a professional philosopher—building housing to provide shelter and care for homeless and poor people is her mission and career—but she loves philosophy and now knows a great deal about the philosophy of Merleau-Ponty. She has been my most important reader, interlocutor, and philosophical friend. To her this book is dedicated, with humble gratitude.

Finally, I am grateful to the philosopher Maurice Merleau-Ponty (1908–1961), whose writings and thought have guided my work for more than twenty-five years, and who has become to me more than a teacher and philosophical guide, more like an older brother, though we never met. I am grateful for conversations with several philosophical friends who did know him in person: Forrest Williams, Jacques Taminiaux, Paul Ricoeur, and Claude Lefort. Of these, I thank in particular Paul Ricoeur and Claude Lefort, who assisted me with guidance and introductions on my very first sabbatical leave to study the writings of Merleau-Ponty in Paris in 1983–84, who remained friends, and whose writings remain an inspiration. As I came to the end of this work, I realized that the last chapter was not really an "ending" and that this work will continue in one form or another, very likely more beauty, definitely more Merleau-Ponty, whose works, though left so incomplete, have a richness and openness thereby that calls for their continuance in others.

THE RETRIEVAL OF THE BEAUTIFUL

Part 1

Thinking Through Merleau-Ponty's Aesthetics

1

Beauty in Eclipse

> Beauty—that is, the love of ideal sensations—creates in us today sheer physical embarrassment.
>
> —Barnett Newman, "The New Sense of Fate"

> As an attuning, beauty thoroughly determines the state of mankind.
>
> —Martin Heidegger, "Rapture as Form-Engendering Force"

The disappearance in our times of the concept of the beautiful from philosophical reflection is a profound loss. It has abandoned us to the dangers of bifurcated thinking and living: thinking in which the separation of subject from object dominates philosophy and science, and living in which humans are separated from nature and from one another. The philosophical dualism of subject and object underlies the divisions in Western civilization between spirit and matter, self and world, mind and body, humans and animals, nature and technology, landscape and property, domination and dominated. By contrast, the experience of the beautiful transcends the subject-object dichotomy, and in it both union and difference are philosophically integrated. Other domains of experience may ultimately lead beyond epistemic and metaphysical dualism as well—the experiences of truth and of goodness, for example—but these are riven with immediate divisions between the true and false, between good and evil, whereas the beautiful is neither purely subjective nor purely objective but occupies that in-between that is the interworld, the intersubjective, the intercorporeal. It may strike us that beauty also is riven with bifurcation, for example between the beautiful and the ugly, and is merely another way for subjects to separate, classify, and dominate objects. In fact, as we will shortly see, the confusion of beauty with hierarchies of perfection has fueled much of the critique of beauty in our times. However, it is not the ranking and conceptualization of the beautiful and its distinction from the ugly that is of immediate concern in this book, but the experience of the beautiful itself that is beyond any concept, and where we discover a "pleasure of reflection" or appreciation of the world and of others that is the signature of a unique openness to the world and the other in thinking and living.

This is the "puzzle" about the beautiful that initiated Kant's *Critique of Judgment.* What Kant calls a judgment of taste, which means the aesthetic judgment regarding the beautiful, occupies a curious "strange and different" space in between pure subjectivity and pure objectivity (*CJ* 7/41). On the one hand, the judgment is rooted not in concepts, but in a subjective feeling of pleasure. As such, it does not add any genuine information about the thing in question, be it nature or a work of art, for this would require the structure of the theoretical understanding within which a particular is subsumed under a given rule or universal. As Kant puts it, a unique feature of aesthetic judgments is that "these judgments do not by themselves contribute anything whatever to our cognition of things" (*CJ* preface/6). On the other hand, though they are rooted in the subjective feeling of pleasure and as such are *conceptless,* yet judgments of the beautiful bear an urgency that requires others—Kant contends *everyone*—to concur or agree with the judgment. To give but simple examples, if one describes the particular form of a butterfly or goldfinch in flight, or Cézanne's late Mt. Sainte-Victoire watercolors or a performance of Bach's *Goldberg Variations,* as beautiful, this is an expression of personal pleasure and delight at the same time as it "invites" another into this same experience. Again, in Kant's language: "What is strange and different about a judgment of taste is only this: that what is to be connected with the presentation of the object is not an empirical concept but a feeling of pleasure (hence no concept at all), though, just as if it were a predicate connected with cognition of the object, this feeling is nevertheless to be required of everyone" (*CJ* 7/31). Though Kant overstates the range of this "everyone" into a presumed universality of aesthetic judgment, we are persuaded that the experience of beauty combines features of both subjectivity and objectivity; it occupies a space in between this bifurcation, or perhaps we should even say *prior to* the division between the purely subjective and the completely objective. What is gained from this unique presence to the world and to others is a peculiar, remarkable openness that is not found in theoretical understanding or in the ethical imperatives of practical reason. Beauty opens us up to the world and others in a way available nowhere else in the range of our powers as human beings.

Aesthetic judgment, Kant writes, "compensates" the philosopher "by revealing to him a property of our cognitive power which without this analysis would have remained unknown" (*CJ* 8/57). In a beautiful commentary on this Kantian insight, Hagi Kenaan has written that

> though Kant understands that unless he could bring the judgment of taste under unifying principles it would threaten the cohesiveness of his project, he remains committed to elaborating the intuition (the discovery) that the form of our encounter with the beautiful is truly unique, that with beauty we open up to meaning (to the meaningfulness of the world) in a manner that is out of the ordinary in terms of our common patterns of engaging the intelligible.[1]

Also commenting on these matters in the context of his lectures on Nietzsche, Heidegger stated the essential point: "By having a feeling for beauty the subject has already come out of himself; he is no longer subjective, no longer a subject. On the other side, beauty is not something at hand like an object of sheer representation. . . . The aesthetic state is neither subjective nor objective."[2] Kant and Heidegger here give us the essential theme of this study. We will be developing our philosophical reflection on the beautiful primarily through the thought and writings of the French philosopher Maurice Merleau-Ponty, for it is our view that no other philosopher has gone further in developing an original ontology beyond the dualism of subject and object. This book will think through the ontology and aesthetics of Merleau-Ponty for the retrieval of the beautiful, and our theme is the experience of the beautiful beyond the subject-object divide.

Artists and philosophers today write and speak of the beautiful as if it is a concept and experience from another time, a time of the eighteenth century when the beautiful commanded the analysis of Burke and Kant. Artists and philosophers now speak of beauty as embarrassing and irrelevant. Is beauty dead, with all the repercussions for living and thinking which that death would entail? Has the twentieth century initiated an epoch of the death of beauty as the nineteenth century and Nietzsche's own thinking initiated the epoch of the death of God? At the beginning of this study seeking the retrieval and reconfiguration of the beautiful, it would be important to listen to an artist and a philosopher explain their distaste for the beautiful and its eclipse by other concerns, especially the sublime.

Barnett Newman and Jean-François Lyotard have developed an anti-aesthetic that erases the beautiful, or even more strongly, seeks to destroy it, in favor of an aesthetic of the sublime that is thought more relevant to the artistic experimentation of our times. Only three years after Merleau-Ponty published his first essay about modern art titled "Cézanne's Doubt" in 1945, Barnett Newman in New York City painted his signature breakthrough artwork titled *Onement I,* a work of severe nonfigurative minimalism. The painting presented a narrow orange band vertically bisecting a red-brown rectangle approximately in the center of the rectangle; it is a painting of very modest size (27 × 16 inches) and is rudimentary in execution. Newman's was not the kind of artwork that Merleau-Ponty made central to his philosophy of painting; the latter preferred to develop his aesthetics in relation to the artwork of Paul Cézanne, Vincent Van Gogh, Henri Matisse, Paul Klee, Auguste Rodin, and several other French and European artists. Several of us have argued that Merleau-Ponty's aesthetics could well be extended to incorporate abstraction in general and abstract expressionism such as Newman's in particular.[3] Nevertheless, it was Lyotard's 1984 essay entitled "The Sublime and the Avant-Garde," as well as his "Newman: The Instant," that brought philosophical attention to the paintings of Barnett Newman for enabling Lyotard's own aesthetic theory of the sublime.[4] In a later chapter of this study, we will attend in much more detail to that aesthetic and the feeling of the sublime, together with its linkages with the experience of the beautiful.

For Newman working in the 1940s, '50s, and '60s, together with the other members of the now-classic school of New York abstract expressionism—Rothko, Motherwell, Pollock, de Kooning, Still, and others—the problem of subject matter was everything. After the horrors of two world wars and a depression, in an American culture now beset by a consumerism no longer disguised, including the commodification of the artwork itself, what could be painted now? "It was impossible at that time to paint the kind of painting that we were doing—flowers, reclining nudes, and people playing the cello. . . . So that we actually began, so to speak, from scratch, as if painting were not only dead but had never existed."[5] Unwilling as well to turn to an aesthetic of sensations as had the later Cézanne or the cubists, the outcome for Newman and his colleagues was a radical break with the history of European painting and a turn toward rigorous nonfigurative composition based only on the minimums of color, line, and the principles of geometry and biomorphic, organic forms and shapes.

I have chosen to begin my discussion of the eclipse of the beautiful with Barnett Baruch Newman not only because his views are so extreme, and not only because I find *Onement I* and so much of his artwork personally quite moving, but because he theorized his art so rigorously and persistently, taking every advantage of his education as a philosophy major at the City College of New York, including study of his namesake,

Baruch Spinoza, as well as the Kabbalist tradition. We have many Newman essays in aesthetics such as "The Sublime Is Now," "Prologue for a New Esthetic," and "The First Man Was an Artist." Newman even involved himself in an extended public dispute with the art historian Erwin Panofsky regarding the etymological origins of the Latin title of his painting *Vir Heroicus Sublimis.*[6] In these writings, Newman articulated his own difficulties with the aesthetic of the beautiful precisely in terms of this post-World War II moral crisis of subject matter. The fact of the matter is that several decades before Newman, skepticism about beauty had crystallized in the art world of the 1920s through Marcel Duchamp's turn away from what he called "retinal art" to conceptual art together with his ready-mades. His *Fountain,* a urinal as ready-made artwork, was shown alongside other works of modern art in the 1917 Society of Independent Artists exhibition in New York.[7] Early in the century, the irrelevance of beauty had become an established current of the twentieth-century art world.

In the world of philosophy too, Lyotard had been preceded by the skepticism of Dewey and Collingwood, both of whom eliminated the term "beauty" from their aesthetic thinking as early as the 1930s. In *The Principles of Art,* Collingwood wrote that there has been a determined attempt to make beauty "stand for that quality in things in virtue of which when we contemplate them we enjoy what we recognize as an aesthetic experience. There is no such quality."[8] Collingwood's abolition was preceded by four years in John Dewey's *Art as Experience:* "Beauty is properly an emotional term," which has "unfortunately been hardened into a peculiar object; emotional rapture has been subjected to what philosophy calls hypostatization, and the concept of beauty as an essence of intuition has resulted . . . it is surely better to deal with the experience itself and show whence and how the quality proceeds."[9] Mikel Dufrenne took a similar road in his *Phenomenology of Aesthetic Experience:* "We shall avoid invoking the concept of the beautiful, because it is a notion which, depending on the extension we give it, seems either useless for our purposes or dangerous." Dufrenne explains that too narrow an understanding of the term is inevitably rooted in ancient Greek classicism and produces an arbitrary and sterile dogmatism. If the understanding of the term is broadened to include Enlightenment and Romantic conceptions, the notion "ceases to be dangerous only to become useless: it names rather than solves the problem."[10] When George Santayana published *The Sense of Beauty* in 1896, he could not have known that the nineteenth century would mark the end of systematic and serious treatment of the beautiful in Western thought, that the concept and entire problematic would simply drop out of twentieth-century philosophy.

Indeed, in the popular literature beauty has gone into eclipse as passé and sterile, commonly regarded as one of the most transcendental of concepts and therefore a throwback to the imposition of the allegedly universal and necessary upon what is diverse, multiple, individual, and cultural. One finds works like Naomi Wolf's *The Beauty Myth,* which elaborates in detail how images of beauty have been used to objectify women in everything from work and religion to body types, food, sex, and pornography.[11] Paul C. Taylor has accused the aesthetic of beauty of racist aestheticism, captured by Toni Morrison in *The Bluest Eye* as well as in what Taylor called the "straight hair rule" of beauty resulting in practices such as Malcolm X's hair-straightening conk.[12] Michel Foucault, in "Friendship as a Way of Life," has said that one of the reasons our society refuses to understand homosexuality as anything deeper, richer, and more complex than an immediate fifteen-minute sexual gratification is that trivializing homosexuality in this way "responds to a reassuring canon of beauty" in which, presumably, beauty circulates only throughout the male-female relationship in sexual attraction and attractiveness.[13] In "Enter the Dragon: On the Vernacular of Beauty," Dave Hickey argues that beauty is disdained by artists because it has become associated with the "corruption of the market." Art dealers traffic in objects and appearances and, simply put, "beauty sells." It sells commodities like cars and clothes in the world of advertising, but it also sells art as the kind of attractive commodity sought by collectors and dealers.[14] An exhibition was mounted in March 2005 at the Boston Museum of Fine Arts called "Speed, Style, and Beauty" and featuring cars from 1929 to 1996, from Bugatti to Porsche, many owned by the designer Ralph Lauren. Included were the 1929 Bentley Blower from Ian Fleming's original James Bond novels, the Mercedes-Benz 300SL Gullwing Coupe favored by Sophia Loren and Zsa Zsa Gabor, and the 1955 Porsche 550 Spyder, the model of car that James Dean was driving when he suffered his fatal car accident. The artistic and philosophic rejections of beauty, together with its commercial and celebrity exploitation, do indeed demand a hesitation, a halting of any headlong rush toward recovery (*reprise*) of the concept of beauty when it has been reduced to such trivialization and philosophic silence.

We do have a recent literature attempting to restore or at least reconsider beauty's status. This begins with the 1984 study of Kant and post-Kantian aesthetics by Mary Mothersill titled *Beauty Restored,* and continues with Elaine Scarry's study of the politics and ethics of beauty entitled *On Beauty and Being Just* (1999), originally delivered as the Tanner Lecture on Human Values at Yale University in 1998. Arthur Danto has been immersed in this debate for some years now, culminating in his 2003 Paul Carus Lectures published as *The Abuse of Beauty: Aesthetics and the Concept of Art.*[15] Within the Continental tradition, we have Hans-Georg Gadamer's extended essay on "The Relevance of the Beautiful" (1986), and within Merleau-Ponty studies, Stephen Watson has recently published an essay on Paul Klee's *Notebooks* and *Diaries* in relation to Heidegger, Adorno, and Merleau-Ponty and titled "On the Withdrawal of the Beautiful." Umberto Eco's anthology of the *History of Beauty* (2004) is a remarkable contribution.[16]

Two art exhibitions have also added weight to the notion of a new life for the concept of the beautiful. "Regarding Beauty: A View of the Late 20th Century," organized by the Hirshhorn Museum of the Smithsonian Institution in 1999 in Washington, D. C., presented an array of ninety works to argue that beauty has not disappeared from the dialogue of art and is an essential part of the evolution of art in the twentieth century. The exhibition featured works from the 1960s by well-known artists, such as Roy Lichtenstein's *Sinking Sun* (1964) and Sigmar Polke's *Bunnies* (1966), but also work from the 1980s and '90s by Cindy Sherman, Janine Antoni, Gerhard Richter, and Beverly Semmes.[17] The Fifth Istanbul Biennial in spring 1998 mounted an important exhibition titled "Life, Beauty, Translations and Other Differences."

Nevertheless, it is apparent that the aesthetic of the beautiful in the contemporary climate is a topic fraught with dangers. In this regard, let us say at the outset that what will be at stake here is less restoring an old philosophical tradition and theme than attempting to articulate what is at stake within it.[18] The term "retrieval" is not to be taken to mean an archaic history of a past that is dead and gone, but what Heidegger meant by authentic or "proper historicality" based upon the temporal template of past-present-future: not merely to repeat, but to repeat, review, and revise, as we have mentioned in our preface. The English term "reenactment" may better capture this sense of Heidegger's German term *Wierderholung.* Heidegger's *Being and Time,* in its early section on the history of ontology, says that the past "is not something which *follows along* after Dasein, but something which already goes ahead of it." Or in the same paragraph: "Dasein 'is' its past in the way of *its* own Being, which, to put it roughly, 'historizes' out of its future on each occasion."[19] Commenting on Heidegger in his chapter on "Temporality" in *Phenomenology of Perception,* Merleau-Ponty summarized the Heideggerian meaning this way: "The future is not posterior to the past, or the past anterior to the present. Temporality temporalizes itself as future-which-lapses-into-the-past-by-coming-into-the-present" (*PP* 420; *PhP* 480–81). All hyphens: future-past-present. Later Merleau-Ponty puts it in his own terms: "The past, therefore, *is* not past, nor the future future. . . . A past and a future spring forth when I reach out towards them [*je m'étends vers eux*]. I am not, for myself, at this very moment, I am also at this morning or at the night which will soon be here, and though my present is, if we wish so to consider it, this instant, it is equally this day, this year, or my whole life." Shortly after this text Merleau-Ponty says: "I am myself time" (*PP* 421; *PhP* 481).

The question that matters is therefore what beauty means now, if it means anything of import, in this place, at this time, at the onset of the twenty-first century. It is a question of the reworking, reenactment, or *reprise* of the tradition. The argument of this book is that there is, indeed, a great deal of import at stake; there is an effort at thinking and living beyond the subject-object divide, for, as Heidegger states in the second epigraph of this chapter, in our attunement to beauty much about "the state of mankind" is determined. The sense of integration between self and world that marks the aesthetic also establishes genuine community of oneself with others, and therefore a protest against fragmentation, isolation, and boredom or despair. This may not be as obvious in the arts of painting and sculpture that Merleau-Ponty made the focus of his aesthetic thinking, but it is obvious if one brings to mind the art of music and its power to establish identities and blend personalities and peoples, both for the performers and participants as well as for listeners. The role of music in Merleau-Ponty's aesthetic and ontological thinking has long been underestimated, and the musical theme will be part of our discovery and trajectory: in relation to Paul Klee's musical paintings, and in relation to Merleau-Ponty's conception of the beautiful as a certain "radiant image" and "particular *rhythm,*" as he puts it in a passage from *The World of Perception* (*WP* 99; *C* 58). There is much work to do, first in analyzing and interpreting "Eye and Mind," next in studying the aesthetic thinking of "Merleau-Ponty's artists"—Cézanne, Rodin, and Klee—and finally in working somewhat systematically, architecturally, toward a philosophy of the beautiful, though one always hesitates more toward fragments with a thought as elusive as the beautiful: desire, repetition, difference, radiance, rhythm, pleasure, and the sublime. In thinking through Merleau-Ponty, we will seek a retrieval of the beautiful.

2

Thinking Through "Eye and Mind"

What I am trying to convey to you is more mysterious; it is entwined in the very roots of being, in the impalpable source of sensations.

—Joachim Gasquet, *Cézanne,* cited by Merleau-Ponty in "Eye and Mind"

The eye . . . through which the beauty of the universe is revealed to our contemplation is of such excellence that whoever should resign himself to losing it would deprive himself of the knowledge of all the works of nature.

—Leonardo da Vinci, *Treatise on Painting,* cited by Merleau-Ponty in "Eye and Mind"

"Thinking through" Merleau-Ponty's aesthetics means, first, giving his aesthetics a careful, detailed, and systematic reading, and, second, moving through his aesthetic thinking as a trajectory or vector for thinking about aesthetics today and the current controversy regarding the eclipse and retrieval of the beautiful. We find no direct aesthetic of the beautiful in Merleau-Ponty's writings, only glimpses here and there nested within his broader phenomenology and ontology of perception (*aisthesis*). This leaves to us the retrieval of the beautiful from this philosophy of *aisthesis* and the late ontology, as well as from the sources with which he was working, particularly the aesthetic texts of Cézanne, Rodin, and Klee. The questions that drew Merleau-Ponty to the study of modern art were located elsewhere than our theme of the beautiful: what is the meaning of painting for understanding human perception; for understanding history, expression, and language; and for understanding immanence, transcendence, and the deep structure of reality? Merleau-Ponty deployed the study of modern art as something like a laboratory to energize his overall philosophical thinking in much the same way modern science energized the philosophies of the Renaissance and Enlightenment. Each of these three sets of questions motivated three essays on the meaning of modern art across the philosopher's career: "Cézanne's Doubt" (1945) on the phenomenology of human perception; "Indirect Language and the Voices of Silence" (1952) with its response to Malraux's views on history, Sartre's theory of literature, and Saussure's structuralism; and "Eye and Mind" (1960) with its original ontological ideas of chiasm, reversibility, dehiscence, *écart* (gap, spread), and Flesh (*la chair*).

No doubt Merleau-Ponty's signature contribution to aesthetics, and the last work he saw published before his early death in 1961, is "Eye and Mind," and that work will be our primary focus here. Taken together, the three aesthetic essays exhibit two quite remarkable and distinctive features: the arts are the gateway for philosophical thought above the physical sciences; and modern art, more than classical or Renaissance art, uniquely merges with the effort of phenomenology "by reason of the same kind of attentiveness and wonder, the same demand for awareness," as Merleau-Ponty wrote in the preface to *Phenomenology of Perception* (*PP* xvi; *PhP* xxi).

To understand something of what we mean by saying that Merleau-Ponty used his study of modern art to fuel his philosophy, we can consider the chronology of his work on *The Visible and the Invisible.* As is now well known, upon Merleau-Ponty's death the new ontology was left unfinished. It was published posthumously in its fragmentary condition by Claude Lefort as *The Visible and the Invisible* (1964) together with selections from Merleau-Ponty's rich working notes (*notes de travail*); these comprise 112 pages in the published text, which Lefort selected from the 386 handwritten pages of Merleau-Ponty's working notes.[1] Merleau-Ponty wrote chapters 1–3 of *The Visible and the Invisible* from March to June 1959, then took a sixteen-month hiatus, during which we have only his working notes for that book, before writing the rich and evocative chapter 4: "The Intertwining—The Chiasm." In chapter 4 we find the philosophical advances, thought, and vocabulary that are years ahead of us still and that gave fertile inspiration to much in French philosophy in the years to follow in the work of Foucault, Lyotard, Derrida, Deleuze, Irigaray, and others. Recently Jacques Derrida, even while expressing hesitations and counterarguments, also expressed his high regard for *The Visible and the Invisible* for giving us "pages so strong, so alive, which have contributed so much to open a pathway for the thinking of its time, and our time."[2] During that sixteen-month interim before writing chapter 4 of *The Visible and the Invisible,* Merleau-Ponty worked on "Eye and Mind" and the philosophy of modern art, and we find many of the key ontological ideas from that highly original, unfinished chapter of *The Visible and the Invisible* being worked out in "Eye and Mind"; for example, the central ideas of depth and Flesh. He also produced other crucial essays during the sixteen-month interim, including "Bergson in the Making" (May 1959), "The Philosopher and His Shadow" (October 1959) which is a rich study of Husserl, and the preface to *Signs,* part 1 (February 1960) and part 2 (September 1960). Each of these is deep and important, and each also provides the context within which "Eye and Mind" developed. Yet it is not too much to say that "Eye and Mind" was the centerpiece of Merleau-Ponty's studies that provided the hinge between chapters 1–3 and chapter 4 of *The Visible and the Invisible.* Moreover, we find that the essay was the focal point of Merleau-Ponty's writing during the summer of 1960 and that there were preparatory notes, reading notes, and three complete drafts of the work in manuscript prior to the published version; the first two drafts were in handwriting and the third was in typescript.[3] "Eye and Mind" is, indeed, a focal work, a prolonged and careful work, the key to Merleau-Ponty's late philosophical itinerary, and thereby one of the central keys to understanding twentieth-century aesthetics and philosophy.

The Earlier Aesthetic Essays

Before undertaking a systematic reading of "Eye and Mind," some brief comment on the two earlier essays will be helpful. In "Cézanne's Doubt," Merleau-Ponty was interested in Cézanne for his attempts to paint the "lived" pre-scientific experience of the world as a painterly analogue to phenomenological "seeing." *Epochē* had been Edmund Husserl's word for the famous phenomenological reduction, suspension, or bracketing of the "natural attitude," which is that taken-for-granted habitual assumption that the world exists as objects "out there" separate from its reflection in consciousness "in here." Husserl's phenomenology bracketed out this habitual assumption in order to engage in description of experience as it is lived, not as it is "objectively ordered." The natural attitude leads us into a "commonsense" metaphysics of something like "naive realism" that defeats phenomenological wonder at our experience of the world. There are all the implications of Husserl's transcendental idealism here, a discussion that would take us far afield, but what is important for understanding Merleau-Ponty and Cézanne is that Merleau-Ponty had qualified his endorsement of Husserl's *epochē* in the *Phenomenology of Perception* by writing, in one of the most famous passages from its preface, that "the most important lesson which the reduction teaches us is the impossibility of a complete reduction" (*PP* xiv; *PhP* viii). Nevertheless, Merleau-Ponty was still struck by Cézanne's insistence on a peculiar kind of "germinating" (*germinait*) with nature in which the artist comes to be present "at the world" (*l'être au monde*). The landscape "thinks itself in me" (*se pense en moi*), Cézanne would say. A remnant of the *epochē* appears as well in "Eye and Mind" as Merleau-Ponty would even go so far as to accord to the painter a unique privilege above the philosopher, the scientist, and the writer: "Only the painter is entitled to look at everything without being obliged to appraise what he sees" ("EM" 123; *OE* 14). Merleau-Ponty probably goes too far when he writes that "art and only art" draws upon the fabric of brute meaning "in full innocence," and when he asserts a correlative "secret science" of the painter ("EM" 123; *OE* 13, 15), but in his zeal we understand the fascination, the challenge, and the demand of the painterly vocation for phenomenological philosophy and any philosophy that seeks to experience and know the world. In other words and in plain language, if we are fascinated by modern painting and sculpture, we must ask ourselves what it is about the artist's eye that enables such penetrating vision and provocative visions.

What interested Merleau-Ponty most profoundly about Cézanne was the artist's ability to "work with doubt." Cézanne was beset with "moments of doubt" about his vocation. "As he grew old, he wondered whether the novelty of his painting might not come from trouble with his eyes, whether his whole life had not been based upon an accident of his body." He doubted his talent and did not dare ask his father for support ("CD" 59–60; "DC" 15–16). The critics were after him too, as we know all too well. In "Cézanne's Doubt," Merleau-Ponty cited these sorts of attacks by the critics: "The hesitation or muddle-headedness of his contemporaries equaled this strain and self-doubt. 'The painting of a drunken privy cleaner,' said a critic in 1905.'" "Cézanne's Doubt" continues to speak of Cézanne's uncertainty, his not knowing, his forgetting, his ignorance and his shadows, his isolation and solitude, and his increasing hostility toward the public and rudeness with his friends and models. Cézanne suffered from religious doubts too. After the death of his mother, he found life terrifying and began to practice a Pascal's wager sort of religion: "I feel I will be on earth for another four days—what then? I believe in life after death, and I don't want to risk roasting *in aeternum*" ("CD" 60; "DC" 17).

If Cézanne had his doubts, Merleau-Ponty had doubts too. In fact, as his student Lyotard has written, "Merleau-Ponty certainly would not have been a great commentator on Cézanne if 'Cézanne's doubt' had not been his own."[4] It is an instructive exercise to read "Cézanne's Doubt" in relation to Descartes' doubts. We will see that in "Eye and Mind," Descartes still remains the most telling philosopher and rationalism the most telling philosophy to be analyzed and overcome for Merleau-Ponty's transformation of ontology and aesthetics. Merleau-Ponty made "Cézanne's Doubt" the lead essay in *Sense and Non-Sense,* and in the preface to that book he wrote that "Cézanne is an example of how precariously expression and communication are achieved. Expression is like a step taken in the fog—no one can say where, if anywhere, it will lead" (*SNS* 3; *SeNS* 8). The deep human desire for an unshakeable foundation for our life and our work—which manifested itself in Descartes' philosophy as the quest for certainty—will not avail. We do our work with persistence, rigor, and without fear, and then reap the pleasures and sufferings, joys and defeats, our efforts yield us. That is the lesson of Cézanne. We shall learn much more regarding Merleau-Ponty's interpretation of Cézanne in chapter 3, devoted to Cézanne, strong beauty, and truth in painting.

In "Indirect Language and the Voices of Silence" Merleau-Ponty studied the structures of language and history in relation to the theory of signs developed by Ferdinand de Saussure and the theory of history developed by André Malraux, as well as the existential philosophy of literature articulated by Jean-Paul Sartre in *What Is Literature?* (1947). The essay is obviously multilayered and complex. It appeared originally in the journal Merleau-Ponty founded with Jean-Paul Sartre, *Les Temps Modernes,* and was intended to appear as the third chapter of Merleau-Ponty's unpublished *The Prose of the World,* in which the philosopher was concerned with a general theory of expression, language, and signs. It eventually appeared as the lead essay in *Signs* (1960). Merleau-Ponty argued for an expressive theory of art that rethinks the notion of style and focuses on the artist's working (*peindre*) rather than the works (*les peintures*) that appear in museums and galleries and turn artists into rivals. Institutions should be understood in Husserl's sense as fecund foundations (*Stiftung*) that open fields for investigation. Thus, style is historical and intersubjective, the special way in which our living body experiences, practices, and takes up a tradition of gesture and meaning both to perpetuate it and to challenge it in a "coherent deformation." Sartre was wrong to claim that, in contrast with the writer, the painter "is mute." The silence of painting is not an absence of meaning but a silence pregnant with the style of a painter at work intermingled with the structures of the world that are figured.

There is a struggle going on in both of these earlier aesthetic essays by Merleau-Ponty for a denser and richer philosophical language to account for our confrontation with the world. The prose is elegant and lucid, yes, yet he used as keywords in his philosophy of art in 1945 and

1952 "expression" and "existence." He was seeking a middle way that would overcome the dualisms of modern philosophy and thought, and "expression" was the central word for developing his theory of painting in between the classical imitation theory of art (*mimesis*) and the Romantic imagination theories. Like Schopenhauer before him and Heidegger after him, Merleau-Ponty believed that the painter and the philosopher are working on the same problem: to give expression to existence, to give form to the formless, or to give new form to old forms. This is the "difficulty of the first word," to find the word that is more than a shout or a cry and truly speaks (*la parole parlant*). "Existence" was the rather existential keyword meant to interlace mind and body, self and nature. But this term, "existence," remains in the essays rather unanalyzed, always threatening to pull apart back into the dualities of subject and object, consciousness and world, that the essays and philosophy are meant to conquer. "Existence" retains a subjective hue and tips much too far in the direction of the "I" of subjectivity.[5]

By the time of "Eye and Mind," Merleau-Ponty had shifted the weight of artistic expression from the "I paint" to the anonymous "One paints," thereby articulating a depth or laterality of the self that is at a distance from itself and is dispossessed in the creative event. He had grown more aware of the need to rethink key phenomenological ideas such as intentionality, experience, and expression. What is remarkable about the Husserlian *epochē* as a response to Descartes is that Husserl accepted, rather than challenged, Descartes' desire for certainty. As Husserl's *Ideas I* as well as his *Cartesian Meditations* make clear, Husserl, like Descartes, wanted to be a complete beginner in philosophy and to cast out all doubt in developing a scientific philosophy. Husserl said that were he allotted the span of Methuselah's days—that oldest of all biblical figures who lived to be 969 years of age—he would in his old age finally reach the ideal of the philosopher as a downright beginner.[6] In contrast, Merleau-Ponty and Cézanne sought an art and a philosophy that would be able to "work with doubt," to make the perpetual questioning of the world and of the self positive, creative, and productive.

The Visible and the Invisible begins in its first paragraph from the assertion of a "perceptual faith" common to the ordinary person as well as the philosopher: the faith that we see the things themselves, that there is a world, that the world will speak to those who know properly how to listen and understand. Yet Merleau-Ponty immediately adds that this "seeing," which means the "primacy of perception" that had been the fundamental tenet of his earlier philosophy, is now a problem: "What is strange about this faith is that if we seek to articulate it into theses or statements, if we ask ourselves what is this *we*, what *seeing* is, and what *thing* or *world* is, we enter into a labyrinth of difficulties and contradictions" (*VI* 3; *VIn* 17). Merleau-Ponty's most delicate and difficult philosophical concept becomes, rather than intentionality, passivity. This passivity, anonymity, or generality in both the artist who paints and the philosopher who thinks and writes means that there is a system of exchanges between body and world such that eye and hand become the obverse side of things and the inside of an outside in which both are enveloped. Merleau-Ponty refers to this as a good or profound narcissism in which the seer is caught up in the seen, not to see in the outside the contour of one's own body, but to "emigrate into the world so that the seer and the visible reciprocate one another and we no longer know which sees and which is seen" (*VI* 139; *VIn* 183). We will consider in more detail Merleau-Ponty's idiosyncratic use of this troubled term "narcissism" later in this study. For now, the point we are stressing is that in either temporal sequence in the relation between meditating and creating—whether one meditates first and then creates, or if one creates and then meditates upon what has been done—there is a laterality, a way of being surprised by the work as if the work itself takes over and overtakes us. These are the accidents, the outright mistakes, we could say the chaos of the creative event if this didn't make it sound like the automatism or automatic writing of the surrealists, because these dispossessions are prepared by months and years of study, labor, and discipline. "Eye and Mind" does, in fact, describe painting as "autofigurative," citing Apollinaire's statement that in a poem there are phrases that do not appear to have been created but seem to have "shaped themselves," and Henri Michaux's commentary on Klee's colors saying that they seem to have been slowly born upon the canvas, exhaled at the right spot like a patina or a mold ("EM" 141–42; *OE* 69–70).

Here we find ourselves being plunged into the central ideas of "Eye and Mind," for the preliminary concepts, tensions, and probings of the earlier aesthetic essays lead us into the heart of the later aesthetic philosophy. We need to work patiently and slowly to deepen these ideas. It is therefore time to undertake a more systematic sustained reading of "Eye and Mind."

"Eye and Mind": Merleau-Ponty and Descartes

In its published version, "Eye and Mind" has five parts. Even this organizational structure underwent alteration as Merleau-Ponty worked on the earlier drafts of his text, in the second draft dividing the essay into seven parts. Nevertheless, as we shall see, the structure of the published version is lucid and telling. Parts 1 and 5 are brief. Part 1 is prelude, arguing that modern painting and sculpture bring us closer to Being, the "there is" (*il y a*), than does the operationalism of contemporary science. As already mentioned, part 1 bears some of the remnants of the *epochē* in the innocence and privilege it assigns to the painter's vision and "secret science." Part 5 is postlude, drawing the essay to a close with reflections on the durability of the artistic quest in which, from the cave paintings of Lascaux to our own times, there is never "progress" toward a "universal painting" or a totalization of painting. This is not a disappointment or failure, Merleau-Ponty argues, but the endless quest for the confirmation, exaltation, and re-creation of Being. The published version of the essay deletes the final sentence that was included as late as the third and last draft: "The painter is as far from despair as from self-importance, and one must wish for humanity many persons who, like him, contemplate the world with solidarity and transform it."[7] The deletion may mean many different things, but the sentence is very much like what Merleau-Ponty had said about Cézanne in the concluding sentence of the preface to *Sense and Non-Sense:* "But failure is not absolute. Cézanne won out against chance, and men, too, can win provided they will measure the dangers and the task" (*SNS* 5; *SeNS* 10). Maybe Merleau-Ponty simply did not desire an ending in 1960 so close to a repetition of 1945. Maybe also his own optimism about human history had diminished and the sentence no longer properly expressed his sentiments. The latter interpretation seems more consistent with his newly expressed skepticism about "progress" in human history, his conviction that, as he puts it, "the whole of human history is, in a certain sense, stationary" ("EM" 149; *OE* 91–92).

The philosophically extended and thoroughly developed parts of "Eye and Mind" are parts 2, 3, and 4. Part 2 discusses the meanings and enigmas of vision, particularly the painter's vision. Part 4 initiates us into the original ontology of depth for which modern art provides the inspiration. Part 3 is the hinge between the philosophy of vision of part 2 and the ontology of part 4 and contains the philosopher's critique of the philosophy of vision and metaphysics in Descartes' "Optics."

Let us begin in the middle with part 3 of "Eye and Mind," the critique of Descartes' optics, because it is the hinge swinging the door open from the new theory of vision in part 2 to the new ontology in part 4. We can see how much importance must be accorded Cartesian rationalism, for its critique is the doorway to the new ontology in part 4 of "Eye and Mind," and, as we developed the chronology earlier, "Eye and Mind" itself is the hinge between chapters 1–3 and chapter 4 of *The Visible and the Invisible.* Simultaneously with these writings, the philosopher was also teaching a course in 1960–61 at the Collège de France titled "Cartesian Ontology and Ontology Today."

Why did Descartes' philosophy remain so important and alive for Merleau-Ponty? Descartes had already come in for extensive analysis and critique in *Phenomenology of Perception,* particularly in its chapter on "The Cogito," and one might imagine Merleau-Ponty to have moved beyond Descartes. In that vein, imagine how altered "Eye and Mind" would be if we were to find a critique of Hegel or Heidegger in the swing chapter. Merleau-Ponty had undertaken a close reading of the introduction to Hegel's *Phenomenology of Spirit* in part 1 of the 1960–61 course titled "Philosophy and Non-Philosophy Since Hegel," and had given a reading of Heidegger's *Being and Time* in the 1958–59 course titled "Philosophy Today," so these were thinkers and texts that were very much on his mind.[8] We should certainly look deeper than attributing the renewed focus upon Descartes to a kind of French insularity or provincialism. One of the first points to note is that there were certain philosophers whose writings and thought would not leave Merleau-Ponty alone. We find them at the beginning, in the middle, and at the end of Merleau-Ponty's works. One was Sartre, a second was Marx, another was Husserl, but there was also Descartes. Second, I would argue that "Eye and Mind" itself gives us the explanation for Merleau-Ponty's return one more time to the study of Descartes. Near the end of his critique of Descartes in part 3, we find this sentence: "Our science and our philosophy are two faithful and unfaithful offshoots of Cartesianism, two monsters born of its dismemberment" ("EM" 138; *OE* 58). Contemporary science is the faithful monstrous child through its positivist operationalism that is hostile to any excursion into metaphysics. Contemporary science is the "flatness [*la platitude*] of technicized thought" ("EM" 137; *OE* 57), Merleau-Ponty writes. Contemporary philosophy is the unfaithful monster that maintains itself amidst the culture of operationalist thinking by fleeing the domain of metaphysics as well—"an anxious trembling quickly mastered" ("EM" 137; *OE* 56)—for Cartesianism is "a metaphysics that gives us definitive reasons to leave off doing metaphysics" ("EM" 137; *OE* 56). What is at stake is the loss of any "metaphysics of depth" ("EM" 137; *OE* 56). Contemporary art thus provides a middle way in between contemporary science and contemporary philosophy.

Invoking the language and imagery of monsters not only resurrects the worries about the dangers of unbridled science embedded in an account like Mary Shelley's of Dr. Frankenstein's creature; it also reaches into the deepest concerns and fears of our atomic and nuclear age—ugliness, deformity, the barbarous, the alien—in short, the inhuman. In sum, contemporary science and its twin, contemporary philosophy, threaten our humanity and our world. Both are the children of Cartesianism. This may seem hyperbolic to some, yet it is a signal of the seriousness of the philosopher's desire to find a new theory of vision and ontology that "prospect the actual world" ("EM" 138; *OE* 58) and re-engage human beings with the world. In other words, if the philosophy of consciousness and subjectivity that has dominated Western thought from Descartes through Husserl is going to be turned back, if that means the whole subjective turn in epistemology and metaphysics that locks the mind away from the body and human beings away from nature and the world is going to be defeated, then Descartes' theory of vision and hyper-rationalism must be traced to its roots and exposed for its errors. Some say that Merleau-Ponty and phenomenologists in general never make arguments, they just give descriptions. On the contrary, as we will shortly see, when Merleau-Ponty criticized a philosophy like Cartesianism or existentialism, he really made arguments, and he was relentless and thorough.

There is a third reason for Descartes' importance and Merleau-Ponty's return to him, this time found in a source outside of "Eye and Mind." In 1956 Merleau-Ponty published a history of philosophy titled *Les philosophes célebrès* (*The Celebrated Philosophers*) in which the leading scholars of the day wrote signature essays on philosophy's major figures and Merleau-Ponty wrote the introductions to each of philosophy's epochs; these were collected in *Signs* under the title "Everywhere and Nowhere" ("Partout et nulle part"). As an aside, it is noteworthy that Merleau-Ponty's history of philosophy also included more than one hundred plates of artworks portraying many of Western history's major philosophers and some artworks created by the philosophers themselves. In short, the book is beautiful. In that work, in his commentary on Descartes and the seventeenth century, Merleau-Ponty describes Cartesianism as "major rationalism" (*le grand rationalisme*). Minor rationalism (*petit rationalisme*) is what rationalism had become by 1900, the scientific explanation of Being that presumed that one day science would explain the whole of reality and there would be nothing left to ask. This minor rationalism, Merleau-Ponty says, "seems full of myths to us," the two main myths being that the laws of nature result in total determinism and that modern science can achieve total scientific explanation of the world without gaps and discontinuities. Minor rationalism is "the fossil of a major rationalism (that of the seventeenth century) rich with a living ontology" (*S* 147–48; *Si* 185–86). Major rationalism holds that "science is an aspect or a degree of Being; it is justified in its place, perhaps it is even through it that we learn to know the power of reason. But this power is not exhausted in it" (*S* 148; *Si* 187). These are the philosophies of Descartes, Spinoza, Leibniz, and Malebranche, all of which, in their different ways, recognize another type of Being beneath the chain of causal relations, the Being of a "positive infinite" or an "infinite infinite," and "the idea of the positive infinite is major rationalism's secret" (*S* 149; *Si* 188). In other words, Descartes passed with ease from science to metaphysics and from the light of nature to the light of God, from reason to faith. Our philosophical situation, Merleau-Ponty says, is "entirely different from that of major rationalism." Yet this larger and grander rationalism "is still of major importance for us, and it is even close to us in that it is the indispensable way toward the philosophies which reject it" (*S* 151; *Si* 191). Merleau-Ponty concludes that "passing to the infinite infinite does not seem to us to be the answer," yet it is necessary "to go back to the origins of Cartesianism in order to go beyond it." The philosopher was seeking to take up in a more radical way the Cartesian task of the thinking of Being, but with no expectation of achieving an exhaustive and comprehensive general thought. "The air of improvisation and the provisory, this somewhat haggard aspect of contemporary investigations (whether they be in science or philosophy, in literature and the arts), is the price we must pay in order to acquire a more mature consciousness of our relationships to Being" (*S* 151; *Si* 190).[9] The itinerary of the thinking of Being necessarily goes through Descartes for Merleau-Ponty.

Finally, I would add that the Cartesian text Merleau-Ponty examines in part 3 of "Eye and Mind" is the perfect choice of text that in its own day had revolutionized what had become Merleau-Ponty's lifelong philosophical concerns. This text is Descartes' "Optics," first published together with *Discourse on Method* in 1637, and it contains the central themes that riveted Merleau-Ponty's concern and attention: the theory of vision and a new and far-reaching metaphysics uniquely combined with Descartes' own brief commentary on painting and drawing. This was *the book* for Merleau-Ponty. Some Cartesian scholars dispute the historical reach of the influence of Descartes' "Optics," even if they do not dispute the overwhelming influence of Cartesianism in Western thought and culture. Maragaret Atherton, for example, has criticized the "mythic Descartes" constructed by Martin Jay, Richard Rorty, and others who have used Descartes' theory of vision as emblematic of a "scopic regime in the modern era." According to this version of an "ocularcentric Descartes," "knowing is described as gazing with the mind's eye on mental representations that mirror the exterior world."[10] Mind's eye, mental representations, mirroring—these are taken as the summary of Descartes' optical philosophy. Atherton argues that this is a caricature of Descartes' account of what we see. She admits that Descartes is trapped into positing a "mind's eye" as the true seer, but she argues that representationalism and mirroring are not part of the Cartesian theory of vision, which "so far from being a picture copying an exterior world, in fact bears no resemblance to that world at all."[11] As for influence, Atherton contends that the "mythic" account of Descartes overlooks the greater influence of George Berkeley's *Essay Toward a New Theory of Vision* and *Theory of Vision Vindicated,* both of which disputed Descartes' intellectualist account of vision. Yet, as even Atherton herself admits, though Descartes praised vision at the beginning of the "Optics," "what he produced was an account that encouraged a distrust of vision."[12] For, in the most famous phrase from the "Optics," Descartes says that "it is the mind which sees, not the eye."[13] This above all was what Merleau-Ponty contested. This above all cannot give a proper account of the artist's vision. In the words of "Eye and Mind," "every theory of painting is a metaphysics," and "a closer study of painting would lead to a different philosophy" ("EM" 132; *OE* 42).

The "Optics" itself is a gracefully written and inviting book in which Descartes sets out to "make myself intelligible to everyone, and to omit nothing, nor to assume anything that might have been learned in the other sciences."[14] The book was occasioned by the invention of the telescope about thirty years prior to Descartes' text of 1637. The invention, Descartes narrates, had occurred rather by happenstance by a maker of lenses named Jacques Métius of the city of Alcmar in Holland when he assembled and looked through two lenses, one thicker in the middle and the other thicker at the edges. Thus, the goal of Descartes' optical philosophy is to give an explanation of light and sight that will also explain how sight can be improved with the assistance of optical inventions such as the telescope. This goal sets out the structure for the book: the first discourse is philosophical, titled "Of Light," and the tenth and last discourse is technical, titled "Of the Method of Cutting Lenses." Nevertheless, the very accessibility for the reader that Descartes intends as a virtue is also what Merleau-Ponty argues leads Descartes into certain traps. These are caused through the use of "two or three comparisons" that Descartes says conveniently explain all the properties of our experience of light, rays, and sight.[15] These are comparisons for the effect of light upon the eye, and they are in fact three: the blind man's cane or stick, the wine vat, and the tennis ball. Above all, the blind man's cane as deployed by Descartes leads to modeling sight upon the sense of touch. The blind, says Descartes, "see with their hands":

> Their stick is the organ of some sixth sense given to them in place of sight. And in order to draw a comparison from this, I would have you consider light as nothing else, in bodies that we call luminous, than a

> certain movement or action, very rapid and very lively, which passes toward our eyes through the medium of the air and other transparent bodies, in the same manner that the movement or resistance of bodies that this blind man encounters is transmitted to his hand through the medium of his stick.[16]

To so model vision on touch, Merleau-Ponty says, effectively eliminates the whole problem of vision "at one swoop," which is the problem of action at a distance or the problem of depth ("EM" 131; *OE* 37).

Descartes viewed light as geometrical lines or rays that strike the eye when reflected from the surface of objects. These rays of light are reflected or refracted much like a ball striking surfaces of various porosities and curves, concave or convex, at different angles. This is a purely geometrical account of the nature and behavior of light based on the analogy of the continuous and uninterrupted line, and the various discourses of the "Optics" are filled with line diagrams of light rays striking the eye(s) for both monocular and binocular vision. Shifting from light to vision and the organ of the eye, the account becomes complicated by the question of the images or pictures that are created on the back of the retina. The image or picture, as is well known, is upside down, just like the image produced by the camera obscura, and the image is very small relative to the range of sizes the image represents, from ants to trees to mountains, for example. The problem is to explain how the eye determines the position and situation of objects with respect to us, whether up or down, and also to explain how the eye determines size and distances, near or far, when the image on the retina is inverted and quite small. These dual problems suggest to Descartes that it is not the eye that is making these determinations at all: "It is the mind which sees, not the eye." Thus we find in Descartes' optical philosophy a geometrical account of light, a mechanical account of the eye, and an intellectualist account of vision.

If it is the mind that sees and not the eye, we are now also within range of another of Descartes' famous conclusions, that resemblance between the retinal image and its object is not required for vision. This was Atherton's point regarding Descartes' optical philosophy mentioned earlier. "We must not hold," Descartes writes, "that it is by means of this resemblance that the picture causes us to perceive the objects, as if there were yet other eyes in our brain with which we could apprehend it."[17] Yet, if resemblance is not required, by what mechanisms or laws does the mind correctly interpret the picture or image? Here Descartes suspends his explanation in a mystery, saying only that these relationships are "established by nature" inasmuch as our mind is united to our body.[18] Thus, for example, together with the perception of light the eye also perceives color, but this does not mean that there are colors in the things or in the sky through which the rays of light move from the sun; it means only that upon the occasion of the geometrical and mechanical perception of light through the organ of the eye, nerves, and brain, the mind also perceives color. "There need be no resemblance between the ideas that the mind conceives and the movements which cause these ideas."[19]

The confluence of these three different threads regarding the nature of vision—geometrical-mechanical, pictorial, and intellectual—does not always hang together. The geometrical account of light and the mechanical account of the eye predominate, and the problem of pictorial representation on the retina is "resolved" only through the shift to the intellectual activity of the mind. The problem for Descartes is that he knows that vision is not only a mental event, it is an embodied mental event, yet he never successfully handled the union of mind and body. Thus, we land straightway in Descartes' dualism of mind and body and his intellectualist diminution of the senses and color. Clearly, the one of these three threads in Descartes' model of vision that is most poorly handled is the pictorial. It is here that Merleau-Ponty knew he had something important to say.

The question of the beautiful does not come into Descartes' discussion of vision in the "Optics," but Descartes' *The Passions of the Soul* (*Les passions de l'âme*) includes a section in which beauty is discussed under the heading "Attraction and Repulsion." The same tension regarding embodied mental vision appears in this discussion. Good and evil, Descartes states, are judgments of our "internal senses" or reason, while the beautiful and the ugly are "represented" to us by our "external senses," especially sight. Sight is essential for the judgment of the beautiful (or the ugly) to arise, yet beauty is not seen by the eye but by the mind. The beautiful and the ugly give rise to the passions of attraction and repulsion, the love for the beautiful and repulsion from the ugly, which are "more violent than other kinds of love and hatred, because what enters the soul through the senses affects it more strongly than what is represented to it by its reason." For the same reason, Descartes adds, the passions aroused by the beautiful and the ugly "contain less truth than the others."[20] As judgments of reason, the desires awakened by judgments of good and evil are less violent to the soul and contain more truth. One sees immediately that in these Cartesian analyses regarding the beautiful are embedded the same traces of intellectualism, mind-body dualism, and rationalism that we encounter in the optical philosophy. Again, Descartes omits any account of the union of external and internal senses or reason.

Of the ten discourses that comprise Descartes' "Optics," Merleau-Ponty studied most intensely discourse 1: "Of Light," discourse 4: "Of the Senses in General," discourse 6: "Of Vision," and discourse 7: "Of the Means of Perfecting Vision." From his reading, Merleau-Ponty presents in "Eye and Mind" a rapid and sustained series of counterarguments to the Cartesian optical philosophy, several of which we have already been drawn into elaborating. For one thing, this philosophy is modeled on a few brief and rather crude comparisons: the stick, the wine vat, and the ball. These seek to praise vision and render its explanation accessible, but in the end have the effect of diminishing and trivializing vision. For another thing, the claim that it is the mind, not the eye, which sees is contradicted by the mind's necessary reliance on the body, and this interrelationship is relegated to the mystery of "natural laws." And last, a theory of sight that is modeled on touch ignores that vision occurs at a distance. Descartes treats light as rays, largely straight, like the blind man's stick that "feels" the object, thus eliminating the depth, latency, and thickness of luminosity.

In general, Merleau-Ponty argues, Cartesian intellectualism was unable to grasp the central dimension of depth, either bringing the world too close to the eye by reducing vision to thought or shifting to the divine perspective of God in which the world is surveyed from above (*survol*). Yet, as Merleau-Ponty writes, "something about space evades our attempts to survey it from above" ("EM" 135; *OE* 50). When one is too close to things, as in sight modeled on touch, or too far away from things, as in the perspective of God, the outcome is the same: Being is flattened. "We are [as Cartesians] always on the hither side of depth, or beyond it" ("EM" 133; *OE* 45–46). The visible world is reduced to mere images or icons for the mind to know as ideas or thoughts, rendering problematic the relation of mental representations and things. Descartes, Merleau-Ponty concludes, "was right in liberating space: his mistake was to erect it into a positive being, beyond all points of view, all latency and depth, devoid of any real thickness" ("EM" 135; *OE* 48).

These ontological-epistemic counterarguments are brought to bear in "Eye and Mind" on what Descartes has to say about paintings and engravings, and lead on to exposing at least two central aesthetic errors on his part. Because Descartes considers light as lines rather than colors, color is "an ornament, mere coloring, and the real power of painting lies in drawing" ("EM" 133; *OE* 43). Thus, Descartes' first aesthetic error was that he assumes the truth and finality of linear perspective drawing. The perspectival techniques of the Renaissance, Merleau-Ponty argues, "were false only in that they presumed to bring an end to painting's quest and history, to found once and for all an exact and infallible art of painting"

("EM" 135; *OE* 49). Cartesianism mistakenly takes for granted the perspectival techniques of the Renaissance as an exact solution, while Leonardo da Vinci's own studies of linear perspective themselves involve competing and sometimes contradictory claims. Here Merleau-Ponty enters into a rather technical discussion of perspectival technique based upon the historical studies of Panofsky, intended to demonstrate that even the artists of the Renaissance such as Leonardo fell back upon the disdained *perspective naturalis* of apparent size over the Renaissance *perspective artificialis* of angular size when it was convenient to do so. Merleau-Ponty refers to the inconvenience of Euclid's eighth theorem, which notes that "equal and parallel sizes, unequally distant from the eye, are not seen in direct or inverse proportion to their distances." Euclid's point was that angular size, to which he subordinates apparent size, does not vary in a simple direct or inverse proportion with changing distance. Leonardo was equivocal concerning the relationship between angular and apparent size. He tends to follow Euclid's assumption that apparent size is determined by visual angles but, nonetheless, there are occasions in his works that make the visual angles themselves vary inversely with distance. Amidst the philosophical complexities of "Eye and Mind," this addition of another layer of technical discussion of perspectival painting within the history of art may seem bewildering, but its importance is to reinforce the philosopher's argument against the geometricity of Cartesian optics. Merleau-Ponty writes: "The painters knew from experience that no technique of perspective is an exact solution and that there is no projection of the existing world which respects it in all aspects and deserves to become the fundamental law of painting. They knew that linear perspective was far from being an ultimate breakthrough; on the contrary, it opened several pathways for painting" ("EM" 135; *OE* 50).

We find in Descartes' "Optics" a brief discussion of drawings and etchings in which he states his clear preference for these arts over painting and sculpture. In Cartesian optics, light is primary over color, as words or signs are primary over resemblances. Therefore, "there are no images that must resemble in every respect the objects they represent." In point of fact, Descartes argues, "often, in order to be more perfect as images and represent an object better, they must not resemble it."[21] In the world of contemporary painting, such remarks might easily be taken as a prologue for abstraction in painting and sculpture, not the vibrant colors of the abstract expressionism of Barnett Newman or Mark Rothko to be sure, but more the geometrical abstraction of a painter like Mondrian. Of course, this is not the direction Descartes went in the seventeenth century. Rather, he concludes that engravings best represent the things and the world to us; engravings which are "made of nothing but a little ink placed here and there on paper," and in which "only in shape is there any resemblance" to forests, towns, men, and battles and storms.[22] Here we find another Cartesian aesthetic error. Descartes reduces the meaning of painting to that of a text to be read, a text, Merleau-Ponty says, "totally free of the promiscuity between the seeing and the seen" ("EM" 132; *OE* 40). For the Cartesian, the lines and shapes of engravings are like words, intellectual signs to be read by the mind with a univocal reference.

We should dwell for a moment on this surprising term "promiscuity" (*promiscuité*), for it is a key to unlocking Merleau-Ponty's own theory of light and vision worked out in part 2 of "Eye and Mind," as well as being interwoven into the discussion of Cartesianism in part 3. The term means a mixture or mingling (*mélange*), but usually one that is indiscriminate, disordered, or even confused, and in the sexual domain it is contrasted with the ordered relationship of marriage. It is not for its connotation of disorder and confusion that the term came into Merleau-Ponty's text, but for the notion of the intermingling of seer with the seen, the mixing together of self and world. It is chosen to designate the full range of sensuality in our contact with paintings and with things. In fact, the word *promiscuité* has a very precise meaning in French, where it refers to being mixed together with others in a space that is too constrained for too long a time: "too close." It is a topological or relational term regarding the topological paradox of a space that is without space, and thus an impure mixture with others, whether those others are familiar or strangers. The term began to appear in Merleau-Ponty's 1955 course on passivity ("The Problem of Passivity: Sleep, the Unconscious, Memory"), and particularly in his long analysis of the disturbing case of Dora from Freud's psychoanalysis.[23] Thus, "promiscuity" is a technical term in Merleau-Ponty that refuses the separation of mind and body, self and world, that is at the heart of the Cartesian philosophy. It is a term that refuses the reduction of the meaning of painting to a single univocal meaning, but retains the openness of multiple and multivocal meanings. It also refuses the reduction of the meaning of painting to any one of its single elements, for example, the Cartesian line. Even the Cartesian view of line is too prosaic, too geometrical and reduced. Merleau-Ponty emphasizes the flexuous line and cites Klee's ability to "let a line dream" (*laissé rêver une ligne*), "to go line" (*aller ligne*), in the famous phrase of Henri Michaux ("EM" 143; *OE* 74). The promiscuity between seer and seen means that "the whole of painting is present in each of its modes of expression; there is a kind of drawing, even a single line, that can embrace all of painting's bold potential" ("EM" 132; *OE* 42). Light too is best conceived in terms of such a meaning of promiscuity, including the play of shadows with things and with the eye, the oneiric world of the eye and dusk, the night, and dream space, and the metamorphosis of things into the sight of them. In short, "light must have its own power to generate the imaginary" ("EM" 138; *OE* 59).

From these anti-Cartesian analyses and arguments, we can understand what Merleau-Ponty means when he writes that painting "scrambles all our categories" ("EM" 130; *OE* 35): essence and existence, real and imaginary, visibility and invisibility, and activity and passivity. Rather than the prosaic geometrical line, light is an undulating, flexuous line like a wave. Yet in our experience, both line and wave are abstractions, for in experience and life light is a presence, a thickness, an atmosphere that bathes the world and renders it awash in colors: the hazy light of summer heat, the clarity of high blue skies in the fall, the shadows of falling dusk. In our chapter 5 on Paul Klee, we will study Klee and Merleau-Ponty seeking a "new idea of light" as a "rhythmic simultaneity," an idea introduced by Klee's friend and fellow-artist, Robert Delaunay. Turning from light to vision, rather than a one-way action from light to the eye, we should understand vision as the reversibility or circular exchange between painter and world that has led painters so often to say, as did Cézanne and Klee, that the landscape or the forest was speaking in them. Vision is an integral and integrated system of exchanges between body and world such that eye and the movement of the eye become the obverse side of the things seen. Thus, vision should not be reduced to a linear relation between light and the eye, but rather vision results from movement, not only eye movement, but the movement of eye, head, neck, arms, and legs together. Each of these, Merleau-Ponty argues, is not an isolated part but "total parts" because they are inter-referential within the organic whole of the living body ("EM" 125; *OE* 19). Eye and body move and work together within a visual field in which the things stand out or recede as they play against each other as foreground, background, and horizon, creating difference and depth.

The reversibility of seer with seen, or chiasm, is at the heart of Merleau-Ponty's philosophy of vision and ontology. This is not a logical and linear reversibility of the biconditional, "if and only if." This is an aesthetic reversibility that is best exemplified in the phenomenon of the mirror and in self-portraiture where there is reversibility with difference, without the logical implication of symmetry or substitutability. In the mirror, the right hand is transposed as the left. He who sees is also visible, yet there is no coincidence between seer and seen. In chapter 4 of *The Visible and the Invisible,* Merleau-Ponty named this envelopment, generality, and anonymity by the term "Flesh" (*la chair*). There he compared Flesh to the Greek idea of element, which is not substance, nor mind, nor matter. In "Eye and Mind" the philosopher preferred the term "Being" to speak of the *il y a,* the "there is," and nowhere in that work is the term "flesh" capitalized as it is in *The Visible and the Invisible.*

Therefore, "Eye and Mind" shows us a progression, a development, in Merleau-Ponty's use of "flesh" that foreshadows what will happen with the term in *The Visible and the Invisible.* In "Eye and Mind," "flesh" (*la chair*) makes it first appearance in the context of the philosophy of vision in part 2. Thus, flesh is most originally the flesh of our bodies, human bodies in which we find the literal optic nerve chiasm at the back of the eye as the nerve fibers cross over one another. The anatomy of this crossing creates both the possibility of vision and, at the same time, a blind spot in the vision of each eye, since there are no photoreceptors that can respond to light stimulation at this juncture. The optic chiasm may serve as a paradigm for other more figurative bodily chiasms, the crisscrossings of touching and being touched, seeing and being seen, feeling and being felt, hearing and being heard. In each sensory modality, each in its own way, we find both contact and distance, a drawing-close that is not a perfect simultaneity or synthesis but retains a gap (*écart*). Merleau-Ponty writes: "When I say then that every visible is invisible, that perception is imperception, that consciousness has a *punctum caecum* [blind spot] . . . one has to understand that it is the visibility itself that involves a non-visibility—in the very measure that I see, I do not know *what* I see" (*VI* 247; *VIn* 300). The human body exhibits this unique doubling and self-reflection that would not be possible, Merleau-Ponty points out, if our eyes were made in such a way as to prevent us from seeing any part of our own bodies, or if we had lateral eyes, as do some animals in which there is no cross-blending of visual fields ("EM" 125; *OE* 20). Reversibility is also a "chiasm" in the sense of the Greek letter *chi* (X) and as found in the rhetorical form of the chiasm when the ordering of phrases is reversed: "the snow falling, the falling snow."

Immediately after speaking of the "flesh of the body," Merleau-Ponty adds that "the world is made of the very stuff [*l'étoffe même*] of the body" ("EM" 125; *OE* 19). Thus, there is a "flesh of the world" that Merleau-Ponty would come to speak of as dimensionality, continuation, latency, and encroachment by the time of *The Visible and the Invisible,* where he wrote: "That means that my body is made of the same flesh as the world (it is a perceived), and moreover that this flesh of my body is shared by the world, the world *reflects* it, encroaches upon it and it encroaches upon the world . . . they are in a relation of transgression or of overlapping" (*VI* 248; *VIn* 302). This phrase, "made of the same stuff," is a problem for us because it seems to lend itself exactly to those very terms it is meant to replace—substance, matter, or stuff. In analyzing this philosophy that is about movement and process, not substance, we would better translate *étoffe* as "cloth" or "fabric" and speak of the "fabric of the world" rather than its stuff, for fabric has some life and movement as it folds, rustles, and moves together with the actions of the body. Nevertheless, the point is that there is a progression, a development in the meaning of "flesh" in "Eye and Mind" from human flesh to the more general meaning of the flesh of things. In part 4, describing the thickness of water in a swimming pool, Merleau-Ponty refers to the water as "flesh" ("EM" 142; *OE* 70) and later speaks of "all flesh": "All flesh, and even that of the world, radiates beyond itself" ("EM" 145; *OE* 81). Thus, "flesh" became, for Merleau-Ponty, ever more self-consciously, the most comprehensive and general term that he would eventually prefer to the word "Being."

The meaning of that most general term, Flesh, is the meaning of both carnality and reversibility. What is "out there" in the world is also the same thing that is "here" at the heart of vision. The mountain, Merleau-Ponty puts it, "makes itself mountain before our eyes" ("EM" 128; *OE* 29) when we or the painter interrogate the world with our eyes. Our eyes are the interrogative metamorphosis of the world into vision. "The interrogation of painting in any case looks toward this secret and feverish genesis of things in our body" ("EM" 128; *OE* 30). Thus vision is a reversibility, a circle of eye and mountain, a circuit of seeing and seen, an interrogative conversation of asking and listening, the circulating of Being which is the movement of Flesh, that is, reversibility. The circle, too, as well as the chiasm, expresses the meaning of reversibility. "If one wants metaphors . . . the body sensed and the body sentient are as the obverse and the reverse, or again, as two segments of one sole circular course which goes above from left to right and below from right to left, but which is one sole movement in its two phases" (*VI* 138; *VIn* 182). The world and the painter are the inverse and obverse of one sole power that breaks open in an unending generosity of creation and expression. We are held by a speech and a thought that have us, and a call for that speech and thought to find new and original forms.

Surely the most surprising text in part 4 of "Eye and Mind" is the paragraph in which Merleau-Ponty speaks of the water in a swimming pool (*piscine*) as flesh. I want to draw out several points from this passage, so it would be good to have the philosopher's text before us in full:

> When through the water's thickness I see the tiled bottom of the pool, I do not see it *despite* the water and the reflections; I see it through them and because of them. If there were no distortions, no ripples of sunlight, if it were without that flesh that I saw the geometry of the

> tiles, then I would cease to see it *as* it is and where it is—which is to say, beyond any identical, specific place. I cannot say that the water itself—the aqueous power, the syrupy and shimmering element—is *in* space; all this is not somewhere else either, but it is not in the pool. It inhabits it, is materialized there, yet it is not contained there; and if I lift my eyes toward the screen of cypresses where the web of reflections plays, I must recognize that the water visits it as well, or at least sends out to it its active, living essence. ("EM" 142; *OE* 70–71)

Merleau-Ponty is here speaking of vision, that is, *seeing* the water in the pool, and thus he describes the water in the pool from the point of view of a *seer* who is not immersed in the pool's water. Of course, a person can open his eyes underwater and see the water in this different way, as well as experience the buoyant tactility of being held by the water; however, in this passage Merleau-Ponty is interested in light and the play of light on the water and the pool's surroundings. In fact, he has preceded his description of the pool with a citation from Hermes Trismegistus regarding the "voice of light": "It [art] is truly the 'inarticulate cry,' as Hermes Trismegistus said, 'which seemed to be the voice of the light'" ("EM" 142; *OE* 70). If it seems unusual to introduce the water and pool in this context, the shift from light to water also occurs in "Pimander," the creation story of Hermes Trismegistus which begins from light, moves to darkness, and then to something of a watery nature out of which comes the inarticulate cry of the voice of fire (light).[24] Later, in our chapter on Paul Klee, we will spend some time studying this important new concept of light as voice, as what Klee and Robert Delaunay refer to as "rhythmic simultaneity," vibration, pulse, and measure. The concept mixes together different sensory modalities in a way that Merleau-Ponty often did, the way of synesthesia. Nevertheless, for the present, we want to establish certain emphases within the swimming pool passage in order to bring to the forefront the significance of the water as flesh for articulating Merleau-Ponty's ontology of flesh.

We first see that water as flesh is *event and process* rather than a substance fixed in place. The water is an "aqueous power," active, acting on the pool, the tiles, sidewalks, and screen of cypress trees. This means that this is an *ontology of verbs and adverbs* above nouns and adjectives. The force of water as power is best felt linguistically in expressions such as: to water, to water wetly, to water reedily, shimmeringly, quickly, or slowly. Nietzsche once said that to name the lightning as the nominative lightning and then say things like the "lightning flashes" creates an illusion in which the noun-verb grammar "doubles the doing." Lightning just is the flash in the sky; there is not something separate and substantive, lightning, that then causes the flash in the sky.[25] The hypostatization of actions into nouns is an illusion of language: a person's lap is not a thing, it is just the act of sitting, and there is no mystery to be solved when the sitting person rises and stands, such as "where did the lap go?" The fist just is the act of clenching the hand, and there is no deep problem about the ontology of the fist when the hand unclenches, as long as we remain in the domain of the life-world, which is a verbal and adverbial reality. Stones, rocks, and mountains last a long time, and their life of events and actions is quite slowed down compared with water in a pool, let alone living-and-dying beings such as plants, animals, and persons. Yet the mountain is also this power of making its forests, animals, and peaks "mountainous" and "stony," and the durability of the mountain is not an excuse for freezing events and actions into an ontology of permanent substances.

The most challenging part of this altogether challenging account is its escalation to the statement that the water as flesh is "not in the pool," or again, that "it is not contained there." The French is completely straightforward: "elle n'est pas dans la piscine. Elle l'habite, elle s'y materialize, elle n'y est pas contenue." What is at stake here is the meaning of that little word "in" that has been the source of so many philosophical difficulties and perplexities, such as the mind is "in" the body. Merleau-Ponty does not mean to be obfuscating or coy here, but rather to oppose those philosophies of substance, matter, and space that view the world as consisting of various substance-containers of various spatial sizes that are then filled "in" by other substances, such as a liquid of water "in" a solid made of concrete the size of a swimming pool. There has been a pervasive fault in the philosophical use of the term "in" to construe the inside in a spatializing sense. Thereby we are led to think of consciousness, thought, word, and significance as located in a space or container, such as "wine is in the jar." Merleau-Ponty's point is that the water, the tiles, the sidewalks, and the cypresses *live* in a network of meanings in which each is an expression of all the others, and therefore the ontology of flesh is *a logic of internal relations*. The world does not consist of separate and discrete objects, each bearing its own definition independently and then entering into external causal relationships; rather, the meaning of one action or event is internal to the meaning of the others. That is why the water is as much shimmering on the cypresses, rendering them "all watery," as the water is "in" the pool, for the water that is "in" the pool is also at its reflections on the screen of cypresses, just as it is rippling the geometry of the tiles on the pool bottom. In accord with Aristotle's analysis of the eight uses of the word "in" from the *Physics,* this is the sense in which we use the word "in" to designate encompassment or inclusion as the part/whole relationship; for example, when we say that "she is in the family," "health is in the body, "science is in her soul," or "metaphysics is in his blood."[26] Water is "in" the pool as two elements in a family of relationships that are water, pool, sidewalks, and cypresses.

Neither the term *difference* nor *écart* appears precisely in this text on the flesh of water because Merleau-Ponty is working on light, place, space, and relatedness. Nonetheless, it is well to remind ourselves that this logic of internal relations, which is a *logic of reversibility or of chiasm,* is also one that resists synthesis or the famous "night in which all cows are black." Though the cypresses are "watery" and the pool is "watery," as are the tiles, it is different to be a cypress tree than a pool or tiles, and this is an *ontology of difference* as well as relatedness. A child is "in" the family just as are the parents and grandparents, but it is different to be a child than to be a parent or grandparent. The senses of these differences do not override the "unity" of the network of internal relatedness, but render the unity less tightly knit, more flexuous, flexible, and multi-sided. The parent is also a child in relation to the grandparent, and the network of meanings overlaps and deepens into layers or dimensions. .

Where, then, does Merleau-Ponty stand in respect to the old dilemma of dualism and monism? It would be best to avoid this question, for it is one handed down in modern philosophy from all the old Cartesian "bric-a-brac," as Merleau-Ponty would call it: inside versus outside, reason versus sensation, reason versus emotion, mind versus body, and spirit versus matter. Yet we know the question is not merely a Cartesian one, but one that has haunted Western thought from its beginning as the problem of the one and the many, the form and the particular. The term "monism" is a problem for us today, but at the same time, not to be evasive, let us fall back on the term "non-dualism," for Merleau-Ponty's new ontology of the one Flesh remains loosely knit. It both preserves the gaps (*écarts*), strife, and differences among colors and things and between self and world, and prioritizes genesis and process over substance. Verbs and adverbs replace nominatives. The incarnate principle of Flesh imbues life and the world with a longing for unity that is deferred, but a deferral that keeps open the genesis and metamorphosis of meaning. This is an "oneiric naturalism," for it is a philosophy of life and nature that preserves within it mystery, wonder, and dream, or equally, a "visceral spiritualism," for it is a philosophy of invisibility yet one that is rooted within our bodily incarnation.[27]

It is at this point that we find ourselves on the brink, as it were, of the unfolding of this new optical philosophy and ontology into a reconfiguration of the beautiful. We almost expect it to appear somewhere in the writings even as we hold our breath seeking it. The provocation of this more promiscuous and porous account of our relation with things, with others, and with the world invites us to wonder how the key elements of this ontology—reversibility, Flesh, *écart*—and the key elements of this theory of painting—color, the flexuous line, mirrors, self-portraits, motion, depth—could become the architecture of a new philosophy of the beautiful. Exactly here, on the brink, we encounter what is, for us then, the aching absence of beauty in "Eye and Mind." I want to explore the reasons for this aporia but also to argue that it should not deter us from seeking to unfold for ourselves a retrieval of the beautiful by thinking through and thinking by way of Merleau-Ponty's ontological and aesthetic architecture.

Glimpses of Beauty

There are only two occurrences of the word "beauty" (*la beauté*) or its cognates in all three of Merleau-Ponty's essays on painting: one in "Indirect Language and the Voices of Silence," one in "Eye and Mind," and none at all in "Cézanne's Doubt." Moreover, both mentions of "beauty" occur in quotations from other writers, one from Malraux and the other a mixture of Rilke with Leonardo. In his citation from Malraux's *The Voices of Silence,* Merleau-Ponty in "Indirect Language" strongly criticizes Malraux's view that "because painting is no longer for faith or beauty it is for the individual; it is the 'annexation of the world by the individual'" ("ILVS" 88; *Si* 64). Though Merleau-Ponty rejected Malraux's individualist and subjectivist interpretation of modern art expressed in these citations, he remained silent in the 1952 essay on the aesthetic of beauty. In an earlier essay from 1947 titled "A Scandalous Author," defending the writing and philosophy of Jean-Paul Sartre against his critics, Merleau-Ponty had spoken of a "religion of the beautiful." Our habit has been to define art by the beauty of its objects, he says, a habit inherited from ancient times with its cult of the beauty of the Greek gods. Judged against such a habituated beauty of purity and perfection, Sartre's writing produces scandal, for it dwells with ugliness, alienation, prostitution, lynching, war, and horror. Yet in our own times, living in a post-Romantic epoch, "if inner and outer are reunited, their meeting will not be harmonious or beautiful but will have, rather, the violence of the sublime" (*SNS* 43; *SeNS* 76). This is a "minor sublimity" (*un petit sublime*), Merleau-Ponty says, which means "a sublimity without eloquence or illusions which is, I believe, an invention of our times" (*SNS* 43; *SeNS* 76). Sartre's critics lack the boldness of Pascal to mix the angelic and bestial in mankind. "They need something above and beyond human disorder, and if they do not find this in religion, they seek it in a religion of the beautiful" (*SNS* 77; *SeNS* 43). Though this text demonstrates Merleau-Ponty's familiarity with the categories and history of the aesthetic terms "beauty" and "the sublime," as well as the tradition's tendency to bifurcate them, he does not enter into his own explicit comment and analysis. The text would lead one to suppose that Merleau-Ponty's aesthetic, at least of the 1940s and early 1950s, elevated "minor sublimity" above the "religion of the beautiful," with no common ground between them.

We find the second occurrence of the word "beauty" in part 4 of "Eye and Mind," in a citation that begins with Leonardo's *Treatise on Painting* and concludes with material from Rilke's book on *Auguste Rodin.*

> Da Vinci invoked a "pictorial science" which does not speak in words (and still less in numbers) but in works that exist in the visible just as natural things do—yet pass on that science "to all the generations of the universe." A silent science, says Rilke (apropos of Rodin), that brings into the work the forms of things "whose seal has not been broken"; it comes from the eye and addresses itself to the eye. We must understand the eye as the "window of the soul." The eye . . . through which the beauty of the universe is revealed to our contemplation is of such excellence that whoever should resign himself to losing it would deprive himself of the knowledge of all the works of nature. ("EM" 146; *OE* 82)

Merleau-Ponty's text is not entirely clear regarding its mélange of da Vinci and Rilke in this citation. As best we can determine, the first sentence of this quotation is from Leonardo's *Treatise,* next comes the second sentence from Rilke, then the third and fourth sentences return to Leonardo. In developing this intertextual linkage of the "science" of painting, beauty, and the eye, Merleau-Ponty does not comment further on the element of the beautiful, but rather returns to his critique of the Cartesian theory of vision.

Since Leonardo's conjunction of the "science" of painting with beauty and praise of the eye above all other senses appears in this text, it might be important here to comment that we should not shy away from the fact that Merleau-Ponty does find in vision a very unique feature not found in other senses such as touch or hearing. This, as we have seen in his critique of Cartesian optics, is "distance" or "depth." Merleau-Ponty writes: "We must take literally what vision teaches us: namely, that through it we touch the sun and the stars, that we are everywhere at once. . . . Vision alone teaches us that beings are different, 'exterior,' foreign to one another, are yet absolutely *together,* are 'simultaneity'" ("EM" 146; *OE* 83–84). Merleau-Ponty has been criticized extensively of late for "privileging" vision in this way, particularly by Derrida, and for diminishing other sensory modalities, especially touch.[28] It would be distracting here to enter fully into this disagreement, yet I do want to say that I do not interpret Merleau-Ponty's focus upon what is unique and special about vision to be a kind of "privileging" that ruins a "democracy of the senses." It is one thing to take cognizance of what is unique in a given sensory modality, that is, to take seriously the differences among the gifts of the various senses, and it would be another thing to forget the contributions of the other senses or to model or remake all of them in terms of sight, in a sort of bad "ocularcentrism" or "scopic regime." Hearing and listening are prominent from *Phenomenology of Perception* right into *The Visible and the Invisible,* and touch is nearly ubiquitous in Merleau-Ponty's philosophy, beginning from the centrality of the motif of right hand touching left hand and reciprocally, which is the very model for reversibility learned from Husserl. In this case, if anything, vision is modeled on the reversibility of touch, though that is too strong, for we have seen that Merleau-Ponty does not want a model of vision as touch like that of Descartes. Vision is "at a distance" and touch is not. Rather, it is better to say that reversibility is a multiple and varied principle, as is the Flesh, that manifests differences to be described and understood as one shifts from vision to touch to hearing, and so on. We simply must agree that Merleau-Ponty's point is well taken, that the unique gift of sight is to be able to judge the distance, size, and location of things in the world immediately in a way that touch or hearing cannot, which is not to say that touch and hearing do not have their own special and unique gifts, nor that among the blind, hearing or touch cannot be sensitized and sharpened to take over much of vision's unique functions.

To return to the theme of beauty in Merleau-Ponty's texts, in the recently published transcripts of Merleau-Ponty's 1948 radio lectures for French national radio, *The World of Perception* (the English translation of *Causeries*), we encounter a brief set of comments on beauty, and the context is surprising. In the sixth lecture on "Art and the World of Perception," Merleau-Ponty raises the question of beauty in relation to cinematography. Beauty in a film, he says, does not manifest itself in the story itself or in the "tics, mannerisms, and devices" of a particular director. What matters is an "overall cinematographic rhythm" that has a kind of unity and necessity, though not one that could ever be reduced to a rule book. It is a rhythm that appears in already successfully completed works and inspires other attempts. The viewer experiences "the unity and necessity of the temporal progression in a work of beauty without ever formulating a clear idea of it. Then, as now, this viewer will be left not with a store of recipes but a radiant image, a particular rhythm" (*WP* 99; *C* 58). Beauty is an experience without a cognitive concept, without a formal rule book, and later we shall argue that the beautiful is a "sensible idea," a notion Merleau-Ponty worked out in relation to Proust. Beauty has to do with rhythm and radiance. These remarks strike us as ringing true, but of course, they are all too abbreviated. We shall take advantage of the notion of rhythm in particular in relation to beauty in studying the musicality of many of the works of Paul Klee, as well as in expanding the concept of rhythm far beyond the musical context, even toward Nietzsche's notion of the Dionysian element in art.

There are many reasons we could give for Merleau-Ponty's texts offering us only glimpses of beauty rather than a full-on direct study. First, he was not thematizing anything like a comprehensive aesthetic theory in his essays on art, nor even a comprehensive philosophy of painting. If anything, as we indicated in the opening of this chapter, we find in "Eye and Mind" an aesthetic philosophy more in the ancient and wider sense of *aisthesis,* referring to the full range of our sense experiences rather than the more modern sense of a philosophy of aesthetic judgment beginning with Baumgarten's *Aesthetica* in 1750.[29] Similar to "beauty," the term "aesthetics" is nearly absent from "Eye and Mind" as well as the earlier aesthetic essays.[30] The philosopher was working on the philosophy of vision and ontology. Some philosophers, most noticeably Sibley, have regarded beauty as a "supererogatory quality" that supervenes on perception—when the light, the line, the color, the depth, and the movement are just right, then the painting, the drawing, the sculpture, the photograph, and the dance are just right, and then there may be beauty.[31] Though it is certainly helpful to distinguish beauty from empiricist accounts that treat it like a sense *qualia* such as color, in phenomenological language, beauty is not a quality at all but an experience that happens between the thing and the one who appreciates it. In the language of "Eye and Mind," beauty is something itself quite elemental within the element of the Flesh itself as the chiasm, the between that blends self and artwork, self and nature. We are getting ahead of ourselves here, and all of this will be developed slowly and carefully in part 3 of this study. For now, we only emphasize that the experience of beauty is relational between subject and object, self and thing, and its presentation depends upon the life and history of the perceiver brought into relationship with the colors, lines, shadings, and excellence of the well-made object. No one makes beauty directly, and if we attempted to do so it would only mar the work, and we think, as well, that no philosophy ever describes or conceptualizes beauty directly, and if it attempted to do so it would ruin the philosophy. Rather, we make well-made things that then may be experienced as beautiful, both by the artist and other appreciators. I think that no one has put this better than Rilke in his second essay on Rodin:

> It bears repeating that beauty is not "made" at all. No one has ever made beauty. . . . The artist who is guided by this knowledge does not need to think of beauty; in fact, he knows no better than anyone else what it consists of. Directed by an urge to fulfill a purpose far beyond himself, he knows only that there are certain conditions under which beauty may come to the things he makes. And his calling consists of getting to know these conditions, and gaining the ability to produce them.[32]

Rilke adds that art, relieved of philosophical and rhetorical burdens, can return to its "humble, dignified place in everyday life."[33] Beauty and the philosophy of beauty are indirect, and that philosophy will emerge from Merleau-Ponty's philosophy of vision and ontology, which is also an indirect ontology.

Second, beauty is not a defining characteristic of works of art, so there is no necessary reason that would have required Merleau-Ponty to include it in a study of modern painting, drawing, and sculpture. Many artworks are not beautiful—for example, Picasso's much-traveled *Guernica.* This painting's images of a shrieking horse, dead children, and terrorized wraiths has become an icon of the twentieth century that Gijs van Hensbergen calls, in his recent book on *Guernica,* the modern equivalent of the Crucifixion. The mural has had its own "biography" of war associations, from its anti-Franco origin through World War II, the Korean War, and the Vietnam War, with world tours and installations at the Museum of Modern Art in New York City and the United Nations.[34] No one would think to call this monochromatic portrait of "existential terror" beautiful. The closest I have seen anyone come to such an ascription is Crispin Sartwell, who finds in *Guernica* what he calls the "beauty of power," which he calls an "insane" beauty that wants "to see people torn to bits."[35] For myself, *Guernica* remains a most unbeautiful work, or at least one in which beauty is simply not the point. For Barnett Newman, *Guernica* was "a totem to the idea of the sublime," which he so sharply differentiated from beauty.[36]

Moreover, if beauty is not a defining characteristic of artworks, neither should beauty be limited to the realm of artistic productions, thereby denying the quality of beauty to nature, as have philosophers from Hegel to Maritain in what strikes most as a philosopher's prejudice against common usage and in favor of the purity of abstract Spirit. In the political and economic realms, such a bifurcation between beauty and nature deprives us of the full deployment of aesthetic qualities in pursuing environmental protections of oceans, forests, and animals. It is philosophically odd not to speak of the beauty of the curve of a blue marlin or the smell of patriarchal cedars. In other words, we might just as much expect a treatment of beauty in Merleau-Ponty's courses on "Nature" in 1956–60 as in his study of modern art, "Eye and Mind." Indeed, in the second "Nature" course of 1957–58, Merleau-Ponty does discuss several linkages of animal coloring, behavior, and ritual with art and music, and we will come to these later. Additionally, the well-made objects of the "third realm" in between nature and fine art are also often beautiful, such as furniture, glassware, fabrics and clothing, jewelry, a tattoo or a hairstyle, or a delicious bread or wine.[37] All this is simply to say that there is no necessary reason for Merleau-Ponty to have undertaken a consideration of beauty in a philosophic study of art.

Finally and above all, I would say that rather than giving us a direct philosophy of beauty in "Eye and Mind," Merleau-Ponty gives us a "lyric experience of beauty" in the expressive language of his innovative and experimental reasoning and thought, which blends ontology with a kind of Proustian lyricism. It is a philosophy that recognizes beauty without creating an overt theory about it. In Kant's third *Critique* he had famously written, "Beautiful is what, without a concept, is liked universally" (*CJ* 9/64). Beauty, in some sense, is one of those ultimate elementals that resists conceptualization. There is a "system of equivalences, a Logos of lines, of lighting, of colors" that make for "a conceptless presentation of universal Being" ("EM" 142; *OE* 71). In the chapters that follow, we will trace the crossings, interlacings, and folds of the architecture of the beautiful in developing its claims on desire, memory, feeling, and difference.

It is difficult to work from what are only glimpses. Nevertheless, we can approach this question of retrieval and reconfiguration through the aesthetic and ontological architecture of "Eye and Mind" as well as by studying the sources from which Merleau-Ponty was working, especially those of Paul Cézanne, Auguste Rodin, and Paul Klee. The impact of Rodin in particular upon "Eye and Mind" has been underappreciated. Certainly Klee is the most influential artist upon the overall thinking we find in Merleau-Ponty's text, but it is Rodin who theorized the beautiful (and ugly) with explicit connections to the aesthetic of Charles Baudelaire. Therefore, in the next chapters we turn to the explication of the aesthetic that we find in Rodin, and of the other artists whose thought and work are stitched into the structure of "Eye and Mind," most importantly Cézanne and Klee. Rainer Maria Rilke is also important for us throughout, for, as we have mentioned in our Preface, it was Rilke who wrote two lengthy essays on Rodin, engaged in a correspondence with his wife, Clara, about Paul Cézanne published as *Letters on Cézanne,* and visited with Paul Klee (*DPK* 317/959).

Part 2

Merleau-Ponty's Artists

3

Paul Cézanne: On Strong Beauty

> In paintings themselves we could seek a figured philosophy of vision—its iconography, perhaps.
>
> —Merleau-Ponty, "Eye and Mind"

> The goal of the artist is to work without worrying about anyone and to become strong; the rest isn't worth the word of Cambronne.
>
> —Émile Bernard, *Conversations with Paul Cézanne*

> I can tell how I've changed by the way Cézanne is challenging me now.
>
> —Rainer Maria Rilke, *Letters on Cézanne*

Cézanne stood at the doorway to the twentieth century, and he is the colossus we have yet to comprehend. On beauty, Cézanne is our problem and our challenge. One wonders immediately why we should even raise the aesthetic and language of beauty in relation to Cézanne. For the most part, that aesthetic seems simply beside the point. "He had no conception of beauty," Bernard reported; "he possessed only the idea of truth."[1] Cézanne himself wrote, "I owe you the truth in painting and I shall give it to you."[2] We will need to return to this statement regarding truth in painting in the last section of this chapter. Yet at least two of Cézanne's contemporaries, Émile Bernard, in spite of the statement just cited, and Rainer Maria Rilke, insisted on the term "beauty" when speaking of the works of Cézanne, and we will therefore examine Bernard's Cézanne writings and Rilke's letters. Our goal is to articulate a concept of "strong beauty" in which works of art are not judged on classical requirements but are judged on the basis of their power to challenge perceptual experience. Kurt Badt has captured our theme on truth and strong beauty in *The Art of Cézanne:* "The artistic beauty of his work—the harmony and melody evolved through the medium of configuration alone—is strong." Moreover, Badt continues, strong beauty is directly linked with truth: "As this same beauty is preserved in Cézanne's pictures throughout the whole process of creation, in all the phases of realization right to its fulfillment, the fully realized work has also the quality of being true."[3] Badt concludes regarding Cézanne's "realizations" of truth in painting that "in the process of giving truth a form," the everyday outlines of things "are, as it were, burned in fire, and out of the fire of truth the objects emerge in new form."[4] It will be our contention that in this day and age, the beautiful must be permitted expansion of its meaning to include, and even accent, experimentation, the new, and the different. For beauty is in some measure about fire and desire, and desire seeks what is other. Beauty belongs to works that make the apple all "appley," and draw us out of ourselves and altogether into "appleyness," as if we had never experienced apples before.[5] That is Cézanne, and he knew apples. Also a few old jugs and a mountain.

We shall first preface our discussion of Cézanne, Bernard, and Rilke by introducing Merleau-Ponty's notion of a figured philosophy.

Figured Philosophy

Merleau-Ponty built his aesthetic thinking through close readings of artworks and artists. This is apparent from his published aesthetic writings, and it becomes even more apparent with the opportunity to study the preparatory notes and three drafts of "Eye and Mind" prior to its final published version.[6] There we find reading notes on the writings of Auguste Rodin and Paul Klee that are cited in the footnotes of "Eye and Mind," together with notes on Paul Cézanne, whose influence never wanes. Merleau-Ponty studied the writings, conversations, and interviews of artists themselves to develop his ideas, invent new vocabulary, and draw his conclusions. In addition to working from Leonardo's *Treatise on Painting,* he drew on the letters, interviews, and writings of Cézanne, Matisse, Klee, and Rodin. Some philosophers of art, such as Malraux in *The Voices of Silence,* have dismissed the statements of artists about their own work; when they talk about what they are doing they sound like "house painters." Not Merleau-Ponty, who found in these sources a rich archive for the development of his own ontological and aesthetic vocabulary and thought.

In "Eye and Mind," Merleau-Ponty proposed the idea of a figured philosophy and mentions this thought three times. We hear it in the first epigraph for this chapter, which is taken from part 2 of "Eye and Mind":

"In paintings themselves we could seek a figured philosophy of vision—its iconography, perhaps."[7] The reference is to an essay by Bergson in *The Creative Mind* on "The Life and Work of Ravaisson" that reads: "The whole philosophy of Ravaisson springs from the idea that art is a figured metaphysics, that metaphysics is a reflection of art, and that it is the same intuition, variously applied, which makes the profound philosopher and the great artist."[8] Ravaisson had sought a resemblance or convergence between the thought of Aristotle and the aesthetics of Leonardo da Vinci. In contrast with the early physicists who saw in things only their material mechanism, and with the Platonists who saw only their abstract general type or form, Aristotle sought in the heart of individual beings the characteristic thought impelling them. For Ravaisson, Aristotelianism was the very philosophy of art conceived and practiced by Leonardo, "an art which neither emphasizes the material contours of the model, nor tones them down to the advantage of an abstract ideal, but simply centers them around the latent thought and generative soul."[9]

Merleau-Ponty's suggestion of a "figured philosophy" would delineate and amplify itself in at least four ways. First, its language would be indirect; it would be one in which metaphor, allusion, the implicit, and silence would bring philosophy closer to the written style of literature, to the lyricism and lacunae of Proust with "tufts of meaning" like thickets that we explore, never finished, always "on the way," never thin and reduced. In this regard, Jenny Slatman has called our attention to a passage in Merleau-Ponty's courses on "Nature" in which he is commenting on the relation between art and philosophy in the thought of Schelling. "There is still a difference between philosophy and art: the philosopher looks to express the world, the artist seeks to create it. . . . Philosophy does not sublimate itself in art. There is simply a possible relation between the experience of the artist and the experience of the philosopher, insofar as the experience of the artist is open, an *ek-stasis*" (*N* 46; *NN* 72).[10] The key word here is "open" (*ouverte*), and it means that the philosopher and artist enter into their experience of the world in the same manner; their work is never closed, but remains ever open and porous to the call of the world. Second, the content of figured philosophy would be interlaced with non-philosophy, especially with the arts, and most especially with the visual arts of drawing, painting, sculpture, photography, and film. The flexuous lines of the written philosophical word would parallel and double the flexuous lines of the artist that render works provocative or sublime or beautiful. Third, a figured philosophy would be a philosophy of nature, interlaced with nature and its art and poetry, for nature is figured as the grain and burl of wood, the undulating lines of sand dunes in the desert or at the shore, and the encroachment of ocean onto sand that we call shoreline, which is really not a line at all but a depth or dimension. Fourth, and finally, figured philosophy would be connected with mathematics, especially with geometric figures born from the angle and curve of the line—circles, and also spheres and spirals.

The second thread in this fabric of figured philosophy is most in play here: the intimate relation between philosophy and non-philosophy, the arts. "Eye and Mind" deploys a gallery of artists to develop the new theory of vision and new ontology that is further elaborated in *The Visible and the Invisible,* and which we analyzed in the last chapter. "Eye and Mind" includes photographs of eight artworks by Giacometti, Cézanne, Nicolas de Staël, Matisse, Klee, Germaine Richier, Rodin, and the unknown Alain de la Bourdonnaye. The range of artists upon whom Merleau-Ponty draws is remarkable in spite of his own humble comment that he is a "layman" who lacks "both competence and space" ("EM" 139; *OE* 63) to draw upon art history properly. He writes:

> If the historian unearths beneath its manifest content a surplus and thickness of meaning, a texture which held the promise of a long history, then this active manner of being, this possibility he unveils in his work, this monogram he finds there—all are grounds for a philosophical meditation. . . . I lack everything for its execution, both competence and space. But since the power or the fecundity of works of art exceeds every positive causal or linear relation, it is not illegitimate for a layman such as myself, speaking from his memory of a few paintings and books, to express how painting enters into his reflections. ("EM" 139; *OE* 63)

In addition to the eight artworks that Merleau-Ponty chose as photographs, he refers throughout "Eye and Mind" to at least another dozen artworks, including the Lascaux cave paintings and works by Rembrandt, Henry Moore, Duchamp, Gericault, Caravaggio, Roualt, Ingres, and the photographic research of Étienne-Jules Marey regarding capturing movement on film. We begin in this chapter with Cézanne, and the chapters following will discuss the aesthetic thinking of Rodin and Klee.

Cézanne and Émile Bernard

We know that it takes only a moment to hear the word "ugliness" hurled in the direction of Cézanne's paintings, certainly from his contemporaries, and even today in the museums. "The crowd was particularly amused by the head of a man, dark and bearded, whose cheeks were sculptured with a trowel and who seemed to be the prey of an eczema. . . . The love of physical and moral ugliness is a passion like any other."[11] It is undeniable that, measured by classical standards, scarcely any masterful painter has produced more ugly works than Cézanne, with the possible exception of Van Gogh. There is a strong element of primitivism or *gaucherie,* that is, awkwardness, in the execution of many of his works. Richard Shiff has summed this up: "Cézanne felt certain that he possessed an artistic 'temperament' and had 'strong' sensation; but he continued to search after the 'means of expression,' the required artistic technique."[12] The famous "distortions" Merleau-Ponty discusses disqualify many Cézannes from the classical and neoclassical conception of beauty stressing formal qualities of harmony, balance, and proportion, even though Cézanne liked to refer to himself as a "classical" painter.[13] However, he did not mean by this adherence to the Greek ideals of proportion, harmony, balance, and the Golden Section, but rather that he drew on the old masters and that he drew on nature and his own sensations. His portraits of the card players and many of the late bather studies do display a classical kind of symmetric, harmonic architecture in their construction. Yet Cézanne presents "an unfamiliar world in which one is uncomfortable and which forbids all human effusiveness" ("CD" 66; "DC" 28).

Bernard's 1904 article in *L'Occident* repeatedly insists that Cézanne's paintings are beautiful: "they reveal the miraculous vein from which would spring total beauty"; Cézanne "sees things, not in themselves, but in their direct rapport with painting, or through the concrete expression of their beauty"; the work of Cézanne "imposes its vision by the essence and originality of its insight, the beauty of its substance."[14] Yet Bernard knows that the beautiful presents a problem in relation to Cézanne, and he admits that it "demands an explanation." He writes: "I would, in this case, define it thus: '*the fullest development of the art employed.*'"[15] He explains that Cézanne's models were not sophisticated people (whom he hated for their corrupt taste and duplicity), but rather his wife, his son, and simple people—the gardener Vallier, a peasant in a blue smock. With these before him, he set to work seeking beauty "inside the very means of painting itself: lines, tones, colors, thick paint, style, presentation, character."[16] This is far from a conventional or material beauty, Bernard concludes, and Cézanne's paintings will only be beautiful for those who possess a "very elevated sensibility" capable of "making us lose sight of the thing represented in order to enjoy it in the aesthetic sense."[17] To these three elements—proletarian and vernacular models, the fullest development of the art deployed, and an aesthetic sensibility—Bernard also mixes in a fourth, mystical element. Bernard claims that the true artist closes his door "in order to plunge himself into the absolute."[18] Here Bernard enters into what we can hear as an echo or read as a reminiscence of Hegel's spiritualization of the artwork, in which the work of art is a "surface or semblance of the sensuous." Beauty has nothing to do with desire or pleasure; but instead the work is apprehended for its own sake with the purpose of satisfying higher spiritual interests. "It is thus that, in art, the sensuous is *spiritualized,* i.e., the *spiritual* appears in sensuous shape."[19]

It seems that Bernard gets some of it right, specifically the part about beauty as *the fullest development of the art employed,* and that is Cézanne indeed. However, his claims about an "elevated" aesthetic sensibility and mysticism do not seem to us to ring true—they are truer, really, of Bernard's own symbolist paintings, and not of Cézanne. Bernard represented one of the two established schools of painting out of which the work of Cézanne emerged, the other being impressionism. We give Merleau-Ponty great credit for recognizing in the work of Cézanne an art beyond impressionism, for most of Cézanne's early admirers attached his work either to symbolism or impressionism. Typical of the latter, for example, the critic Gustave Geffroy had the opportunity to watch Cézanne in action when he was at work on Geffroy's own portrait in 1895. The transition from painting the "impression" to what Cézanne always called "sensation" was all too easy to make, for the words *sens* and *sensation* in French have a double meaning referring to perception but also to feeling. Geffroy described what he took to be Cézanne's "impressionism" in a passage like this: "Art does not proceed without a certain incompleteness, because the life that it reproduces is in perpetual transformation. . . . This is the truth of art everywhere and always, the truth affirmed with such power and charm by impressionism. Cézanne is one of the representatives of this fugitive and eternal vision."[20]

Merleau-Ponty argued that Cézanne was attempting to paint, not the fleeting impression in a precise momentary atmosphere of light, but the "lived-perspective," which includes depth and "thingliness" or a certain monumentality, even if that is not always easy to see standing before the works. In the portrait of *Madame Cézanne in a Red Dress* (1888–90), she looks distorted; the arms are immobilized, and the curtain next to the red chair is right on the picture plane but the chair is not. Her hands are composed of bizarre colors—red, green, blue, violet, flesh—in a way that must have influenced Matisse. (See figure 1.)

Even if sorting all this out is not as easy as "lived-perspective" might suggest, what is required is not something like an elevated aesthetic sensibility. Cézanne was not trying to paint like the classical Renaissance

1. Paul Cézanne, *Madame Cézanne (née Hortense Fiquet, 1850–1922) in a Red Dress,* 1888–90. Oil on canvas. 45 7/8 × 35 1/4 in. (116.5 × 89.5 cm.) The Metropolitan Museum of Art, New York. The Mr. and Mrs. Henry Ittleson Jr. Purchase Fund, 1962, 62.45. *IAP/ Image copyright © The Metropolitan Museum of Art, New York, N.Y.*

painters, like a Raphael or David for example, in which every single corner and piece of the painting is crystal clear in sharp focus. That is not the way vision works, even when an object is fixed immobile before us, let alone if the object is moving, let alone if we are moving too. Cézanne was attempting to paint the way we actually see, with a focal point of some clarity and peripheral perception that is shadowy and vague, with the plane of the focal point beyond the picture plane, and above all with a monumentality that lends things their proper respect and permanence. Mme. Cézanne's face is the focal point, and I must say, in spite of the lack of conformity to fineness and delicacy expected of traditional portraiture, the result is really quite tender. One keeps in mind, of course, that she has been sitting and sitting, days on end, so we can forgive the slightly bored expression and the arched eyebrow. "It took him one hun-

2. Paul Cézanne, *Madame Cézanne (née Hortense Fiquet, 1850–1922) in the Conservatory,* 1891. Oil on canvas. 36¼ × 28¾ in. (92.1 × 73 cm.) The Metropolitan Museum of Art, New York. Bequest of Stephen C. Clark, 1960, 61.101.2. *IAP/Image copyright © The Metropolitan Museum of Art, New York, N.Y.*

dred working sessions for a still life, one hundred fifty sittings for a portrait" ("CD" 59; "DC" 15), Merleau-Ponty writes in the first sentence of "Cézanne's Doubt." The hands are below the focal point and fall into the shadows, with various lightings and colors at different times of day, but they are peripheral so the edges are vague and shadowy. In the portrait of *Madame Cézanne in the Conservatory* (1891), the hands are not even painted at all, the kind of "painting in reserve" that paints only the spaces around the hands. (See figure 2.)

We need to understand some things like these in order to grasp Cézanne's art, but we need not be an "aesthete."

Bernard's spiritualization of a "mystical" Cézanne seems true in one sense, namely that the painter was searching for nature itself, for the means to bring himself to the origin of the world and the work of the Creator in the genesis of things. Already in 1895, Thadée Natanson wrote that Cézanne "is the painter of apples and he makes apples his own. . . . They belong to him as much as an object belongs to its creator."[21] Cézanne was a maker of worlds, and he himself said that he left the museum to "study Nature in all its beauty."[22] Cézanne was asked, "What is the ideal of earthly happiness?" He replied: "To have my own beautiful way of painting [*belle formule*]."[23] For this, Cézanne was always searching, struggling, never satisfied. The phrase *belle formule* mystified and frustrated his fellow-painters, who recognized in Cézanne's search what they themselves also sought. Bernard tells the story of showing Cézanne in 1904 a little still life Cézanne had painted fifteen years earlier that Bernard owned and treasured: "It's terrible," Cézanne responded.[24] He always believed that the art he had produced in the past was only the beginning of the art he would someday be able to create.

There is another sense in which we might agree to a "spiritual Cézanne," and that is with regard to the late watercolors. Merleau-Ponty selected a watercolor of Mt. Sainte-Victoire as one of the images for "Eye and Mind," and he comments that "in the watercolors of Cézanne's last years, space radiates around planes that cannot be assigned to any place at all: 'a superimposing of transparent surfaces,' 'a flowing movement of planes of color which overlap, advance and retreat'" ("EM" 141; *OE* 68). It has been a matter of much comment that the painter who searched out local color, solidity, and monumentality for almost all of his life should have turned to watercolors in these late works that are so transparent, so full of light, with painterly brushwork and pencil lines of such fineness and delicacy. The watercolor painting of Mt. Sainte-Victoire (1902–06) composed of delicate blues and violets is utterly ethereal and transcendent. (See figure 3.)

Cézanne's chromatic color theory, developed in the still lifes especially, had included red-violet and blue-violet as half-tint transitions from orange to blue. Nevertheless, this ethereal violet laced through the foreground of Mt. Sainte-Victoire is like the purer violet that ends the visible color spectrum. Violet rays have the shortest wavelength of any visible color, and therefore violet might be called a "really metaphysical color," for "beyond it lies the invisible."[25] Though so different in object, construction, and color, there are ways in which Cézanne's late watercolors are not unlike Bernard's *Madeleine dans le Bois d'Amour* (1888), showing a girl lying across the path before the woods with her eyes leading us right off the canvas to an invisible beyond. Cézanne's late watercolors "dematerialize" objects and the world with their transparency and illumination.

However, the idea of a mystical Cézanne does not carry all the way through for us because Cézanne's paintings are mostly about noth-

3. Paul Cézanne, *Mont Sainte-Victoire,* 1902–6. Watercolor, graphite, and gouache on paper. 12 1/5 × 18 9/10 in. (31.1 × 47.9 cm.) Louvre, Paris, France. *Scala/Art Resource, N.Y.*

ing other than themselves as paintings. Unlike the flowers of Degas or Renoir, which make us see right through the works to flowers, Cézanne stops us at the canvas. His struggles are right there for us to see, and every one of them, even the most successful, is an "attempt," an experiment. If he was or was not seeking the absolute, it remains hidden. Cézanne's paintings are mostly about painting. Yes, you have to paint something, but it is not really about the something, so an apple will do nicely, or a pear, or a blue vase. In the Cézanne room of the museums, viewers scrutinize. Seminars break out spontaneously. The fundamental relation to the works is *interrogative.* Where is the edge of Mme. Cézanne's hands? Why are both adjacent sides of the table leg painted in the same flat plane? Why is the fireplace edge not in the same plane as the drapery? Is it even the edge of a fireplace? In Cézanne, we never "lose sight of the thing," just as Bernard himself claimed.

This is not to say that Cézanne's paintings are inexpressive: in his observation that "expressing what *exists* is an endless task" ("CD" 66; "DC" 26), Merleau-Ponty summed up Cézanne's life and work. To take one example, the 1866 portrait *The Artist's Father, Reading "L'Événement"* shows us a large and imposing father even though he sits in an upholstered chair reading the newspaper. (See figure 4.)

The image itself is life-size, approximately six and a half feet tall

4. Paul Cézanne, *The Artist's Father, Reading "L'Événement,"* 1866. Oil on canvas. 78 1/8 × 47 in. (1.985 × 1.193 m.); framed size: 88 1/4 × 57 × 4 in. (2.242 × 1.448 × .101 m.) Collection of Mr. and Mrs. Paul Mellon, 1970.5.1. (2369)/PA. *Image courtesy of the Board of Trustees, National Gallery of Art, Washington, D.C.*

by four feet wide, and the predominant colors are black and white: the white upholstery of the chair offsets the father's black jacket and cap. This father is not relaxed, but upright on the edge of the chair even though he is reading the newspaper. There is clear space between his body and the back of the chair on which he could have been resting. He is dressed somewhat formally, wearing a skullcap, jacket, and white collar, and the newspaper he is shown reading is not his own favorite, *Le Siècle,* but Cézanne's own preferred paper, *L'Événement,* in which favorable art reviews and opinions appeared by Cézanne's friends. The paint is applied thickly with a palette knife, giving the whole scene an edgy, rough feel. This image, created when Cézanne was twenty-seven, captures the authoritarian and stern relationship of father to son, a father who did not trust his son's chosen career as an artist. A man of practical affairs who was first a hatmaker and then a banker, the father made enough money to leave a "respectable income" to Cézanne and his two sisters when he died. In the background of the painting, hanging on the wall above and behind the chair, appears one of Cézanne's own still lifes of apples, pears, and a sugar bowl, hovering over this father's reading like a haunting resistance to the father's desires for his son. Cézanne said: "My father, who was intelligent and good-hearted, said to himself: 'My son is an artist who will die in misery. I'm going to work for him,' and my father left me enough to live on and paint until I die."[26] Bernard reports that "thinking about his father brought tears to Cézanne's eyes. When he was young, he thought his father was severe, but in the end he understood the generous wisdom that guided him."[27] The painting is expressive, and it expresses that tension, the reserved dignity and authority of the father who judges and maintains a distance, but who is also a practical figure who can be counted upon for support.

As these cases illuminate, when Merleau-Ponty speaks in this way of expression in painting, or in language, for that matter, especially fiction and poetry, he is thinking of what he calls in *Phenomenology of Perception,* in the chapter on "The Body as Expression, and Speech," original art and speech (*une parole parlante*) that "sings the world's praises" (*chanter le monde*), not the more deadened and leaden "spoken speech" (*une parole parlée*) handed down as a language system (*PP* 197; *PhP* 229). For original speech there is no externality or exteriority in the sign-signified relationship. Merleau-Ponty writes of the experience of becoming engrossed in a book and no longer seeing letters on the page or even being aware of turning the pages; we are literally "at," or perhaps even "in," the imaginative landscape of the work. In *The Prose of the World,* this is what Merleau-Ponty calls the "perfection of language," which is its capacity to pass unnoticed. Between the author and reader, as between the painter and viewer, there is a "meeting of minds" in which the author and painter "come to dwell in my world." Merleau-Ponty analogizes the expressive relation between author and reader to a love relation in which one partner is dominant for a time—this would be the reader or viewer—but subsequently, with a truly great author like Stendahl or a painter like Cézanne, the relationship reverses and the other partner, the author or painter, takes over. Merleau-Ponty says that "the expressive moment occurs where the relationship reverses itself, where the book takes possession of the reader" (*PW* 13; *PM* 9–13). Adopting Husserl's language on intersubjectivity, Merleau-Ponty speaks of a "complicity of speech and its echo, or to use Husserl's lively phrase referring to the perception of others, through the 'coupling' of language" (*PW* 13; *PM* 21). The work, Merleau-Ponty says, "catches fire" and "my thoughts are ablaze." This metaphor of "catching fire" from *The Prose of the World* echoes Kurt Badt's account of truth in Cézanne's pictures in which the things are "burned in fire," and anticipates Merleau-Ponty's discussion of the paintings of Paul Klee in "Eye and Mind" in which he quotes Klee: "A certain fire wills to live; it wakes. Working its way along the hand's conductor, it reaches the canvas and invades it; then, a leaping spark, it arcs the gap in the circle it was to trace: the return to the eye, and beyond" ("EM" 147; *OE* 86).

Rilke knew Bernard's account of Cézanne mainly from Bernard's *Souvenirs sur Cézanne* and dismissed him as a "not very likeable painter behind whose back one may glean a few factual data."[28] Rilke could not have known that Bernard would become quite critical of Cézanne, for that was only recorded in a publication in 1921, long after Rilke's letters were written in October and November 1907. According to Bernard's account in 1921 of his last conversation with Cézanne, Bernard had told Cézanne that the Italian art of the Renaissance obeyed a "superior logic and that is what made it alternately mystical, Platonic, and imaginative." In response, Cézanne "regarded Bernard with a terrible look in his eyes" and answered through apparent tears, "The truth lies in nature; I will prove it!" Then he walked away. Bernard watched him recede into the distance and felt, he says, that he "had just stood up for Art against the stubbornness of a solitary man who blocked his own path through the absolutism of his research."[29] Such a traumatic and contrary ending between Cézanne and Bernard means that Rilke will bring us closer to an interpretation of the beautiful in Cézanne that will be productive for us.

Cézanne and Rilke

From Rilke's letters, we know that he spent the month of October 1907 engaged in an almost daily face-to-face study of the paintings by Cézanne displayed in the Cézanne room of the Salon d'Automne in the Grand Palais on the Champs Élysées, a retrospective exhibition of sixty-two works organized in the year after Cézanne's death. Rilke's first impressions agree very much with Bernard regarding the humbleness of all the objects painted: "The apples are all cooking apples and the wine bottles belong in the roundly bulging pockets of an old coat."[30] These are presented by Cézanne not as edible or potable; they are "things" that are "simply indestructible in their stubborn thereness."[31] Rilke argues that Cézanne makes "saints" out of these humble things and "forces them—*forces them*—to be beautiful, to stand for the whole world and all joy and glory."[32] So there is a beauty that has to do with thingliness, indestructibility, and sheer monumentality. This shining presence of the most humble of things is the presence of beauty, and it is found, not in words or in reflection, but in the physicality and layering on of the paint, working and reworking it over and over again, stroke upon stroke. In "Eye and Mind," Merleau-Ponty puts this thought about Cézanne's "things" in his own way:

> It is too little to say that it [the thing, the object, the smile] is there as an image or essence; it is there as itself, as that which was always most alive about it, the moment I look at the painting. The "world's instant" that Cézanne wanted to paint, an instant long since passed away, is still hurled toward us by his paintings. His Mt. Sainte Victoire is made and remade from one end of the world to the other in a way different from but no less energetic than in the hard rock above Aix. ("EM" 130; *OE* 35)

Rilke himself shied away from attempting to write an essay about Cézanne, which he still admitted was a "great temptation" for him.[33] Yet his second essay on Rodin (1907) gives us much of what we can imagine he would also have said of the "beautiful things" of Cézanne. In everyday talk, the word "thing" means almost nothing to us and we pass right by it without a thought. Yet the thing is something precious, and from our childhood it is associated with many memories. Try to remember some precious thing, a piece of wood perhaps, that once required your love, trust, and devotion, Rilke asks. This small forgotten object once was the primary relationship with the world; it was tree, king, and child. Such a thing struck us by its urgency, the particular, "almost desperate earnestness" all things have. Rilke imagines that the urgency of things led to the making of tools and vessels and the earliest images of the gods. He writes: "No thing can move you if you do not allow for it to surprise you with an unimaginable beauty. Beauty is always something we come to, but we don't know what this something is."[34]

This emphasis on the monumental, shining presence of things therefore enables us to understand why Rilke made so much of Cézanne's colors. In his letters, this is the dominant theme linking beauty with Cézanne. Rilke wrote that no one before Cézanne "ever demonstrated so clearly the extent to which painting is something that takes place among the colors, and how one has to leave them alone completely, so they can settle the matter among themselves. Their intercourse: this is the whole of painting."[35] No one before had ever used color as had Cézanne, simply for making the object. This is what Cézanne called the "realization" (*la réalisation*) of the work, the way in which the harmony, the balance, the "logic" of the colors makes the things come forth. Rilke thinks this is like a glandular activity in the mouth of a dog whose secretions anticipate the approach of different things, nutrients or poisons. Everything gets settled among the colors themselves, and a color only comes into its own in response to another color. Rilke writes of Cézanne's "very unique blue," which, when set against a "self-contained blue" such as we find in Van Gogh, presents us with a "listening blue," and a "thunderstorm blue," a blue "full of revolt, Blue, Blue, Blue."[36] "All of this is very beautiful," Rilke wrote.[37]

To beautiful things and beautiful colors, Rilke adds one further stone in the arch of beauty: beautiful character, and this is about the integrity of Cézanne himself as shown in the works. Bernard, Merleau-Ponty, and others have told us all the tragicomic stories: Cézanne's paranoia that everyone was trying to "get their hooks" into him, how he found life terrifying, especially near the end, how he raged against his works and his critics, how he suffered from diabetes and had trouble with his eyes, how he would not allow anyone to watch him working, how he could not stand to be touched physically by anyone, how the children ridiculed him on his way to his studio, how Zola, his own Provençal childhood friend, had misunderstood him and misrepresented him to the world in his novel *L'Oeuvre*. Cézanne commented: "One fine day I received *L'Oeuvre*. It was a real blow to me to see his innermost feelings about me. When all is said and done, it is a very bad book and completely false."[38] Rilke writes: "I know a few things from his last years when he was old and shabby and children followed him every day on his way to his studio, throwing stones at him as if at a stray dog. But inside, way inside, he was marvelously beautiful."[39] Rilke thinks that Cézanne was an artist who truly loved the world, and did not leave that love outside or alongside the works as an extraneous sentiment, but put the love into the works themselves. He would not have known how to show another human being his genuine love for them, but perhaps precisely due to his cross temperament and insular life, he knew how to put his love to rest in every apple and every object.

He knew how to put his love to rest in the portraits of his wife as well, Hortense Fiquet Cézanne. These have been neglected or discredited as portraits due to their sitter's lack of beauty, her sour disposition, her failure to smile and ingratiate herself. These works have been treated with hostility, as if Cézanne painted his wife "all appley," like just another still life.[40] The portraits have been thought to express what seemed to the critics the incredulous, if not ridiculous, relationship and marriage of Paul Cézanne and Hortense Fiquet, a woman known as a superficial "chatterbox" with whom the painter did not live after the birth of their only son, also named Paul.[41] The wife and child lived mostly in Paris, while the artist lived mostly with his housekeeper and sister in Aix. Yet the sheer number of portraits insists that we look again: almost thirty portraits of this woman, his wife, twenty-six of them cataloged, stretching over twenty-two years from 1872 to 1894. We can tell a different story: there is in these paintings not just "a woman" or "an unhappy woman." We find what Merleau-Ponty calls a "style of being," and this has much less to do with feeling than with "the emblem of a way of inhabiting the world, of treating it, and of interpreting it by her face, by clothing, the agility of the gesture and the inertia of the body" ("ILVS" 91; *S* 54; *Si* 68).[42] Not one of these paintings is the same. From one to another, the colors of her clothing change and the colors of the highlights on her cheeks and lips and in her eyes also change, the pose and posture shift, the setting alters, and through it all, there remains a tenderness that, though apparently aching and melancholy, is also deep and full of care. Rilke said it was a tenderness full of love, and if Cézanne's fears and worries and petulance prevented him from putting it overtly into the relationship, he could put it all into the works.

There is a portrait of Mme. Cézanne that seems to us to confirm indisputably Cézanne's tenderness for his wife, titled *Hydrangea Blossom with Portrait of Hortense Cézanne* (1885). (See figure 5.) As the painting's French title—*Hortensia avec portrait de Hortense Cézanne*—reveals, Hortense Fiquet Cézanne's first name means "hydrangea," and Cézanne has linked his wife with the flower symbolically in the work, something highly unusual in his oeuvre. In the upper right-hand corner we see a simple, elegant pencil line drawing of Hortense's face and neck, with her head reclining and resting on what appears to be a pillow. In the entire left side of the picture is a watercolor in green, white, and violet of the hydrangea blossom with its leaves. The expression on the face of Hortense is one of serene repose, and Cézanne has captured her without the least "distortion" or "appleyness." The eyes gaze at us with a kind of melancholy tenderness clearly drawn by an artist who has put his feelings for her into the work. John Rewald, in his *Catalog Raisonné* of Cézanne's watercolors, writes that while the work "is a statement of remarkable delicacy, the true miracle is the exquisite tenderness revealed by the head of Hortense Cézanne," and Ruth Butler's recent study of the "model-wives" of Cézanne, Monet, and Rodin says that this work is simply Cézanne's "most beautiful facial rendering of Hortense. . . . There is a delicacy and gentleness here seldom

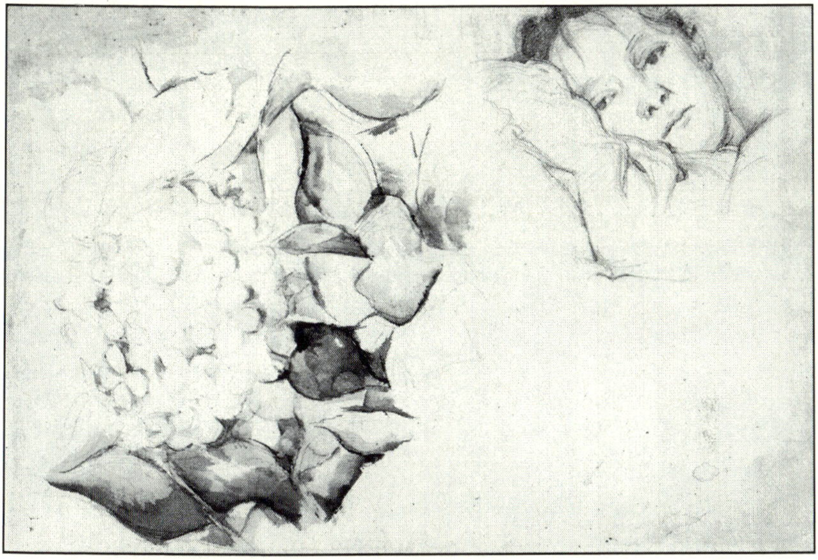

5. Paul Cézanne, *Hydrangea Blossom with Portrait of Hortense Cézanne* (*Madame Cézanne aux hortensias*), circa 1885. Pencil and watercolor on white paper. 12 × 18⅛ in. (30.5 × 46 cm.) The owner of this work wishes readers to view it in color. It is Plate 22 in John Rewald, *Paul Cézanne: The Watercolors, a Catalogue Raisonné* (Boston: Little, Brown, 1983). An online digital image is available at www.paul-cezanne.org. *Private collection, Zürich.*

seen."[43] Butler describes the hydrangea drawing with its green and violet wash as Cézanne's "bouquet for his wife." The dating of the work places it in the period just prior to the marriage of Paul and Hortense in 1886; however, the two had met in 1869 and their son, Paul, had been born in 1872, so their relationship had seen some seventeen years of development. The work is definitely not the work of an early infatuation but is drawn from mature feelings of care and tenderness.

We find the same tender attention in the portraits of the gardener, Vallier. The gardener sat repeatedly, and the earlier portraits of Vallier filled with blues, greens, and light give way to the darkness and black of the last portrait, the painting on which Cézanne worked on the day he was caught in a storm and, already sick with bronchitis, collapsed and died. Meyer Shapiro has compared these late Vallier portraits with the work of Titian and Rembrandt: "It concerns an aristocracy which is not founded on power or accomplishment, but on inner strength. This plain man is big without swagger or self-consciousness, at peace with himself without resignation."[44] This is what Rilke calls Cézanne's "sainthood." "This lying-down-with-the-leper and sharing all one's warmth with him, including the heartwarmth of nights of love; this must at some time have been part of an artist's existence, as a self-overcoming on the way to his new bliss."[45] Cézanne had no other devotion than to his work, the abundance of his tasks, and the steadfastness of this love. Perhaps in this way, Rilke meets Bernard on the mystical path, but Spirit is not placed in a heavenly beyond nor the works reduced to a surface or semblance, but is realized in a man and in the works.

Rilke gives us the clue to another idea that he does not develop in the Cézanne letters, and this emerges from Rilke's discussion of Cézanne's colors: Rilke links Cézanne's colors with something about time. Cézanne, he writes, "so incorruptibly reduced a reality to its color content that it resumed a new existence in a beyond of color, without any previous memories."[46] Rilke found in Cézanne's touches of color that paradox of a time before time: a new existence, a beyond of color, with no previous memories. In his second essay on Rodin (1907), Rilke began with much the same: "I come before you to remind you of your childhood. For it should be possible to awaken memories that are not yours, memories that are older than you."[47] There is something going on in Cézanne that has to do with the folding over of time, with repetition and desire, the desire for the "again," and all of this has something to do with beauty about which we must say much more later. We hear the echo of that almost magical phrase written by Merleau-Ponty in *Phenomenology of Perception,* "an original past, a past that has never been present" (*PP* 242; *PhP* 280). Rilke and Merleau-Ponty converge upon passivity, repetition, and archaic time in experiencing the beautiful. What is it about all those Cézanne repetitions—those apples, that mountain, that woman, and those bathers? What is it about all those sittings? What is the desire that kept all of this going? We must speak carefully and patiently here, for we are aware of all the reasons—from Kant, from Hegel, from current political critiques—to dissociate desire from beauty, and we will address those reasons directly in part 3 of this work. We need to speak of an aesthetic desire that is not controlling, possessive, or objectifying, but a cooler and more positive desire like Cézanne's color blue, that gives us the world and respects the otherness of things.[48] First, there is simply a desire for the work, a desire for the paint itself and its textures and smells, and the strokes over and over and over, so reassuring and satisfying, to make that same movement that carries the brush from the palette to the canvas to bear down on that edge until it gives in to the shadow. Nothing could be more satisfying than the materials and the tools, to be with them in insular solitude with nothing but the work, to repeat those movements. Second, there is a desire for the struggle as well, to work at the problem of edge and shadow, focal and peripheral, picture plane and object plane, near and far, what Merleau-Ponty called the problem of depth. All these are questions, not to be worked out as beliefs or opinions, but to be answered in and by the work itself. The artist desires the same as the philosopher, Merleau-Ponty argues: "No longer is it a matter of speaking about space and light, but of making space and light which are *there,* speak to us. There is no end to this questioning." And speaking directly to the question of desire, he adds: "This philosophy, which is yet to be elaborated, is what animates the painter—not when he expresses opinions about the world but in that instant when his vision becomes gesture, when, in Cézanne's words, he 'thinks in painting'" ("EM" 138–39; *OE* 60). Something like this must have been what also led Merleau-Ponty to say that "the very first painting in some sense went to the farthest reach of the future" ("EM" 149; *OE* 92). Time folds over and we can picture Cézanne at the caves of Lascaux in "a beyond of color, without any previous memories." Lost in the work, transported in time, the meaning of Cézanne is the desire for the work and to be at the world; this is a strong beauty.

Some have said that beauty is an effeminate concept, filled with fragility and delicacy, and that is why it must give way to the more masculine, stronger concept of the sublime. In the eighteenth century, Edmund Burke had this to say: "An air of robustness and strength is very prejudicial to beauty. An appearance of *delicacy,* and even of fragility, is almost essential to it."[49] All of the qualities Burke ascribes to the beautiful are of this genre: smallness, smoothness, softness, delicacy, clarity. Of colors, he wrote that "they must not be of the strongest kind. Those which seem most appropriated to beauty are the milder of every sort: light greens; soft blues; weak whites; pink reds; and violets," and moreover, absolutely no black.[50] Still today, Gilbert-Rolfe, writing of the contemporary "technological sublime," argues that beauty is a feminine concept due to its "implicit powerlessness."[51] Such notions entirely miss the point of Cézanne. He shows us another way: strong beauty.

There is desire for an "again" in us, the viewers, as well. We want to see what Cézanne saw, to repeat his vision and be at the mountain. We want his mountain to be our mountain, and so we look at the paintings and we go back, over and over again, to scrutinize, to question, to be puzzled. Eventually the galleries and museums are not enough. Merleau-Ponty himself, in the summer of 1960, headed for that road where Cézanne's studio is still located just east of the Aix town center. There he finished the third and last draft of "Eye and Mind" and signed it from "Le Tholonet, juillet-aôut, 1960." Willem de Kooning says that sometimes, at a certain moment, he would "catch a glimpse." That is what we, the successors, desire from Cézanne; just a glimpse.

Cézanne and Heidegger: Truth in Painting

If there is in Cézanne a desire for the work and a desire for the struggles of painting, there is also a third desire, and this is the desire for truth in painting. Famously, Cézanne wrote in a letter to Bernard of October 23, 1905, as we cited in our introduction to this chapter: "I owe you the truth in painting and I shall tell it to you" (*Je vous dois la vérité en peinture, et je vous la dirai*).[52] In the "Indirect Language" essay, Merleau-Ponty makes it eminently clear that modern painters "want nothing to do with a truth defined as the resemblance of painting and the world. They would accept the idea of a truth defined as a painting's cohesion with itself." Modern painting, like modern thought, he adds, "obliges us to admit a truth which does not resemble things, which is without any external model and without any predestined instruments of expression, and which is nevertheless truth" ("ILVS" 93–94; *S* 56; *Si* 71–72). Such statements mean that Merleau-Ponty does not theorize truth in terms of a mind picturing an external world, or of an artist representing external things and objects. In fact, he is opposed to the entire philosophical tradition's efforts to speak of mind and truth on a representational model of reality, as we have seen in his critique of the "Optics" of Descartes.[53] Together with Heidegger, Merleau-Ponty thinks that the meaning of truth has to do with unconcealing and rendering visible, which means that if we must speak of "correspondence," we do so only as cor-respondence, or an attunement that opens up and expresses the world.

Although this much is quite clear, Merleau-Ponty was guarded in his references to truth in art, in comparison with a philosopher such as Heidegger in "The Origin of the Work of Art." Therefore, it will be helpful to develop this thought of truth in painting for Cézanne and Merleau-Ponty in relation to Heidegger, first from "The Origin of the Work of Art" and subsequently from what we know of Heidegger's later confrontation with the paintings of Cézanne. Our argument will show a movement in Heidegger's philosophy of art from an initial distance from and set of contrasts with Merleau-Ponty toward a growing closeness to Merleau-Ponty's philosophy of art; this movement was inspired by Heidegger's discovery of Cézanne, and also by his discovery of Paul Klee, which we will add later in chapter 5. It has become customary to note Merleau-Ponty's growing proximity to the thought of Heidegger in Merleau-Ponty's later writings; I want to argue that in their philosophy of art it worked the other way around, with Heidegger becoming more like Merleau-Ponty.

In "The Origin of the Work of Art" Heidegger had concluded: "The nature of art would then be this: the truth of beings setting itself to work."[54] "The Origin" posits an explicit link between beauty (*Schönheit*) and truth, beauty being one of truth's modalities. Heidegger states: "This is how self-concealing being is illuminated. Light of this kind joins its shining to and into the work. This shining, joined in the work, is the beautiful. *Beauty is one way in which truth occurs as unconcealedness.*"[55] A reading of "The Origin" in comparison with "Cézanne's Doubt" and "Eye and Mind" discloses a set of initial differences between Heidegger and Merleau-Ponty, of which three are prominent. While Merleau-Ponty worked from specific artists, nearly all modern—Cézanne, Rodin, Klee, and so on—Heidegger preferred different and more eclectic artworks: a Van Gogh painting, a Greek temple, a poem by C. F. Meyer titled "Roman Fountain," and the late hymns of Hölderlin. Second, whereas Merleau-Ponty argued in "Eye and Mind" that painting best "draws upon the fabric of brute meaning . . . and does so in full innocence" ("EM" 123; *OE* 13), Heidegger makes it clear that all art as the advent or happening of truth "is, as such, *essentially poetry*."[56] "The nature of art is poetry," Heidegger writes, and "the nature of poetry, in turn, is the founding of truth."[57] There is an important sense here in which this contrast should not be overdone, for texts by Merleau-Ponty other than "Eye and Mind" show deep comprehension of the philosophical importance of poetry as well as music, which is also seemingly diminished in "Eye and Mind." To give just one example with respect to poetry, and not even referring to the deep influence of Proust on *The Visible and the Invisible,* in the justly famous passage from *Phenomenology of Perception* on "singing the world" (*chanter le monde*) that we have discussed in relation to the concept of expression, it has been too little noticed that Merleau-Ponty makes poetry exemplary of this unique "singing." Verbal forms in different natural languages, he argues, would no longer appear so arbitrary if we took into account the word's "'gestural sense,' which is all-important in poetry, for example. It would then be found that the words, vowels and phonemes are so many ways of 'singing the world'" (*PP* 187; *PhP* 218). A third contrast brings us to the horizon of a deep philosophical tension between the aesthetic thinking of Heidegger and Merleau-Ponty: whereas Merleau-Ponty was steadily more interested in the artistic *act* (to paint, *peindre*), with its unique vision and creativity, that in the artwork (the painting, *la peinture*), Heidegger stresses the artistic *work,* the artwork as such, its essence and function. This last difference brings into view Heidegger's central notions of "world" and "earth."

For Heidegger, the nature of a work as a "thing" is its equipmentality as serviceable and reliable. This is the same stress that we found in Rilke's treatment of the "thingliness" of the objects in Cézanne's works. Heidegger explains his own meaning through a narrative of one of Van

Gogh's paintings of what Heidegger took to be a pair of shoes that belonged to a peasant woman: "this equipment belongs to the *earth,* and it is protected in the *world* of the peasant woman."[58] It would be too distracting here to go into all that has been written and thought about these shoes: how Meyer Shapiro contended that they were Van Gogh's own shoes—boots in fact—disclosing not the rural world and plowed fields of Bavarian peasant farming but the winter worlds of Paris and Montmartre in the late 1880s; and how then Derrida wrote a book beginning with Cézanne titled *The Truth in Painting* in which he questioned whether Van Gogh even shows us a "pair" of left and right matched shoes and whether they are the shoes of a man or of a woman.[59] In fact, the whole Heideggerian narrative regarding Van Gogh is anomalous in an essay in which Heidegger argues against the museum conception of art and in favor of one in which great works of art create and preserve a community of peoples.[60] Be all that as it may, whereas what Heidegger means by "world" is only moderately troubled, from a Merleau-Pontean point of view, the meaning of "earth" is much more difficult and troublesome.

Every human being, Heidegger argues, is born into a fundamental horizon of disclosure and it is this that he calls "world," the background and usually unnoticed understanding that determines for a historical people what, for them, fundamentally *there is.* Thus, "world" in "The Origin" is continuous with *Being and Time* where Heidegger identifies it as an "ontological structure" that emerges from the ready-to-hand.[61] "World" is also what Heidegger has in mind when later in "The Origin" he speaks of "the clearing" or "the open." The Heideggerian concept of "world" is fairly resonant with Merleau-Ponty, for as a reader of Husserl, Merleau-Ponty continuously understood the perceived world as a temporal region "that endures only through the reflections, shadows, levels, and horizons between things (which are not things and not nothings, but on the contrary mark out by themselves the fields of possible variation in the same thing and the same world)" (*S* 160; *Si* 202). Merleau-Ponty also, at least from the middle period of his thought onward, if not before, thought of "world" or horizon as historically and culturally made rather than as a structure given purely naturally or biologically, whatever that could mean. Thus, I think it would be largely correct to see an agreement between Merleau-Ponty and Heidegger regarding truth in painting with respect to "world": an artwork renders visible or unconceals the invisible horizons of perception that everyday perception takes for granted, and thus overlooks. This is one way, a mild way, I would say, to understand the artwork as, in the words of Paul Klee, "rendering visible," which means rendering the invisible visible.

When we come to Heidegger's concept of "earth," we truly see a distance open up between the aesthetic thinking of these two figures. "The temple work," Heidegger writes, "standing there, opens up a world and at the same time sets this world back again on earth, which itself only thus emerges as native ground."[62] Heidegger himself rules out a literal reading of "earth" or the native "ground" either as a mass of matter deposited somewhere or as the idea of a planet in the solar system. Rather, the meaning of "earth" circulates between two thoughts in the "Origin" essay: the first is the thought of sheltering and stability, that earth has more solidity and durability than either world or artwork and thus offers them shelter and protection; the second is the thought of concealment, even ineffability, in the work of art, that leads in the direction of Heidegger's language of the sacred and the "holy." The notion that artworks disclose a world must be given its other side of darkness, unfathomability, depth, and mystery. Being also "withdraws," "closes," and "conceals itself," and this thought is part of the meaning of "earth." "The earth is essentially self-secluding. To set forth the earth means to bring it into the Open as the self-secluding."[63] Scholars have also found in "world" and "earth" an echo of Nietzsche on the Apollonian and Dionysian elements in great art.[64] In volume 1 of *Nietzsche,* Heidegger refers the original meaning of these word pairs, world-earth and Apollonian-Dionysian, to the German poet Hölderlin, who "had seen and conceived of the opposition in an even more profound and lofty manner," for Hölderlin draws the contrast between "holy pathos" and the Occidental "sobriety of representational skill."[65] These terms from Hölderlin are much closer to the language of "The Origin," which cites explicitly Hölderlin's hymn "The Rhine" and often speaks of earth as site of the "holy."[66]

Now I would be one of the last to say that there is no sense of the artwork as the site of the holy or sacred in Merleau-Ponty, and as part of our chapter on Paul Klee and "mortal beauty" we will take up the meaning of transcendence for Merleau-Ponty in relation to beauty. However, I do want to emphasize here that Merleau-Ponty's philosophy of art is much more guarded with respect to any "spiritualization" of the artwork or mystical ineffability of earth. Such a stress would drive Merleau-Ponty's philosophy of art away from Cézanne and back toward Bernard. Though Merleau-Ponty does speak of an "eternal Cézanne" ("CD" 71; "DC" 35), whenever Merleau-Ponty was drawn into speaking of spiritual life, it was always a spirituality of this world of which he spoke, not a transcendent world that is other and beyond. Citing Claudel, who said that God is not a supersensible idea but "another ourself which dwells in and authenticates our darkness," Merleau-Ponty drew his own conclusion against any notion of vertical transcendence: "Transcendence no longer hangs over man: he becomes, strangely, its privileged bearer" ("ILVS" 108; *S* 71; *Si* 88).

Transcendence has to do with humanity's own embodied incarnation and reaching out toward the other and the world; it is transcendence on the "plane of immanence," in the language of Deleuze and Guattari.[67]

Turning back to Heidegger, when Merleau-Ponty came to address explicitly the relationship of world and earth in "The Philosopher and His Shadow," following Husserl he spoke of the "circularity between Nature and persons" (*S* 176; *Si* 222). With Husserl, when Merleau-Ponty speaks of the Earth, he does not speak of it poetically but as the planet that is our native soil, the "stem of our thought as it is of our life" (*S* 180; *Si* 227). Husserl's awakening of a "wild-flowering world [*l'être sauvage*] and mind [*l'esprit brut*]" is, Merleau-Ponty says, a "renewal of the world that is also mind's renewal, a rediscovery of that brute mind which, untamed by any culture, is asked to create culture anew." And Merleau-Ponty then wrote the last sentence of his Husserl essay in the "down-to-earth" language of the craft of woodworking and cabinetry: "that 'teleology' Husserl speaks about which is written and thought about in parentheses—that jointing and framing of Being which is being realized through mankind" (*S* 181; *Si* 228).

Heidegger describes the world-earth disjunction as "strife" (*Urstreit*), "conflict," and even "warfare" between the forces of disclosure and those of concealment. The world or truth aspect of the work is pitted against the earth or concealment aspect. The "Origin" text emphasizes that "the conflict is not a rift [*Riss*] as a mere cleft is ripped open; rather, it is the intimacy with which opponents belong to each other."[68] Even thus qualified, it is far from obvious that such a strife or agitation is to be found in every great work of art, including those others that Heidegger himself mentions, such as Van Gogh's paintings and Hölderlin's late hymns.[69] In these works we find much more harmony of colors and sounds than strife. Heidegger imported the notion of strife rather directly from Heraclitus, and thus truth in the work of art does not just "happen," it must be won.[70]

"The Origin of the Work of Art" dates from the mid-1930s; it was originally given as a lecture in Freiburg in 1935, then repeated in Zurich in early 1936, and subsequently reworked as three public lectures in Frankfurt in late 1936. A decade after the "Origin," in the late 1940s, Heidegger had his first confrontation with the meaning of Cézanne, and this occurred precisely through his own study of Rilke's *Letters on Cézanne* in preparation for Heidegger's 1946 lecture on Rilke, "What Are Poets For?"[71] Shortly after, he had the opportunity to view several Cézannes in the Basel Art Gallery, especially late Mt. Sainte-Victoire watercolors (*Mont Sainte-Victoire Seen from Les Lauves,* 1902–06) and portraits of the gardener Vallier. Heidegger began to visit Cézanne's homeland around Aix-en-

Provence in the mid-1950s and is reported to have said: "Cézanne's path is the path to which, from beginning to end, my own path as a thinker responds (corresponds) in its own way. . . . These days in Cézanne's homeland are worth more than a whole library of philosophy books. If only one could think as directly as Cézanne painted."[72] Regarding Heidegger's journeys to Aix, Heinrich Petzet reports on a photograph that shows Heidegger sitting in front of Mt. Sainte-Victoire. His position was on one of Cézanne's paths, along which one reached the edge of a precipitous rock face with the dark green of trees, the red of the earth, and the water of the Zola dam far below, and on the other side of the dam was the mountain range. "He sat very still, over against St. Victoire, looking at the mountains. He sat there like that for a long time. I could not say just how long; this kind of time is nonmeasurable."[73]

What Heidegger meant in saying that Cézanne's path was the one to which his own path as a thinker responded is not entirely clear. For one thing, the language of strife between world and earth in "The Origin" was much more suited to an architectural work such as a Greek temple, with its placement on rocky soil and terrain, than to the paintings of Cézanne with their rigorous color logic. But for another, some illumination is available in a poem Heidegger wrote, or a "thing thought," as he called these poems of his, about one of Cézanne's final portraits of the gardener Vallier. It begins with a description of the painting:

> The thoughtfully serene, the urgent
> stillness of the form of the old gardener
> Vallier, who tends the inconspicuous on the
> *Chemin des Lauves.*

After these lines about the work, Heidegger seeks to set forth the philosophical meaning of Cézanne:

> In the late work of the painter the twofoldness
> of what is present and of presence has become
> one, "realized" and overcome at the same time,
> transformed into a mystery-filled identity.[74]

In Cézanne, Heidegger experienced an overcoming of the duality of time between present and presence, between beings and Being, as well as the duality of the world-earth strife, not altogether so, but something closer to what Merleau-Ponty meant when he said that in Cézanne's late mountain landscapes "the mountain makes itself mountain before our eyes" ("EM" 128; *OE* 29). The curious point about Cézanne's last paintings of his mountain, as we have noted about the late watercolors, is that his late painterly vision disassembles the mountain, dematerializes it, and then reassembles it. It is as if we have the color field nearly absent of meaning (*sens*), or as wild meaning (*sens sauvage*), out of which quite suddenly emerges the mountain. Beginning with the experiments of Cézanne's middle paintings, Merleau-Ponty says, "the things began to move, color against color; they began to modulate in the instability" ("EM" 140; *OE* 66). Merleau-Ponty names this the "deflagration of Being" ("EM" 140; *OE* 66), by which we can understand the rapid combustion of Being becoming world before our eyes. "It is the painter," Merleau-Ponty says, "to whom the things of the world give birth by a sort of concentration or coming-to-itself of the visible" ("EM" 11; *OE* 69). This is a stronger meaning of rendering visible; not that weaker meaning of showing us what in our world has been overlooked, but rendering visible what has never been visible before, in which we are at the birth of meaning and the twofoldness of time is overcome. This is what Heidegger, too, had come to experience in his confrontation with Cézanne's portrait of Vallier, and what Heidegger contemplated as he also, like Merleau-Ponty subsequently, sat in quiet repose before Mt. Sainte-Victoire.

In these ways having to do with truth as unconcealing or rendering visible, Merleau-Ponty argued that there is an affinity between art and philosophy: the philosopher is the one who "wakes up and speaks" (*IPP* 63; *EP* 73). Of Cézanne, he said the artist "speaks as the first man spoke and paints as if no one had ever painted before. . . . The artist launches his work just as a man once launched the first word, not knowing whether it will be anything more than a shout" ("CD" 69; "DC" 32). In his inaugural lecture at the Collège de France, Merleau-Ponty confessed that "philosophy limps. It dwells in history and in life, but it wishes to dwell at their center, at the point where they come into being with the birth of meaning" (*IPP* 58; *EP* 67–68). Cézanne found that center at the fold of time and memory. He was still limping too, but far ahead of us. If the "limping of philosophy is its virtue" (*IPP* 61; *EP* 71), the limping of Cézanne is our challenge, for we can see him on the horizon before his mountain, and in our ears we can hear the echoes of Cézanne's shout, and it is the shout of beauty.

4

Auguste Rodin: Beauty and Its Doubles

> Nothing equals in splendor this terrible opposition of the Beauty, which one wishes were eternal, and the atrocious disintegration, which actually awaits it.
>
> —Auguste Rodin, *Art: Conversations with Paul Gsell*

> Beauty is always and inevitably of a double composition, although the impression that it produces is single.
>
> —Charles Baudelaire, *The Painter of Modern Life*

> My body is that meaningful core which behaves like a general function, and which nevertheless exists, and is susceptible to disease.
>
> —Merleau-Ponty, *Phenomenology of Perception*

The aesthetic of Rodin is a "mixture." It mixes earth and artist, classical and modern, empirical and transcendental, immanence and transcendence, temporal and eternal, eros and corruption, pleasure and pain, banal and transgressive, power and impotence.[1] Beauty is the mixture of these doubles. In Rodin, these are not opposites but secret pairings. Sculpturally, they are the two dancers intertwined as mirror images in Rodin's lovely *Dance Movement, Pas de deux "B"* (1910–11). Merleau-Ponty would have called these doublings "chiasms." In "Eye and Mind," he cites Rodin on creating movement in works of art and on truth and lies in art, and Merleau-Ponty comments on the surprising convergences between sculptural fragments produced by quite different sculptors such as Rodin and Germaine Richier. The reference in "Eye and Mind" to the "beauty of the universe" is from Rilke's essay on Rodin. Indeed, Rodin comments extensively on the meaning of the beautiful in his *Art: Conversations with Paul Gsell.* Merleau-Ponty selected photographs of two female nudes for inclusion in "Eye and Mind": one by Matisse, *Bather with Long Hair* (1942; *Baigneuse aux cheveux longs*), the other by Rodin, *The Crouching Woman* (1880–82; *La femme accroupie*). Rodin's aesthetic is far from whole cloth, but it most assuredly begins from an erotics of the flesh. Erotic desire ranging from the banal to the transgressive is transcribed almost everywhere in Rodin's works, and this connects Rodin with the Romanticist symbolism and erotic poetry of Charles Baudelaire. Our argument will be that the erotics of Rodin yield to deeper aesthetic meanings having to do with movement, mortality, transcendence, and a crossing between beauty and the sublime.

Beauty, Eros, and the Feminine: *The Crouching Woman*

In Rodin, beauty is a site of pleasure and of power. Even today, if *The Kiss* has grown banal, *I Am Beautiful* (*Je suis belle*) is still transgressive.[2] So are many of Rodin's drawings and watercolors of female nudes in the most intimate and trusting sensual poses: *Reclining Female Nude, Two Women Embracing, Love Sleeping, Sapphic Couple,* and *Psyche,* to name but a few. *I Am Beautiful* (1882) is a dynamic work positioned on the portal of *The Gates of Hell* at the top of the right bas-relief. Rodin repeated the work as a disturbing, beautiful freestanding bronze: a powerful, muscular male figure, upright and legs apart, clutches at a crouching woman above him whom he is only able to reach and hold on his chest, forever denied physical union. (See figure 6.) The title of the work derives from the first line of Baudelaire's "La Beauté" in *Flowers of Evil:* "I am beautiful, O mortals! like a dream of stone" (*Je suis belle, ô mortels! comme un rêve de pierre*).[3] Here beauty is a woman, the object of desire. During his earlier years as a designer at a factory in Sèvres, Rodin had sketched a similar image as a decorative motif for a porcelain vase. Only then, it was a mother holding her child to her chest.[4]

I Am Beautiful combines two figures originally produced separately: the male figure is the *Falling Man* (1882), and the female figure he grasps and holds on his chest is *The Crouching Woman* (see figure 7), produced by Rodin in the same year of 1882 and selected by Merleau-Ponty for inclusion in "Eye and Mind." *The Crouching Woman* (*La femme accroupie*) displays a woman crouching in extreme, almost corkscrew torsion. Octave Mirbeau referred to the work as "the frog," and Merleau-Ponty correlates it with Richier's crouching *La Sauterelle* (*The Leaper*).[5] The work is remarkable not only for Rodin's departure from conventional, classical

6. Auguste Rodin, *I Am Beautiful* (*Je suis belle*), 1882. Bronze. 27 × 14 × 11 in. (68.58 × 35.56 × 27.94 cm.) The Dallas Museum of Art. The Wendy and Emery Reves Collection. *The Dallas Museum of Art. The Wendy and Emery Reves Collection.*

poses, but for the model's ability to make her body available in a way hardly imaginable.[6] The elongation of the right arm wrapped around the figure's chest clasping her left leg as she crouches gives the figure the sensation of a turning, spinning movement. The movement is a gesture toward the world in the lower part of the body that shows the woman's vulnerability and at the same time a covering-up in the upper body, a motile intentionality that prevents a static, frozen posture. The backward tilt of her head onto her right shoulder, eyes closed, in combination with the reach and clasp of the arm and hand create a moving melancholy pathos of expression. These integrate with the lights and darks in the highlights and hollows of the surface. It was customary for

7. Auguste Rodin, *The Crouching Woman* (*La femme accroupie*), conceived 1880–82; cast 1925. Cast by the founder Alexis Rudier, Paris. Bronze. 33 × 21 × 18 in. (83.8 × 53.3 × 45.7 cm.) Rodin Museum, Philadelphia, Pennsylvania. Bequest of Jules E. Mastbaum, 1929. *The Philadelphia Museum of Art/Art Resource, N.Y.*

bronze casts to be made off-site from studios in foundries, and each was known for a signature patina. However, for *The Crouching Woman,* Rodin worked the surface of the bronze cast himself using tools, acids, and a soft chamois to elicit the balance he sought of browns, greens, and black. Albert Elsen has written: "*The Crouching Woman,* characteristic of his best patina, has an unpredictable allocation of color accents, irregular in intensity and shape, which have become more brilliant rather than darker with age." It is simply "aesthetically beautiful."[7]

The primary reason Merleau-Ponty introduces Rodin into his discussion in part 4 of "Eye and Mind" is for Rodin's thinking and achievements pertaining to movement, and we know that movement for

8. Auguste Rodin, *The Walking Man* (*L'homme qui marche*), 1907. Bronze statue. 84 1/10 × 28 1/5 × 61 3/5 in. (213.5 × 71.7 × 156.5 cm.) Musée Rodin, Paris, France. *Vanni/Art Resource, N.Y.*

Merleau-Ponty is about transcendence and life. "The movement of one's own body is to touch what lighting is to vision. . . . Even on the most sensitive parts of our tactile surface, pressure without movement produces a scarcely identifiable phenomenon" (*PP* 315; *PhP* 363, 364). Rodin knew how to make stone come alive and move. The idea of dynamic or kinetic art challenged the very possibility of the sculpture of nature and life and eventually would arrive in the mobile-like sculptural works of Calder, in which the parts literally move and circulate with the movement of the air. Rodin's success with movement in *The Crouching Woman* is also powerfully on display in *The Walking Man* (1907; see figure 8), the figure without arms or head upon which Rodin built *St. John the Baptist Preaching* (1878).[8]

In *The Walking Man,* if one follows the line of the back leg upward toward the torso and then downward into the line of the front leg, we can actually feel the power of striding through space, or, as Merleau-Ponty described it, we feel that the walker "*bestrides* space" (*enjambe l'espace*). The sculpture "makes movement visible by its internal discordance" ("EM" 145; *OE* 79). Discordance means that arms, legs, trunk, and head are each presented at a different instant, an image which the body never at any moment really held and which, Merleau-Ponty says, "imposes fictive linkages between the parts, as if this mutual confrontation of incompossibles could—and alone could—cause transition and duration to arise in bronze and on canvas" ("EM" 145; *OE* 79). The sculptor or painter, Rodin says, "makes visible the passage of one pose into the other; he indicates how imperceptibly the first glides into the second. In his work, one still detects a part of what was while one discovers in part what will be."[9]

Movement is the metamorphosis of time. Merleau-Ponty wrote: "At each successive instant of a movement, the preceding instant is not lost sight of. It is, as it were, dovetailed into the present, and present perception generally speaking consists in drawing together, on the basis of one's present position, the succession of previous positions, which envelop each other" (*PP* 140; *PhP* 164). "Dovetailed" is the English translator's interpretation of *emboité,* the French term for fitting, jointing, or clamping. It is a good choice, for "dovetailed" is a woodworking or craft metaphor. Tails and pins are fitted together at a right angle in a well-made dovetail joint, most often in the right angle of a drawer, and this is the strongest joint in cabinet-making. So too are past and present dovetailed together in movement; so too are self and world dovetailed together in movement, for movement is the gesture of transcendence. This is not otherworldly vertical transcendence, the reach toward God and angels, but a horizontal reach toward others and things. Transcendence is the experience of primary or primordial perception that exports us out of everyday secondary perception into a world beyond the safety of personal history and subjectivity, a world that is a stranger, "alien, no longer an interlocutor, but a resolutely silent Other" (*PP* 322; *PhP* 372). *The Crouching Woman* and *The Walking Man* give us access to silent, resolute realities; in their posture and movement they capture the sculptural equivalent of transcendence.

Rodin was famous for populating his studios with multiple meandering naked male and female models whose movements energized the sculptor's work. He was constantly studying their postures, poses, and movements as close to nature as possible, searching for the feelings expressed in every part and muscle of the body, the whole scene thereby creating the atmosphere of a Greek bacchanal.[10] Rodin adored the Greeks, not for Diotima's Form of Beauty taught to Socrates in the *Symposium,* but precisely for their sensuality. He surrounded himself with Greek sculpture and other artworks. Once, holding up to the light an ancient sculpture of the Medici Venus, Rodin excitedly pointed out to Paul Gsell the nearly infinite projections and depressions on the surface needed to produce the undulations and curvatures. "This is real flesh," he said, and "on every occasion the ancients fervently bore witness to their adoration of the flesh. It is folly to believe they disdained it. With no other people has the beauty of the human body aroused a more sensual tenderness."[11]

Rodin also adored the female form, and he poured that love into a study of every detail and nuance of the female body and female sexuality—physiognomy, color, and form. He created repeated and numerous line-drawing studies of the female nude. Few artists exemplify this facility in different media more forcefully than Rodin, whose watercolors and drawings are multiple and marvelous, achieved rapidly in bursts of insight. In 1887 the publisher Paul Gallimard commissioned Rodin to draw illustrations for Baudelaire's *Flowers of Evil,* and Rodin produced twenty-seven drawings, among which we find a drawing of a nude female figure, this time titled by Rodin simply "La Beauté," his illustration of Baudelaire's poem of the same title cited earlier. His drawing of an embracing couple he titled "Desire."[12] It is undeniable that Rodin was a student of the male form as well as the female, beginning with the astonishing realism of *The Age of Bronze* (1876–77). Yet Rodin's aesthetic makes beauty feminine and the artist masculine, the male-female doublet.

This is dangerous, particularly for us today. In the hands of Burke and Kant in the eighteenth century, it had been disastrous. It opens aesthetics to the attack on "beauty discourse" which, in the words of one critic, elevates the naked white female body "as the most consistent (if contentious and highly charged) trope of aesthetic beauty" and an instrument for the containment and regulation of female sexuality.[13] Burke dwelt upon the female neck and breasts as the apex of beauty and proceeded to develop an aesthetic of softness, smoothness, delicacy, and fragility.[14] We have already seen in the last chapter that Cézanne's "strong beauty" had put that to rest, along with his numerous portraits of Mme. Cézanne. Kant had argued that the "fair sex" has just as much understanding as the male, but it is a "*beautiful understanding,*" whereas that of the male is a "*deep understanding,* an expression that signifies identity with the sublime."[15] For Kant, the woman will learn no geometry, nor the principle of sufficient reason, nor the monadology. "In history, they will not fill their heads with battles, nor in geography with fortresses, for it becomes them just as little to reek of gunpowder as it does the males to reek of musk."[16] They will need to know nothing more of the cosmos than is necessary to make the heavens a beautiful sight to them. In matters of moral principle, "the virtue of a woman is a *beautiful virtue,* that of the male sex a *noble virtue,*" and Kant did not hesitate to draw the conclusion of this binary: "I hardly believe that the fair sex is capable of principles, and I hope by that not to offend, for these are also extremely rare in the male." In place of knowledge of moral principles, "Providence has put in their breast kind and benevolent sensations, a fine feeling for propriety, and a complaisant soul. One should not at all demand sacrifices and generous self-restraint."[17] For Kant, the Maker has given the female a sense of the beautiful that is a substitute for the male's sense of rightness and moral principle. The virtues of woman are therefore neatness, modesty, simplicity, and innocence. Kant offered these observations in his pre-critical discussion of beauty from 1763, decades before the *Critique of Judgment,* but when projected forward they exclude the woman from a proper understanding and practice of the moral law of the categorical imperative and right action undertaken from duty alone. Kant had just completed a reading of Rousseau's *Emile* in formulating these opinions, and we very much discern Rousseau's influence from the educational curriculum set out for Emile's intended, Sophie.[18] All in all, rendering beauty feminine has all too often been a way of diminishing both beauty and the feminine and elevating the masculine as the sublime.

I want to argue that Rodin's identification of beauty with the feminine opposes Burke and Kant, who confuse genuine beauty with an aesthetic of beautification or the cultural "properness" of the eighteenth century. There is a lot going on with respect to Rodin and women, and we should not attempt to oversimplify or gloss over the elements of power, class, and money—and perhaps obsession as well—in Rodin's relationships with his models and in the very public affair he had with Camille Claudel, to the despair of his "common-law wife," Rose Beuret, whom he would marry legally only shortly before her death.[19] Like the painter Degas, who drew from live scenes at the Paris ballet and its practice rooms where many lower-class young girls were brought by their mothers, Rodin's models came from the lower classes, with few other options for life and work. He employed them and for the most part treated them generously financially. Rodin met Camille Claudel when she was but twenty, he an older forty-four; she was from a financially established middle-class country family, and he saw in her talent and sculpture his potential equal who might even surpass his own work. During the early years of their relationship, Camille was a faithful assistant and collaborator on *The Gates of Hell* and *The Burghers of Calais* before breaking with Rodin to pursue her own work with magnificent outcomes such as *The Wave* (1898), *Psalm* (1899), and *The Waltz* (1905). Their fifteen-year affair grew ever more public and tumultuous and ended in the ruin of Camille, who was committed in 1913 to a psychiatric hospital for the last thirty years of her life.[20] Is the male-female aesthetic doublet reversible? What happens when the woman becomes the artist of this most "unwomanly" art of clay, marble, hammer, chisel, water, and fire and she is the one who makes the *Bust of Rodin,* as did Camille in 1892? In the lives of these two, Claudel and Rodin, situated in the late nineteenth and early twentieth centuries, reciprocity and respect strained, then fractured, and then became hostility and enmity. Camille's famous literary brother, Paul Claudel, pronounced their work "antithetical." The art of Rodin, he wrote, "is the heaviest, the most material there is; indeed, certain of his figures cannot release themselves from the clay in which they are enmeshed. When they do not crawl, embracing the mud in a kind of erotic frenzy, it seems as if each of these embracing bodies is trying to return to the primal lump." Of his sister's work, he wrote that "it glistens . . . with an ingenuous joy, forming, in all the meanings of these adjectives, the world's most 'animated' and most 'spiritual' art."[21] If Paul Claudel was wrong about Rodin, whose name he refused to pronounce, no one has spoken better about the art of Camille.

With the tangled complexities of philosophy, art, and life in full view, I nevertheless want to argue, in the first place, that Rodin challenges the "moralized aesthetics" of the feminine that dominated previous generations. He gives us whole, robust, vital, naked female bodies, complete with angularities of limbs and the torsion and expression of living movement. Rodin's sculptures of women look forward to the way Robert Mapplethorpe photographed Lisa Lyon in muscular bodybuilding poses on the edge between femininity and androgyny.[22] The pose of *The Crouching Woman* approaches this muscularity and strength in managing to achieve and hold such an impossible position. The scandal in his own day of Rodin's couples such as *The Kiss* and *Eternal Springtime* is that the female is consumed by erotic desire as much as her male partner. Rilke wrote:

> The desire of men and women for each other had become the passion of human relations. And this is the way it appears in the work of Rodin. There is still the eternal battle of the sexes, but here the woman is no longer an animal who submits or is overpowered. She too is awake and animated by desire, as if they had both joined forces to search for their souls.[23]

Many of Rodin's drawings and watercolors replace the male altogether: Two Female Nudes, Arm in Arm, Back to Back; Three Women Embracing; Female Nude Inclining Toward a Kneeling Female Nude, and many more.

Second, Rodin challenges as well the youthfulness and perfection of the idealized female form with both its constancy and variations across the ages. He is interested in what he calls "character" that is more deeply expressed in maturity and old age. The youthful body of puberty that is full of brand-new vigor and svelte pride, he wrote, "hardly lasts more than a few months." Without even speaking about childbearing and fatigue, the tissues of the youthful girl slacken and the lines relax. "I will not say that woman is like a landscape that is constantly modified by the position of the sun, but the comparison is almost right." The girl becomes a woman, and "this is another type of beauty."[24] Rodin's *The Old Courtesan (She Who Was Once the Helmet-Maker's Beautiful Wife)*, from 1885, shows an aged and haggard woman, breasts fallen, belly swollen, posed fully nude in a seated posture, with knees bent and arms behind her back. (See figure 9.)

Her pose "confronts with mingled despair, resignation, and defiance the evidence life had inscribed on her body."[25] This is Rembrandt brought to life. "The vision of the great Dutchman," Rodin says, "focuses on the coarseness of clothing, on the irregularities of old faces, on the callosities of plebeian hands. To Rembrandt, beauty is only the acknowledged antithesis between the triviality of the physical envelope and the inner radiance."[26] Apparent ugliness is the expression of moral grandeur. Rodin and Rembrandt are the utter contrast with Kant, who saw in age "the great destroyer of beauty" that threatens all of a woman's charms. Whereas the Kantian masculine matures into nobility and sublimity, the epoch of growing old is "terrible to every woman," Kant wrote.[27] This account is not "just." That is the very word Rilke finds himself writing of Rodin: Rodin's work is "just." "Filled with the animating burden of his vast knowledge, he looked like a seer into the faces of those living around him. . . . This is not what is commonly called beautification, nor would it be accurate to speak of giving something characteristic expression. It is more a matter of separating the enduring from the transitory, passing judgment, being just."[28]

Philosophically, Rodin really sets forth two different, though related, ideas on the relationship of the beautiful and the ugly. Discussing *The Old Courtesan* with Gsell in *Art: Conversations with Paul Gsell,* he argued that there is nothing in nature that is ugly, but rather everything in nature is beautiful. This is an *ontological doctrine* of natural beauty that expresses Rodin's positive affirmation of all of nature and life as it has

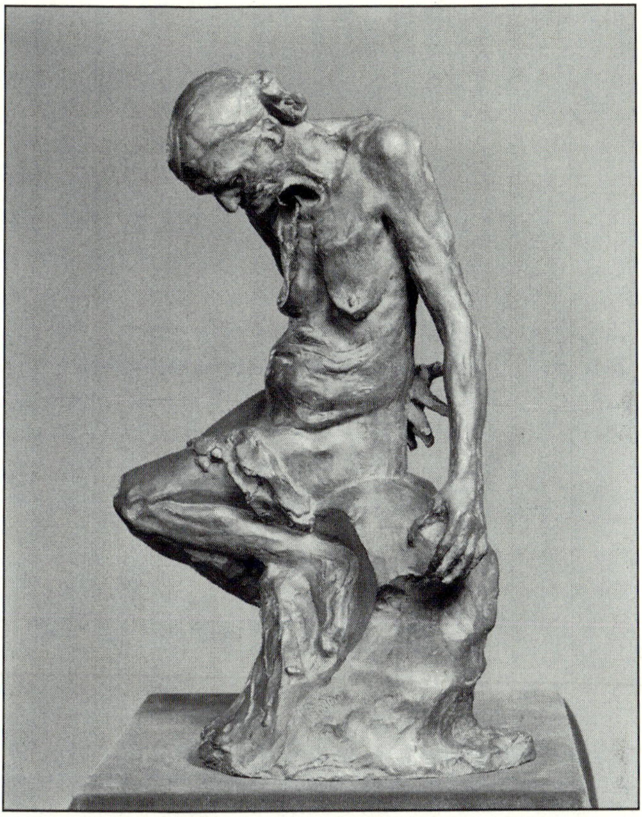

9. Auguste Rodin, *The Old Courtesan* (*La belle qui fut heaulmière*), modeled circa 1885; cast 1910. Bronze. 19¾ × 11 × 8 in. (50.2 × 27.9 × 20.3 cm.) Made in France. The Metropolitan Museum of Art, New York. Gift of Thomas F. Ryan, 1910, 11.173.3. *Image copyright © The Metropolitan Museum of Art, New York, N.Y.*

come from the hand of the maker across its manifold forms and ages, from young to old, birth to death. Yet Rodin knows that this is a minority opinion across time and culture and that the human condition is marked by a penchant for naming and classifying the repulsive, disgusting, low, and base, all that is meant by "ugly." Against this, Rodin argues that the artist is the one best capable of displaying the natural beauty in what humans persist in thinking and naming "ugly." This is an *anthropological doctrine* about human language, thinking, and classification, and about the role of the artist in transfiguring common language and vernacular practices; it is a doctrine that puts the artist in the place of the priest and the social worker. We call "ugly" that which is deformed or unhealthy, that which suggests illness, debility, and suffering, such as a hunchback, a bowlegged person, or a poor person in rags. We also call "ugly" the soul and conduct of one who is immoral, vicious, or criminal; the parricide, the traitor, and ambitious people without scruples. However, Rodin argues that "when a great artist or great writer gets hold of one of the types of 'ugliness,' he instantly transfigures it . . . it is solely the power of 'character' that creates beauty in Art, and it often happens that the one who is the most ugly in Nature is the most beautiful in Art."[29] Because Rodin's ontological doctrine has asserted the universality of beauty in nature, we should read this last phrase anthropologically—"*what is called* 'ugly in Nature' is yet most beautiful in the hands of Art."

"Character" links the ontological and anthropological doctrines as the central concept of the aesthetic. In *Art,* Rodin says that "character can even be called a 'dual truth'; for it is internal truth translated by the external truth. It is the soul, the feeling, the idea expressed by the features of a face, the gestures and actions of a human being, the colors of a sky, the line of a horizon." Therefore, "the contortion of a sickly physiognomy, the scoring of a vicious mask, in every deformity, in every blemish, the inner truth bursts forth more easily than from regular and wholesome features."[30] Rodin sought exactly this in his modeling: the outer sculptural forms of inner emotions. We should not imagine that any of this—duality, internal and external, soul, feeling—is philosophically unproblematic and transparent, and we shall soon take it up again in relation to Baudelaire and Rodin's *The Burghers of Calais.* Nevertheless, in these ontological and anthropological doctrines devolved upon "character," Rodin asserts a firm stand against the prescription that beautiful art must represent only those subjects commonly classified as "beautiful" in a certain culture at a certain place and time. In this regard, in a similar vein, Aristotle is to be given great credit, I believe, for recognizing beauty in the Greek tragedies. He found beautiful characters in the tragedies and praised some plots as more beautiful than others.[31] Beauty is not limited to what is shining and filled with glory. The searing beauty of tragic poetry and plot are found amidst the failings and flaws of the characters, and it is these very flaws that "accomplish by means of pity and terror the catharsis of such emotions."[32]

Rodin's aesthetic rebellion violated the precepts of academic beauty still predominant at the time, to which we have access through nineteenth-century editions such as Charles Blanc's *Grammar of the Arts of Drawing, Architecture, Sculpture, Painting.* According to these precepts, gestures and facial expressions had to seem natural and to express pride, majesty, and grace derived from Greek and Roman prototypes; postures were to be simple, uncomplicated, and stable; deformity or strenuous movement was heresy; ugliness was simply not permissible, since it would compromise the immortality of true beauty and have negative moral influence; the sculptor was always to be emotionally reserved and express no "inner fire."[33] According to these canons, Rodin would have to be regarded as an "academic *manqué*," as Elsen has put it so well, which means that he remained classical in reaching back to the past for his models and inspirations but was "missing" from the classical ranks in his modern rejection of the sterility and rigidity of the accepted canons and the demand for youthful suppleness and perfection in the female body.[34] Unlike Cézanne, for example, who simply turned his back on the schools and Salons and went his own way, Rodin worked within the public institutions and competed for public commissions. He did not seek to overthrow the classical models, and he saw himself linked backward to biblical figures, Greek and Roman antiquity, and to Michelangelo, as reflected in so many classical and Renaissance figures that bear the names of his works: Adam, Eve, St. John the Baptist, Venus, Narcissus, Romeo and Juliet, Paola and Francesca, and so forth. Nevertheless, he sought an art that brought itself closer to the primacy of feelings and to the natural, uncorseted human figure. This "modern classicism," if we may so call it, is evident from Rodin's reach backward toward antiquity and Michelangelo and forward to the sculptors who were to follow: Maillol, Lipchitz, Picasso, Matisse, Brancusi, Duchamp, Calder, Giacometti, Moore, Arp, and others.[35]

The beautiful transfiguration of the ugly is paramount in Rodin's much earlier, important but maligned, *Mask of the Man with the Broken Nose* (1863–64), which he attempted unsuccessfully to exhibit in the Salon of 1864. (See figure 10.) The broken nose of this ugly, aging man, "smooshed" to the right, heightens the pained expression on his face. He is the neighborhood handyman, Bibi. Rodin shows us only a mask, not the full head, for Rodin was working on this portrait at age twenty-three in an unheated stable, and the back of the clay head froze and broke off. Thus, an accident made its contribution to the history of beauty. In an incomparable account, Rilke writes that its beauty comes from

> the sense of proportion, the balance of the living planes, and from an understanding of the fact that all these moments of ferment come to rest within the thing itself. And while one can't help but be moved by the protean pain of this face, one also has the unmistakable sense that it utters no accusation. It makes no appeal to the world. It seems to carry its own justice within, the reconciliation of all its contradictions, and patience sufficient for the weight of its burden.[36]

10. Auguste Rodin, *Mask of the Man with the Broken Nose,* conceived 1863–64; cast 1925. Cast by the founder Alexis Rudier, Paris. Bronze. 10 1/4 × 6 7/8 × 9 3/4 in. (26 × 17.5 × 24.8 cm.) Rodin Museum, Philadelphia, Pennsylvania. Bequest of Jules E. Mastbaum, 1929. *The Philadelphia Museum of Art/Art Resource, N.Y.*

Mask of the Man with the Broken Nose "comes out of nowhere," it seems, for only a few years earlier Rodin had produced his first portrait, a bust of his father, *Bust of Jean Baptiste Rodin* (1860). It shows the father with tightly pursed lips and a prominent nose, looking straight ahead, with mustache and beard deleted. The effect is completely classical, showing the pride and composure of someone who could have been a Roman senator. If there is character, it is imagined or constructed. On the other hand, the character of Bibi, the handyman, is expressed in the indelible wrinkles that age and life have inscribed in his face and in the lines creased into his cheeks. Rodin explicitly draws the corollary of his position that character is the meaning of the beautiful: the only ugliness that exists in works of art derives from the absence of character. This is art that is false and superficial, that seeks to be pretty rather than expressive, that is affected and precious, that smiles without motive or that is pretentious without reason, the person who throws out his chest and swaggers without cause. "All that is without soul and truth; all that is only a parade of beauty and grace; all that lies."[37]

This theory of ugly art and the artist's transfiguration of "ugliness," the entire beautiful-ugly dyad that informs the aesthetic of Rodin, though a great advance over Kant and Burke, still does not countenance the uglification of the world as it confronts us today. Rodin's ontology of natural beauty does not consider the boundary region between nature and the arts more widely construed, namely the arts and crafts of architecture, industry, and technology, that wider meaning of "poiesis" upon which Heidegger insisted in "The Origin of the Work of Art" and "The Question Concerning Technology." Only Theodor Adorno has developed this aesthetics of the ugly with the importance it deserves in consideration of industrial, urban, and suburban sprawl, industrial waste, abandoned warehouses, and strips of blacktop parking lots adjoining fluorescent-lit malls with their cheap and poorly made commodities, together with the dehumanization of life and the destruction of human community they have created.[38] The art world itself suffers from the uglification of art as commodification and kitsch, the pursuit of shock and what sells. Rodin caught a glimpse of all this that was to come in his very first recorded conversation with Gsell, in which he responds that already in his day "artists are fossils" and "art is dead." Formerly in France, he says, middle-class persons as well as peasants "used only objects that were beautiful to behold," but now everything had become ugly, manufactured hastily without grace by "stupid machines."[39] It is too much to assert the positive thesis that beautiful spaces and places, beautiful art and music, create beautiful character and uplift the human soul, for we know of too many mixtures of aesthetic life with monstrous character such as Nabokov's Humbert Humbert in *Lolita*. Yet we can with confidence assert the negative, that ugly spaces and places cheapen human life and render it mean and low.

We know that there is much more to be developed here, but we are in danger of losing sight of eros and the feminine in Rodin, and so we return to the third strand of that argument, to which Rilke gives the clue with his mention of faces: "He looked like a seer into the faces of those living around him." It was in the faces of women, as of men, that Rodin searched for what he meant by soul and character. He sought the pleasures and strength of female sexuality, but when he sought a woman's soul, he sought her face. Speaking to Gsell, Rodin remarked: "You speak of an expressionless face. There is no such thing for the artist. For him,

11. Auguste Rodin, *Mignon,* conceived 1867–68; cast 1925. Bronze. 15½ × 12 × 19½ in. (39.4 × 30.5 × 49.5 cm.) Rodin Museum, Philadelphia, Pennsylvania. Bequest of Jules E. Mastbaum, 1929. *The Philadelphia Museum of Art/Art Resource, N.Y.*

every human head is interesting. . . . Even in the most insignificant head there dwells life, magnificent power, inexhaustible material for masterpieces."[40]

Rodin's portraits of women stretch across his career, and they include many of Rose Beuret and several of Camille Claudel. Their sensitivity and beauty are immediate and do not require the long investigation demanded by the portraits of Mme. Cézanne before one perceives the emotional coloring and tenderness in the highlights of the face. An early, small bust of Rose Beuret made by Rodin shortly after they had met in 1864 is utterly disarming and appealing, showing her quite informally with shoulder-length hair let down in a sweeping spiral. (See figure 11.) The irises of the eyes are hollowed out and the lips slightly parted, lend-

12. Auguste Rodin, *Thought,* 1886–89. Marble. Height: 29 1/8 in. (74 cm.) The Philadelphia Museum of Art, Philadelphia, Pennsylvania. John G. Johnson Collection, 1917. *The Philadelphia Museum of Art/Art Resource, N.Y.*

ing a living, breathing feeling to the face's expressive gesture. The bust is unabashedly named *Mignon,* which when said to or of a young child (*très mignon*) means "delicate," "pretty," "precious," or even "cute," but when addressed to an older one bears the connotation of "darling." An 1884 bronze of Camille Claudel's head and face is similarly tender and refined. She looks directly ahead and holds the viewer's gaze; the hair is short and curled and asks to be touched. Another of her from 1886 shows only her head emerging from a rough uncut block of marble; there is no neck or body below, only uncut stone, as if the mind is a disembodied reverie. (See figure 12.)

If the uncut marble below brings to mind a gravestone, the face above breathes with life. Her chin rests directly on the marble, and she wears a kerchief kind of cap over her close-cut hair. This sculpture of Camille's face Rodin named *Thought*. She is as much "the thinker" as the male who would occupy the chair atop *The Gates of Hell*. Rilke wrote that these later images of women "have a different, more deeply grounded and less common beauty." This less common beauty is the beauty of soul in a woman's face, eyes, mouth, and lips. "Rodin always inclines toward a representation of a woman's face as a part of her beautiful body, as if her eyes were the eyes of her body and her mouth the mouth of the body. Where he sees and creates in this organic way, the face often takes on such a strong and moving expression of unexpected life that it completely supersedes the portrait as a whole."[41] Thought, soul, character, life: feminine beauty. Maybe, with Rilke, we are giving Rodin the benefit of the doubt. But the portraits insist otherwise.

Difficult Beauty: *The Burghers of Calais*

The flesh as eros portends the flesh as corruptible, the front and back, the outer and inner, the visible and the invisible of the flesh. Rodin's erotics of the flesh are reversible with suffering and mortality. Rodin knew Baudelaire's *Flowers of Evil* intimately and could recite entire poems from it. He returned repeatedly to "Une Charogne" ("A Carcass," number 29), which describes decaying, filthy flesh eaten away by worms and then imagines the adored mistress in this condition:

> Yes! This is what you'll be, O queen of every grace,
> When, last rites said, you lie alone;
> Beneath the sod and fat bouquets, you'll find your place
> And, moldering, become dry bone.
>
> Then, O my beautiful, repeat this to the worm
> Whose kisses eat your face away:
> That I preserve the sacred essence and the form
> Of all my loves as they decay.
>
> *Oui! Telle que vous serez, ô la reine de grâces*
> *Après les derniers sacrements,*
> *Quand vous irez, sous l'herbe et les floraisons grasses,*
> *Moisir parmi les ossements.*

Alors, ô ma beauté! dites à la vermine
Qui vous mangera de baisers.
Que j'ai gardé la forme et l'essence divine
De mes amours décomposés![42]

The form and divine essence of the beautiful mistress, preserved in the last lines, are the only tolerable protection from the ugliness and horror that precede them.[43]

Baudelaire's prose poems in *Paris Spleen* include a poem that I have cited before[44] that is entitled "The Desire to Paint," and when Merleau-Ponty taught his course on modern poetry at the University of Lyon in 1947, he undoubtedly encountered it.[45] Part of it goes like this: "Unhappy perhaps is the man, but happy the artist torn by desire. I burn to paint her who came to me so rarely and fled so rapidly . . . How long it is since she disappeared. She is beautiful, and more than beautiful; she is astonishing. In her, all is dusk, and all that she inspires is nocturnal and profound."[46] Baudelaire links beauty with dusk and the nocturnal rather than with sunrise and the clear light of day. His aesthetic, like Rodin's, pairs beauty with the aged, the old, the used, the worn, all those phenomena customarily relegated to the ugly and even what is evil. "The Desire to Paint" has this for an ending: "There are some women who inspire a desire to conquer them and possess them; but this one rouses the desire to die slowly while she watches." In Baudelaire and Rodin, the flesh that is erotically desirable is simultaneously corruptible and mortal; beauty seeks the permanent and discovers the transient, beauty seeks transcendence of time and discovers the pervasiveness of time. "If there is anything more beautiful than a beautiful thing, it is its ruin."[47] Of *The Old Courtesan* William Gass has written, "the body is our first grave; it is the bronze that is glorious."[48]

In *The Painter of Modern Life,* Baudelaire writes this: "Beauty is always and inevitably of a double composition, although the impression that it produces is single." He explains: "Beauty is made up of an eternal, invariable element, whose quantity it is excessively difficult to determine, and of a relative, circumstantial element, which will be, if you like, whether severally or all at once, the age, its fashions, its morals, its emotions. . . . I defy anyone to point to a single scrap of beauty which does not contain these two elements."[49] Rodin's dualistic language of outer forms revealing inner feelings, combined with Baudelaire's appeal to the "forms" and "divine essences" of the beautiful mistress, could easily be philosophically misinterpreted as an apparent Neoplatonism. In fact, this has been done to Baudelaire.[50] In our view, that would be a mistake for a work like *Flowers of Evil,* a work that in its very title disputes the equation of beauty—flowers—with the Good. Baudelaire's account of beauty's doubles is immediately preceded by the assertion of the need for a "historical" theory of beauty: "This is in fact an excellent opportunity to establish a rational and historical theory of beauty, *in contrast to the academic theory of an unique and absolute beauty.*" Forms or divine essences are not the otherworldly originals that this world instantiates, and this "historical aesthetic" could not be Platonism. What then is it? Perhaps it will be best first to investigate this question less directly as a philosophical idea and more directly as a sculptural idea.

Rodin sought character in *The Burghers of Calais,* one of his greatest artistic mixtures of beauty, suffering, and mortality. The other is *The Gates of Hell.* For *The Burghers,* it is necessary to know the story because it is a narrative work that expands the scope of sculpture into a literary event. Calais is the small town in the northernmost region of France of which Lille is now the capital. It was a seaport and during the Hundred Years' War was vulnerable to attack and embargo. In 1347 King Edward III of England laid siege to Calais for eleven months, blockading its increasingly hungry and starving citizens. At last word came to the mayor of the town that the English king would agree to lift the siege on condition that six of its leading citizens volunteer as hostages, wear nothing but sackcloth, be bound together by rope, and bring the key of the city to King Edward, most likely to be killed. The material evidence regarding the event of the burghers is scant, based upon a brief account in the late medieval *Chronicles* of Froissart, which Rilke has summarized. The mayor assembled the burghers in the town square, where they heard the terrible news and stood in stunned silence. Gradually, the heroes among them began to stand up. Only four are named: Eustache de Saint Pierre, the oldest, followed by Jean de Fiennes, Pierre de Wiessant, and Jean d'Aire.[51] The first is recorded as the richest man in town; the second had power, prestige, and two beautiful young daughters; the third was said to be rich in possessions and inheritance; and the fourth is recorded only as the brother of the third. The *Chronicles* report how they removed their shirts, tied ropes around their necks, and set out; how they arrived in the king's camp and how harshly they were received; how the executioner came up behind them; and how, at the last minute, they were spared at the request of Edward's queen. "He heeded the words of his wife," Froissart writes, "because she was with child."[52]

Rodin sought the character of these men. He seized upon only one moment in this story, the moment of their departure.[53] Each one of these six men had come to a decision, but each lived through it in his own way. (See figure 13.) The anguish of this moment was something unknown

13. Auguste Rodin, *The Burghers of Calais,* 1884–95. Bronze. 91 1⁄10 × 96 1⁄2 × 79 9⁄10 in. (231 × 245 × 203 cm.) This is one of twelve original casts. It was purchased by the British government in 1911 and placed in 1915 in Victoria Tower Gardens, London. The sculptural group was commissioned to Rodin by the city of Calais in 1884. It represents the sacrifice of Eustache de Saint Pierre and five fellow citizens that offered themselves to Edward III of England to spare Calais during the siege of the city by the English in 1347. Westminster Palace, London, Great Britain. *Vanni/Art Resource, N.Y.*

in the sculpture of classical antiquity. The medieval adoration of the Passion of Christ and the religious art of the church offered hundreds of heroes and scenes of sacrifice to the mind of Rodin, though as Elsen has written, it is "fruitless" to attempt to search out all the medieval sources in the *Pietàs* of the Middle Ages, Gothic monuments throughout France, and sculptures in the Louvre showing the head of Christ as the Man of Sorrows.[54] In studies and models for the work, Rodin formed each of the sacrificial heroes nude in the "shivering expressiveness of their bodies," and then draped the figures as befitted the resolve of each. (See figure 14.) Rilke writes:

> He created the old man with arms hanging down as if his joints were loose, and he gave him a heavy, dragging stride, the worn-out gait of an ancestor. . .

14. Auguste Rodin, *The Burghers of Calais,* 1884–95 (detail). Bronze. 91 1⁄10 × 96 1⁄2 × 79 9⁄10 in. (231 × 245 × 203 cm.) Musée Rodin, Paris, France. *Vanni/Art Resource, N.Y.*

He created the man who carries the keys. There is life in him for many years to come, and it is all concentrated in this last hour. He can hardly stand it. His lips are pressed together. . .

He created the one who bows his head and holds it in his hands, as if to collect himself, to be alone for one more moment. . .

He created the two brothers, one of whom looks back, while the other lowers his head in a motion of decisive submission, as if he were already offering it to the executioner. . .

And he created the vague gesture of the man who "passes through life" . . . His right arm is raised, bent ambivalently at the elbow; his hand opens in the air and releases something, as if he were setting a bird free. . . . This figure, placed by itself in a dark, forgotten garden, would make a fitting monument for all who have died young.[55]

As crucial as their individuality, each with his own thoughts and emotions, so too was the necessary unity of these six figures in their shared moment. Each of the figures has its own fullness, posture, and planes. "They stood side by side, like the last trees of a felled forest."[56] Yet unity is achieved through the low, rectangular, ground-level base that replaces the traditional high, exalted pedestal. These burghers live and breathe together, and they could walk right off the base and through the gates of the town, as if the tragic procession could recommence at any moment. Rodin also places them against the same sky. This is what he himself said of the significance of silhouettes and sky in this work: "These people live through their legendary expressions, and their grouping must be found through their silhouettes in the atmosphere, and of necessity against the background of the sky made possible by a low pedestal."[57] The town of Calais rejected the low pedestal and refused the sculpture's placement in the town square. The elders had hoped for a classic statue of only the oldest burgher, Eustache de Saint Pierre, to be placed on the traditional high base before the town hall. Rodin responded with a request that the *Burghers* be placed on the coast on a high rough-hewn scaffolding looking out to sea, framed against the sky and unending horizon.[58]

The infusion of beauty with suffering shown us in *The Burghers* is spoken in the language of Rodin, as of Baudelaire, in a Romanticism governed by emotion and imagination. Baudelaire asserted that Romanticism did not consist of a choice of a subject nor of exact truth, but "in the manner of feeling."[59] "Feeling" means more than mere empirical bodily sensations; it means the participation in the sufferings of another creature, and this *horreur sympathique,* as far as Baudelaire is concerned, applies to this world and the next:

> A cortege in my reveries,
> Your far off flickering the lights
> Of Hell in which my heart delights.
>
> *Sont les corbillards de mes rêves*
> *Et vos lueurs sont le reflet*
> *De l'Enfer où mon coeur se plaît.*[60]

However, Baudelaire stretches the fabric of Romanticism to the breaking point. He locates beautiful forms in those that bear the significance of the most extreme human suffering, not only sadness and melancholy, but grief, anguish, bitterness, and even despair. Despair brings Baudelaire, and Rodin with him, to the brink of nihilism in its pessimistic form.[61] Rodin certainly does not take that last leap, though there are no halos circulating above the burghers and there is no easy salvation or glory. Speaking of Rodin's bust of Berthelot, the great chemist, fashioned in 1907, Gsell comments: "His tormented forehead, his lowered eyes are painfully melancholy. This beautiful head is like the emblem of modern intelligence, which, sated with thinking, almost weary of thought, ends by asking: 'What's the use?' . . . Yours seem to put in question the value of human life itself and to feel the anguish of unrealizable desires."[62] This might well be the thought of the mysterious *Thinker* atop *The Gates of Hell.*

Yet *The Burghers* combines grief and agony with resolve and defiance. Rodin's idea of beauty is a mixture of Romanticism, toying with the edges of nihilism, anticipating the fragmentations of modernity. In the end it is best to see in "character" and "feeling" less fully worked-out philosophical concepts and more a sculptural idea, a comprehension of living bodies through eye and hand in modeling. The sculptural idea is to create a volume from the inside out so the surface expresses the energy, structures, movements, strain, fatigue, and everything else that is going on beneath it. Rodin put it this way: "Instead of imagining the various parts of the body as more or less flat surfaces, I represented them as projections of interior volumes. I endeavored to express in each swelling of the torso or the limbs the presence of a muscle or a bone that continued deep within the skin."[63] This explains why Rodin first created each burgher nude "in the shivering expressiveness of their bodies" before he re-created them draped in sackcloth. The time and effort were not wasted. The surface is not a mere surface but the expression of movement, energy, and pain, the whole gamut of human passions. The body, Merleau-Ponty wrote in the third epigraph for this chapter, "is that meaningful core" or expressive space that "nevertheless exists and is susceptible to disease" (*PP* 147; *PhP* 172). Difficult beauty.

Beauty, Institution, and the Sublime: *Balzac*

Once Cézanne met up with Rodin. Gustave Geffroy's early book on Monet recounts the scene. It happened when Cézanne had gone to stay awhile at Monet's home in Giverny in 1894. It is not surprising that Cézanne was there, despite his insular and solitary ways, for he regarded Monet as "the most gifted painter of our times" in capturing local colors.[64] Monet invited several friends in Cézanne's honor, among them Rodin.[65] With tears in his eyes, Cézanne told Octave Mirbeau and Geffroy: "He's not proud, Monsieur Rodin; he shook my hand! Such an honored man!!!" After lunch, Cézanne actually knelt before Rodin in the middle of a path, to thank him again for shaking his hand.[66] What is the meaning of those tears and that kneeling down, Cézanne to Rodin? In that riddle lies the mystery of Rodin. It said something about Cézanne's own social awkwardness and self-doubts, of course. But more: respect, admiration for the work, and gratitude for the lessons, for Cézanne's planes and volumes are often those of Rodin. Cézanne gives the painterly mirror of Rodin's sculptural idea of working from the inside out: "Nature is seen more as depth than as surface."[67] But Cézanne's gesture meant still more: something about the "myth of Rodin" and honors.

Like Cézanne, Rodin had also experienced early rejection. In spite of the rejection three times of Rodin's application as a sculpture student for the Grand École des Beaux-Arts, the rejection by the jury of the Salon in 1864 of his first masterwork, *Mask of the Man with the Broken Nose,* and the rejection of his first real showpiece, *The Age of Bronze* (1877) for its "excessive" realism,[68] so well did Rodin eventually come to understand the terms of success in all its public aspects that on the last day of December 1887, New Year's Eve, he was awarded membership in the French Legion of Honor and received its Cross of the Legion of Honor at the initial rank of chevalier. Ruth Butler's *Rodin: The Shape of Genius* reports that Rodin had "mixed emotions," since at the time a scandal had come to public knowledge of lesser artists and others buying the decoration. Nevertheless, Rodin accepted, and he was celebrated with a banquet given by his friends in early 1888; much later, in 1910, he was promoted to the second highest rank in the Legion of Honor, that of *grand officier,* of whom there were only about two hundred in the country.[69] Rodin's decoration with the Cross of the Legion of Honor in 1887 was no doubt a crucial part of what Cézanne meant when, in 1894, he met Rodin and knelt down before "such an honored man." Merleau-Ponty himself was offered membership in the French Legion of Honor at the rank of chevalier, but he declined in a letter of April 30, 1957:[70]

> This distinction attests to the goodwill of the government. Now, I am convinced as a citizen that the government has avoided doing its job, and compromised as never before the very idea of government. Its goodwill toward me is misdirected, and it would be wrong of me to accept it. I therefore do not intend, in the present state of affairs, to act upon the letter you inform me of from the Grand Chancellor, nor to be received into the Order [of the Legion of Honor].[71]

Merleau-Ponty refused identification with the French government of Charles de Gaulle at the time of the Algerian War. Rodin, at work on

Balzac and decorated by the French state, hesitated to declare his anti-government support for Alfred Dreyfus in the Dreyfus affair, though the majority of those fellow-artists who supported Rodin had done so.[72] Here is yet another doublet in the mystery of Rodin, for he was the artist and rebel outsider who fought and succeeded in becoming the celebrated political insider. For many reasons, I would not draw the personalities, art, and life of Merleau-Ponty and Rodin together too tightly—Rodin said "yes," Merleau-Ponty said "no"—yet this paradox is not unlike what we find in Merleau-Ponty's life and career, for he also faced the dilemma of philosophy and politics and fought successfully against the academic politicians who had attempted to deny him the chair of philosophy at the Collège de France.[73]

All of this comes together in Rodin's commission for the magnificent *Balzac,* and much more to the credit and enduring influence of Rodin than not. This commission did not come from the French state as did *The Gates of Hell,* nor a municipality as did *The Burghers of Calais,* but from the Société des Gens de Lettres in 1891, the literary society founded by Honoré de Balzac himself. The commission called for the work to be completed within eighteen months, but the final plaster version was not completed and exhibited until 1898. Rodin faced challenges he had never before encountered, including creating the public monument of a man who had died in 1850 and whom Rodin had never known. He read and reread Balzac's own works, and, guided by Mirbeau, he worked from photographs, journalistic accounts, and the typical features of inhabitants of Balzac's hometown near Tours. He went to the extreme measure of ordering a suit of clothes from Balzac's old tailor and finding a likely model to pose wearing it. All in all, Rodin produced fifty studies on the way to arriving at the statue. In the middle of those seven years of labor, with Rodin alternating between despair and enthusiasm for the work, Cézanne knelt to Rodin.

I recount these stories and events in order to inquire briefly about the mixture of aesthetics and politics: the power of art for the formation and perpetuation of political communities, and the power of politics to influence and manipulate public art. The artist is central, even paradigmatic, in the interchange between the personal and the institutional. All of Merleau-Ponty's artists played out their lives in this crossing: Cézanne dodged the draft and turned his back on the schools and Salons; Paul Klee served in the army and saw his artwork included in the 1937 exhibition of degenerate art mounted by the Nazis; and Rodin was rejected by the schools and fought back for public acclaim and commissions. In his 1954–55 course on "Institution in Personal and Public History," Merleau-Ponty offers a distinction between instituting and instituted, and he pursues this distinction in particular for the history of art. The problem is that there is a difference of temporal position. For us today, Renaissance planimetric perspective appears as a settled, even inexorable, acquisition possessing both logic and durability, just as Rodin's sculptural procedure of working with volumes from the inside out is now established wisdom and practice. However, and on the other hand, for the Renaissance painters, as for Rodin's sculptural procedure, all this was instituting and risk. Merleau-Ponty's French word is *hazard,* which as well as meaning "risk," "peril," "danger," or literally "hazard," also bears the sense of "chance" or "accident." Merleau-Ponty writes: "There is a subject instituted and instituting, but inseparably, and not a subject constituting." He adds that constituting is "almost the contradictory" of instituting (*IP* 37). For instituting, there is a different model of time: passivity-activity. There is a different sense of self, really a sense of displacement of self. The relation to the past is also different, as is the relation to the future; the relation to others is also changed, for others are on the "inside" of self, as Merleau-Ponty puts it, and not on some supposed "outside." Instituting has a logic, but it is indirect and non-achieved: "For the artist, the work is always an attempt" (*IP* 79). In sum, instituting is "a mixture [*mélange*] of hazard and reason" (*IP* 83). The painter makes a "decision," but this is an "ethical-social decision and not a law of nature or even the acquisition of a critical pictorial consciousness that would be ultimate" (*IP* 84). This means that the artist stands on the threshold of public institutional life, but in the end, the artist's work remains within the domain of personal institutions closest to the meanings and significations of love. Merleau-Ponty concludes the section on art in the "Institution" course with these words: "The institution of a work, like a love in the sense of open signification, develops by budding [*bourgeonnement*], turning and bending [*virage*], decentering and recentering, zigzag, ambiguous becoming [*passage ambigu*]" (*IP* 87).[74] In the résumé of the course, Merleau-Ponty sums things up in terms of a "subterranean logic": "A painter learns to paint other than by imitating his predecessors. Each of his works announces those to follow—and makes it so that they cannot be the same. Everything hangs together, and yet he cannot say in which direction he is going" (*IP* 124–25; *IPP* 110).

We recall that the 1954–55 course on "Institution" is situated in between Merleau-Ponty's work on the unfinished *The Prose of the World* (1951) and *Adventures of the Dialectic* (1955). In the former, from the "Indirect Language" essay, we find the philosopher's statement that the true concept of history should be modeled "after the example of the arts and language" (*PW* 85; *PM* 120). Thus, we connect the concepts of instituting and instituted, prospective and retrospective, hazard and reason, to the concepts of a historicity of life and historicity of death that we find in the "Indirect Language" essay. In the subsequent work on *Adventures of the Dialectic,* we find the philosopher's critique of Marxism and the dialectic of history as a sterile adventure and his movement toward the more flexible and open thought of Max Weber and his Marxist student, Georg Lukács. Thus, the "Institution" course anticipates *Adventures of the Dialectic,* where Merleau-Ponty would write that "the adventures of the dialectic are errors through which it must pass. . . . Revolutions are true as movements and false as regimes" (*AD* 204, 207; *AvD* 299, 303).

Balzac was not installed as a public work of art at the Grand Palais for which it was commissioned, nor was it ever cast into bronze in Rodin's lifetime; the statue was rejected by the Société des Gens de Lettres, and Rodin returned the money from the commission and placed the work in the private solitude of his garden at Meudon.[75] He was accused in the press and by the critics of having depicted Balzac as a penguin, a snowman, a sack of coal, and a shapeless larva, of presenting him as if he had just gotten out of bed to confront a creditor. The work was said to possess "too much philosophy and not enough modeling."[76] Too much philosophy: what does it mean to call the *Balzac* statue "philosophical"? For one thing, *Balzac* is an abstraction. Rodin made the decision to suppress detail in favor of highlighting the silhouette. Rodin himself said: "I sought in *Balzac,* as in *Victor Hugo,* to render in sculpture what was not photographic."[77] In the context of discussing movement, Rodin had said to Gsell that "it is the artist who tells the truth and photography that lies."[78] The head of Balzac is what rivets our attention first; it is enlarged, thrust back, gazing upward and outward in line with the strong curvature of the back. (See figure 15.)

The rest of the body is entirely draped in Balzac's customary monk's robe; this includes the hands and arms, which are also placed under the robe, lending, as some have said, a sense of sexual mystery and power to the work.[79] For another thing, "philosophical" means that what matters are the lines of force and rhythm that function like lines of thought or lines of argument. One is reminded of Ralph Waldo Emerson's statement that a poem is not simply meters, but "a metre-making argument."[80] What a good sculptor models, Rodin said to Gsell, is "not only the muscles but the life that moves them . . . he represents the power that formed them and granted them grace, vigor, amorous charm, or untamed fire."[81] For *Balzac,* it is mostly power and untamed fire. This *Balzac* imposes his presence upon us as a disturbing wisdom that requires our attention, the demands of characters and times and places. For a third thing, this *Balzac* is framed by background sky and its lighting and the unending horizon. We experience the statue in different lightings in different at-

15. Auguste Rodin, *Monument to Balzac,* 1898. Bronze. 106 3/10 × 47 2/5 × 50 2/5 in. (270 × 120.5 × 128 cm.) Musée Rodin, Paris, France. *Vanni/Art Resource, N.Y.*

mospheres dependent upon dawn, high noon, and dusk, and different climates from sun to rain to snow, and different seasons from summer to winter. It calls to mind the beginning of the world and the beginning of life as well as the end of life and mortality. Finally, "philosophical" means discussion and debate. *Balzac* is as much an interrogative work as Cézanne's portrait paintings or the late landscapes and watercolors. The work poses the mystery of Balzac, and also the mystery of Rodin and the mystery of life itself.

All of this was too much for the Société, the professional critics, and the public who demanded a heroic portrait of an intellectual giant of the Republic. Rather than calling together the community of French letters, the community of Paris, and the community of humankind, the community ruptured, fragmented, and dispersed. In this reaction against the work, *Balzac* gives us a negative image of the powers of public art for the formation of shared opinion, history, and community, for what it failed to do also shows us the possibilities for what it might have been able to do. The work was too far ahead of its time; it is a work for our time. In its time it was misconstrued as cynicism and farce; in our time, it is thought, rhythm, force, and mystery. It is figured philosophy.

Cézanne liked *Balzac.* His praise of Rodin in general was cautious and qualified: "No one knows what he is like deep down. He is a man of the Middle Ages who does make great pieces, but he doesn't see the whole. He needs to be framed, like these old sculptors, in the portal of a cathedral. Rodin is a prodigious stone cutter, and with all his modern *frissons,* he will be successful in making all the good statues anyone could ever want; but he lacks ideas."[82] Against such an overall assessment, Cézanne's evaluation of *Balzac* is all the more remarkable. After beginning negatively with the suspicion that the ideas for *Balzac* really came from Mirbeau, Cézanne turns appreciative, even enthusiastic:

> He captured him, held him with great intelligence, with his eyes that take in the world and close passionately on it. . . . And his hands, under his great cape, dominate the whole life of this chaste man. It's wonderful! . . . And this massive block, you know, is made to be seen at night, lit violently from below, at the exit of the Théatrè Français or the Opera, in the late-night fever of Paris in which we imagine the novelist and his novels![83]

Cézanne concludes with a more subdued identification with the common struggles he, the painter, shared with Rodin, the sculptor: "I don't want to belittle Rodin by what I'm saying, but listen. I like him. I admire him a lot; but he's very much of his time, like all of us. Well, we only make pieces; we don't know how to compose."[84]

Cézanne's recognition of the ideal placement of *Balzac* amidst the city of Paris framed by lighting from below against the night sky correlates almost precisely with Edward Steichen's stunning photograph of the work, *Balzac, Towards the Light, Midnight* (1908). Steichen had traveled from America to France to meet Rodin in 1900 after he had seen a newspaper reproduction of *Balzac;* their meeting resulted in the Steichen portraits of Rodin himself that many count among "the masterpieces of photography," as well as Steichen's sublime portraits of *Balzac* framed against the night sky.[85] This reminds us that we found ourselves using the term "sublime" in speaking of *The Burghers of Calais.* So did Rilke, and this is not accidental.[86] We also find ourselves addressing that term

16. Edward Steichen, *Balzac, Towards the Light, Midnight,* 1908. Direct carbon print. 14⅜ × 19 in. (36.5 × 48.2 cm.) The Metropolitan Museum of Art, New York. Alfred Stieglitz Collection, 1933, 33.43.38. *The Metropolitan Museum of Art/Art Resource, N.Y. Reprinted with permission of Joanna T. Steichen. Additional copyright Edward Steichen © Carousel Research.*

to *Balzac,* for there is a chiasm between the beautiful and sublime when beauty grows powerful, transcendent, and majestic. (See figure 16.)

This is the horizontal transcendence that draws us out of ourselves and into the things and the world, even trans-descendence into desire, dreams, and eros, "the oneiric universe of carnal essences" ("EM" 130; *OE* 35). Kant disjoined the disinterested beautiful from the dynamic, terrifying and awe-inspiring sublime, and we shall return in detail to his analysis in the last chapter of this book. Here it is enough to see, in the cases of the *Burghers* and *Balzac,* that beauty and the sublime blend into one another when the beautiful grows powerful and mysterious. "Mystery," Rodin wrote, "is like the atmosphere in which very beautiful works of art bathe. . . . Every masterpiece has this mysterious characteristic. One always finds in it a little bewilderment. Remember the question mark that hovers over all the paintings of Leonardo."[87] Mystery, simplicity, power, and transcendence enable the linkage of the beautiful and sublime.

Balzac was homeless. Rodin left the monument standing alone in the private space of his garden. Rodin's things, Rilke said, "could not wait; they had to be made. He foresaw their homelessness long ago. The only choice he had was whether to suffocate them or to give them the sky around the mountains."[88] Rodin requested that the town of Calais place his *Burghers of Calais* on a high, rough-hewn scaffolding looking out to sea, framed against the sky and unending horizon. The town refused. I can see *Balzac* on the coast of Calais looking out to sea, poised like a masthead on a mighty ship framed against the expansive sky and unending horizon. Like Rodin himself, *Balzac* interweaves power and mystery, immanence and transcendence, earth and sky, the beautiful and sublime. These are the mixtures of the beautiful.

5

Paul Klee: Mortal Beauty

> Often I said that I served Beauty by drawing her enemies (caricature, satire). But that is not enough. I must shape her directly with the full strength of my conviction. A distant, noble aim. Half asleep, I already set out on that path. When I am awake, it will have to be accomplished. Perhaps the road is longer than my life.
>
> —Paul Klee, *Diaries*

> Music, for me, is a love bewitched. . . . I have always been on good terms only with music.
>
> —Paul Klee, *Diaries*

> Then, as now, the viewer will experience the unity and necessity of the temporal progression in a work of beauty without ever forming a clear idea of it. Then, as now, this viewer will be left not with a store of recipes but a radiant image, a particular rhythm.
>
> —Merleau-Ponty, *The World of Perception*

Paul Klee described the meaning of modern art as "rendering visible," and when Merleau-Ponty discovered these words in Klee's "Creative Credo," it must certainly have confirmed the motif, as Cézanne used to call it, for Merleau-Ponty's last book, which came to be titled *The Visible and the Invisible.*[1] "Rendering visible" means rendering the invisible visible, which means the end of art as mimesis and the turn toward presentation and experimentation, in short, toward abstraction. Yet this end of representation is not an erasure or crossing out, for abstraction retains forms and sometimes reference. Klee's "Credo" takes us on what he calls "a little journey to the land of better understanding" which leads us down a road to a river, a boat, a bridge, an unplowed field, a dense wood, past a running dog, basket-weavers, and a child with the merriest curls. This "schematic fairy tale of the imaginary" includes the things Klee loved to paint, and along the way of this journey, Klee introduces us to the formal elements of graphic art: all sorts of lines—articulated, interrupted, bundled, and doubled, and the origin of art in genesis and movement: "The pictorial work springs from movement, it is itself fixated movement, and it is grasped in movement."[2] There is also the story of Creation and the discovery of Fire: "A certain fire flares up; it is conducted through the hand, flows to the picture and there bursts into a spark."[3] Merleau-Ponty wove all this from Paul Klee into the texture of "Eye and Mind."

Tunisian Beauty: Color and Light

Klee himself freely uses the language of beauty and the beautiful in his *Diaries* to describe his experiences of a shining island, of Tunisia, of colors and watercolors, but when he pauses to theorize the experience of beauty, he hesitates and writes with ambivalence and reticence, and beauty was often connected for him with thoughts of mortality. In the words of our opening epigraph: "I must shape her [Beauty] directly with the full strength of my conviction. A distant, noble aim. . . . Perhaps the road is longer than my life" (*DPK* 49–50/142). Later, on his trip to Tunisia in 1914 with the war on the horizon, he began to speak of himself as a "crystal-clear soul," but a crystalline-type with a heart that bleeds: "The heart that beats for this world seems mortally wounded in me. As if only memories still tied me to 'these' things. . . . Am I turning into the crystalline type. . . . But then: the whole crystal cluster once bled. I thought I was dying, war and death. But how can I die, I who am crystal? I, crystal. . . . I remain in this ruined world only in memory" (*DPK* 313–15/950–52). Indeed, Franz Marc, Klee's dear friend and fellow artist, was fated to fall in the war at Verdun on March 14, 1916 (*DPK* 323–24/965).[4] Klee himself was drafted into the German army on March 11, 1916, and served in the infantry, air corps, and as a paymaster until his request for discharge in December 1918.[5]

These references regarding beauty from Klee's *Diaries* make it evident that beauty was, for Klee, on the one hand, a whimsical notion about the play of color and light, but on the other, one of the deepest, most profound, and most searing notions touching on mortality and ultimate things: mortal beauty. In between these extremes, we find a classical beauty in a very early painting of Paul Klee's sister, Mathilde, *Untitled* (*Portrait of the Artist's Sister*), 1903 (*Ohne Titel: Die Schwester des Künstlers*). The painting stands out in a number of ways. For one thing, the work was created during the period of time when Klee had been focused almost exclusively on drawing and graphics. As well, the painting is an experiment in combining oil and watercolor painting. However, above all, the portrait is simply beautiful in an almost ancient Greek sense, harmonious and beautifully proportioned. The head is shown in a strict profile, and the dark blue of the background creates an atmosphere that gives the face an air of calmness and serenity. This early very beautiful and moving painting of his sister foreshadows Klee's later successes as a truly great colorist. On the whimsical, playful side of beauty, we find a pencil drawing and several variations of the *Head of a Society Woman* (*Mondäner Frauenkopf*) from 1932 as well as several earlier 1927 pencil line sketches of ethnic feminine faces: *Chinese Beauty* (*Chinesische Schönheit, Praecision*), *Semitic Beauty* (*Semitische Schönheit, Praecision*), and *Negroid Beauty* (*Negride Schönheit, Praecision*). A small painting on jute from Klee's last year, 1940, is titled *Beautiful Nest* (*Schönheit Nest*) and reflects Klee's lifelong study and collection of natural objects.

Klee also augmented his artistic studies of beauty with their counterpart, sketches of the ugly. From 1924 we find *Portrait of Faded Beauty* (*Bildnis vergangener Schönheit*), from 1928 we find a drawing titled *Ugly Woman* (*Die Hässliche*), and from the following year, 1929, one titled *Ugly Child* (*Hässliches Kind*). *Ugly Woman* shows a person's neck and head in profile that, without the title, could as easily appear to be a man. The head is balding on top, there is the stubble of a beard on the face, and the left eye, eye socket, and upper cheek are darkened with marks of aging or exhaustion. *Ugly Child* shows the head, upper body, arms, and hands of a child sketched first in pencil and finished in ink. The lower half of the body's legs are shown in unfinished miniature and are only sketched in pencil. The child is looking boldly out directly at us. A full head of curls sits atop eyes that are strangely mismatched, and other features of the face, especially the nose, lips, and teeth, are weirdly and somewhat grotesquely distorted. The child is shown smiling widely, lips parted, with three separated teeth on top but only one on the bottom; this seems a "wicked smile." The hands are shown at the front of the picture, one on top of the other and nearly touching in obvious kinetic motion that makes one think immediately of the saying about idle hands as "the devil's workshop." This child is up to something and it is up to no good; the picture is a portrait of the child as menace. In 1939, the year before his death, Klee intensified his "ugly" drawings with *Me, Ugly?* (*Ich hässlich?*), *Ugliness* (*Hässlichkeit*), *Ugly Angel* (*Hässlicher Engel*), *She Remains Ugly* (*Sie bleibt hässlich*), and another *Ugly Woman* (*Die Hässliche*). In 1940 Klee created *Angel, Still Ugly* (*Engel, noch hässlich*), which also appears in his *Last Still Life* (1940). We will discuss Klee's angel drawings and this important one in particular in the third section of this chapter when we turn to the theme of transcendence and beauty.

In comparison with Rodin, whose theory of ugliness we analyzed in the last chapter, Klee does not theorize the ugly as much as he draws it. In Klee's *Diaries,* we do find his view that the beautiful and the ugly are a paired dyad. He wrote: "To emphasize only the beautiful seems to me to be like a mathematical system that only concerns itself with positive numbers" (*DPK* 198/759). In Klee's experiments in drawing the beautiful and the ugly—and nearly all the works we have cited are drawings—he was leaning on his strength as a draftsman. In this, he was deeply influenced by Rodin's minimalist sketches of female nudes, which Klee referred to as "caricatures":

> Rodin's caricatures of nudes!—caricatures!—a genre unknown before him. The greatest I have ever seen were among them, a stupendously gifted man. Contours are drawn with a few lines of the pencil, a brush filled with watercolor contributes the flesh tone, and another dipped in a greenish color, say, may indicate clothing. That is all, and its effect is simply monumental. (*DPK* 105–6/397, April 13, 1902)

Klee's drawings were also influenced by Cézanne, whom he calls "the teacher *par excellence,* much more of a teacher than Van Gogh" (*DPK* 237/857). Klee found Cézanne's primitivism appealing and thought that this was a matter of discipline rather than clumsiness: "If my works sometimes produce a primitive impression, this 'primitiveness' is explained by my discipline, which consists in reducing everything to a few steps. It is no more than economy; that is, the ultimate professional awareness. Which is to say, the opposite of real primitiveness" (*DPK* 237/857). Klee's early, somewhat more "representational" imaginary drawings such as *Virgin in a Tree* (1903; *Jungfrau im Baum*) and *Hero with a Wing* (1905; *Der Held mit dem Flügel*), through his later disciplined, economic, and "primitive" drawings, demonstrate his mastery of line and drawing. One cannot sufficiently stress that Klee was a brilliant draftsman. We have already cited in our second chapter Merleau-Ponty's fascination with Klee's "flexuous line" and his praise for Klee's ability to "let a line dream" (*laissé rêver une ligne*), "to go line" (*aller ligne*), in the famous phrase of Henri Michaux ("EM" 143; *OE* 74).

All the while that Klee was doing brilliant work in drawing and graphics in his early years as an artist, he felt defeated, nearly despairing as an artist because of his comparative lack of success with color. The 1903 portrait of his sister stands out as an exceptional success and achievement in this regard. Yet we know that Klee went on to become one of the greatest colorists and theorists of color in the twentieth century, indeed of all time, standing alongside another truly great master of color, Henri Matisse. There are two highlights of the beautiful with which Klee came to terms in a nearly unrivaled way. They are light and color. In 1913, Klee translated from French to German the artist Robert Delaunay's "Light" (1912; "La lumière") and published it in *Der Sturm*.[6] In 1914 Klee traveled to Tunisia, where for the first time he felt at one with color and felt that he had become a painter. We will approach these one at a time.

Delaunay's "Light" is a brief essay of only a few pages presented in poetic form. Even as brief as it is, the essay doubles back and repeats itself almost verbatim on the back side of the pages on which it was drafted. The drafts of the essay are preceded by a thought taken from the closing sentence of Guillaume Apollinaire's essay on "Modern Painting": "I love Art today because I love above all the light and all men love light above all. They invented Fire."[7] Most fundamentally, what Klee took from Delaunay was the idea of light as movement and what Delaunay called a "rhythmic simultaneity." Delaunay wrote: "Reality is endowed with Depth (we see as far as the stars) and thus becomes *rhythmic simultaneity*. Simultaneity in light is the harmony, the color rhythms which give birth to Man's sight."[8] Thinking of light in nature and in art in terms of rhythm and the simultaneity of color rhythms was very appealing to the musician, as well as artist, in Paul Klee and provided a fertile analogy between music and painting, linking together time and rhythm, light and color. Klee wrote that "Delaunay strove to shift the accent in art onto the time element, after the fashion of a fugue, by choosing formats that could not be encompassed in one glance" (*DPK* 374/1081). Delaunay's essay goes on to say that for art to "attain the limits of sublimity," it must approach a harmonic vision with *clarity:* "Clarity will be color, proportions; these proportions must be representative of harmony, *the synchromatic movement (simultaneity) of light,* which is the only reality."[9] Delaunay's conclusion is that "painting in fact is a luminous language": "This voice of light, is it not drawing, that is to say, line? And when light expresses itself completely, all is color. Painting is in fact a luminous language."[10]

All of these ideas sank into the mind and work of Klee: light as rhythm, synchromatic movement, harmony, proportion, and painting as a language of light. We can see the force of Delaunay's thought of light as "rhythmic simultaneity" in so many of Klee's paintings containing alternating squares of colors of different hues arranged in horizontal rows, somewhat analogous to Delaunay's own *Window* series of "stained glass" abstracts. Among such artworks by Klee we find the famous *Ancient Harmony* (1927; *Alter Klang*). As well, we find the works explicitly titled in the name of rhythm. *Rhythmical* (1930; *Rhythmisches*) is a truly radiant work filled with light; it sets vibrating horizontal rows of alternating fields of black, then gray, then white, all painted on a background of brown. *Rhythmical, Stricter and Freer* (1930; *Rhythmisches strenger und freier*) presents horizontal rows of alternating fields of purple, black, gray, and red, four colors, but each occurring in groupings of three. Musically, both of these paintings express the rhythm of a three-beat bar in 3/4 time signature.

In the only text in which Merleau-Ponty speaks directly to the question of the beautiful, it is remarkable how precisely his thinking mirrors that of Delaunay and Klee, for Merleau-Ponty stresses two elements: radiance and rhythm. We have mentioned this text in our introduction and have made it one of the epigraphs for this chapter. In the chapter on art in *The World of Perception,* Merleau-Ponty is discussing beauty in cinematography, which he stresses does not reside in the story being told, which could quite easily be recounted in prose, nor in the mannerisms and devices of a given director. What matters is the selection of episodes, the choice of camera shots, the length of time allotted to each, the order in which they are presented, and the sound or words with which they are or are not accompanied. All of this taken together creates an "overall cinematographical rhythm [*un certain rhythme cinématographique global*]" (*WP* 98; *C* 58). Thus, Merleau-Ponty thinks there is a "sort of logic, grammar, or stylistics" of beauty in film that consists of the "precise weight to accord each element in a typical structural grouping," though this is never reducible to an explicit recipe or rule book. This brings us to Merleau-Ponty's concluding text that we want to highlight: "Then, as now, the viewer will experience the unity and necessity of the temporal progression in a work of beauty without ever forming a clear idea of it. Then, as now, this viewer will be left not with a store of recipes but a radiant image, a particular rhythm" (*WP* 99; *C* 58). We will do much more with this element of rhythm in our next chapter, as well as the pairing of radiance and rhythm in relation to Heidegger and Nietzsche, but for now we will keep our focus on radiance and light.

In "Eye and Mind," Merleau-Ponty refers explicitly to Delaunay's essay "Light" by way of the citation found near the end of Delaunay's piece from Hermes Trismegistus, "Pimander." Delaunay wrote: "It is the voice that the Light causes to be heard and of which Hermes Trismegistus speaks in his *Pimander.* 'Soon'—one reads in the *Pimander*—'the shadows will descend . . . and from them came an inarticulate cry which seemed to be the Voice of light.'"[11] In "Eye and Mind," Merleau-Ponty incorporates a fragment of this text and writes in part 4: "Art is not construction, artifice, the meticulous relationship to a space and a world existing outside. It is truly the 'inarticulate cry,' as Hermes Trismegistus said, 'which seemed to be the voice of the light'" ("EM" 142; *OE* 70). Merleau-Ponty's paragraph then continues by discussing the "flesh" of the water in the pool (*piscine*) that we analyzed in chapter 2, truly the most enigmatic but also one of the most revealing passages in all of "Eye and Mind." Then the paragraph ends with something like a definition of the goal of painting given in terms of radiance: "This inner animation, this radiance [*rayonnement*] of the visible, is what the painter seeks beneath the words *depth, space, and color*" ("EM" 142; *OE* 71, translation altered).

The critical phrase and idea in these texts from both Delaunay and Merleau-Ponty is "the voice of the light." It is clear why Merleau-Ponty and Klee both would find the phrase enchanting, for by giving light voice, it ascribes to light both sound and rhythm, resulting in something quite like "rhythmic simultaneity" as vibration, pulse, and measure. The other aspect of the text, the "inarticulate cry" of this voice of light, also succeeds nearly perfectly in expressing the task of painting in seeking to render the voice of light radiant and articulate. Painting, Merleau-Ponty writes,

> has made for itself a movement without displacement, a movement by vibration or radiation [*rayonnement*]. . . . The painting itself would then offer to my eyes almost the same thing offered them by real movements: a series of appropriately mixed, instantaneous glimpses along with, if a living thing is involved, attitudes unstably suspended between a before and an after. ("EM" 144; *OE* 77)

Again, thinking of the voice of light, Merleau-Ponty wrote that "no longer is it a matter of speaking about space and light, but of making space and light which are *there,* speak to us" ("EM" 138; *OE* 59). In these texts we can hear an echo of what Merleau-Ponty had already written in "Cézanne's Doubt," that "the artist launches his work just as man once launched the first word, not knowing whether it will be anything more than a shout [*un cri*]" ("CD" 69; "DC" 32).

Merleau-Ponty's citation of Hermes Trismegistus invokes hermeticism, the controversial tradition of writings and literature descended from the *Corpus Hermetica* that began with the Egyptian god-priest, Hermes Trismegistus, and established African sage philosophy.[12] The very identity of Hermes Trismegistus is a matter of dispute: whether there was such a historical individual, whether he was a god related to the Greek god Hermes, or whether a priest, and whether he is the author of all the writings found in the *Corpus Hermetica.* Rather than a last name, "Trismegistus" is a title that means "thrice-blessed" or "thrice-greatest," and the most consistent characteristic of this figure is that of a sage or wise teacher. "Pimander" is the creation story in the hermetic tradition and stands alongside Genesis in the Jewish and Christian traditions. Pimander (Poimandres), who is Nous, appeared to Trismegistus when his "bodily senses were restrained, like someone heavy with sleep," and revealed to him the nature of ultimate reality. First appeared a limitless light, clear and joyful, that invited love, followed by a separate darkness, fearful and gloomy, "coiling sinuously" so that it looked like a snake. Then the darkness changed into something that appeared of a watery nature, "agitated and smoking like fire" that produced "an unspeakable wailing roar. Then an inarticulate cry like the voice of fire came forth from it." This "holy word" is the inarticulate cry of the voice of fire, the "voice of the light."[13]

In his last lecture course, on "Philosophy and Non-Philosophy Since Hegel" ("PNP" 40; *RC* 305), Merleau-Ponty referred to "a new idea of light" (*une nouvelle idée de lumière*) that is closely connected with a new idea of truth. Like the voice of the light that comes with its colors, shadows, and darkness that lend it its rhythm, "the true is of itself ambiguous. . . . The true cannot be defined as coincidence and outside of all difference [*écart*] in relation to the true" ("PNP" 40; *RC* 305). Merleau-Ponty uses the German word *Vieldeutigkeit,* meaning "polysemy," or the capacity of a word or sign to have multiple meanings, and says that this capacity for multiplicity "is not a shadow to eliminate true light" ("PNP" 40; *RC* 305). In the unfinished course of 1960–61, "Cartesian Ontology and Ontology Today," as part of a critique of Descartes' theory of vision, Merleau-Ponty repeats the phrase "the cry of light [*cri de la lumière*]" and pairs it with "natural light [*lumière naturelle*]" (*RC* 182). Therefore, we conclude that we are to take very seriously, indeed, the notion of light as "rhythmic simultaneity" that Merleau-Ponty acquired from Delaunay and Klee, though it is not nearly as clear how far down the path of hermeticism Merleau-Ponty would have us go, for that path becomes very much interwoven with Neoplatonism.[14]

With thoughts such as these from Delaunay resounding in his mind, the very next year, 1914, Klee undertook his trip to Tunisia, where in the light of the Tunisian sky and the colors of the sea, landscape, and architecture, he made his breakthrough with color. Klee traveled to Tunisia in April 1914 with his friends and fellow artists August Macke and Louis Moilliet. The trip, which had been delayed and was renewed at Klee's insistence, is outlined in detail in Klee's *Diaries* and has been discussed many times.[15] The references to color and beauty permeate Klee's Tunisian writing and thinking in the *Diaries* and infuse his painting in the cities of Tunisia in which he stayed: Tunis, St. Germain, Hammamet, and Kairouan. Klee described the first approach to Tunis: "The sun has a dark power. The powerful clarity on shore full of promise. Macke too feels it. We both know that we shall work well here. . . . Reality and dream simultaneously, and myself makes a third in the party, completely at home here. This will be fine" (*DPK* 286/926e). He described his first somewhat ineffective attempts to paint in Tunis and to synthesize the urban architecture and pictorial architecture as "not yet pure, but quite attractive, somewhat too much of the mood" (*DPK* 286–87/926e). He seemed to mean that these early attempts were too much filled with his own feelings and enthusiasm and not enough with the things, or as he says, not yet "objective." He spoke of the green-yellow terracotta of some very peculiar plantings in a Tunis park precisely in terms of sound: "The sonority of it strikes deep and will remain with me, even though I don't paint on the spot" (*DPK* 287/926f). In St. Germain near Tunis a few days later in the evening, by the water and under a full moon, when Moilliet urged him to paint the scene, Klee said: "Naturally I am not up to this kind of nature. Still, I know a bit more than I did before" (*DPK* 290/926k), and he reflected on the moon as his bride, an alter ego. Indeed, in 1915 upon his return from Tunisia to Munich, Klee created the painting *Moonrise, St. Germain* (*Mondaufgang, St. Germain*). In this work and the other Tunisian watercolors, Klee worked for the first time using color to fashion objects and architecture without the aid of lines. The colored rectangles and curve-sided squares form the fabric of the work in what Will Grohmann names "an oriental lyricism." Grohmann writes: "The modulation of contrasting colors is pushed to the extreme limit, giving rise to rhythmic movement in all directions of the plane as well as vibrations, that is space and time, the assimilation of dream and reality."[16] In Hammamet, Klee found that the reeds and bushes provide "a beautiful rhythm of patches" (*DPK* 292/926m), and he painted a lovely watercolor, *Hammamet with Its Mosque* (1914; *Hammamet mit der Moschee*), composed of pink, green, and red triangular abstracts of landscape in the foreground, with the purple and white mosque, green trees, and the southern light of white-blue sky in the background. (See figure 17.)

In Kairouan Klee painted one of the last watercolors of the Tunisian trip, *Before the Gates of Kairouan* (1914; *Vor den Toren von Kairouan*), in which the varying shades of watercolors in brown, blue, and yellow are applied one on top of the other in washes to form a brilliantly colored architecture out of which emerges a view of the town. It was here, in Kairouan, near the end of the journey, that Klee experienced his color epiphany which he expressed in metaphysical-mystical terms: "Color possesses me. I don't have to pursue it. It will possess me always, I know it. That is the meaning of this happy hour: Color and I are one. I am a painter" (*DPK* 297/926o). The depth of emotion and sentiment Klee

17. Paul Klee, *Hammamet with Its Mosque* (*Hammamet mit der Moschee*), 1914. Watercolor and pencil on paper. 8 ⅛ × 7 ⅝ in. (20.6 × 19.4 cm.) The Metropolitan Museum of Art, New York. The Berggruen Klee Collection, 1984, 1984.315.4. *Copyright ©2009 Artists Rights Society (ARS), New York / VG Bild-Kunst, Bonn. Image copyright © The Metropolitan Museum of Art / Art Resource, N.Y.*

felt for Tunisia, color, and beauty could not be contained as Klee's ship departed: "Something shouted in me, shouted a reply to them and could not shout, simply because it could not. And yet all of me cried out in a tearful voice that came from the depths of my being" (*DPK* 304/926s). Klee summarized the meaning of the trip in terms of creation, genesis, and creativity: "The creation lives as genesis beneath the visible surface of the work. All intelligent people see this after the fact, but only the creative see it before the fact (in the future)" (*DPK* 308/932). Rendering the invisible visible is the meaning of painting.

Klee's Tunisian experience did sink down into his soul and did, indeed, remain with him and nourish his painting back in Munich and far beyond. In the years of his Bauhaus teaching (1921–30) and pedagogical notebooks, Klee turned the study of color into a formal theory of the color circle.[17] Merleau-Ponty wrote that Klee's colors seem to have been born slowly upon the canvas, to have emanated from some primordial ground, "exhaled at the right place" ("EM" 141; *OE* 69–70), and that "the return to color has the virtue of getting somewhat nearer to 'the heart of things'" ("EM" 141; *OE* 67). Klee believed deeply that the creative process is one in which an unconscious power seizes us such that a work of art is the expression of a spiritual energy not subject to our will or concentration. Yet in the creative genesis, the work must be anchored to an intricate comprehension of the formal elements of line, shading, and color, and of the formal properties of each of those elements. There is a formal order and necessity among color relationships, Klee argued, and Merleau-Ponty agreed that colors have formal properties that give them a life and force worthy to be called a "*Logos* of colors" ("EM" 142; *OE* 71), in which it is possible to speak about true and false pairs, complements, oppositions, balance, and equilibrium. The nature of color relationships is expressed by the color wheel, the circular form of the multilinear arc of the rainbow, in which there are the three primary colors, red, yellow, and blue, with their secondary complements, green, violet, and orange, respectively. Color relationships are in the first instance diametrical oppositions between the three primary colors and their complements: red-green, yellow-violet, and blue-orange. Thus, color can be used antithetically, with passages from red through gray to green or from yellow to violet, and whole ranges of meaning can be expressed in this oppositional way. The logical sense of contradiction is not misplaced here, for red and green when combined cancel each other out and produce gray, in the same way that the meaning of A is canceled in combination with its contradictory not-A. By considering the peripheral relationships as we move around the circumference of the color circle from a primary color to its adjacent secondary color, we generate six major tertiary colors: red-orange, yellow-green, blue-violet, and so on. In contrast to oscillating diametrical color movement, the peripheral movement of color along the circumference of the circle creates gradual, nuanced, fluid transitions as complements rather than oppositional pairs. We may have passages of color along the circumference of the wheel from yellow through orange to red, or from red through violet to blue, or running the entire circumference.

All this regarding a formal logic of color relationships should not be overdone from the point of view of Merleau-Ponty's aesthetics, and

Klee had a somewhat alarming tendency to overly formalize these relations arithmetically in his Bauhaus course notes, using circles, triangles and proportions to create what he named the "Canon of Color Tonality."[18] It was probably against this excess of formal totalization in Klee's color theory that Merleau-Ponty wrote that "there is no one master key to the visible [*il n'y pas de recette du visible*]" ("EM" 141; *OE* 67). Be that as it may, when Klee spoke of the "Canon of Color Totality," the term "canon" here is to be understood not only as a general principle or rule, which it is, but also musically, as in Pachelbel's well-known Canon in D Major. Klee wrote that the Canon of Color "permits us to follow the three-part movement" from the three primary colors as the first voices, to their complements, to the tertiary colors on the periphery. "The voices come in successively as in a canon. At each of the three main points one voice reaches its climax, another voice softly begins, and a third dies away. One might call this new figure the canon of totality."[19] Color thus leads us to melody and the theme and questions of musical painting.

Melody and Beauty: Musical Painting

Merleau-Ponty did not include musicality among what he discovered in Paul Klee, the painter who made the most musical paintings of the twentieth century. Sometimes Klee painted musicians: pianists, singers, harpists, kettledrummers. Sometimes he incorporated elements of musical notation: notes, staffs, key signatures, and the fermata. More often he deployed the structural elements of music as pictorial elements in his paintings: tone, harmony, sonority, polyphony, and above all, pictorial rhythm. Klee painted *Kettledrummer* (1940; *Paukenspieler*) in the last year of his life, and it brings together all of his accumulated mastery of color, line, and depth. It is a broad-brush, red, orange, and black abstraction of the arms and face of the tympanist performing the crashing beats of the kettledrums at the end of Mozart's *Requiem,* a consummate blend of music and painting. We will return to this artwork shortly.

Merleau-Ponty's quick bypass of music early on in "Eye and Mind" is well known and has been taken as a diminution of music among the ranks of the arts. Indeed, it has given rise to an interpretive literature that sets music and painting, sound and image, in opposition in Merleau-Ponty's aesthetic and ontology. However, there are many sources in Merleau-Ponty's writings that lend themselves to a different interpretation that is interested in the crossovers between music and pictures, audibility and visibility. The theme of music and painting in Klee has a long history in both the academic and art worlds. It was the subject of full-length books by Andrew Kagan in the 1980s and Hajo Düchting in the 1990s, and Klee was included in a mid-1980s Stuttgart exhibition that engaged in a comprehensive survey of the relations between music and the visual arts in the twentieth century.[20] The theme was also the subject of a stand-alone exhibition titled "Klee and Music" at the Pompidou Center in Paris in 1985–86, and the Paul Klee Zentrum organized an exhibition titled "Paul Klee—Melody and Rhythm" in the winter and spring of 2007.[21] The composer Gunther Schuller has created a symphonic work for full orchestra titled *Seven Studies on Themes of Paul Klee* that offers musical interpretations in separate movements for seven Klee paintings, including *The Twittering Machine* (1922), *Abstract Trio* (1923), and the monumental *Ancient Harmony* (1927).[22] Thus, our intent here will be an appreciative study of what is rather well known regarding Klee on music and painting, while arguing that Merleau-Ponty's elevation of Klee equal to and even above the status of Cézanne signals that Merleau-Ponty had a deep understanding of the ontological significance of music.

"Music," Merleau-Ponty wrote in the text from "Eye and Mind" that seems to diminish music, "is too far on the hither side of the world and the designatable to depict anything but certain schemata of Being—its ebb and flow, its growth, its upheavals, its turbulence" ("EM" 123; *OE* 14). "Too far on the hither side of the world" (*trop en deçà du monde*) places music "on this side of" the world, or "short of" the world, which is to say, I take it, that Merleau-Ponty experienced music and sound as too much on the subject side of sense experience and not enough on the world side, the "yonder" side, too much "inside" and not enough "outside," to be a reliable guide to the true nature of aesthetic experience and Being. This is similar to what the philosopher had also said about the sense of touch and the Cartesian theory of vision modeled after the sense of touch: "We are [as Cartesians—and as touchers] always on the hither side of depth" ("EM" 133; *OE* 45–46). We will have to return to this assessment later in this chapter, but for now it is enough to know that we find a contrary moment in Merleau-Ponty's newly published working notes from *The Visible and the Invisible,* written on November 15, 1959, after he had attended a concert that included Beethoven's *Leonore* overture: "Music as the model of meaning—of this silence from which language is made. . . . To interpret every perception, all its *eloquence* in this silence. In any case, music, like painting, is to the sensible world what philosophy is to the entire world."[23] As well, in the second lecture course on "The Concept of Nature," 1957–58, on animality, Merleau-Ponty adopted Jacob von Uexküll's account of the relationship between the animal and its *Umwelt* as the playing or singing of a melody: "the unfurling of an *Umwelt* as a melody that is singing itself." Later, we will attach great significance to the passivity or dispossession of the subject that is suggested here, one in which "the melody sings in us much more than we sing it; it goes down the throat of the singer, as Proust says . . . the melody is incarnated and finds in the body a type of servant" (*N* 173–74; *NN* 228). Such philosophic attention to music is much more in tune with the art of Paul Klee, for one of the lifelong threads in the development of Klee's aesthetic was the problem of the convergence, even convertibility, between painting and music. Klee grew up with parents who were both musicians, and his father was a professor of music who specialized in teaching voice; Klee himself was a violinist, and he married Lily Stumpf, a pianist.[24] Therefore, the musical-pictorial interrelationships and the sound-image chiasm or "between" were deeply rooted in Klee's personality as well as in his art.[25]

Rather early on, Klee had to come to philosophical terms with one possible way to think this "between" that arose among his artistic friends, Wassily Kandinsky and Franz Marc, who formed the core of the avant-garde Blue Rider group in Munich (1911–12). In *Concerning the Spiritual in Art,* Kandinsky strongly endorsed the sound-color chiasm based on the amazing crisscrossings among the various sensory modalities in synesthesia, and argued that synesthesia could not be explained by the empiricist psychology of associationism. "The sound of colors is so definite that it would be hard to find anyone who would try to express bright yellow in the bass notes, or a dark lake in the treble. . . . It is evident therefore that color harmony must rest only on a corresponding vibration in the human soul."[26] Kandinsky set out a virtual catalog of color-music correlations. Blue is the most heavenly color; in music a light blue is like a flute, a darker blue is a cello, a still darker blue is a thunderous bass, and the darkest blue of all is an organ. Green is the bourgeoisie—self-satisfied, immovable, narrow, the color of summer with its equanimity and restfulness. Absolute green is the placid, middle notes of a violin. Light warm red gives a feeling of strength, vigor, and triumph. It is a sound of trumpets, strong and ringing. A cold light red is like the fresh beauty of the face of a young girl. It is the singing notes of a violin. Orange is like an old man, convinced of his own powers; its note is that of an old violin. Violet is a cooled red, sad and ailing, the color of mourning; in music it is an English horn or the deep notes of wood instruments like the bassoon.[27] In these ways, Kandinsky set forth the experiences of color as sound.

Synesthetic sense experiences came in for strong support in Merleau-Ponty's *Phenomenology of Perception.* Merleau-Ponty gives many examples, for example, viewing a film: "The sounds modify the consecutive images of the colors: a louder note intensifies them, the interruption of the sound produces a wavering effect in them, and a low note makes blue darker and deeper" (*PP* 228; *PhP* 263). Such ordinary and everyday synesthesia is most often unnoticed and taken for granted, but it is very common, which we recognize when suddenly the film's sound is turned off as the images continue. "One sees the hardness and brittleness of glass," Merleau-Ponty writes. "One sees the springiness of steel, the ductility of red-hot steel, the hardness of a plane blade, the softness of shavings. . . .The form of a fold in linen or cotton shows us the resilience or dryness of the fiber, the coldness or warmth of the material" (*PP* 229; *PhP* 265). He also gives the examples of hearing the hardness and unevenness of cobbles in the rattle of a carriage, and how we speak appropriately of soft, dull, or sharp sounds. We are all familiar with the temperatures of colors in which colors are experienced as a range from the warmth of red and orange to the coolness of blue, just as red and orange are the colors of fire and blue is the color of water and ice. Klee charted these color temperature shifts with great precision.[28] From such ordinary synesthesias, Merleau-Ponty relied on the psychiatric research reported by Mayer-Gross and Stein in the 1920s on the heightening of synesthesia in the altered awareness produced by mescaline: the sound of a flute gives a bluish-green color, trees grow greener, and "the barking of a dog attracts light in an indescribable way" (*PP* 228; *PhP* 263, 264).[29]

What is remarkable about Merleau-Ponty's account is that he argues that such multimodal synesthetic crisscrossings are not extreme or bizarre. "The sight of sounds and the hearing of colors exist as phenomena," he writes. "Nor are these even exceptional phenomena. Synaesthetic perception is the rule" (*PP* 229; *PhP* 265). Merleau-Ponty grounds this argument in the nature of the human body as a system of equivalents and transpositions from one sense to another. Our bodies are a "permanent *sensorium commune*" (*PP* 235; *PhP* 271), and we perceive the inter-sensory object just as our two eyes communicate to produce one optical image. "When I say I see a sound," Merleau-Ponty writes, "I mean that I echo the vibration of the sound with my whole sensory being, and particularly with that sector of myself which is susceptible to colors" (*PP* 234; *PhP* 271). Merleau-Ponty speculates that the explanation for the infrequency of our synesthetic perception, or perhaps better, the infrequency of *our awareness of the reality* of synesthetic perception, is the influence of scientific knowledge. Through the analytic methods of modern science that associate each sense with a particular organ, a separate neurological sensory pathway, and a particular region of the brain, "we have unlearned how to see, hear, and feel" (*PP* 229; *PhP* 265). This is a cultural learning account, and we should interject that it is probably not rich enough, for Aristotle had already differentiated the five outer sensory modalities long before modern science, and the debate over the privilege of vision versus touch extends from Aristotle through Leonardo right into the modern period. Though Kandinsky developed exercises to increase synesthetic perception,[30] lending credence to the learning theory of sensory crisscrossing, we do seem to be on the terrain of one of those abilities that are "gifts" or in some sense more neurologically available for certain individuals.[31]

Merleau-Ponty believes that the same crossover exists between words and sense experiences. He writes: "The word 'warm' induces a kind of experience of warmth which surrounds one with something in the nature of a meaningful halo. The word 'hard' produces a sort of stiffening of the back and neck." A word is first of all "an event which grips my body" (*PP* 235, *PhP* 272). It is easiest to grasp this notion of the word as event with vocal speech, in which there are physical sound-wave vibrations of the air produced by the sound that reach and interact with, not only our ears, but our whole bodies. I would also like to associate this notion of word as event with Merleau-Ponty's notion of advent: in addition to secondary speaking using words as given and received from a natural language tradition, there can occur a primary speaking that is an original founding (*Urstiftung*) of a new life with its historicity and tradition ("ILVS" 105; *S* 68; *Si* 85). Words as advents have the power to stop us in our tracks, knock us off our feet, sweep us away, and all the other physiological expressions we use to designate the power and lightning of original speaking. "Words have a physiognomy," Merleau-Ponty argues, because the body "reverberates to all sounds, vibrates to all colors, and provides words with their primordial significance" (*PP* 236; *PhP* 272, 273). Poets write the physiognomies and rhythm of words, which are best felt when poetry is spoken aloud rather than read silently.

Although Klee took support from Kandinsky's efforts to integrate music and picture-making, Klee was ambivalent if not skeptical of such a subjective and psychological approach. It reminds a person of the ancient sort of dream books that claimed to offer one-to-one univocal translations of dream symbols and that Freud found so deplorable. For one thing, it is reported that Scriabin claimed the key of C minor was red, while Rimsky-Korsakov perceived it as white.[32] For another thing, there is only one place I know of in which Klee speculated on the interrelations of forms, colors, and instruments, and in this he suggested combinations that are at odds with the Kandinsky catalog: a correlation of Veronese green with the detached timbre of the flute, and one of brown mixed with a light blue or red tint with the oboe or clarinet.[33] In addition to such issues of personality and subjectivity, a synesthetic approach to particular isolated hues and tones seems at odds with what Merleau-Ponty and Klee called the logos of colors: the interactive effect of colors with one another, the rhythms of polar opposition between the three primary colors and their complements (red–green, yellow–violet, blue–orange), and the peripheral relationships as we move around the color circle from a primary color to its adjacent secondary color to generate the six major tertiary colors (red–orange, yellow–green, blue–violet, and so on). Finally, a talented violinist, clarinetist, or French horn player, to take examples from strings, winds, and brass, is capable of whole ranges of colorings with one and the same instrument, so it seems odd altogether to designate a univocal correlation between one color and a particular instrument.

Klee sought a more formalist and arithmetical method for translating a musical work into a picture, and he found it not in the psychology of color responses, but in the idea of quantitative and qualitative pictorial rhythms. He wrote: "Abstract formal elements are put together like numbers and letters to make concrete beings or abstract things; in the end a formal cosmos is achieved."[34] Klee emphasized the element of intuition in making art in order not to become rigid and rule-bound, but he also stressed exact research, and he believed that music was far advanced beyond the visual arts in its quantitative methods: "What was accomplished in music before the end of the eighteenth century has hardly been begun in the pictorial field. Mathematics and physics provide a lever in the form of rules to be observed or contradicted. They compel us—a salutary necessity—to concern ourselves with the function and not with the finished form."[35] Thus articulating the philosophy and methods of the Bauhaus, Klee indirectly challenges the ambivalence within phenomenology regarding the sciences and formal languages. Though Merleau-Ponty, probably above all other phenomenologists, appropriated the psychological and biological research of his day, ultimately, like Husserl, he also demanded that formal structures be secured in the anchor of the life-world, which for Merleau-Ponty meant bodily experience, intersubjectivity, and history. Such a movement elevates intuition over calculation and inverts the Bauhaus theory and practice, which seeks the form only by way of function and measurement, art only by way of sustained study of the crafts of building and making.

As examples of Klee's approach, we might consider *Fugue in Red* (1921; *Fuge in Rot*), or *Heroic Strokes of the Bow* (1938; *Heroische Bogenstriche*), which is also sometimes translated as *Heroic Fiddling*. *Fugue in Red* is a watercolor that vibrates or reverberates as gradual changes in color ranging from pink to violet spread across the work and are repeated like the full steps and half steps of a chromatic musical scale. (See figure 18.)

18. Paul Klee, *Fugue in Red* (*Fuge in Rot*), 1921, 69. Watercolor and pencil on paper on cardboard. 9⅗ × 12⅖ in. (24.4 × 31.5 cm.) Privatbesitz Schweiz, Depositum im Zentrum Paul Klee, Bern. *Copyright ©2009 Artists Rights Society (ARS), New York/VG Bild-Kunst, Bonn.*

The beat of the colors on the flat surface is stabilized rhythmically, thus evoking musicality through subtle coloration. Four main thematic elements, one of which is recognizable as a jug or vase, appear on different lines like a musical staff, and the rhythm of the painting has the precision of a metronome. About this work, Klee wrote: "The repetitive factor characteristic of structures is here the concept of increase or decrease which is repeated at every step. If the naturally ordered movement perceived with the ears instead of the eyes is comparable to the movements of natural tones, the artfully ordered movement is reminiscent of the structured division of tones we find in musical scales."[36]

Heroic Strokes of the Bow is a work painted as homage to great violin playing.[37] (See figure 19.) The background is a deep blue approaching violet, against which appear in black the downstrokes of the violin bow in varying thicknesses or dynamic weight. Opening and closing arrows express the crescendo and decrescendo. Alongside the flying bow also appear the scroll and bridge of a violin and a hammer that may remind us of the tuning hammer. Dots are reminiscent of musical notes on a score, and circles and straight lines of various lengths create rhythm.

19. Paul Klee, *Heroic Strokes of the Bow* (*Heroische Bogenstriche*), 1938. Colored paste on newspaper on dyed cotton fabric on board. 28¾ × 20⅞ in. (73 × 52.7 cm.) The Museum of Modern Art, New York. Nelson A. Rockefeller Bequest, 958.1979. *Copyright ©2009 Artists Rights Society (ARS), New York/VG Bild-Kunst, Bonn. Digital image copyright © The Museum of Modern Art/Licensed by SCALA/Art Resource, N.Y.*

Near the right side in the lower half appears the resemblance of a fermata, that symbol for a long hold of a note or chord.

We find a repetition and variation on many of these elements in the work from the same year titled *The Gray Man and the Coast* (1938; *Der Graue und die Küste*). (See figure 20.) Here Klee reversed the color harmonies between blue and violet to create what appears as a seacoast, and the dots that functioned as musical notes now appear as a boat bobbing on the sea. In the upper right corner, a ghostly figure hovers over the whole scene. The addition of a single black dot at the top center

20. Paul Klee, *The Grey Man and the Coast* (*Der Graue und die Küste*), 1938, 125. Colored paste on burlap. 41 3/10 × 28 in. (105 × 71 cm.) Zentrum Paul Klee, Bern. Livia Klee Donation. *Copyright ©2009 Artists Rights Society (ARS), New York/VG Bild-Kunst, Bonn. Photo copyright ©ADAGP, Paris.*

turns what were the strokes of the violin bow and decrescendo into the jaws of a sea monster. Klee always enjoyed such humor and whimsy. Such works as these play on pictorial rhythms and the analogies between the formal elements of music and those of painting. A line is also a melody, thickness of line is weight or dynamic ranging from the pianissimo to the double forte, and arrows of varying length and angles are crescendos and decrescendos. Color is musical intonation, whether sweet and gentle or harsh and edgy. In painting there are color harmony, contrast, and opposition, just as in music there is harmony in the chords and counterpoint in the voices.

Indeed, it was both polyphony and pictorial rhythm that most deeply invaded Klee's aesthetic thinking and picture making, derived from his love for the eighteenth-century works of Bach and Mozart. "Mozart and Bach are more modern than the nineteenth century," Klee wrote. "Polyphonic painting is superior to music in that, here, the time element becomes a spatial element. The notion of simultaneity stands out even more richly" (*DPK* 374/1081). Given these musical preferences, it is therefore somewhat ironic that it would be Gunther Schuller who would reverse the direction from music to pictures and translate Klee's pictures into music, all but one of the seven movements being based upon the twelve-tone system in his symphonic composition *Seven Studies on Themes of Paul Klee.* We find an example of what Klee means by pictorial translation of music in the pedagogical *Notebooks* from his Bauhaus years. It is the translation of a sonata for piano and violin by J. S. Bach, No. 6 in G Major, consisting of a three-part passage, or polyphony in three lines or voices, and Klee executes the musical theme pictorially for each of the voices for each bar or measure. Each voice is represented first by a quantitative length of line corresponding to short lines for the quick sixteenth, thirty-second, and sixty-fourth notes in the upper registers, and longer lines for the more sustaining eighth and quarter notes in the lower register. Each of the lines is then interpreted qualitatively as a certain thinness or thickness to represent the dynamic of each voice, whether soft or loud. Finally, crescendos and decrescendos appear as the increasing and decreasing angles of each of the lines, an opening angle to express increasing volume and a closing one to express diminishing volume.[38] This is the sort of pictorial transposition of a musical passage that is exemplified in the formal elements of *Heroic Strokes of the Bow.* Of course, the shades of blue are still chosen on the basis of the coolness of their color temperature, that remnant of synesthesia that Klee studied and trusted. With this background work on painting and musicality before us, we should now return to the question of music in "Eye and Mind" as well as Klee's most powerful musical work, *Kettledrummer.*

Transcendence and Beauty: Klee's Drummer Paintings

It is now time to reverse the field with respect to Merleau-Ponty's judgment that music, sound, and touch give us only a hazy outline of the spatial depth of the world and occur too much within the physiological space and subjectivity of our own bodies. *Phenomenology of Perception* had argued otherwise, claiming that just as for color, there is also an objective, an atmospheric, and a subjective bodily experience of sound. There is the objective sound that "reverberates in the instrument," an atmospheric sound that is in the air and space "*between* the object and my body," and finally a last stage in which the acoustic element becomes "the highly precise experience of a change permeating my whole body" (*PP* 227; *PhP* 262–63). Even so, what Merleau-Ponty says in "Eye and Mind" about music being too much "hither" could be taken otherwise than as a criticism, namely as an articulation of a peculiar strength of music, as well as touch, to engage with and portray the life of feelings. We do not mean to claim that emotions are entirely "inner" and not worldly, forgetting their intentional-cognitive and behavioral structure in addition to their "inner sensations." However, Merleau-Ponty's words "ebb and flow" remind us very much of the rolling waves and crests in the life of feelings and in the unfolding of a musical work. This foreshadows what Merleau-Ponty would write about sonority and listening in *The Visible and the Invisible:* "I am a sonorous being; . . . my voice is bound to the mass of my life as is the voice of no one else. But if I am close enough to the other who speaks to hear his breath and feel his effervescence and his fatigue, I almost witness, in him as in myself, the awesome birth of vociferation" (*VI* 144; *VIn* 188).

In one of my earlier writings on Klee, I made the audacious suggestion that the painting by Paul Klee I wish Merleau-Ponty had included in "Eye and Mind" was not *Park near Lu(zerne)* (1938; *Park bei Lu*) but *Kettledrummer* (1940; *Paukenspieler*), the painting that Klee created in his last year as he was dying, a work inspired by Mozart's *Requiem,* which was written as Mozart also was dying and that he left unfinished.[39] It was perhaps right that Merleau-Ponty, the philosopher of nature, life, and natality, should have preferred *Park near Luzerne* as a monogram of his philosophy, for it is a pictographic painting that can be read as the map of a park or read more figurally as a park with its bending trees, soccer balls and a soccer player, a visitor on a park bench, and those playful eyes directly in the center looking out at us. (See figure 21.) Merleau-Ponty's is a philosophy for the most part overflowing with a sense of joy, generosity, and hope.

Moreover, reading from Merleau-Ponty's philosophy of nature, the painting appears as a suggestion of beginnings, the description of a pattern of growth: a start, a branching, further branching, a new start, here and there sterility without branching, but then through the form in the center, the suggestion of a tree, the concentration of growth in the possible development of fruit with potentialities for further growth.[40] Yet *Kettledrummer* gives us Klee's reflections on mortality without morbidity and with a sense of transcendence that is not at odds with life, metamor-

21. Paul Klee, *Park near Lu(zerne)* (*Park bei Lu*), 1938, 129. Oil and colored paste on paper on burlap; original frame. 39 3/10 × 27 3/5 in. (100 × 70 cm.) Zentrum Paul Klee, Bern. *Copyright ©2009 Artists Rights Society (ARS), New York / VG Bild-Kunst, Bonn.*

phosis, and growth. Of death, Klee wrote in his *Diaries* even as a young man: "I philosophize about death that perfects what could not be completed in life. The longing for death, not as destruction, but as striving toward perfection. On the whole, a stage between striving and despair" (*DPK* 52/143).[41]

Martin Heidegger encountered these late works of Klee in St. Alban, a suburb of Basel, in the home of Ernst Beyeler, who, with his wife Hildy, had amassed eighty-eight oil paintings, watercolors, and drawings by Klee, part of their collection that would grow to become today's stunning gallery, the Fondation Beyeler, in Basel, Switzerland. Heinrich

22. Paul Klee, *Death and Fire* (*Tod und Feuer*), 1940, 332. Oil and colored paste on burlap; original frame. 18 2/5 × 17 3/5 in. (46.7 × 44.6 cm.) Zentrum Paul Klee, Bern. *Copyright © 2009 Artists Rights Society (ARS), New York / VG Bild-Kunst, Bonn.*

Petzet, who was present at the Beyeler home, reports that the little gouache *Ein Tor* (1939; *A Gate*) "brought a deep silence upon Heidegger. After a while he said in a somber tone, 'This is the gate through which we all must at some time pass: death.'"[42] Heidegger also encountered *Death and Fire* (1940; *Tod und Feuer*) on his visit to the Klee Foundation in Bern, among all the Klee riches of that collection. (See figure 22.)

Heidegger said that Klee's works "are not paintings, but feeling. Klee was capable of making moods 'visible' in pictures. . . . The less we think of Klee's paintings as presenting objects, the more they 'appear' (in the sense of the Greek *phainestai*)." Regardless of the enjoyment that we get from Klee's work, "hidden in the paintings of Klee is the thorn of a claim that is not easy to satisfy."[43]

Kagan has written that *Kettledrummer* is "the death-drum image refined to a potent essence."[44] Yet even as Klee gave us his painterly reflections on mortality in late works such as *Death and Fire* and *Kettledrummer,* he did so without loss of his lifelong sense of humor and irony, and he paired his *Drummer* series with a vast increase in the production of his light and ethereal *Angel* works.[45] Klee had made angel pictures for twenty-five years since 1915, including *Angelus Novus* (1920), which presents us with a young, novice angel, wings upraised in what might be taken as a stop sign. It was purchased by Walter Benjamin, who saw in it the angel of history, but a history that "piles wreckage upon wreckage" which the angel is unable to prevent because "a storm is blowing from Paradise."[46] In his last two years, Klee continued to invent angels of a mixed type that dwell between this world and the next: an amusing *Angel Applicant* (1939; *Engel Anwärter*; see figure 23) that seems like it might be a dog, a poor angel, an ugly angel, or a doubting angel, and the touching *Forgetful Angel* (1939; *Vergesslicher Engel*).

Despite their wings, Klee's angels retain the traits, weaknesses, and feelings of being human; they are hopeful yet filled with uncertainty. For Gert Schiff, it is clear that "certain procedures, or even bureaucratic formalities, must be honored before one becomes an angel proper."[47] Grohmann has written that the angel series is a set of variations on the theme of "the gradual process of formation and transformation of every living thing." For Klee, "the end was rooted in the beginning."[48] This may overstate the case, for there is no transparency or anything like absolute redemption in these transformations and repetitions, and if Klee is somewhat of the crystalline soul, the crystal is impure, just as his abstract visions of the invisible angel world are necessarily created from fragments of this visible world. Klee called the visible world "a junkyard of unauthentic elements for the creation of impure crystals" (*DPK* 313/951). It is doubtful if Klee had fully worked-out theological views, and there is much to say about his debates with Kandinsky and Marc on spirituality and what Klee called the inner "divine ego," which he distinguished from a "self-seeking ego" (*DPK* 318/961).[49] Klee introduced these terms in a dispute with Marc's wife about the theory of art, a dispute he later regretted, and even as he used the terms he "protested forcefully against the notion of theory in itself" (*DPK* 318/961). If Klee did have a theology, it seems it would be a theology of finitude, or that paradox of a finite divinity, a flawed and suffering divine limited in perfection and its capacity to create and command supremely. In his *Notebooks* Klee described "the tragedy of spirituality," which derives from "the simultaneous helplessness of the body and mobility of the spirit" which is the dichotomy of human existence. "Man is half a prisoner, half borne on wings. Each of the two halves perceives the tragedy of its halfness by awareness of its counterpart."[50]

23. Paul Klee, *Angel Applicant* (*Engel Anwärter*), 1939. Gouache, ink, and pencil on paper. 19 ¼ × 13 ⅜ in. (48.9 × 34 cm.) The Metropolitan Museum of Art, New York. The Berggruen Klee Collection, 1984, 1984.315.60. *Copyright © 2009 Artists Rights Society (ARS), New York / VG Bild-Kunst, Bonn. Image copyright © The Metropolitan Museum of Art, New York, N.Y. / Art Resource, N.Y.*

Kettledrummer is the culmination of a series of drummer works from 1940. Klee was profoundly affected by the image of Mozart on his deathbed imitating the kettledrums of his *Requiem* during his final delirium, and Klee found in the kettledrummer a pictorial metaphor for death that was not really "about" death in the descriptive sense, but about the power and transcendence of sound, color, and life. One of the first of these works, *Force of the Drummer,* is reminiscent of Klee's cubist-influenced abstract drawings, and the lines are rather brittle and timid, tipping the image toward the intellect and the interrogative in a way that seems to intellectualize the metaphor and diminish its emotive power.

Knaueros, Former Drummer is an expressive eulogy that moves toward a more monumental, powerful image as the head is raised upward and the mallets are raised independently as extensions of human anatomy and energy.[51] The barrel chest, bulging muscles, and compressed figure heighten the monumentality. Kagan has suggested that the breastbone line, "hyperbolically extended rightward from the thrust-back head," is a repetition of the sculptural lines of classical sculpture, such as the *Dying Niobid*.[52] *Amateur Drummer* introduces the dynamic musical weight of the heavy, thick line, but treats this line as in children's art, one of Klee's lifelong studies and styles. There is a child's way of drawing a house, drawing trees, dogs, and cats, as of drawing drums, and as adults we can all repeat them. They remain inscribed beneath more artistically sophisticated works by a universality that Klee called prehistory.

All these precedent studies are synthesized in the culminating *Kettledrummer,* and it is the musical elements that lend the emotive sense of mystery, strength, and transcendence to this work. (See figure 24.)

The scale of the work is quite small, its dimensions roughly those of a page of legal-size paper, yet it is unrivaled in force, monumentality, and daring. The contrasting warm colors of red and orange signify the two different musical notes of the tympani in the *Requiem;* the thick lines sound the thundering dynamic double forte; the arms and mallets are merged into one, and the energy of the mallets is the same as the energy of the arms and hands. Then we suddenly also recognize, peering out from that one central eye, the musical sign of the fermata with its instruction to the kettledrummer to hold the notes in an indefinite sustain, holding, holding, and holding—holding into the pregnant silence as the orchestra subsides and the sound waves yet fill the air, still holding into that silence which is an "openness" onto another stage and mystery that might be, as Klee wrote, not destruction, but "striving toward perfection." We know that Merleau-Ponty concluded the important ontological part 4 of "Eye and Mind" with a phrase from Klee's *Diaries* that came to be inscribed as the epitaph on Klee's tomb: "I cannot be grasped in immanence." The entire epitaph reads as follows: "I cannot be grasped in the here and now. For I live just as well with the dead as with the unborn, somewhat closer to the heart of creation than usual, but far from close enough" (*DPK* 419).

With the full English version of Klee's epitaph before us, we observe something interesting and important, namely Merleau-Ponty's use of the word "immanence," which suggests its pairing with "transcendence," and the attribution of transcendence to the artwork of Klee. Merleau-Ponty gives us a very free translation of the German original with these terms, which are more philosophical than a literal rendering

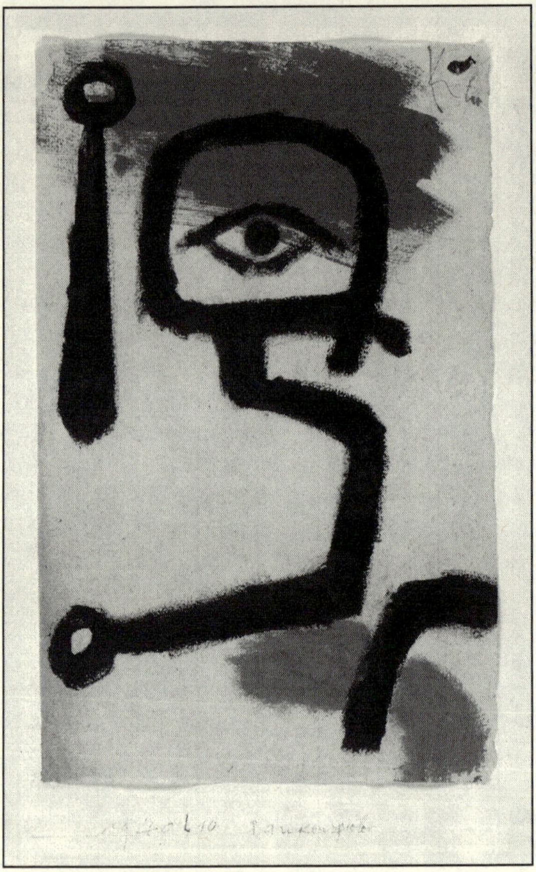

24. Paul Klee, *Kettledrummer* (*Paukenspieler*), 1940, 270. Colored paste on paper on cardboard. 13 3⁄5 × 8 3⁄10 in. (34.6 × 21.2 cm.) Zentrum Paul Klee, Bern. *Copyright ©2009 Artists Rights Society (ARS), New York / VG Bild-Kunst, Bonn.*

would suggest. The German original of the epitaph—*Diesseitig bin ich gar nicht fassbar*—is more down to earth, so to speak, when rendered as "here and now" rather than "immanence." Furthermore, we know that "immanence" is Merleau-Ponty's own translation, for it differs from the French translation by Klossowski that Merleau-Ponty cited in "Eye and Mind"; Klossowski's translation uses the expression "*ici-bas*" ("here below").[53] We point this out to stress that when Merleau-Ponty speaks of transcendence and attributes the term to Klee, the context is Merleau-Ponty's own philosophy of painting, and the specific context is a discussion about depth—depth in painting, depth in the postural latencies of our bodies, and depth in Being. Klee's epitaph, Merleau-Ponty says, gives us the "ontological formula of painting." The full sentence reads: "And to give the ontological formula of painting we hardly need to force the painter's own words, Klee's words written at the age of thirty-seven and ultimately inscribed on his tomb: 'I cannot be grasped in immanence'" ("EM" 147–48; *OE* 87).

The primary meaning of "transcendence" throughout the thought of Merleau-Ponty is horizontal and refers to our reach toward the outside, there to be related to and even shattered by others and by the world. This is transcendence that means reaching out beyond the insular self toward others and world; a beyond, therefore, that does not necessarily invoke an otherworldly "above," but is the thrust of life itself. There is also a second meaning of "transcendence" in Merleau-Ponty's thought as "trans-descendence," which is invoked with the thought of depth within the postural latencies of the body. Whereas the first meaning has to do with the world and depth in three-dimensional space, the second has to do with desire and the depths of dream space. Merleau-Ponty wrote that there is a "profound postural latency" ("EM" 187; *OE* 86) submerged in the heaviness of our bodies that trans-descends from below, as there is the transcendence toward the light, like the phenomenon of flight that "participates no longer in the heaviness of origins" ("EM" 187; *OE* 86). We will need to spend much more time pondering the meaning of this trans-descendence into the depths of our bodies and lives when we take up the problem of beauty in relation to the unconscious and Merleau-Ponty's idea of a "good narcissism" suggested in *The Visible and the Invisible.* "There is a fundamental narcissism of all vision" (*VI* 139; *VIn* 183), he wrote. This word "narcissism" is a problem for us today, and we will necessarily explore what Merleau-Ponty means by a "second" or "good" narcissism in contrast with what Freud means by "secondary narcissism."

Nevertheless, while we stress these two meanings of "transcendence" that go beyond the self toward an outside and toward an "under" that is a generality and "anonymous One," we would not give Merleau-Ponty's thought its full due if we were to omit all sense of "sacramentality" in this philosophy of the beautiful. Though Merleau-Ponty broke with his Catholic upbringing in his twenties and with the Catholic personalism of Emmanuel Mournier and the journal *Esprit* in 1936, still, Merleau-Ponty would never declare himself an atheist and remained deeply attached to the thought of incarnation, undoubtedly much to the consternation of Jean-Paul Sartre. "The Incarnation changes everything" (*L'Incarnation change tout*), Merleau-Ponty wrote in "Faith and Good Faith" (*SNS* 174; *SeNS* 310). He says that the Incarnation means that "God has been externalized" in human history and, in this sense, "Christianity is directly opposed to spiritualism" (*SNS* 175; *SeNS* 310). In his last lecture course of 1960–61, "Philosophy and Non-Philosophy Since Hegel," speaking of Nietzsche's teaching of the death of God, Merleau-Ponty agreed with Heidegger that the statement "God is dead" "means everything, except: there is no God" ("PNP" 13; *NC* 279). In Nietzsche, God is an aching absence in Being that cries out for "new gods" and "new tablets of values," not a Being who merely does not exist as if there were simply one less item in the universe that would not be missed. Writing of Bergson in *Signs,* Merleau-Ponty did not flinch from speaking of God as element; God is, Merleau-Ponty wrote, "the element of joy or love in the sense that water and fire are elements. Like sentient and human beings, he is a radiance, not an essence" (*S* 190; *Si* 239). Again with reference to Bergson, from Merleau-Ponty's inaugural address at the Collège de France in 1952, we find these words: "Everything happens, according to Bergson, as if man encountered at the roots of his constituted being a generosity which is not a compromise with the adversity of the world and which is on his side against it" (*IPP* 25–26; *EP* 33). To us, though Merleau-Ponty attributes these views to Bergson, he seems to speak somewhat of himself as well, and certainly they reflect the tenor and tone of his philosophy, a philosophy that speaks in the creedal phrase of "things visible and invisible," and whose central ontological notion, Flesh, is an icon of the prologue of the Gospel of John: "And the Word became Flesh and dwelt among us."[54] In 1960, at the time he was at work on both "Eye and Mind" and *The Visible and the Invisible,* Merleau-Ponty stated: "The question for a philosopher is not so much to know *if* God exists or does not exist . . . as to know what one understands by God, what one wishes to say in speaking of God."[55] "Eye and Mind" speaks of the artist's work that changes the world into pictures as "transubstantiations" ("EM" 124; *OE* 16).

Merleau-Ponty was invariably reticent to articulate openly a philosophical theology; nevertheless, one of the texts in which he reveals somewhat undisguisedly what he understands by God is from the "Indirect Language" essay. One cannot help but note the religious analogies that seem to inspire Merleau-Ponty in this text: transfiguration and priest, miracles and grace. The truth in Hegel's dialectic, Merleau-Ponty finds, is that there is "something like a grace in events which draws us away from the evil toward the good" ("ILVS" 110; *S* 73; *Si* 91). Yet the religious imagery, suggestive though it may be, must be brought down to earth. The Hegelian dialectic, Merleau-Ponty argues, "is what we call by another name the phenomenon of expression." The philosopher adds that we would doubly misstate the problem of history as an order of advent if we construe it as an order of vertical transcendence: "Christianity is, among other things, the recognition of a mystery in the relations of man and God, which stems precisely from the fact that the Christian God wants nothing to do with a vertical relation of subordination." There is, he says, "an impotence of God without us." Merleau-Ponty cites Paul Claudel, who said that "God is not above us but beneath us—meaning that we do not find him as a supersensible idea but as another ourself which dwells in and authenticates our darkness" ("ILVS" 108; *S* 71; *Si* 88). We have cited Merleau-Ponty's conclusion earlier in relation to Cézanne and Heidegger's sense of earth as hidden and "holy": "Transcendence no longer hangs over man: he becomes, strangely, its privileged bearer" ("ILVS" 108; *S* 70–71; *Si* 88).

The weakness or impotence of God in the world without us brings us back to Paul Klee's thought of a God of finitude and the "tragedy of spirituality," not in the sense that so many events in life are tragic, meaning unhappy events, disasters, and calamities. But there is a tragedy of spirituality in the older Greek sense of tragedy (*tragōidia*), meaning that there are flaws, weaknesses, and destinies that are part and parcel of human life to be faced and lived with knowledge of our own suffering, but more especially, the suffering of others. "Indirect Language" speaks of King Oedipus ("ILVS" 109; *S* 72; *Si* 90), good King Oedipus, we would say, who suffered but whom the gods exonerated at the end at Colonus and led to a beautiful and mysterious resting place to be at peace at last. Only the Athenian king Theseus was present at Oedipus's departure from this earth, and in the words of Sophocles, Theseus reported: "It was not lightning, bearing its fire from Zeus, that took him off; no hurricane was blowing, but some attendant from the train of Heaven came for him; or else the underworld opened in love the unlit door of earth. For he was taken without lamentation, illness or suffering; indeed his end was wonderful if mortal's ever was."[56] Oedipus, at the end of more than twenty years of exile from Thebes, wandering, and suffering, aided and attended by the loving but doomed daughter who was also his sister, Antigone, at last found a mortal beauty.

At the beginning of the chapter on "Sense Experience" in *Phenomenology of Perception,* Merleau-Ponty speaks of "the gap which we ourselves are" (*cette lacune que nous sommes*), since "perception itself is the 'flaw' in this 'great diamond' [*la perception est le 'defaut' de ce 'grand diamant'*]" (*PP* 207; *PhP* 240). We also encounter this expression in Merleau-Ponty's essay on Sartre in *Sense and Non-Sense* titled "A Scandalous Author": "Matter, sky, harvests, animals are beautiful. Man's attitudes, his very clothes, bear witness to the fact that he is of a different order. He is a flaw in the diamond of the world" (*SNS* 45; *SeNS* 79). Thus, the "flaw" of which Merleau-Ponty speaks is we ourselves, the order of humanity, and it is this "gap" (*lacune*) that prevents philosophy and the world itself from being a pure crystalline diamond, to use Klee's term. Merleau-Ponty's philosophy means to undo the conception of the world as unchanging and immutable and the conception of philosophy as a system of fixed concepts for grasping the fixed world. The perceptual world is inherently "flawed," if one wishes to speak this way, for indeed, this "flaw" might also be recognized as a positive value. We ourselves are inherently limited, finite, and mortal, and thus philosophy can only be thought from the inside, from within perception itself, from within finitude and mortality. Merleau-Ponty's text contains an implied literary reference to Paul Valéry's long poem *Le cimetière marin* (*The Cemetery by the Sea*):

> My doubts, my strivings, my repentances,
> These are the flaw in your great diamond.
>
> *Mes repentirs, mes doutes, mes contraintes*
> *Sont le défaut de ton grand diamant.*[57]

Merleau-Ponty returned to this thought of "the flaw in the diamond" in a late working note from January 1960 for *The Visible and the Invisible* that refers back to his text in *Phenomenology of Perception* but connects it explicitly with the thought of incarnation: "What we have said at the start concerning perception as integration-differentiation . . . makes of my incarnation no longer a 'difficulty,' a fault in the clear diamond of philosophy—but the typical fact, the essential articulation of my constitutive transcendence" (*VI* 233; *VIn* 287). The "flaw" is not a fault at all, but simply the "typical fact" of human existence. This working note includes as part of its heading or title: "Transcendence synonym of incarnation" (*VI* 229; *VIn* 283).[58]

Valéry preceded his long and beautiful *The Cemetery by the Sea,* which is about time, dream, sleep, and sea, with an epigraph from Pindar's *Pythian Odes:* "My soul, do not seek immortal life, but exhaust the realm of the possible."[59] With Merleau-Ponty as well as Valéry, it seems to us, the epigraph does not deny immortal life, gods, or God, but urges us not to seek them in the sense of a direct striving, and not to seek them in a beyond. Like the painting and thought of Klee, art and life are not limited to the realm of the here and now, immanence, and the visible, but are meant to be saturated with what is possible, not seen, invisible, and transcendent. God and immortal life are not so much above us as before us and below us in the faces, bodies, and lives of those who are most vulnerable: children, the poor, the ragged, the homeless, the sick—and also in landscapes, seascapes, mountains, valleys, and canyons where there lives a sublime stillness and wonder.

It is well known that Paul Klee died of scleroderma with which he was diagnosed in 1935, a rare disease that hardens the skin and makes the mucous membranes dry up, almost always resulting in early death.

25. Paul Klee, *Untitled, Last Still Life* (*Ohne Titel, Letztes Stilleben*), 1940. Oil on canvas. 39.4 × 31.7 in. (100 × 80.5 cm.) Zentrum Paul Klee, Bern. Livia Klee Donation. *Copyright ©2009 Artists Rights Society (ARS), New York/VG Bild-Kunst, Bonn.*

Klee suffered from the progress of the disease for five years until it overtook him on June 29, 1940. The last two years of his life saw a drastically accelerated outpouring of his artworks, and we find several in which he reflected openly on his mortality: *Early Sorrow* (1938), *A Sailor Feels the End Is Near* (1938), and *Fear Erupting* (1939). His large *Untitled, Last Still Life* (1940; *Ohne Titel, Letztes Stilleben*) was left unfinished, unsigned, and unnamed, and is apparently the work he left as his legacy on his easel when he departed from Bern, Switzerland, for the last time to be admitted to the hospital in Locarno. (See figure 25.)

In the foreground to the right is a yellow-orange circle that suggests a tablecloth, with a green jug and an abstract sculptural form on it.

The sculpture seems to suggest somewhat the human form. The surface of the circle is strewn with hieroglyphic symbols that might also be read as flowers. In the dark background is the disk of the moon. Grohmann writes that the picture "becomes even more disquieting if we look at the rigid shapes of the cut flowers which suddenly look as if strewn on a grave. Thus the still life is transmuted into a ghostly nocturne."[60] What interests us even more than this foreshadowing, premonition, or anticipation of the grave is on the front of the picture plane on the left. There appears a sheet of white paper with one of Klee's angel drawings. This one is *Angel, Still Ugly* (1940; *Engel, noch hässlich*). Though strangely formed with hands and legs too heavy for the angel body and angel wings, thus still in the process of maturing from carnality to spirituality, yet this angel smiles out at us from the canvas. There is only one important respect in which this angel picture in *Last Still Life* differs from its original that Klee had drawn separately a few months earlier. In the original, a short horizontal line near the bottom of the angel torso evidently indicates the angel's female sex. In *Last Still Life,* this short horizontal line is combined with a short vertical line to form a cross. This may be the cross of Christian faith, but more likely it is simply a crossing out of the female sex to indicate the angel's progress toward a more complete spirituality.[61] Nevertheless, faced with his own demise, Klee remained ironic and whimsical, still attached to a sense of transcendence as a "mid-world." We conclude these reflections on transcendence and beauty by recalling the words from Klee's *Diaries:* "I philosophize about death that perfects what could not be completed in life. The longing for death, not as destruction, but as striving toward perfection. On the whole, a stage between striving and despair" (*DPK* 52/143).

Egyptian Beauty: Klee's Pyramids and Mythical Time

In writing and thinking about Klee's art, we should not let our reflections end in death but in life. Thus, it will now be important to bring our study of Klee and Merleau-Ponty full circle by a countermovement from Tunisia to Egypt, from color and abstraction to the hieroglyphs of Klee's *Last Still Life.* This will enable a discussion of the symbol and mythical time. In a very dense working note from April 1960 from which we cite only a fragment here, Merleau-Ponty returns to the discussion of mythical time: "This 'past' belongs to a mythical time, to the time before time, to the prior life, 'farther than India and China'" (*VI* 243; *VIn* 296).

The note is extremely cryptic and complex, beginning with Freud and moving through Proust, Piaget, and Husserl, and is worthy of an entire study itself.[62] Here we can only say some things about a mythical time in relation to Paul Klee. The desire to know and express the non-origin of birth and death is a fundamental desire of Klee's art, and this is the entrance to the time before time, which can only be the time of myth that is given us in symbols. Earlier in this chapter we cited Klee's statement on abstraction from the "Creative Credo"; now we extend this text to the symbol: "Abstract formal elements are put together like numbers and letters to make concrete beings or abstract things; in the end a formal cosmos is achieved, so much like the Creation. . . . The relation of art to creation is symbolic. Art is an example, just as the earthly is an example, of the cosmic."[63] This model of abstraction based in the formal elements of painting is analogous to the method by which children learn, first letters, then syllables, and then finally how to read and write, and it is no accident that we find in Klee this sustained link between his symbolic art and the drawings of children.[64] In his course of 1958–59, "Philosophy Today," Merleau-Ponty cites at length from Klee's 1924 Jena lecture titled "On Modern Art" in which Klee says that the artist "is a philosopher, perhaps, without exactly wanting to be one."[65] Merleau-Ponty quotes the following text in full:

> What artist would not yearn [*désirerait*] to dwell near the mind, or heart, of creation itself, that prime mover of events in space and time? In nature's own womb, the soil whence all creation springs, which holds the key to every riddle? But not all of us are destined to go there. Each must obey the command [of his heart] within him, wherever it may lead. . . . Our own [pounding] heart, however, urges us to go deeper, down to [primordial] bedrock. (*NC* 56–57)[66]

Commenting on this passage from Klee cited by Merleau-Ponty, Emmanuel de St. Aubert has written that "the Merleau-Pontean movement is that of a patient, enduring research for a depth more and more synonymous with a desire for desire, essential to his conception of Being."[67] This is the philosopher's desire to know and express the fundamental yearning within Being itself, to express the non-origin of birth and death within the heart of Creation. For some, this reading of Merleau-Ponty that stresses expressing the non-origin "of the first day" may bring Merleau-Ponty's ontology too near the Romanticism of Hegel, or even more so, of Schelling. I would rather associate it with what Klee himself calls the "cool Romanticism" of his style of abstraction: "One deserts the realm of the here and now to transfer one's activity into a realm of the yonder where total affirmation is possible. Abstraction. The cool Romanticism of this style without pathos is unheard of" (*DPK* 313/951).

Klee experienced this yearning as a magical attraction to the south, first to Tunisia in 1914, as we have discussed in the opening section of this chapter, but more than a decade later in a trip to Egypt from December 1928 through January 1929. We know so much of the former trip to Tunisia through Klee's detailed chronicle and reflections in his *Diaries, 1898–1918,* but so little of the details of this trip to Egypt, since he painted and wrote almost nothing during the trip, preferring to soak up impressions of the landscape of the Nile River valley and its peoples that became themes for his work. We know through his son, Felix, that he had gone on tours of the pyramids and the Sphinx and took an enchanting nocturnal trip to Aswan and the tombs of the pharaohs, carried there by donkey.[68] Grohmann wrote that Klee had an instinctive bond with the Near East, and though his "previous knowledge of Egypt was no greater than his knowledge of Tunis, on arrival he felt as though he had been there before. 'Where are we going? Always home.'"[69] Egypt represents that intermingling of history and landscape in which "the responsive mind can read humanity's destiny in time and space," and Klee had at his disposal the necessary array and flexibility of means for its picture-making.[70] An outpouring of Egyptian pictures followed Klee's return to Dessau and, after the Bauhaus years, in Switzerland, marked by the elements of an ancient symbolics—birds, cats, fishes, water, boats, mountains, crescent moon, and sun—and above all by the colored striped patterns of his landscapes expressing the polyphonic interplay between earth and light: from *Monument in the Fertile Country* (1929; *Monument im Fruchtland*) on through *Legend of the Nile* (1937; *Legende vom Nil*). (See figures 26 and 27.)

What Klee found in Egypt was a presence of a past, "of origins and changes in time," of "the genius of the land" that he "transmuted into a fabric of contrapuntally interwoven colored motifs that expand into fields and paths, pyramids and monuments."[71] All of this came together in the great masterwork of *Ad Parnassum* (1932), a divisionist work akin to pointillism in which the graphic elements show an arched gate or door dominated by the triangular lines of a massive pyramid above it and, overarching all, the shining sun. From the title, the door may be the gate to Mount Parnassus, home of Apollo and the Muses, but in the doubling of its meaning it also invokes the pyramids of the ancient pharaohs. This painting also returns us to the thought of musical painting, since any graded sequence that attempts to teach students mastery through a series of steps with compositions of increasing difficulty could be called a "Gradus ad Parnassum." For example, in Debussy's *Children's Corner*

26. Paul Klee, *Monument in the Fertile Country* (*Monument im Fruchtland*), 1929, 41. Watercolor and pencil on paper on cardboard. 18 × 12 1/10 in. (45.7 × 30.8 cm.) Zentrum Paul Klee, Bern. *Copyright ©2009 Artists Rights Society (ARS), New York/VG Bild-Kunst, Bonn.*

(1906–08), there is a movement called "Dr. Gradus ad Parnassum" that seems to poke fun at five-finger exercises. If Klee had such a musical meaning partly in mind, it undoubtedly would point in the direction of a Bach fugue, and it is purely speculative on our part to suggest that the actual Bach composition best referenced might be *The Art of the Fugue.* For although this work displays the kind of mastery at which a "Gradus ad Parnassum" might aim, it is still unfinished, so we are already there yet still on the way at the same time.[72]

Though Merleau-Ponty links mythical time with India and China (as in the poem of Baudelaire, "Moesta et Errabunda" in *Flowers of Evil*)

27. Paul Klee, *Legend of the Nile* (*Legende vom Nil*), 1937, 215. Pastel on cotton on colored paste on burlap. 27 1/10 × 24 in. (69 × 61 cm.) Kunstmuseum Bern, Hermann und Margrit Rupf-Stiftung. *Copyright ©2009 Artists Rights Society (ARS), New York/VG Bild-Kunst, Bonn.*

rather than Egypt, the former are not meant to be taken as geographical-political entities that for us, today, would not be that far away at all. Merleau-Ponty inherited the India-China pairing from Hegel and Husserl, both of whom had demeaned them, though Husserl less so, Merleau-Ponty wrote in "Everywhere and Nowhere" in *Signs*. Husserl had included India and China as part of the "historical whole of the life-world" (*S* 137; *Si* 173), whereas Hegel had found in the pyramids "only philosophy in itself" (*S* 135; *Si* 170–71), which is to say, matter insufficiently spiritualized. What Merleau-Ponty finds in the metaphors of India and China is akin to what Klee found in Egypt: "Indian and Chinese philosophies have tried not so much to dominate existence as to be the echo or the sounding board of our relationship to being" (*S* 139; *Si* 176). At least twice in important texts on time, Merleau-Ponty wrote of a pyramid of time rather than a line or a river. The *Phenomenology* tells us that "we are, as Proust declared, perched on a pyramid of past life" (*PP* 393; *PhP* 450) and "every present as it arises is driven into time like a wedge and stakes its claim to eternity" (*PP* 393; *PhP* 450–51). This may in itself be a double reference, for a wedge is a triangle, yet there is a second text found in the introduction to *Signs:* "I am installed on a pyramid of time which has been me" (*S* 14; *Si* 21).[73] A pyramid, among other things, is an image of verticality, monumentality, and durability. If the pyramid is a symbol of the durability of the past in presence, we do not forget that it is also the fate of a future, for a pyramid is also a tomb.

Klee explains the formal meaning of the triangle in his pedagogical notebooks: "The triangle came into being when a point entered into a relation of tension with a line and, following the command of its Eros, discharged this tension. The tension between point and line is characteristic of the triangle."[74] There is a painting by Klee titled *Eros* (1923) that shows two triangles—two pyramids—one inverted on top of the other, with horizontal bands of blue, green, yellow, and orange, and in the middle of the bottom pyramid that forms the base, two black arrows move upward to meet the inverted pyramid moving downward toward it. One is reminded of someone like Barnett Newman who created the massive sculpture *Broken Obelisk,* which depicts the point of contact between the enormous triangular form at the base and the immense triangular form poised above it, that point of contact, tension, and desire at the moment of Creation. Of mythical time and space, Merleau-Ponty has written: "There is a mythical space in which directions and positions are determined by the residence in it of great affective entities. . . . In dreaming as in myth we learn *where* the phenomenon is to be found, by feeling that towards which our desire goes out, what our heart dreads, on what our life depends. Even in waking life things are no different" (*PP* 285; *PhP* 330). In Klee, as in Merleau-Ponty, the topological space that seeks to express the non-origin of birth and death is become the libidinal space of mythical time. The time of the artwork is the "time before time," the "time of the first day," it is logos-eros. This is the "cool Romanticism" of Paul Klee, and, we dare say, it bears many signs of a searing mortal beauty, above all, color and light, melody and rhythm, transcendence and something about the time before time.

Part 3

The Retrieval of the Beautiful

6

Beauty, Shape, and Desire

> And henceforth movement, touch, vision, applying themselves to the other and to themselves, return toward their source and, in the patient and silent labor of desire, begin the paradox of expression.
>
> —Merleau-Ponty, *The Visible and the Invisible*

> Now for the first time the object comes to the fore as pure object and that coming forward into appearance is the beautiful. The word "beautiful" means appearing in the radiance of such coming to the fore.
>
> —Martin Heidegger, *The Will to Power as Art*

We now turn our attention to developing the architecture of the beautiful, working to prolong the lines of Merleau-Ponty's key aesthetic concepts and insights for the contemporary debate. We have inherited themes from Merleau-Ponty's own texts and from his artists: desire, radiance, rhythm, repetition, difference, and the intertwining of the beautiful and the sublime. We speak of an architecture of the beautiful rather than a system, hierarchy, or architectonic in order to indicate a certain understanding of the relation of parts and wholes in the meaning of the beautiful. In the "Indirect Language and the Voices of Silence" aesthetic essay, Merleau-Ponty refers to the stones in an arch and the relation between individual stones as parts to the whole of the arch. He is discussing the philosophy of language developed by Saussure that "rejects any other than a 'diacritical' meaning of signs" ("ILVS" 77; *S* 39; *Si* 50). In the view developed by Saussure, words gain their meanings through an internal articulation and divergence from other words. Language is not a logical totality like a philosophical system, all of whose elements can be deduced from a single idea. Rather, the unity of language is a "unity of coexistence, like that of the sections of an arch which shoulder one another" ("ILVS" 77; *S* 39; *Si* 50), Merleau-Ponty writes. In similar fashion, there is not a philosophical system or logical totality of the beautiful in which we can expect to deduce the various parts of its meaning from a positive general idea. Rather, the various features within an architecture of the beautiful shoulder and support one another. As architecture, there are openings, hinges, windows and doorways, nooks and hollows. We want to live in the house of beauty and make it our home.

The logic of architecture shows up as well in *The Visible and the Invisible* as part and parcel of the visible present. Visible things can fill me and occupy me because "the weight, the thickness, the flesh of each color, of each sound, of each tactile texture, of the present, and of the world" emerge by a sort of coiling up or redoubling. "What there is, is a whole architecture, a whole complex of phenomena 'in tiers,' a whole series of 'levels of being'" (*VI* 114; *VIn* 153). Like time and space themselves, the beautiful comes into view by "piling up, by proliferation, by encroachment, by promiscuity . . . which are the nodes and antinodes of the same ontological vibration" (*VI* 115; *VIn* 155). One imagines a larger home, coiling and spiraling staircases that open onto levels with encroaching, overlapping, and proliferating spaces and times, filled with light and air, bodies and desires, repetitions and differences awakening the most intense feelings of pleasure and sublimity. Something like that is the architecture of the beautiful. Let us begin with the question of desire, both its nature and its relationship with the beautiful.

Beauty and desire were essential, and essentially linked, in the aesthetic of all three of Merleau-Ponty's artists, Cézanne, Rodin, and Klee, and in a central passage of *The Visible and the Invisible* cited in the opening epigraph for this chapter, Merleau-Ponty places desire at the origin of all expression, artistic and linguistic: "In the patient and silent labor of desire, begin the paradox of expression" (*VI* 144; *VIn* 189). We are nevertheless aware that there are reasons that speak against desire bearing a strong relationship, or any relationship at all, with beauty. As we have seen, Kant demanded that the experience of beauty be "disinterested," and he sharply differentiated the kind of "liking" involved in aesthetic judgment both from the sensuous "agreeableness" of a color or a sound that gratifies us and from a moral liking for the goodness of an object that endorses the existence of something. For Kant, the pure or disinterested form of liking peculiar to the beautiful arises neither from desires nor from needs, but aesthetic judgment is a disinterested judgment of "free beauty" (*CJ* 5/51–52). We will devote our last chapter of part 3 to a study of Kant's *Critique of Judgment* and undertake its evaluation from the point of view of Merleau-Ponty's aesthetic. Hegel, too, argued that the apprehension of the beautiful is a kind of regard that has nothing to do with desire but apprehends the world or the work for its own sake with the purpose of higher spiritual interests. "In art, the sensuous is *spiritualized,* the *spiritual* appears in sensuous shape."[1] These sentiments are also reflected more recently in the opening of Umberto Eco's *History of Beauty,* wherein he equates beauty with "a detached attitude" toward some good that "does not arouse our desire." "We talk of Beauty when we enjoy something for what it is, irrespective of whether we possess it or not."[2] Eco's word "possess" expresses an implicit assumption of a concept of desire that has held sway throughout the Western tradition, from Plato to Hegel to Sartre, namely that desire is a kind of negation. According to this majority tradition, to desire the beautiful would be to hold some good as the object of regard, even of admiration, out of a lack or absence in oneself. This is necessarily to demean that object—so this line of thought goes—for it reifies or objectifies the object as a possession, if not a literal possession that one seeks literally to own, then at the least an object "possessed" by the desiring gaze or "look."

In this chapter, we seek to develop an account of aesthetic desire that is not lack or need, a cooler and more positive notion of desire that begins elsewhere than from negation or possession, and one with a more nuanced account of our relations with the world and others. We think again of Paul Klee's devoted attention to the temperature of colors, which brings us again to the coolness of Cézanne's blue, especially in the late Mt. Sainte-Victoire landscapes. We recall Rilke's praise of Cézanne's "very unique blue," which, unlike a "listening blue" or a "thunderstorm blue" or a blue "full of revolt," is simply "Blue, Blue, Blue."[3] "All of this is very beautiful," Rilke wrote.[4] Aesthetic desire is the coolness of blue, therefore a desire that is not a destructive negation, but a productive singularity that is the birth of art and expression. We will find beneficial the notion of aesthetic desire as shape and take up the parallels and analogies between aesthetic and erotic desire. The intertwinings among love and beauty will lead us into the most elemental aspects of Being itself, the Flesh. Aesthetic desire (*aisthesis*) is our opening to the world, and within Being is the rhythm and radiance of the beautiful itself. At the conclusion of the "Temporality" chapter of *Phenomenology of Perception,* Merleau-Ponty wrote of "a 'Logos of the aesthetic world,' an 'art hidden in the depths of the human soul,' one which, like any art, is known only in its results" (*PP* 429; *PhP* 490–91). Ontology is aesthetic-ontologic, for there is a "logos of the aesthetic world."

The Critique of Desire: Sartre and Hegel

In the aesthetic and ontology of Merleau-Ponty, there is a reworking of the concept of desire. In chapter 4 of *The Visible and the Invisible,* "The

Intertwining—The Chiasm," desire (*désir*) is presented as productive of singularities, and indeed as the source, the origin of all expression, of all things beautiful. Before we turn to a full engagement with this passage and its context, it will be useful to explore the background from which it emerges in Merleau-Ponty's critique of Sartre in the preceding chapters of *The Visible and the Invisible.*

Merleau-Ponty's thinking with regard to desire grows out of a dialectical engagement with Sartre's views in *Being and Nothingness.* In order to remain focused on the construal of desire as negation, we can only be cryptic here with what is a richly layered and suggestive phenomenological description from Sartre. He asks us to consider the situation of a man in a public park when suddenly another person comes onto the scene. In the park, Sartre contends, the Other arises in my perceptual field as a threat conveyed by "the Look." Sartre writes: "Thus suddenly an object has appeared which has stolen the world from me. . . . The appearance of the Other in the world corresponds to a fixed sliding of the whole universe, to a decentralization of the world. . . . It appears that the world has a kind of drain hole in the middle of its being and that it is perpetually flowing off through this hole."[5] The French phrase translated here as "drain hole" is *trou de vidange,* a hole or gap that is empty. *Vidange* is related to *vide,* meaning "empty," "void," "vacant," "blank," or "chasm." *Trou de la serrure* is a keyhole, *trou d'homme* is a manhole. Thus, according to Sartre, the Look of the Other introduces nothingness as the "disintegration of my universe" (*désintrégration de mon univers*) in which my world is threatened with "draining off" into the world of the Other. In concrete relations with others, this means that there is a contest between my universe with my project over against the universe and project of the Other. Only two outcomes are possible, Sartre argues: either I will succeed in subordinating the Other as an object-for-me in my universe, or the Other will succeed in subordinating me as an object in his or her universe. The first possibility is sadism, Sartre says, and the second is masochism. Both are negations. The attempt to maintain an attitude of indifference between oneself and an Other is inherently unstable and ambivalent, reverting to the sadistic or masochistic negations, as Sartre demonstrated so brilliantly in the triangular relationships among the central three characters of *No Exit.* Therefore, concrete interpersonal relations founded upon negation have as their inner (secret) structure the Look, threat, power, and domination. The ideal of love as a mutual exchange of care and intimacy between individuals is an impossibility. Love is in fact "a conflict," Sartre writes. "The lover demands a pledge, yet is irritated by a pledge. He wants to be loved by a freedom but demands that this freedom as freedom should no longer be free."[6] Love is an "unrealizable ideal," and desire as this negation or "drain hole" is the desire for mastery of the Other.

Sartre's philosophical focus upon "the Look" in the engagement with the Other and the desire to subject the other to one's own project presents one version of what we might call the "reification" or "objectification" argument against the beautiful. To fix an other with one's gaze, even with the fascination and elevation that calls the other beautiful, it is argued, is necessarily to reify, objectify, and reduce the full individuality of the other. As Elaine Scarry put it in her recent *On Beauty and Being Just,* this complaint against beauty did not mean that beautiful things themselves had to be banished from the humanities and arts—the poems, the stories, the paintings, the sculptures, and the films—but only that conversation and discussion of beauty had to take place "in whispers."[7] According to Scarry, this political argument against beauty goes along these lines: "When we stare at something beautiful, make it an object of sustained regard, our act is destructive to the object. . . . The complaint has given rise to a generalized discrediting of the act of 'looking,' which is charged with 'reifying' the very object that appears to be the subject of admiration."[8]

We do want to say that it is all too easy to dismiss Sartre's analysis of desire and love as pessimistic and extreme, yet it is a courageous phenomenology of human relationships, *if* we grant its origin in the subject's Look and the threat from the Other, together with the premise that posits desire as negation. Nevertheless, what is the meaning of this negation? What is the logic of this nothingness, of being and nothingness? To this Merleau-Ponty has responded directly and at length in *The Visible and the Invisible* in the second chapter titled "Interrogation and Dialectic," the first section of which is called "Perceptual Faith and Negativity." From the moment Sartre conceives the self or subject as negativity and the world as positivity, there is no longer any interaction between them. Merleau-Ponty writes of Sartre's position: "Between it [the world, the Other] and myself there is neither any point of encounter nor point of reflection, since it is Being and I am nothing" (*VI* 52; *VIn* 78). Furthermore, the very language deployed by Sartre undermines his own description. Merleau-Ponty argues that the "agnosticism" or negation with respect to the Other "suddenly appears as the worst of infringements. For he who states it implies that it is applicable to all those who hear him. He does not speak only of himself, of his own perspective, and for himself; he speaks for all. . . . His description implies the power to speak for all, whereas the description contests this power" (*VI* 79; *VIn* 111). In contrast, the only way to think the negative is "to see it out of the corner of one's eye" (*VI* 53; *VIn* 79), says Merleau-Ponty. Any direct, frontal approach collides with the truth that "nothing is not," thereby negating itself and converting the thought of the negative into the very plenitude of positivism. To dramatize his point, Merleau-Ponty writes this phrase, "nothingness is not," with the crossed-out line: "to ~~be~~ truly non-being [*pour ~~être~~ vraiment non-être*]" (*VI* 60; *VIn* 88). In other words, "the negativism, if it is rigorous, absolute, is a sort of positivism. . . . An absolute negativism—that is, one that thinks the negative in its originality—and an absolute positivism—that is, one that thinks being in its plenitude and its self-sufficiency—are exactly synonymous; there is not the least divergence between them" (*VI* 64, 65; *VIn* 94).

The view of desire as a negation had been prepared by Hegel long before Sartre as an ontological principle that elevated negation as a "not" or absence present in the very heart of Being. In the famous chapter of *Phenomenology of Spirit* titled "The Truth of Self-Certainty," in the second section on "Self-Consciousness," Hegel had brought Desire onto the stage in the history of Spirit by asserting that "self-consciousness is *Desire* in general." The immediate object of Desire that is the object of sense-certainty and perception, he writes, has for self-consciousness "the character of a *negative*."[9] Hegel's word translated here as "Desire" is the German *Begierde,* meaning animal appetite such as animal hunger, but in Hegel's context it carries a much wider meaning. What self-consciousness fundamentally desires is not the object of immediate sensation, perception, or feeling but self-knowledge. *Begierde,* as Hegel puts it—and this is what justifies the translation "Desire"—has a double object: the first is the immediate object of desire, but the second, which he says is "the true essence," is the self-consciousness that "stands opposed to the first object." This second object of Desire, the desire for self-knowledge, means that Desire must be understood as a negativity, namely the negation of the immediate object of desire, whether thing or person. Jean Hyppolite has interpreted this negation in the following way: insofar as something is an object of desire, "we can just as well say of it that it exists as that it does not exist. It exists, but soon it will no longer exist; its truth is to be consumed and negated, in order that self-consciousness might gather itself up through this negation of the other."[10] Because it is self-consciousness that the desiring subject ultimately seeks, it is necessary that another self-conscious being, a person, become the object of desire rather than an inert object. Self-consciousness originates from the struggle for mastery of another self-consciousness in which I see myself in the other person. I recognize the Other as also seeking self-awareness just as I am. This ushers in the transition to Hegel's account of the "struggle to the death" in the dialectic of lordship and bondage that influenced so many, among them Jean-Paul Sartre, particularly through the lectures of Alexandre

Kojève.[11] It is to be emphasized that Desire does not disappear from the dialectic of lordship and bondage, but rather it raises the dialectic of Desire to a higher level, the intersubjective or interpersonal level, or as Hegel would say, lordship and bondage is "the truth" of Desire.

It is not accidental, therefore, that in his *Introductory Lectures on Aesthetics* Hegel excludes desire from the realm of the beautiful. The lowest mode of apprehension, he says, and the least appropriate for the human mind is the purely sensuous apprehension found in desire. In this kind of relation to the world, the particular individual relates to things also as particulars and seeks to preserve himself in them "inasmuch as he uses them, consumes them, and puts in act his self-satisfaction by sacrificing them to it. In this negative relation . . . its impulse urges it just precisely to destroy this independence and freedom of external things, and to show that they are only there to be destroyed and consumed."[12] In the realm of the beautiful and the artwork, Hegel argues, desire is not appropriate, for the work must be regarded as an object that appeals only to the theoretical aspect of the mind. What Hegel means by this theoretic interest is not the interest of science, which eliminates the particular in favor of universality and scientific principle and law. Rather, it is an apprehension that cherishes the object for its individual existence, but permits the object to exist freely and independently, free of desire. Therefore, the apprehension of the beautiful regards the work of art as a "surface or semblance of the sensuous."[13] This is a kind of regard that has nothing to do with desire, or pleasure as well, but apprehends the work of art for its own sake and with the purpose of satisfying higher spiritual interests. "It is thus that, in art, the sensuous is *spiritualized,* i.e., the *spiritual* appears in sensuous shape."[14] We had reasons to invoke Hegel's view earlier with regard to Émile Bernard's questionable efforts to create a "spiritual Cézanne."

Though Hegel's account of desire in terms of negation of the object and its resulting exclusion of desire from the apprehension of the beautiful runs counter to the philosophy of Merleau-Ponty, yet there is a philosophical gain in Hegel's phenomenology of desire in the clear differentiation it affords between desire and need. We learn that desire is not about the satisfaction of some animal appetite, such as hunger, that can be fulfilled or satisfied by some particular, finite object. Desire is an excess that supersedes a finite need, for desire is a restlessness in the subject that comes to rest for a moment at a particular point but does not end there in that particular thing. In the aesthetic realm, one sonata does not satisfy the musical ear, nor one poem the literary ear. In his book *Desire and Distance: Introduction to a Phenomenology of Perception,* augmenting and extending Merleau-Ponty's own *Phenomenology of Perception,*

Renaud Barbaras has explicated this restlessness of desire that ultimately speaks of depth, self, and world. Need refers to a definite lacking, Barbaras writes, but "desire, on the other hand, is not based on a lacking and strictly speaking it does not lack anything," for in a certain sense, "*nothing can fulfill it.*" "Desire thus refers to an originary incompleteness that exceeds everything that can satisfy it, that is renewed to the exact degree that it is fulfilled."[15] It is as if the object of desire is split in two between the object providing satisfaction and a sudden incompleteness, as if the true object of desire is beneath the surface and remains absent. "The characteristic of desire is that the desired object fulfills it only by inflaming it." Barbaras argues that the origin of this phenomenology of desire is really to be found in Husserl's turn, in the 1920s, to a genetic phenomenology in which he uncovered beneath positing, perceptual intentionality a teleology of the "drive," in Husserl's terminology.[16] As the perception of a presence that is in principle unpresentable, "desire opens up the pure transcendence of the world; its inextinguishable thirst is pure reception." Thus, this incompleteness within the structure of desire, as distinguished from need, is the desire for the world: "The life of the living subject is accomplished only as an unfolding of the world."[17] Therefore, we should understand desire less as the gaze and more as movement outward toward the outside. There is an overflow or excess in desire that marks, as Barbaras puts it, "the very condition of the world's transcendence."[18] The living subject has no desires but simply *is* desire.[19] Desire is the movement of life itself seeking a world, seeking beauty in the world. In light of these arguments and this gain for a phenomenology of desire in terms of movement, life, and surplus, we yet need a further account of desire as a productive power rather than a negation of the Other, life, and beauty. To this we now turn.

Beauty, Love, and Desire

Experiences such as desire, or love as the desire for the beautiful beloved, must be conceived differently than absence or nothingness. Desire itself is formed or shaped. Let us rethink first the question of how the Other arises alongside and together with us, otherwise than as negation or threat, and then give some more specific meaning to this notion of desire as shape. When we think of the Other, it must be the case that there is a divergence (*écart*) between the opening onto the world experienced by each of us, but also a fundamental common envelopment shared between us from which the divergence originates. Merleau-Ponty expresses this in terms of interrogation, the question mark. The other is a question mark that puts to the test the right I might arrogate to think the world for all: "The other's gaze on the things is a second openness. Within this openness which I am, it is a question mark opposite the *solipsist* sphere, it is the possibility of a divergence [*écart*] between the nothing that I am and being" (*VI* 58; *VIn* 86). With this argument, Merleau-Ponty introduces the shift from the philosophy of negation to a philosophy of interrogation. In desiring the beautiful, one is not experiencing a void or lack within oneself, but is being interrogated by the world. One's universe is being put in question by the outside, being challenged by the luminous alterity of an Other. This challenge is not a threat but a welcoming, a generosity, and hospitality toward the stranger as friend. This is precisely what happens when those seminars break out in the Cézanne room of the museums: those bathers, that gardener and this wife, and that mountain look otherwise than any such seen before. Cézanne's paintings made the world look strange and make us feel uneasy. Yet this unease and discomfort initiate opportunities and openings onto new horizons and ways of seeing through experiencing others and the world. Merleau-Ponty's stress is upon a common and shared origin of self and other that precedes both. Consider this passage from Merleau-Ponty's analysis of Sartre in which he disputes Sartre's claim that the Other arises in our experience through the Look at someone over there. "Whatever be the common opinion, it is not in their bodies, nor *anywhere,* that I see the others. It is not from a point of space that the other's gaze emanates. The other is born *from my side,* by a sort of propagation by cuttings or by subdivision" (*VI* 59; *VIn* 86). This is confirmed in a text from the introduction to *Signs:*

> Before others are or can be subjected to my conditions of possibility and reconstructed in my image, they must already exist as outlines, deviations, and variants of a single Vision in which I too participate. For they are not fictions with which I might people my desert—offspring of my spirit and forever unactualized possibilities—but *my twins or the flesh of my flesh* [my emphasis]. Certainly I do not live their life; they are definitively absent from me and I from them. But that distance becomes a strange proximity as soon as one comes back home to the perceptible world. (*S* 15; *Si* 22)[20]

Here Merleau-Ponty articulates a conception of Being itself that is prior to the split between self and others, between nothingness and world. He speaks of a "single Vision" in which I and others participate, in which others appear not as negations but as "outlines, deviations, and variants of one sole Vision" (*reliefs, écarts, variants d'une seule Vision*). This single Vision that is pre-Being, prior to the division between self and others, is the "flesh of the world" (*la chair du monde*). This account conceives the world as a primordial ontogenesis that bears within itself deviations and variants in which each of us is a twin of others, flesh of our flesh.

The sensitive and expressive language Merleau-Ponty develops is all-important. He speaks of others as propagations, twins, doubles, "younger sisters of my own," and "other myselves" (*VI* 71; *VIn* 101). Sartre, Merleau-Ponty says, has given us "the abstract portrait" (*VI* 75; *VIn* 105) of desire in which we are frozen by the Look of the other and deceived into thinking that being and nothingness are absolutely opposed. However, on the terrain of experience itself, rather than abstract overview (*survol*), we discover a sort of Hyper-Being of envelopment within which each of us are variants or accents. The power of the philosophy of the negative is that "it described our factual situation with more penetration than had ever before been done" (*VI* 87; *VIn* 120), yet it leaves us with a feeling of uneasiness because our situation "is being surveyed from above" (*survolée*) rather than from the field of appearances with its reliefs and variants. "The principle of principles," Merleau-Ponty concludes his argument, "is that one cannot judge the powers of life by those of death, nor define without arbitrariness life as the sum of forces that resists death" (*VI* 84; *VIn* 117).

In the same way that the ontological principle of Flesh is not a pure monistic positivity, neither in the realm of Desire does the reconceptualization of the negative compel us toward an altogether positivist account. Such an account would be, for example, found in mechanistic readings of Freud: desire as sexual and destructive drives or instincts in the circuits of my body and my brain, Freud's Eros and Thanatos seeded deep in the unconscious inherited from an animal lineage. Another type of positivist account would derive from mechanistic readings of Darwin on natural selection in which desire is always construed as a functionalist adaptation, in which, for example, beauty—perhaps a smile or an ample bosom or a muscular bicep—is a mechanism for the survival of the species hard-wired into our brains and DNA. Where desire is concerned, we need a more subtle blend of positive and negative in a language, thought, and interworld that is more suggestive and flexuous, like the colors of Cézanne. We need word lines that are as philosophically compelling as the lines of Klee's drawings are aesthetically compelling. In fact, Merleau-Ponty himself gives us a line figure for our meeting with the Other and the experience of Desire. My relationship with an Other, Merleau-Ponty writes, "is not a void; it is not the simple or immediate negation of myself and my universe. From the sole fact that I circumscribe it, be it with dotted lines [*pointillé*], it is cut out in my universe; there is an intersection of my universe with that of the other" (*VI* 80; *VIn* 111).[21] The lines of my life are overlaid with the "dotted lines" inscribed by others. Such a figure cancels neither our divergence (*écart*) one from the other nor our shared envelopment. So we are drawn, and in a double sense. We are *drawn upon* by Others as they shape our lives, and we are *drawn toward* Others as we encounter them in our world.

Therefore, the desire awakened by the beautiful brings with it a weight and gravity that is the experience of a *passivity* (*VI* 61; *VIn* 88) within the activity of seeing or listening or feeling, a passivity within the pleasure of the beautiful. We are drawn, and we are drawn in quite specific and singular ways. This is what we seek in saying that desire has a "shape." There are many instances of absence or emptiness other than desire that confirm something like an outline or shape, the dotted lines, present within an absence. An abyss, though bottomless, has sides and contours and thus presents a more or less narrow or broad dimension. Forgetting has its halting false starts and stops, as we grope for the first letter of a forgotten word or the place of something valuable now lost. Desire has a shape in just this way. By this term "shape," we mean to indicate that desire is not satisfied by any available object or just any experience whatsoever. On a field from generality to singularity, desire is more a singularity, which means that desire can be productive, rather than a mere negation. This productive passivity that gives shape to desire is, we shall argue, in large part, the force of memory, the imaginary, and something about the unconscious. These outline the topics and argument of our next chapter.

We are aware that in introducing this word "shape," we are repeating but recasting the very word Hegel introduced for the appropriate apprehension of a work of art as merely a "semblance" or spiritualized surface of the sensuous. The German word translated as "semblance" is *Schein,* meaning a shining, a seeming, or appearance. We mean something quite different than did Hegel in introducing this term "shape." His clarification of what he had in mind harks back to Plato's formalist restriction of the beautiful to the idealities of harmony, unity, balance, and proportion, qualities available only to sight and hearing and not to touch, smell, or the sensations of taste. Hegel writes that the semblance or shape of a sensuous work of art presents itself only to the "visible look and the sonorous vibration of things." For this reason, he argues, "the sensuous aspect of art only refers to the two *theoretical* senses of *sight* and *hearing,* while smell, taste, and feeling remain excluded from being sources of artistic enjoyment. For smell, taste, and feeling have to do with matter as such."[22] For Hegel, the beautiful is the shining and luminosity of light valued for its clarity, rationality, and simplicity manifested in mathematics, logic, and science, a strangely incomplete account in the organic, cluttered, and reconfigured world of art and the beautiful that confronts us today.

Suffice it to say that when we argue that desire has a shape that gives it singularity and makes it productive, with Merleau-Ponty we include the object, the Other, and the world in full sensuousness. Desire is awakened by the smells and tastes and touches of things just as much as by sight and sound. *Sculpture for the Blind* by Constantin Brancusi is a smooth, sleek, elegant, beautiful marble egg. In a photograph of the work, it is available only to sight. But in its full actuality, it is available without sight and without sound. It is available to the blind in the sensuousness of touch. In just these ways, the ways of feeling, smell, and taste as well as sight and sound, desire has a shape—the shape of a face, or a place, or a time, or a pleasure. In short, shape is memory, as it is imagination and dream.

It is also for these very reasons that, though the word "shape" may appear quite close to Kant's stress upon "form," the absence of color and sensuousness from Kant's conception of aesthetic judgment pulls us away from the word "form" toward the domain of the more sensuous term "shape." Kant places secondary qualities such as color, smell, texture, and "taste" (meaning the sense pleasures of the organ of the tongue) within the kind of liking he calls "agreeableness" and sharply differentiates this kind of liking from the contemplative, disinterested liking of a pure judgment of aesthetic taste. "Any taste remains barbaric," he writes, "if its liking requires that *charms* and *emotions* be mingled in, let alone if it makes these the standard of its approval. . . . A *pure judgment of taste* is one that is not influenced by charm or emotion and whose determining basis is therefore merely the purposiveness of the form" (*CJ* 13/69). In this way, Kant reactivates the classical conception of the *kalos* (beauty) as the form of the *kalokagathos* (good-beautiful).

In the *Symposium* dialogue, through the speech offered by Socrates in the name of Diotima, the woman of Mantinea, we encounter the origin of the Western tradition's attachment to a formalist conception of beauty conceived in relation to the supersensible, the purity of vision and thought that is achieved through overcoming the attachment to sense and embodied, sexual life. This Diotima calls the "final and highest mystery" of Love:

> But how would it be, in our view, if someone got to see the Beautiful itself, absolute, pure, unmixed, not polluted by human flesh or colors or any other great nonsense of mortality, but if he could see the divine

> Beauty itself in its one form? Do you think it would be a poor life for a human being to look there and to behold it by that which he ought, and to be with it? Or haven't you remembered that in that life alone, when he looks at Beauty in the only way that Beauty can be seen—only then will it become possible for him to give birth not to images of virtue, but to true virtue.[23]

Merleau-Ponty's conception of desire as the source of all expression effects a reversal of Platonism and a reversal of Kantianism on this point. Erotic desire is not generated by a lack or a "not having," as Socrates had enunciated the concept in his *Symposium* interrogation of Agathon prior to the introduction of Diotima: "Such a man or anyone else who has a desire desires what is not at hand and not present, what he does not have, and what he is not, and that of which he is in need; for such are the objects of desire and love."[24] The Greek word for "desire" that occurs here is *epithumei,* which means longing or yearning for a thing. It is related to that word for the third part of the soul (*psychē*) customarily translated in the *Republic* as "spirit" or "passion," the Greek word *epithumetikon,* the part of the soul that possesses *epithumiei.* Desire, for Plato, then, is neither animal appetite such as thirst nor is it reason, but a third part of the soul separate from both that is the mediator between them. On the one hand, it may side with the appetites, but on the other hand, desire may, and most often does, Plato argues, side with the rational part of the soul, for example, when the spirit (*epithumetikon*) is "boiling and angry, fighting for what he believes to be just."[25] Whether desire sides with the appetites or with reason, it is indicative of a lack or fundamental neediness in the personality, according to the Platonic schematism.

The fourfold Socratic "not" of desire—not at hand, not present, not having, not being—are all reversed by the conception of desire as the fundamental relation of self and Being that is an excess, a surplus that is our opening onto the world. The self incessantly overflows into the world, and the structure of desire includes an inherent depth and richness that is inexhaustible. It will only end, if it should end, when life itself ends. This, as distinguished from need, marks the life of living subjects seeking the transcendence and beauty of the world. Of this beginning of life, Merleau-Ponty remarks: "With the first vision, the first contact, the first pleasure, there is initiation, that is, not the positing of a content, but the opening of a dimension that can never again be closed, the establishment of a level in terms of which every other experience will henceforth be situated" (*VI* 151; *VIn* 196).

Thus, beauty is not about purity and perfection of form, for any notion of "pure ideality already streams forth along the articulations of the aesthesiological body, along the contours of the sensible things" (*VI* 152; *VIn* 197). Yet we could not miss recognizing in the Platonic teaching the truth that aesthetic desire and erotic desire are very closely interrelated, and the parallels have been growing implicitly in our own reflections. Desire has a shape, and just as this means the memory and expectancy of a place or a time or a pleasure, it just as much very often means the memory and expectancy of the shape of a female or male beloved. This is erotic desire properly understood and not crudely cast as the need for sexual satisfaction. As Aristophanes describes in the *Symposium* dialogue, "these are the people who finish out their lives together and still cannot say what it is they want from one another. No one would think it is the intimacy of sex—that mere sex is the reason each lover takes so great and deep a joy in being with the other."[26] Aristophanes offers a mythological "androgynous" explanation of human origins and the "twinning" of humans due to the punishment meted out by Zeus of being split in half. This myth of Aistophanes quietly reverberates in the echoes of Merleau-Ponty's account of others as propagations, twins, doubles, "younger sisters of my own," and "other myselves" (*VI* 71; *VIn* 101), much more than Diotima's praise of the purity and perfection of form.

There are four implicit parallels or analogies that we should attempt to say something about, halting though it must be, regarding the interrelation of erotic desire with a revised Merleau-Pontean concept of aesthetic desire. There is something right about speaking of the love of art and the love of nature together with the love of another person, for all have to do with the love of beauty and all inspire in us a sense of care, protection, and preservation of the precious treasures that render our lives more meaningful and more miraculous. The first likeness has already been remarked, that both are a movement toward the world that is an excess, that in the other of erotic attachment or the object of aesthetic experience there is "this incessant escaping" just as in the touching of the right hand by the left there is not an exact superposition or overlapping of experience. "This incessant escaping," Merleau-Ponty says, "is not a failure" (*VI* 148; *VIn* 192); rather, it means that there is a "hinge" between self and other and not a perfect or exact overlay. In erotic love, in aesthetic joy, we approach, come near, and come closer, yet we are always on this side of perfect intimacy and depth. There is always more to come. My flesh and that of the world involve "clearings," Merleau-Ponty says, "about which pivot their opaque zones" (*VI* 148; *VIn* 192). This is why for both love and beauty it is necessary to "take seriously" Husserl's notion of "horizon." Love and beauty, just as Flesh itself, are experiences and truths of plurivocity, porosity, and pregnancy, and "he before whom the horizon opens up is caught up, included within it" (*VI* 148–49; *VIn* 93). Whether one says horizon or depth, love and beauty are inexhaustible openings onto transcendence. Plurivocity, porosity, and pregnancy replace the Platonic trilogy of purity, perfection, and permanence.

A second analogy lies in the cooling of desire that eschews grasping possession, visual objectification, and conceptual delimitation. Both beauty and love are diminished if not destroyed by overbearing approaches that prefer domination to appreciation, dogmatism to communication, commodification to free circulation. Erotic and aesthetic desire are both forms of openness to the Other and the world that are interrogative, a sensitive questioning of both world and self, and Merleau-Ponty has given us this description in relation to the practice of philosophy, for philosophy is also a kind of loving. For the desire of which we speak, perhaps the warm and caring loving of friendship (*philia,* philosophy) is a better pointer and guide than the hot passion we often associate with eros (*erosophy*). The things, Merleau-Ponty says,

> offer themselves therefore only to someone who wishes not to have them but to see them, not to hold them as with forceps, or to immobilize them as under the objective of a microscope, but to let them be and to witness their continued being—to someone who therefore limits himself to giving them the hollow [*le creux*], the free space they ask for in return, the resonance they require. (*VI* 101; *VIn* 136)

This dense yet precise text on philosophical methodology is immediately transferrable to the interrogative desire of *aisthesis* and eros, and within it we cannot help but recognize the prominence of Heidegger's phrase "letting be"—"to let them be and to witness their continued being"—as just above we found Heidegger's term "clearing" (*zones claires*)—my flesh and that of the world involve "clearings, about which pivot their opaque zones." In between the heat of grasping and the cold of indifference, there is a kind of caring for things and others that opens up both self and other to an uncharted, inexhaustible richness.

These Heideggerian appropriations by Merleau-Ponty direct us to Heidegger's texts both on the essence of truth throughout the 1930s and on the beautiful in the Nietzsche lectures at the University of Freiburg from 1936 to 1940. Heidegger claims that both Schopenhauer and Nietzsche misinterpreted Kant's requirement that the beautiful is "devoid of all interest" to mean indifference, a pure repose: "The aesthetic state is one in which the will is put out of commission and all striving is brought to a standstill," according to Schopenhauer.[27] In contrast, Heidegger contends that Kant means that "comportment toward the beautiful as such is *unconstrained favoring.* We must release what encounters us as such to its way to be; we must allow and grant it what belongs to it and what it brings to us."[28] Here the essential relation to things and others comes into view not as indifference, or as grasping, whether physical or intellectual, but as letting appearances, aspects, perspectives, and nuances—what Merleau-Ponty noted as the hollows, free space, and resonance of things—be nourished in the process of sensitive questioning and appreciation. In "On the Essence of Truth," Heidegger is explicit that engagement or activity, rather than indifference, is required in "letting-be": "To let beings be does not refer to neglect and indifference but rather the opposite. To let be is to engage oneself with beings."[29] The kind of engagement at issue for Heidegger contrasts most importantly with technical mastery over things, what he calls "the leveling and planning of this omniscience, this mere knowing" that flattens things out one-dimensionally. He uses the word "attunement" for the kind of engagement with things and others that is open to their freedom and multidimensionality: "Letting beings be, which is an attuning, a bringing into accord, prevails throughout and anticipates all the open comportment that flourishes in it."[30] With the engagement and openness of letting be, Heidegger says, "for the first time the object comes to the fore as pure object and that such coming forward into appearance is the beautiful. The word 'beautiful' means appearing in the radiance of such coming to the fore."[31] In this refined reading, we only demur from the word "pure" in the phrase "pure object" that yet slips its way into Heidegger's text. Reflecting on these textual interlacings between Merleau-Ponty and Heidegger, Mauro Carbone has recently written that "the attitude of philosophy implies the renunciation of the claims to an intellectual possession of the *Begriff*. . . . In fact, aesthetic behavior would be freed from the metaphysical stamp to which it has always been traditionally subject."[32]

The analogies between erotic and aesthetic desire thus are now twofold: both involve an abundance or excess and both are a kind of attunement, letting-be, and care of the other. We now approach a third likeness or analogy, a demand for expression and the "paradox of expression." If neither love nor beauty can possibly be intellectual concepts, they yet require expression; nevertheless, expression requires recasting as the "sensible idea," in Merleau-Ponty's language. Here the link between love and beauty is explicit in Merleau-Ponty's text as a triangulation among literature, music, and love. The reader of this book, and its writer, must be patient here with the development of this point because this third analogy is the most complex one, involving both the philosophy of expression and philosophy of language. Both love and beauty demand expression and birth into language, yet that expression and that birth are fragile, forever skating near the abyss of marring, even ruining, its treasure. In fact, with the notion of "sensible idea" we touch what Merleau-Ponty calls "the most difficult point, that is, the bond between the flesh and the idea, between the visible and the interior armature [*l'armature intérieure*] which it manifests and which it conceals" (*VI* 149; *VIn* 193). Immediately, Merleau-Ponty announces a remarkable path for thinking this most difficult question, namely that "no one has gone further than Proust in fixing the relations between the visible and the invisible, in describing an idea that is not the contrary of the sensible, that is its lining and its depth" (*VI* 149; *VIn* 193). Thus, Merleau-Ponty conjoins literature with philosophy in citing Proust as exemplary on the meaning of "sensible ideas," specifically volume 1, *Swann's Way,* from Proust's seven-volume masterpiece, *Remembrance of Things Past.* What is true of the dialectic of love is also true, in Proust, of many other notions such as the musical idea, light, sound, touch, and physical voluptuousness, namely that these exist "without equivalents" intellectually, yet manifest "their logic, their coherence, their points of intersection, their concordances" (*VI* 149; *VIn* 194). It is essential to these sensible ideas that they are known in and through the aesthesiological body and, in fact, would be entirely inaccessible if we were "pure mind," disembodied. In the sensible idea, body and mind, visible and invisible are necessarily commingled, and thus sensibility and particularity are necessary to this kind of knowing. Merleau-Ponty puts it this way: "They could not be given to us *as ideas* except in a carnal experience. . . . It is that they owe their authority, their fascinating, indestructible power, precisely to the fact that they are in transparency behind the sensible, or in its heart" (*VI* 150; *VIn* 194). Here Merleau-Ponty's phrase regarding sensible ideas known "behind the sensible" (*derrièr le sensible*) expresses the meaning less well, we would argue, than his subsequent phrase, known "in its heart" (*en son coeur*), which resonates with Pascal's famous *pensée* that "the heart has its reasons, which reason knows not."[33] Love and beauty, like musical ideas, are matters known by the heart. In *Phenomenology of Perception,* at the beginning of the chapter on "The Body in Its Sexual Being," Merleau-Ponty had written:

> If then we want to bring to light the birth of being for us, we must finally look at that area of our experience which clearly has significance and reality only for us, and that is our affective life. Let us try to see how a thing or a being begins to exist for us through desire or love and we shall thereby come to understand better how things and beings can exist in general. (*PP* 154; *PhP* 180)

Love and beauty involve a double opening and sensitivity, both to the other and to ourselves, that is an awareness and "knowing by sentiment"

(*VI* 249; *VIn* 297). The French phrase here, "connaissance par sentiment," and the term *sentiment* itself indicate that Merleau-Ponty is conjoining perception or sensibility with "feeling" in coming to know sensible ideas, and the relevant meaning is more like "having a feel for" something than the mere state of pleasure or pain. We have a feel for a relationship or personality or for a particular artist and style, which means a specially cultivated sensitivity. Speaking conceptually, this is preintellectual knowing, but nevertheless it is intelligent knowing sunk deep into the sedimented layers and levels of our bodily comportment. Sensible knowing is less precise conceptually than intellectual ideas of "pure ideality" and necessarily is somewhat "veiled with shadows" (*VI* 150; *VIn* 195), yet for all that sensible ideas are far richer and deeper, and also more fragile due to their lubricity.

In addition to musical ideas, Merleau-Ponty explicated the notion of sensible ideas by way of color. He wrote in a working note of May 1960 that the essence of a certain color of red "is a *Wesen* that in principle is accessible only through the seeing, and is accessible as soon as the seeing is given, has then no more need to be *thought:* seeing is this sort of thought that has no need to think in order to possess the *Wesen*" (*VI* 247; *VIn* 295–96). He immediately appends an example from Proust: the essence is in the red like the memory of the high school building is in its odor. Heidegger's *Introduction to Metaphysics* had already offered the high school example in consideration of the problem of essence: "You can, as it were, smell the being of this building in your nostrils. The smell communicates the being of this essent far more immediately and truly than any description or inspection could ever do."[34] "Essent" is the English translator's effort to render Heidegger's philosophical invention of the word *seiend,* which Heidegger himself says is alien to everyday speech and is his approximate equivalent to Merleau-Ponty's "sensible idea," the idea of an essence that can be known only through the particularity of sensible contact. Heidegger's invention and the English translation are intended to combine the meanings of "essence" and "existence." In addition to the high school that is known immediately through its odor, Heidegger offers as examples of the "essent" the swarming crowd of people in a busy street, the Japanese, Bach's fugues, the Strasbourg cathedral, and Hölderlin's hymns. Already in the preface to *Phenomenology of Perception,* long before he began to use the language of "sensible ideas," Merleau-Ponty had commented regarding Husserl's phenomenology that essence and existence cannot be separated, that "Husserl's essences are destined to bring back all the living relationships of experience, as the fisherman's net draws up from the depths of the ocean quivering fish and seaweed" (*PP* xv; *PhP* x).

Merleau-Ponty's culminating description of sensible ideas should be read and heard specifically with both love and beauty in mind:

> The idea is this level, this dimension. It is therefore not a de facto invisible, like an object hidden behind another, and not an absolute invisible, which would have nothing to do with the visible. Rather it is the invisible *of* this world, that which inhabits this world, sustains it, and renders it visible, its own and interior possibility, the Being of this being. (*VI* 151; *VIn* 196)

Love, beauty, color, and music are sensible ideas, they are a level or dimension of life and world, invisibles *of* this world that inhabit it, sustain it, and render it visible, its own and interior possibility.

Merleau-Ponty's philosophy of language is very much implicated in this subtle notion of the "sensible idea," which lives somewhere in between the things and pure ideality. "It is as though," Merleau-Ponty writes, "the visibility that animates the sensible world were to emigrate, not outside of every body, but into another less heavy, more transparent body, as though it were to change flesh, abandoning the flesh of the body for that of language" (*VI* 153; *VIn* 198). Language is like the Pauline notion of the "glorified body" of the afterlife: not a changing of the mortal body for one immortal, yet moving from the frailty and impermanence of sensible things to the more durable and heritable domain of signs. Merleau-Ponty knows that this "glorification" of things in language is fraught with difficulties. No doubt, I would argue, this is why he speaks of a *paradox* in the expressive event: "In the patient and silent labor of desire, begin the paradox of expression." Merleau-Ponty does not mean to refer merely to a logical paradox that could be reduced to a problem to be solved objectively.[35] Rather, he is pointing out a "mystery," "enigma," or "wonder" that belongs to creative expression intrinsically. It will not go away or disappear; rather, it is a constant and ever-present enigma woven into the fabric of the creative event. Fundamentally, this paradox has to do with the passage of experience into expression, whether it would be into the work of art, the work of love, or language itself. On the one hand, it would appear that the experience of love and beauty itself is mute and silent, and thus expression is always an unfaithful impoverishment of experience, but on the other hand, we find in expression genuine innovation and discovery. Everyone who has found themselves before an empty canvas or uncut piece of wood or stone or unshaped clay or blank page or any other unworked medium knows this paradox that links but separates experience from expression. What will happen? Will anything happen? Will it be any good? Everyone who has found themselves in the presence of one truly beloved knows this paradox of expression in between mute inability to express one's feelings and the joy of halting stammering and gesture when they evoke a reciprocal response. Love is expression with others and according to others. It is both inherently incomplete and inadequate yet a wonder and a miracle. Regarding the paradox of expression, Bernard Waldenfels has concluded: "A complete or exhaustive expression, which would say all there is to say, would inevitably have to become master of its own beginnings and be faithful to an 'original text' of experience; only in this way could it become master of its own end. The wonder of language is that language itself is greater than the existing, ready-made language."[36]

Merleau-Ponty himself grew more and more concerned with language and expression as his thinking evolved, and with measuring the gap and distance between language and Being. He writes in the third chapter of *The Visible and the Invisible,* titled "Interrogation and Intuition," that by considering language "we would best see how we are to and how are not to return to the things themselves" (*VI* 125; *VIn* 166). If we hope to find a language that is pure coincidence with the things, then language could only be a "power for error, since it cuts the continuous tissue that joins us vitally to the things" (*VI* 125; *VIn* 166). The philosopher who speaks would then be displaying a weakness, and he would better keep silence as if Being itself is a philosophy "ready-made," just as one might imagine art is already a ready-made in the presentations by Duchamp or Warhol. Yet if coincidence with Being is lost in philosophy or in art or in love, Merleau-Ponty continues his argument, "this is no accident; if Being is hidden, this is itself a characteristic of Being" (*VI* 122; *VIn* 162). The silence and hiddenness of Being (*l'Être est caché*) demands expression, though indirect and subtle that expression need be. One must believe, then, that there is a language that is not a language of coincidence, but a language of which we "are not the organizer," in which through the metaphor, the image, lateral relations and kinships, transfers and exchanges, language is not necessarily deceptive. "Language is a life, is our life and the life of things. Not that *language* takes possession of life and reserves it for itself. . . . Language is not a mask over Being, but—if one knows how to grasp it with all its roots and all its foliation—the most valuable witness to Being" (*VI* 125–26; *VIn* 167). Language and expression are an opening onto the things themselves, "called forth by the voices of silence" (*VI* 126–27; *VIn* 168). Thus it is that, as sensible ideas, the language and expressions of love, beauty, and music are both a summons and a risk—a summons because we are compelled to expression and because the joys and pleasures that accrue when we "get it right" enrich and exalt the ideas and experience, but a risk due to the very real prospects of inadequacy, disappointment, and outright failure.

Expression and the paradox of expression revealed in the musical idea as a sensible idea leads to a fourth and last point of contact between aesthetic and erotic desire, for in musical performance and appreciation, as in love and beauty, we experience a dispossession of the self. "We do not possess the musical or sensible ideas," Merleau-Ponty writes, "they possess us. The performer is no longer producing or reproducing the sonata: he feels himself at the service of the sonata; the sonata sings through him or cries out so suddenly that he must 'dash on his bow' to follow it" (*VI* 151; *VIn* 196). We are "at the service" of the music, of beauty, and of our love. With this, the positions of interior and exterior, and with them both the concept of philosophy and of desire, have been completely reversed from our starting point with Sartre and Hegel. Possession is now become dispossession and activity become passivity: "philosophy cannot be total and active grasp, intellectual possession, since what there is to be captured [*à saisir*] is a dispossession" (*VI* 266; *VIn* 313). We have already encountered Merleau-Ponty's sense of a dispossession in "Eye and Mind" with its emerging emphasis upon passivity in the artistic experience of creation and enjoyment. We recall that "Eye and Mind" describes painting as "autofigurative," citing Apollinaire's statement that in a poem there are phrases that do not appear to have been created but seem to have "shaped themselves," and Henri Michaux's commentary on Klee's colors says that they seem to have been slowly born upon the canvas, exhaled at the right spot like a patina or a mold ("EM" 141–42; *OE* 69–70). As we noted in our analysis of that text in chapter 2, Merleau-Ponty's most delicate and difficult philosophical concept becomes, rather than intentionality, passivity. Just as his thought moves away from the "I" to the "One" who paints or performs, there is an anonymity or generality in the artist who paints, the musician who creates or performs, and the philosopher who thinks and writes.

With this same thought, the text of *The Visible and the Invisible* ends all too abruptly: "And in a sense, as Valéry said, language is everything, since it is the voice of no one, since it is the very voice of the things, the waves, and the forests" (*VI* 155; *VIn* 201). Here is a sort of "echo-phenomenology" of language that does not eliminate the self but displaces the voice of the individual from its assumed centrality in favor of echoes and ancient remnants of sound, inflection, and breath from elders, ancestors, and from primeval Nature herself.[37] The musical performer, the one who paints or sculpts, and the one who loves are swept away by the beauty held in the geological time of the world. "This 'past' belongs to a mythical time, to the time before time, to the prior life, 'farther than India and China'" (*VI* 243; *VIn* 292). The one who holds has become the one held, and we are wind and wave and forest. Thus beauty is now become something elemental at the folding over of time.

Flesh and the Beautiful

Having set out from desire as an intersubjective phenomenon colored by the erotic context the words evoke, we have arrived at Desire and Beauty as deep and primordial ontological aspects of Being itself. Merleau-Ponty had himself originally presented desire as an intersubjective, erotic phenomenon in the chapter of *Phenomenology of Perception* on "The Body in Its Sexual Being." The placement within the intersubjective is similar with the metaphors of fire that appear throughout "Eye and Mind"—spark, flare, burst, incitement (arousal)—as well as in the reflections on interrogation and dialectic from *The Visible and the Invisible* responding to Sartre's account of desire and the Other in the field of intersubjective relationships. In the introduction to *Signs,* Merleau-Ponty had also spoken of desire with regard to our relations with others in which two thoughts converge: "Vision sketches out what is accomplished by desire when it pushes two 'thoughts' out toward that line of fire between them, that blazing surface where they seek a fulfillment" (*S* 17; *Si* 24). Yet in the crucial text regarding desire near the midway point of the fourth chapter of *The Visible and the Invisible,* "The Intertwining—The Chiasm," we were drawn into a gradual shift from the phenomenological intersubjective plane to the ontological. Here desire is presented as the "source," an origin, which means it must be taken as something elemental within the folds and fabric of the world's element, Flesh itself. Merleau-Ponty confirms that the context must shift, that this Desire together with its correlative Beauty, which we should perhaps now capitalize together with Flesh, is said to be patient (*patient*) and silent (*silencieux*), yet productive because it is a labor (*travail*).

Whereas Merleau-Ponty has taught us and shown us much about the call to expression and language embedded in experiences of love and beauty, he also has had much to say about the productive profundity and fecundity of silence, for silence too is a form of expression, a way of being with others and the world in love, care, and the stillness of expectancy. This is similar to the way in which one dwells with an artwork and lets it sink into one's mind, heart, and soul. Painting has a "mute radiance [*rayonnement muet*]" ("ILVS" 115; *S* 78; *Si* 97), and yet this silence and this radiance are treasures: "What is irreplaceable in the work of art," Merleau-Ponty writes, "is the fact that it contains, better than ideas, *matrices of ideas* [*matrices d'idées*]—providing us emblems whose meaning we never stop developing. Precisely because it dwells and makes us dwell in a world we do not have the key to, the work of art teaches us to see and ultimately gives us something to think about as no analytical work can" ("ILVS" 114; *S* 77; *Si* 96–97). Like a painting, "a novel also expresses tacitly," Merleau-Ponty argues. In *The Red and the Black* by Stendhal, Julien Sorel's desire to kill Mme. de Rênal is "not in the words at all. It is between them, in the hollows of space, time, and meaning they mark out" ("ILVS" 113; *S* 76; *Si* 95) as Julien makes that dreamlike journey to Verrières after he has learned that she has betrayed him. "As if in a second life, he made the trip to Verrières according to a cadence of cold passion which itself decided what was visible and what invisible, what was to be said and what to remain unspoken" ("ILVS" 113; *S* 76; *Si* 95). The mute radiance of painting means that the "voices of painting are the voices of silence," but this is not a defect or a disappointment, for just as with the literary work of art with its hollows and lacunae, this silence is the silence of fullness rather than emptiness.

From the depths of stillness spring new and fresh waters of life and language. From silence springs "the birth of speech as bubbling up at the bottom of mute experience." Therefore, the philosopher knows better than anyone that "what is lived is lived-spoken" (*VI* 126; *VIn* 165). This is not the language of the philosopher or artist himself or herself, but this is the language of which each individual is not the sole author or organizer. "It is the error of the semantic philosophies," Merleau-Ponty says, "to close up language as if it spoke only of itself" (*VI* 126; *VIn* 165).[38] Rather, "things *are said* and *are thought* by a Speech and by a Thought which we do not have but which has us" (*S* 19; *Si* 27). This is the voice we encountered earlier that is the "voice of no one that is the very voice of the things, the waves, and the forests" (*VI* 155; *VIn* 203–4). It is also the voice of "all those we have loved, detested, known, or simply glimpsed" and that now "speak through our voice. . . . Our traces mix and intermingle" (*S* 19; *Si* 28).

We need to say that herein subjectivity or selfhood is not eliminated but recast from the outside. Merleau-Ponty's term for this reconceived subjectivity is "dimension" or "level" but also "hollow" (*creux*), rather than the nothingness of self as a hole in Being. In a cryptic working note Merleau-Ponty says, "In short: nothingness (or rather non-being) is hollow and not *hole*" (*VI* 196; *VIn* 246), and later he expands on this meaning: "The soul is the hollow of the body, the body is the distention of the soul" (*VI* 233; *VIn* 282). Subjectivity has the shape of a hollow formed by body and world because self has a history into which beauties and loves and harmonies arrive, we might say, overflow. Carbone has commented: "Here it is important to note that this 'hollow' is not a mere *receptacle* of the idea, but rather is essentially united with, *is one and the same as,* the idea's advent: activity and passivity coupled."[39] The example is once again musical: "the melody sings in us much more than we sing it," Merleau-Ponty says in *Nature,* "it goes down the throat of the singer, as Proust says. Just as the painter is struck by a painting which is not there, the body is suspended in what it sings: the melody is incarnated and finds in the body a type of servant" (*N* 174; *NN* 228). The painter is the servant of the painting not yet made as the singer is the servant of the melody he or she will incarnate. I would say that there is plenty of subjectivity left in this "hollow," in fact all the subjectivity one needs, but it is subjectivity "hollowed out" from the outside rather than an interior master seeking domination of the outside and the other. It is the individual, yet the individual who belongs to others and the outside much more than the individual who makes demands and claims on others and the world.

The interlacings of Desire and Beauty have brought us to the brink of origins, to the wonder and fecund silence of life, love, and beauty. This is the awesome silence of the primeval forest at dawn before the awakening of birdsong, of the windless canyon at sunset, of the calm and quiet sea at daybreak, not a wave lapping. This silence is fullness, a form of stillness and waiting, waiting upon the beauty of the universe. Herein is our fundamental discovery and argument: Merleau-Ponty's philosophy extends the aesthetic realm, by which Kant meant the limited domain of aesthetic judgment proper, over the entire realm of *aisthesis.* The beautiful has been enlarged and opened up as the entire realm of the sensible.[40] The ontology of Flesh as element and the ontology of the Beautiful as elemental are folded together, for Desire, Love, and Beauty are part of the fabric (*étoffe*) of the world's element, Flesh itself. We say that Flesh is element and Desire, Love, and Beauty are elemental, for these are multiple ways in which Flesh manifests itself. Flesh is verbal and adverbial, process and not substance or matter. We remember the swimming pool from "Eye and Mind": to water wetly, to water reedily, shimmeringly, quickly, or slowly. We do not seek to replace the element, Flesh, with the name of another, Beauty. Beauty, Desire, and Love are verbal and adverbial forms of Flesh's appearing. In the living, unfolding reversibilities of Flesh as Being shine forth the radiance and sound forth the rhythm of Beauty, Desire, and Love—and the sublime, a word scarcely yet given its full weight.

7

Beauty, Repetition, and Difference

He who does not grasp that life is a repetition and that this is the beauty of life has pronounced his own verdict. . . . For hope is a beckoning fruit that does not satisfy; recollection is petty travel money that does not satisfy; but repetition is the daily bread that satisfies with blessing.

—Søren Kierkegaard, *Repetition: A Venture in Experimenting Psychology*

Hence reflection does not grasp its full significance unless it refers to the unreflective fund of experience which it presupposes, upon which it draws, and which constitutes for it a kind of original past, a past which has never been a present.

—Merleau-Ponty, *Phenomenology of Perception*

The role of the imagination, or the mind which contemplates in its multiple and fragmented states, is to draw something new from repetition, to draw difference from it. . . . Difference inhabits repetition.

—Gilles Deleuze, *Difference and Repetition*

Repetition and difference, theme and variations, structure the beautiful. Desire's anticipation is shaped by repetitions lending to desire a temporal "from-to" structure. "Projection toward" is future-referring and "retention from" is past-referring. This "again" ranges from the maximal to the minimal as limit experiences. The most robust experiences of beauty—the beauty of a child's face, the lines of character in an elderly set of hands, or the blues, greens, and violets in Cézanne's late Mt. Sainte-Victoire watercolors—these are filled with an insurgence of whole networks of repetitions and anticipations. Nevertheless, even the most contemplative and detached experiences of beauty, I would argue—perhaps reading a poem, or appreciating a line of reasoning, or contemplating a Japanese watercolor—these too manifest this *minimal* desire to return to the experience of the work "again." Even the Zen meditative experience of emptiness, I believe, retains the desire of this "again." These are passivities within our experience of the beautiful. "Things are said and are thought by a Speech and by a Thought which we do not have but which has us" (*S* 19; *Si* 27). In this chapter, we seek to explore these voices and echoes as the latencies within self and world, the latencies of childhood, and the latencies of an "original past that has never been a present." We think again of Paul Klee's polyphonic painting *Ancient Harmony* (1927), as well of the ancient story of Echo and Narcissus that expresses a tragedy in the "repetition complex" or "compulsion to repeat." Our reflections on these passivities will lead us from memory to the imaginary and, finally, the unconscious.

Beauty and Memory

An installation work of art entitled *Echo* (2003) was part of a recent exhibition at the David Winton Bell Gallery of Brown University titled "InVisible Silence" and dedicated by the curator to Merleau-Ponty.[1] The work is a DVD projection loop by the artist Su-Mei Tse, a Luxembourgian artist of Chinese and English origin. The image is projected on a large scale, seven feet by eight feet, in an enclosed empty space, and presents an idyllic view of a woman sitting alone playing the cello. She is placed in a meadow facing a large Alpine mountain, and her solitary appearance in the vast landscape, together with her bright red dress juxtaposed to the fluorescence of the green grass, imbues the scene with a lush, painterly quality. We also hear the cello with its melodic lines echoing in space. She plays and the echo from the mountain answers. The video loop includes five minutes or so of this haunting exchange between cello and mountain. The entire sight and sound evokes a feeling of beauty and peace.[2]

Vision and the senses are structured by temporal depth that informs our appreciation of the beautiful: to touch *again,* to look *again,* to smell and feel and hear and sense *again.* This was Cézanne's desire for the work, for the paint itself and its textures and smells, and the strokes over and over, to repeat those movements and work at the problems of painting. It is also our desire to return to those Cézanne rooms and interrogate those canvases again and again. If desire has shape in specific and multiple ways, it is because desire arises in the world constructed from personal histories and bodily and cultural latencies and language. There is a kind of memory that becomes the immemorial, for once experienced, and even if no longer noticed and far away in time, it is not capable of being expunged. This is not a kind of mental recall so subject to forgetting and forgetfulness: a name, a word, a street. This is a kind of visceral, cellular body memory that Merleau-Ponty calls the "latent consummation of our very being," and it gives the gravity, the depth, and the potential shape for bodily responses to the world. "Eye and Mind" refers repeatedly to the notions of latency and passivity. The references begin in part 3's critique of Descartes and climax in the theory of space and depth in part 4. In contrast with Descartes, it was Matisse, the philosopher argued, who taught us to see shapes "as structural filaments [*des nervures*], as the axes of a corporeal system of activity and passivity" ("EM" 144; *OE* 76). We must realize, Merleau-Ponty argues in a culminating statement, that "in addition to that which reaches the eye head on, the frontal properties of the visible," there is also "that which reaches it from below—the profound postural latency whereby the body raises itself to see" ("EM" 147; *OE* 86). The beautiful is to be reconfigured in terms of latency, passivity, and repetition.

Beauty as repetition naturally reminds us of the argument made by Plato's Diotima that the person in love desires pregnancy and reproduction, be it through begetting in childbirth or in laws, knowledge, or ideas. "The goddess who presides at childbirth—she's called Moira or Eileithuia—is really beauty," Diotima says.[3] Childbirth is the repetition of the "again" in the other, and this is real beauty. Knowledge, as well, on the Platonic account, might be considered beautiful, for it is presented as a kind of recollection in *Meno*. However, by now terms need sorting: repetition, reproduction, as well as recollection are all in play. It is instructive that Søren Kierkegaard has disagreed with the identification of repetition with Socratic recollection. In the "Report by Constantin Constantius" titled *Repetition: A Venture in Experimenting Psychology,* Kierkegaard pursued the question of whether or not repetition is possible, and whether something gains or loses in being repeated. At first he agrees that repetition "is a crucial expression for what 'recollection' was to the Greeks. Just as they taught that all knowing is recollecting, modern philosophy will teach that all life is repetition," Kierkegaard writes.[4] However, almost immediately Kierkegaard draws a crucial distinction between recollection and repetition. They are the same psychic movement, except in opposite temporal directions: "What is recollected has been, is repeated backward, whereas repetition is recollected forward."[5] The phrase "recollected forward" dovetails past and future into a unity as a "from-to" temporal structure embedded in the heart of the desire for the beautiful, not merely and only to remember or recollect, but to recollect creatively with a new horizon of difference and anticipation. Recollection without the possibility of creative repetition expresses a life of loss and profound melancholy, for it is only recollection with the possibility of repetition that is a "happy love."

The text of Kierkegaard's *Repetition* turns into a narrative of a young man who had fallen wonderfully in love but was unable to sustain it in the present tense. He lived in the recollection of the depth, the beauty, and the humility of love's first time. He was deeply and fervently in love, that was clear, says Kierkegaard, "yet a few days later he was [only] able to recollect his love. He was essentially through with the entire relationship. In beginning it, he took such a tremendous step that he leaped over life." Recollection without the possibility of repetition, Kierkegaard concludes, "has the great advantage that it begins with the loss; the reason it is safe and secure is that it has nothing to lose."[6] This is the argument for Kierkegaard's conclusion in this chapter's opening epigraph: "Life is a repetition and that this is the beauty of life. . . . Hope is a beckoning fruit that does not satisfy; recollection is petty travel money that does not satisfy; but repetition is the daily bread that satisfies with blessing."[7]

If repetition is truly the desire expressed in the desire for the beautiful, and if that desire is not only the desire for the retentional "from" but also the desire for the futural "to," then it cannot be that the meaning of repetition is mere duplication. Genuine repetition must include variation, the recurrence of the same with difference. Variation is part and parcel of the very structure of what repetition *means*. Repetition is the *again* but with meaningful, life-giving difference. In *Difference and Repetition,* Gilles Deleuze has given us the details of the argument that "repetition for itself" must be considered an intertwining of old and new, past, present, and future. "We produce something new," he writes, "only on condition that we repeat—once in the mode which constitutes the past, and once more in the present of metamorphosis. Moreover, what is produced, the absolutely new itself, is in turn nothing but repetition: the third repetition, this time by excess, the repetition of the future as eternal return."[8] "The repetition of the future" means that the metamorphosis created in the present brings forward a past but also portends a future by way of excess, by way of echoes, reverberations, and surplus. Repetition is thus a "synthesis of time."[9]

Deleuze's use of the phrase "eternal return" refers us to the problem of what Nietzsche meant by eternal recurrence of "the Same," and this is a problem too big for us to handle fully here. Suffice it to say that within this doctrine, there is a familiar dilemma somewhat like the

Meno paradox with respect to learning: "One cannot search either for what he knows or for what he does not know. He cannot search for what he knows—since he knows it, there is no need to search—nor for what he does not know, for he does not know what to look for."[10] Similarly, if Nietzsche's doctrine means the recurrence of exact, literal sameness, then there would be no way of noticing or identifying it as a reoccurrence. On the other hand, if the doctrine means recognizable recurrence, it cannot mean the recurrence of the exact, literal "same" but of "the same again," which is to say the same with difference.[11] The commentary by Deleuze on Nietzschean recurrence confirms the point:

> Repetition in the eternal return never means continuation, perpetuation or prolongation, nor even the discontinuous return of something which would at least be able to be prolonged in a partial cycle (an identity, an I, a Self), but on the contrary, the *reprise* of pre-individual singularities which, in order that it can be grasped as repetition, presupposes the dissolution of all prior identities.[12]

Moreover, this difference that is necessarily grafted into every repetition can be either quantitative or qualitative. If it is merely a numerical difference, this will be duplication or recollection without genuine repetition, for within genuine repetition there will be found numerical difference as well as qualitative variation in radiance, in rhythm, in color, sound, shape, and the other manifold aspects of the beautiful.

Difference must be part and parcel of the structure of the desire for the beautiful. Recollection without variation could only produce monotony and boredom; variation that refreshes and pleases can be quite minor or witty and filled with humor, as exemplified in a range from Andy Warhol's celebrity silkscreens of Elvis Presley or Marilyn Monroe to Cindy Sherman's history portraits, many of which were included in the Hirshhorn exhibition "Regarding Beauty."[13] To take just Sherman's work as our example from "Regarding Beauty," her "History Portraits" are artistic repetitions and variations on familiar paintings with herself posed as the subject: Sherman as Leonardo's *Mona Lisa* (1989) and as Caravaggio's *Bacchus* (1990). The variations in the artist's repetitions are whimsical, sometimes obvious, sometimes subtle: posed as *Mona Lisa* in her *Untitled #209,* Sherman adopts the ambiguous smile of the Renaissance subject that resembles Leonardo's original, but she wears a different outfit complete with headgear; as Caravaggio's *Bacchus* in *Untitled #224,* Sherman's repetition is nearer to duplication, though there is clear gender ambiguity compared with the original. Barnett Newman's repeated zips created a visual language so spare as to dramatize the very question of originality itself. Newman did not think of *Onement I* as an achievement or end point of years of work, but as an origin. In addition to its lack of reference as nonfigural, Newman believed it lacked sufficient reference to other works in the history of painting to have achieved independence. As an "orphan," in this sense, it needed "siblings" that would share in the family resemblance of the Newman zip. The work was successful precisely due to its repeatability.[14] Almost no one so elevated the "originality of repetition" to the degree of Barnett Newman. *Onement I* created a template for a language that could regenerate itself again and again in the subsequent years. The visual language was so sharply spare in a "Newman" that it dramatizes the question of originality: how is each painting different, an original, despite so many signs of sameness? In 1950, two years after *Onement I,* Newman felt sufficiently confident that *Onement I* foretold a lifetime of work to be done that he could say: "I think the idea of a 'finished' picture is a fiction. I think a man spends his whole lifetime painting one picture or working on one piece of sculpture."[15]

Merleau-Ponty praised Cézanne's repetitions of Mt. Sainte-Victoire, in oils, in watercolors, at different times of day, in different light, from different perspectives. "His *Mont Sainte-Victoire* is made and remade from one end of the world to the other in a way different from but no less energetic than in the hard rock above Aix" ("EM" 130; *OE* 35). The sculptural work of Constantin Brancusi is equally illustrative: "It is no accident that his work takes shape in a sea of repetitions. The repetition occurs both in terms of repeated forms—cylinders, ovals, ellipses—and repeated subjects, most notably the *Sixteen Birds in Space* in marble and bronze." Of his *Sixteen Birds in Space,* Brancusi defended the uniqueness of every seemingly similar bird. "Each is the result of a new inspiration."[16] If we think of those poems that capture our imagination or those musical works that move us, we find this pattern of repetition and variation as part of the very structure of the works. We wait for the thematic lines to come back again as the work unfolds, we search and listen hard for them if we cannot hear them in the variations. We not only anticipate the repetition of thematic lines, but the variation the author or composer creates, as in the richness and variety of a Bach fugue with its restatements of the opening theme with innovations that prevent us from ever becoming wearied or bored with the music.

It is necessary to complicate the repetition-difference problematic one more degree, turning from painting, music, and poetry to the repetitions of nature where our experience is closer to something like wonder, often ineffable, available in the inter-referential repetitions of the flights and songs of birds or the astonishment of sunsets: mountain sunset at the south rim of the Grand Canyon, ocean sunset at the beach in the

British Virgin Islands, desert sunset in the Sahara outside Goram-Goram in Burkina Faso near Mali; repetitions of vastness, color, and light that invoke solitude and wonder, a silent contact of self and Being. Nature is filled with patterns and proportions that repeat: the spirals in mollusk shells, flowers, sunflower seeds, pinecone petals, and the leaf arrangement on plant stalks; the proportions in insect segmentation; the proportions in human bone structure.[17]

With regard to the repetitions we find manifold in nonhuman nature, we need to mark a distinction between order and beauty. It is undeniable that the repetitions of nature constitute a natural "order," exemplified in the great astronomical regularities governed by rules or laws that compel the same event or pattern in all instances and under all circumstances. This amounts to nothing more than a mechanical reproduction under the compulsion of a formula that does not allow for spontaneity, variation, and creativity in nature. If this were all there was to the duplications we find in nature, a kind of machinelike sameness, then this would not be genuine repetition and this would not be natural beauty. We want to argue that there must be something within the repetition that magnetizes and focuses our attention, some element of life and variation that bestows upon the duplication a difference of quality or rhythm that exceeds sheer quantitative sameness, which would be lifeless and dull. Natural beauty exceeds mere natural order, for nature is filled with endless variation and differences even within the order to which it is compelled.

In *Nature,* Merleau-Ponty considers the blending of the aesthetic features of nature with adaptation in several different ways. In the first place, he makes it clear that in his view, the Darwinian theory of adaptation that would reduce the meaning of "fitness" to survival is caught in the Cartesian dichotomy that "joins an extremely mechanistic way of thinking to an extremely subjective way of thinking" (*N* 168; *NN* 221). Merleau-Ponty turns to the biology of Jacob von Uexküll and Adolf Portmann, among others, for alternative formulations of the concept of nature and the interrelations of animal and environment. In studying the question of mimicry within nature, for example, "utility is not a criterion for life" as assumed in the "Darwinian ideology." "Life is not only an organization for survival; there is in life a prodigious flourishing of forms, the utility of which is only rarely attested to and that sometimes even constitutes a danger for the animal" (*N* 186; *NN* 243). For example, polar fauna are white, though nevertheless there are some exceptions to the rule, for some insects at the North Pole are black. Similarly, twenty-seven species of crab in the Barnave Islands manifest twenty-seven different types of sexual display. "Sexuality," Merleau-Ponty says, "if it aims only at utility, could manifest itself by more economic paths" (*N* 188; *NN* 245). This multiplication of variations is a manifestation of sexual ceremony and ritual rather than strict utility, ceremony and ritual that Merleau-Ponty likens to an aesthetic "drama" of inter-animality. Therefore, "it can be perfectly argued that life is not uniquely submitted to the principle of utility, and that there is a morphogenesis in the design of expression" (*N* 184; *NN* 240). This defense of the aesthetic properties of nature irreducible to mechanism leads Merleau-Ponty explicitly to revise Xavier Bichat's definition of life: "Life is not 'the ensemble of functions that resist death,' to use Bichat's expression, but rather is a power to invent the visible" (*N* 190; *NN* 248). In another passage, Merleau-Ponty says "we must understand life as the opening of a field of action" (*N* 173; *NN* 227).

When we consider the animal milieu especially, it becomes clearer that in a certain sense—that of inventing the visible—the animal is not unlike the artist. The environmental situation and animal movement cannot be understood as a simple relation of "push causality." Rather, the milieu should be understood, Uexküll claims, much more in terms of "a melody that is singing itself" (*N* 173; *NN* 228). For a melody, there is a relation of parts and wholes such that there is a reciprocal influence of the notes upon one another and the first note is possible only because of the last, and vice versa. Similarly, the meaning of the melody is inseparable from its expression, for melody is a sensible idea, as we have seen, in which essence and existence are inseparable. Thus, the environment of the animal cannot be understood either mechanistically or moment by temporal, isolated moment, *partes extra partes,* but as an *Umwelt* in which "each part of the situation acts only as part of a whole situation," and between the situation and movement there is a relation of meaning. The philosophical interpretation of the *Umwelt,* often simply translated as "environment"—mistranslated, I would say—means the animal *habitat* is a sort of cohesion between the animal and the outside, no longer a closing off but an opening of possibilities. "The objective universe, from now on plays the role of a sign rather than that of a cause" (*N* 171; *NN* 225), and this is not to be attributed to conscious design or finalism in the animal like a Platonic "species-essence" or to a machinelike compulsion from the outside. The animal's territory is a "privileged emplacement" in which identical exterior conditions bring along different possibilities of behavior. "In other words," Merleau-Ponty says, "there is a beginning of culture. The architecture of symbols that the animal brings from its side thus defines with Nature a species of pre-culture. The *Umwelt* is less and less oriented toward a goal and more and more toward the interpretation of symbols" (*N* 176; *NN* 231). The relation between the animal and its *Umwelt* thus is most like that of a melody with its theme and variations. "The theme of the animal melody is not outside its manifest realization; it is a variable thematism that the animal does not seek to realize by a copy of the model, but that haunts its particular organization, without these themes being the goal of the organism" (*N* 178; *NN* 233).[18] Through this recasting of the animal milieu aesthetically, Merleau-Ponty avoids the twin impasses of mechanism and finalism, as well as a Platonic separation between the theme as model and its individual expressions. Mauro Carbone has written: "Uexküll's perspective seems to characterize the theme as the *absent,* which only its own variations can indirectly make present and which is therefore *inseparable* from and *simultaneous* with them. *The variations constitute the theme* [my emphasis], without, however, exhausting it: they constitute it as their own excess."[19] No theme without the variations; no repetition without differences.

The biology of Adolf Portmann asks that we attend to the exterior of the animal, with its secondary qualities such as color and aesthetic patterning. "The exterior gives the impression of a product of art," Merleau-Ponty says. This is less true in the "lower animal," such as the spiraled mollusk, where the richness of exterior form is mechanically engendered. In higher animals, the expressive capacity is greater and the body becomes a manner of expression. If we consider the frog, for example, as long as the frog maintains its biological position of folded legs, "everything happens as if the frog had been painted by one sole brush stroke" (*N* 187; *NN* 244). Similarly, the feathers of birds are joined in such a way to form a whole design, and the pattern of the zebra's skin is unique to each individual zebra, like the fingerprints of the human hand. Merleau-Ponty argues that these appearances take on interest and significance when we understand them as a language in which animals show themselves to each other. "There are two ways to consider the animal, as there are two ways to consider an inscription on an old stone: we can wonder how this inscription was traced, but we can also seek to know what it means. Likewise we can either analyze the processes of the animal under a microscope, or see a totality in the animal" (*N* 187; *NN* 245). In higher-order animals, physiology is transformed into expression. The sexual relation takes on expressive value; the occlusion or blink of the eye has a utilitarian function, but in higher animals, the muscle is transformed into a means of expression. What the animal shows is not exclusively utility; rather, "its appearance manifests something that resembles our oneiric life" (*N* 188; *NN* 246). Thus, instinct is not reducible to the concept of adaptation, but is more like the fragment of a melody that the animal carries within itself and is an activity for pleasure not comprehensible in terms of innate trigger mechanisms, as Konrad Lorenz seemed to suppose. The eagle, grey geese, and starlings continue to perform movements of diving and ingesting even in the absence of the relevant prey. These behaviors thus refer to a non-actual, oneiric life and are manifestations of a certain style of behavior. Merleau-Ponty concludes:

> It seems that the animal both wants and does not want the object. The instinct is both in itself and turned toward the object, it is both an inertia and a hallucinatory, oneiric behavior, capable of making a world and of picking up any object of the world. To the extent that instinct is a tension that wants to find relief without knowing why, it does not aim so much at the real as at the irreal. Instinct is oriented toward the image or the typical. There is a narcissism of instinct. If it tends to find its identity in fixing on an object, it does not know what it is nor what it wants. (*N* 193; *NN* 252)

This word "narcissism" cannot go unremarked, for Merleau-Ponty chose the very same term to characterize all of vision in *The Visible and the Invisible.* Similarly, we find an echo of this phrase, "it does not know what it is nor what it wants," in Merleau-Ponty's last conceptualization of the meaning of the unconscious in his résumé of the 1959–60 course, "Nature and Logos: The Human Body." The double formula of the unconscious, Merleau-Ponty writes, is: "'I did not know' and 'I have always known it'" (*IPP* 198; *RC* 179).[20] We will delay the consideration of narcissism and the unconscious in relation to beauty until later in this chapter, but for now it is important to note that in higher-order animal life as in human life, there is also a latency or passivity that unites physiology and aesthetic expression. Life and beauty are both formed as theme and variations, repetition and differences, without the theme having to be explicit as a separate model. The theme provides the hinges around which the variations turn. "Phenomena of life turn around certain hinges. Themes are again dimensions, the establishment of a certain field of gravity" (*N* 183; *NN* 240).

Beauty and the Imaginary

Thinking about repetitions, Merleau-Ponty wrote in the preface to *Signs:* "In a sense, the highest point of philosophy is perhaps no more than rediscovering these truisms: thought thinks, speech speaks, the glance glances. But each time between the two identical words there is the whole spread [*tout l'écart*] one straddles in order to think, speak, and see [*qu'on enjambe pour penser, pour parler et pour voir*]" (*S* 21; *Si* 30). Thought thinks, speech speaks, the glance glances, and in that repetition from noun to verb is found all the difference between name and act. In a working note of September 1959, written in the sixteen-month hiatus between chapters 1–3 and chapter 4 of *The Visible and the Invisible,* Merleau-Ponty was thinking about the difference between the child and the adult. He wrote: "When I perceive the child, he is given precisely in a certain divergence [*écart*] (*originating presentation of the unpresentable*) and the same for my perceptual lived experience for myself, and the same for my alter ego, and the same for the pre-analytic thing. Here is the common tissue of which we are made. The wild Being" (*VI* 203; *VIn* 253). Beauty is life-giving, for it gives us wildness, and this wild Being is discovered in the "presentation of the unpresentable," in the very *écart*—gap or divergence—between self and world, self and other, and even within the "dense, open, but rent and tattered" being that is myself ("EM" 149; *OE* 91).

In the thought of Merleau-Ponty, this concept of *écart*—translated variously as "divergence," "spread," and "gap"—was just emerging in the last pages of his thinking and writing and in his working notes. We find the term *différence* in "Eye and Mind," but not the term *écart,* though we do find in that essay the term *abîme*—"God is for us an abyss" ("EM" 137; *OE* 56)—in the phrase appropriated from Schelling; and "philosophy plunges itself into that dimension of the composite of soul and body, of the existent world, of the abyssal Being [*l'Être abyssal*] that Descartes opened up and so quickly closed again" ("EM" 138; *OE* 57–58). Merleau-Ponty's concept of *écart* is not the unlimited and unshaped abyss of Nietzsche in which there is "no day and no night, no up and no down." Neither is it the *Abgrund* of Heidegger, the absence of ground confronted in our being-toward-death. Rather, *écart* in Merleau-Ponty is precisely about experience that is not in full possession of itself, experience in dispossession. This dispossession is found in both the broader sense of *aisthesis* as perception and the sense of the aesthetic as the realm of art and beauty. In our contact with things and the world, differences appear, our seeing and touching and feeling are unable to "catch up" with the radiant presence of things; they are a temporal rhythm that is inevitably one beat late without getting to coincidence with the "somethings" and the "someones" (*VI* 160; *VIn* 213). Thought, Merleau-Ponty says, "does not possess its own premises; there is in its center a mystery of passivity" ("EM" 136; *OE* 52). In *Signs,* Merleau-Ponty immediately connects the concept of *écart* with chiasm, the crossing over from right hand to left hand and all the other crossings and joinings of the Flesh, soul and body, sensible thing and language. "The philosophy which lays bare the chiasma of the visible is the exact opposite of a philosophy of God-like survey. . . . It seeks contact with brute being" (*S* 21–22; *Si* 30–31).

We want to pursue the implications of Merleau-Ponty's concepts of *écart* and chiasm and the passivities they portend, from the phenomenological body to the "original past which was never a present" and on to the material imaginary and unconscious. All of these are in play in our desire for the beautiful with its repetitions and variations.

To make a beginning, let us dwell in more detail on what Merleau-Ponty meant by the postural latencies of our body that underlie vision, sensing, feeling, and desiring. Postural latency directs us first of all to the circuits that comprise our bodily being-in-the-world that Merleau-Ponty described in the chapter on "Space" in *Phenomenology of Perception.* These are the unreflective, operative intentionalities that structure our perception of things: the customary levels by which we take anchorage or grasp the world—how high or how low; the customary sides—the dominance of right or left, front and back; and the typical signs and gestures—the smile or frown or wave. This is the aspect of postural latency bearing on the formation of the habit-body and its perceptions formed during the course of a personal, sedimented history, the myriad remnants of upbringing and training. All this is within the reflective and pre-reflective experience of the phenomenology of perception. From this point of view, to experience an object as beautiful does not mean giving it a certain value and meaning "out of the blue," as it were, but it is to designate a certain typical variation or accent that one finds attractive in a field of experience that is already instituted in a personal history and a way of being-in-the-world.

In the 1954–55 course on "Institution in Personal and Public History," Merleau-Ponty marks a distinction between institution and constitution. Constitution remains within the philosophy of consciousness, whereas institution sets in play the "outside," the passivities that shape our activities, one of which is our historicity. The body instituted rather than the body constituted installs the human biological body itself within a tradition. The human body itself is fragile and vulnerable, as "Indirect Language" says, or as *Phenomenology of Perception* had expressed it, "the body is that meaningful core" or expressive space that "nevertheless exists and is susceptible to disease" (*PP* 147; *PhP* 172), as we found in Rodin's doublet between beauty and corruptibility. We are biological beings, yet the body's birth into a symbolic world of culture introduces an order of relations that pure physiology and biology do not have the slightest idea of, Merleau-Ponty writes. Seeing, touching, hearing, even disease itself now have a history: seeing is a crossing—"strabism" (*N* 72; *NN* 103)—between nature and culture.[21] Seeing, touching, hearing, and disease are not mere biological in-itself things. Now, in this historical moment, we see according to Cézanne, and according to Rodin, and apples and bodies and mountains now are transfigured; our eyes are educated; poppy fields look just as Monet painted them, though they never looked that way before Monet, and it is Van Gogh's starry night that fills my own eyes and heart. Institution means a "historical ontology" in place of any remainder of "ahistorical ontology" in a philosophy of consciousness. In the chapter on "The Thing and the Natural World" in *Phenomenology of Perception,* Merleau-Ponty had drawn a distinction between everyday perception that "alights on things" in their familiar presence and a deeper, more primordial perception that "pays a metaphysical and disinterested attention" to things. Transcendence was found in the experience of this primordial perception that exports us out of everyday secondary perception into a world beyond the safety of personal history and subjectivity, a world that is a stranger, "alien, no longer an interlocutor, but a resolutely silent Other" (*PP* 322; *PhP* 372). Merleau-Ponty even risked calling this the "thing itself." In the "Institution" course and thereafter, it becomes very clear that Merleau-Ponty does not want this deep or primordial perception interpreted within the frame of a philosophy of consciousness. Though there is yet a difference between casual everyday inattention and fully focused attention, what we might have called primordial perception is now also known to be a practiced perception "according to" others and a tradition. Following Cézanne, we can go out into the valley and ask if focused staring assembles the mountain into a whole or breaks it up into fragmentary planes and colors. This is primordial perception, but it is "according to Cézanne." "Perception, history, expression," that was the triptych conjunction announced in "Indirect Language": "It is only by bringing together these three problems that we can put Malraux's analyses in their proper perspective" ("ILVS" 112; *S* 75; *Si* 94).

"Eye and Mind" moves beyond the personal habit-body by contextualizing postural latency within a discussion of depth, as we have seen, depth in painting, depth in vision, in self, and in desire. With the attractions of the beautiful we are dealing with a depth (*la profonde*) deeper than habit and personal history. What this ultimately means, Merleau-Ponty says in the immediately preceding text, is that "the hallmark of the visible is to have a lining of invisibility in the strict sense, which it makes present as a certain absence" ("EM" 147; *OE* 85). Invisibility "in the strict sense" means that we are dealing with a kind of invisibility here that is deeper than that which is merely not noticed but might be pointed out, or that which is hidden but can be seen from elsewhere. Immediately following the passage on postural latency, we encounter the text on fire from Paul Klee discussed in our second chapter on "Eye and Mind." It will not hurt to repeat it and to extend it slightly:

> In the immemorial depth of the visible, something has moved, caught fire, which engulfs his body; everything he paints is in answer to this incitement, and his hand is "nothing but the instrument of a distant will." Vision is the meeting, as at a crossroads, of all aspects of Being. . . . It is impossible to say that here nature ends and the human being or expression begins. ("EM" 147; *OE* 86–87)

The artist's hand is the instrument of a distant will, and we cannot say where nature ends and the human being or expression begins. In the lecture course at the Collège de France that Merleau-Ponty taught in 1954–55 titled "The Problem of Passivity: Sleep, the Unconscious, Memory," he refers to our birth as the point of contact between us and an "outside." "To live," he writes, "is not simply to be constantly conferring meaning upon things but to continue a vortex of experience which was set up at our birth, at the point of contact between the 'outside' and he who is called to live it" (*IPP* 115; *RC* 67).

To think through this "outside within" in our desires and our recognition of beauty, it will be helpful to return to Merleau-Ponty's phrase "an original past, a past which has never been a present." The phrase occurs in the last line of Merleau-Ponty's chapter on "Sense Experience" ("Le sentir") in *Phenomenology of Perception:* "Hence reflection does not grasp its full significance unless it refers to the unreflective fund of experience which it presupposes, upon which it draws, and which constitutes for it a kind of original past, a past which has never been a present" (*PP* 242; *PhP* 280). The immediate context of this sentence and phrase is a consideration of the nature of perception and the ways in which reflective and unreflective experience are interwoven. "Primary perception is a non-thetic [non-positing], pre-objective and pre-conscious experience," Merleau-Ponty writes. In the preceding paragraph, he had said that there would be no present, indeed "no sensible world with its thickness and inexhaustible richness, if perception did not retain a past in the depth of the present" (*PP* 240; *PhP* 277).

There has emerged among Merleau-Ponty's commentators what we might call both a thin and thick, or a weaker and stronger, interpretation of this original past that is present in perception, and by extension, in expression. On the one hand, M. C. Dillon has argued that in the immediate context of the "Sense Experience" chapter and discussion of perception, Merleau-Ponty means only to indicate that this original past is "never present to reflective consciousness, but fully present to prereflective perceptual consciousness." Based upon what the sentence says, "it is possible," he argues, "to refer to that fund of experience."[22] Thus, this original past would only be the ways in which the past sediments itself in my habit-body and its look and touch. It can be explicated "after the fact" (*après coup*) in terms of a sedimented personal history, originally unknown, but knowable in principle. The stronger interpretation, articulated by Leonard Lawlor and also supported by Bernard Waldenfels, argues that the context for interpreting the sentence and phrase should be what Merleau-Ponty had to say about past and present in the "Temporality" chapter of *Phenomenology of Perception.* We must not, Lawlor argues, interpret reflective experience in terms of unreflective experience only, for both of these remain within consciousness. Rather, unreflective experience itself must be interpreted in terms of an originary past that is prior to both reflective and unreflective experience. There must be a "sense of the past" that enables us to recognize something like a carving in a wooden table as past-referring. Without that "sense," the carving would be only present, and thus, this "sense of the past" could not itself be dependent upon the present or upon perception. "Being caused by a present," Lawlor writes, "but not dependent upon it, this type of past amounts to a repetition without original."[23]

I take note that the French word that is translated into English as "refers" in Merleau-Ponty's text—"reflection does not grasp its full significance unless it *refers to* [my emphasis] the unreflective fund of experience which it presupposes"—is actually the word *mentionne* from *mentionner,* which means "to mention" or "to name." It carries a less cognitive and intellectual meaning than the English term "refer." Furthermore, Merleau-Ponty, in the immediate context, has said as well that "perception is always in the mode of the impersonal 'One.' It is not a personal act enabling me to give a fresh significance to my life" (*PP* 240; *PhP* 277). This text immediately adds that this "One" who perceives is "not myself as an autonomous subject, but myself insofar as I have a body" (*PP* 240; *PhP* 277). Thus, if there is an ambiguity in the text from *Phenomenology of Perception* regarding the meaning of the "original past," we do indeed find an opening to the stronger interpretation that the personal body with its experiences, reflective and unreflective, is the launching point, the opening onto an originary past never present within our own personal experience. This reading is supported by Merleau-Ponty's own philosophical development as he moved away from a philosophy of the subject toward an aesthetic of the anonymous One who paints and the ontology of Flesh in "Eye and Mind" and *The Visible and the Invisible.*

Thus, there are "surpluses" within our posture toward the world that are pre-personal and exceed our own origin. Our own living bodies are "bodies in fissure," we might say, in which vision, touch, smell, taste, and hearing are openings to the pre-personal. Since "it is impossible to say where nature ends and human nature or expression begins," as

Merleau-Ponty says, one of these surpluses is our physiological body; for example, that we very early stand upright and walk on two legs rather than crawl on four, or that we have binocular rather than monocular vision. Such physiological features of the human body lend preferences to how we experience the beautiful. Moreover, beyond the physiological, these openings to the pre-personal include, first, the imaginary, and next, something about the unconscious.

Let us approach the imaginary first, and once again, just as in the case of Sartre's description of the Look of the Other and his subsequent analysis of desire as negation, the contrast of Merleau-Ponty with Sartre on imagination is instructive. Sartre had characterized the difference between perception and imagination as the difference between experiencing an existing thing and experiencing a non-existing thing, that is, a mental image. Perception is the experience of an external object, thing, or event, whereas imagination is the awareness of something as *not being*. Images are distinguished from perceptions or sensations by a distinctive nothingness or nihilation, Sartre says. Thus, for his philosophy, perception and imagination are two entirely different modalities of experience, perception having to do with the visible, imagination with the invisible. In parallel with his response to Sartre in relation to the Look and desire, Merleau-Ponty contends that the imaginary is not a nothingness or hole in what exists. It is rather the imminent, latent, or hidden that is interwoven with the real. Our vision of the world is capable of leaping over distances, piercing the perceptual future, outlining hollows, reliefs, distances, and deviations in Being ("ILVS" 103–4; *S* 67; *Si* 83). Daytime "clear space" slips easily into nighttime dream space, as rising and falling are taken over as the movements of respiration and sexual desire. This profoundly mixes up our innocent presumptions about the demarcation between visible and invisible, real and imagined ("EM" 130; *OE* 35).[24]

Thus, there is a latent imaginary in human life that is something other than the spontaneous, free, and magical Sartrean imagination. The French language demarcates a somewhat ambiguous difference between imagination (*l'imagination*), which pertains to the production of mental images, and the imaginary (*l'imaginaire*), which does not necessarily involve the production of images but refers to the legendary, the mythic, and to idealities such as complex and irrational numbers. King Oedipus, King Lear, and the square root of minus 1 are not mental images, but are part of the stock of the cultural and historical imaginary that structures our perceptions. We see a troubled friend as Lear, or as Oedipus, or if those are overladen and overdramatized, simply as father or mother, as uncle or aunt. "Our waking relations with objects and others especially," Merleau-Ponty writes, "have an oneiric character as a matter of principle:

others are present to us in the way that dreams are, the way myths are, and this is enough to question the cleavage between the real and the imaginary" (*IPP* 116; *RC* 69).

This way of accounting for things draws Merleau-Ponty's philosophy away from Sartre and more toward Gilles Deleuze and Gaston Bachelard. In one of the epigraphs for this chapter, we took notice of Deleuze's claim that the role of the imagination "is to draw something new from repetition." "Imaginary repetition," Deleuze adds, "is not a false repetition which stands in for the absent true repetition: true repetition takes place in imagination."[25] Bachelard found a common origin of science and art in a psychoanalysis of the four elements: earth, air, fire, and water. In a working note from *The Visible and the Invisible* titled "The Imaginary," we have Merleau-Ponty's own statement of his preference for Bachelard's view of the latent imaginary: "Being and the imaginary are for Sartre 'objects,' 'entities'—For me they are 'elements' (in Bachelard's sense)" (*VI* 267; *VIn* 320). We have only two references to Bachelard in Merleau-Ponty's published working notes, yet Merleau-Ponty's own use of the term "element" for "Flesh," which is the same as Bachelard's term "element," means that the incorporation of Bachelard must be marked and given its due weight. Bachelard, in his study of *Water and Reveries* (1942; *L'Eau et les rêves*), introduced the concept of a material imaginary (*imaginaire*) related to material, rather than formal, causes. The formal imaginary has to do with the play and pleasure of images on a surface, with shape, balance, and variety, but the material imaginary plumbs the primitive and eternal depths of material substance itself, its weight and its heart.[26] Thus, the material imaginary is not about mental imaging. Rather, it is about a "sense of the past" that is a "feel for" the deep (*la profonde*) and elemental in our attractions to others, objects, and world. It is a fascination that brings us to stare at moving water, leaping fire, deep canyons, cumulus clouds, and the sails of boats riffling in the wind. Such sensing denotes an undividedness between perception, memory, and feeling, such as when we sense danger, or sense the onset of an illness in ourselves or a member of our intimate family, but cannot quite specify the exact symptomatic details of what we are "sensing."

We are attracted to wood, water, fire, and sky, to faces, bodies, children, and the patterns of nature due to our access to a material imaginary that is a "repetition without an original." This was the deep attraction that Rilke found in the works of Rodin, and we remind ourselves here of Rilke's account cited earlier in our studies of Cézanne and Rodin, that begins with an invocation of the imaginary: "I come before you to remind you of your childhood. No, not of yours, but rather of all that ever was childhood. For it should be possible to awaken memories that are not yours, memories that are older than you." Continuing, Rilke refers to a small piece of wood, for example, that had once taken on the qualities of ancient legends:

> This small forgotten object, which was willing to mean almost anything, made you familiar with thousands of things by playing thousands of roles; it was animal and tree, king and child, and when it receded, all these things were there. This something, worthless as it was, prepared the way for your first relationships with the world; it introduced you to life and people.[27]

There is a "sense of the beautiful" just as much as there is a "sense of the past" that must be independent of reflective and unreflective experience, past and present perception. *The Visible and the Invisible* speaks of this in terms of Husserl's notion of horizons of perception, and the "sense of the beautiful" is thus linked with the phenomenological notion of horizon. It is part of what is given on the "edges" and in the margins of perception, in those places where perception and memory cross over with the material imaginary. I am aware that in using this phrase, "sense of the beautiful," we are echoing the title of Santayana's *The Sense of Beauty*. Santayana, following Plato and Kant, also excludes the "lower senses" of touch, taste, and smell from the realm of the beautiful, with which we have found phenomenological reasons to disagree. Yet there is much to admire in Santayana's argument against the empiricist account of beauty as a "sensation" that can be objectively observed on the same order as a color such as red. This leads to "the futility of a dogmatism that would impose upon another man judgments and emotions for which the needed soil is lacking in his constitution and experience."[28] Rather than sensation, the "sense" of beauty in Santayana's meaning, and in ours, is closer to what one means in speaking of a good musical sense, or a sense of rhythm, or a sense of humor, or a sense of shame, or a sense of insecurity as opposed to a sense of well-being. In the last chapter we connected this with Merleau-Ponty's notion of sensible ideas that he says are "known by sentiment" (*connaissance par sentiment*), which means having a "feel for" a certain style or relationship. The sense of beauty is a sense of appreciation, a power of interpolating and having a "feel for" the beautiful, an awareness of beauty that is accessible through the elemental in the material imaginary. The material imaginary is thus, in the realm of the beautiful, an analogous part of the solution of the paradox that surfaced in the *Meno* regarding knowledge and in the Nietzschean paradox of the eternal return of the same, for the material imaginary enables the recognition of beauty in the first time.

The "sense of beauty" bestowed by the material imaginary also illuminates our attraction to the strange, to the deeply different, to the truly new, the unprecedented and "brand new" in our experience. We are not nailed to the conservation of a personal past but open to the freshness of the world and others because perception blends with the imaginary in the passive syntheses of our perceptions of the elements of earth as wood and stone, air and sky, fire and water. In the very same paragraph of *The Visible and the Invisible* that concludes with the statement that we have highlighted regarding desire—"in the patient and silent labor of desire, begin the paradox of expression"—Merleau-Ponty uses the phrase "the first time" five times in a row (*VI* 143; *VIn* 189). The five "first times" build into a crescendo of ideas about self, other, and world that leads us to the climactic line about the "source" of the paradox of expression found in desire. "For the first time, the seeing that I am is for me really visible." "For the first time, I appear to myself completely turned inside out under my own eyes." "For the first time, my movements no longer proceed unto the things to be seen . . . but they address themselves to the body in general and for itself, my own or that of another." "For the first time, through the other body, I see that, in its coupling with the flesh of the world, the body contributes more than it receives." And finally, we arrive at the double forte of the crescendo, the fifth "first time":

> For the first time, the body no longer couples itself up with the world, it clasps another body, applying itself carefully with its whole extension, forming tirelessly with its hands the strange statue which in its turn gives everything it receives; the body is lost outside of the world and its goals, fascinated by the unique occupation of floating in Being with another life, of making itself the outside of its inside and the inside of its outside. (*VI* 143–44; *VIn* 189)

These five first times—in self-understanding, in vision, in movement, in relations with others, and in Being itself "floating with another life"—are confirmed in a working note of *The Visible and the Invisible* from November 1960. Merleau-Ponty commented to himself that "Nature is at the first day: it is there today" (*VI* 267; *VIn* 320), and he repeats this thought from Lucien Herr.[29] This does not mean, Merleau-Ponty adds, "the myth of original indivision and coincidence as *return*." In other words, the ever-newness of Nature does not refer to some lost innocence in a Garden of Eden at the beginning of time that evokes our nostalgia. Rather, "it is a question of finding in the present, the flesh of the world (and not in the past) an 'ever new' and 'always the same'" (*VI* 267; *VIn* 320). These, I think, are some of the most oracular and prophetic words of philosophy that Merleau-Ponty ever wrote. They clearly mark Merleau-Ponty as a philosopher of birth and natality; his philosophy of beauty is a philosophy of birth (*naissance*) and having a "feeling for" the world which is a kind of knowledge (*con-naissance*). Cézanne, Merleau-Ponty said, converts into visible objects "the vibration of appearances which is the cradle of things" ("CD" 68; "DC" 30).

Beauty and the Unconscious

It is perhaps troubling that Merleau-Ponty concurs that the desire for the repetitions of the beautiful also brings us back to ourselves, or as he himself says, "there is a fundamental narcissism of all vision" (*VI* 139; *VIn* 183). Here we recall as well Merleau-Ponty's construal, in the "Nature" courses, of animal instinct as a kind of "narcissism" that has as much to do with the oneiric and the "irreal" as with the real. This is a term and these are claims that are a problem to us today for their suggestion of self-absorption. Nevertheless, Merleau-Ponty wrote in *The Visible and the Invisible* that there is a "second and more profound sense of narcissism: not to see in the outside, as the others see it, the contours of a body one inhabits, but especially to be seen by the outside, to exist within it, to emigrate into it, to be seduced, captivated, alienated by the phantom" (*VI* 139; *VIn* 183). At stake here is the relationship of the aesthetic and ontology of beauty, desire, and repetition, fashioned through the work of Merleau-Ponty, with Freudian psychoanalysis. We can make an approach to interpreting this relationship through the ancient myth of Echo and Narcissus from which Freud took so much.

Repetition was a punishment rather than a joy in the tragic life of Echo. She was condemned always to do no more than repeat and thereby be left to mourn her inability to express her love to Narcissus. He only refuses her approach, which forecloses the possibility of repeating his words to express her love for him. There are several versions of the story, including the oldest from an early Homeric hymn of the seventh or eighth century BC, and another from Ovid's *Metamorphoses,* worth retelling for its small but significant details. The story is one of the flower myths told to account for the beauty of wild flowers in the austere stony hills and rugged mountains of the Greek countryside. In Ovid's retelling, a suspicious Juno had come to discover Jove's amorous pursuits among the nymphs of the mountainside, but Echo detained her in such long, garrulous chatter that the nymphs had run away and Jove's misdeeds went undiscovered. To punish Echo, Juno cut off Echo's power of originating speech, leaving her only with the power to repeat, to answer in the words she had last heard. "You will always have the last word but no power to speak first."[30] The day Echo saw Narcissus she was fired with love and slipped out from the shelter of the trees to throw her arms around him in an embrace. Narcissus ran from her, crying out, "No, you must not touch—Go, take your hands away, may I be dead before you throw your fearful chains around me." Echo answered, "O fearful chains around me," and turned away in melancholy sorrow,

> Which, sleepless, turned her body to a shade,
> First pale and wrinkled, then a sheet of air,
> Then bones, which some say turned to thin-worn rocks,
> And last her voice remained. Vanished in forest,
> Far from her usual walks on hills and valleys,
> She's heard by all who call; her voice has life.[31]

Narcissus continued in his way of spurning all loves—girls of the rivers, women of the mountains, boys and men—until one lovesick boy prayed to heaven: "O may he love himself alone and yet fail in that great love."[32] The curse was heard in the heavens by the goddess Nemesis, which means "righteous anger," and as Narcissus looked into a pool, "well-deep and silver-clear,"

> Beauty caught his eyes that trapped him;
> He loved the image that he thought was shadow,
> And looked amazed at what he saw—his face.[33]

The rest of the story follows apace, how his love was cursed as grasping at a glancing mirror of reflections, how he became "half-mad" with the self-made image he could not possess, how his tears stirred the pool to waves, how he tore his clothing and beat his breasts, and how he drowned in his own image. Gazing down the well, his last word was "Good-bye," and the voice of Echo answered, "Good-bye."

> As he crossed the narrows
> Of darkest hell he saw the floating image
> Of his lost shade within the Stygian waters. . . .
> As they built up his pyre and waved their torches
> Across his bier, they searched; his body vanished.
> They saw a flower of gold with white-brimmed petals.[34]

The story is done, and the new and lovely flower they named, of course, Narcissus. There remains a mystery of the bodies—two bodies—Echo's bones dispersed among the stony hills as air and thin-worn rocks but yet alive as an inextinguishable voice that answers for all who call out, not in forests, hills, and valleys but in stony mountains; and Narcissus simply vanished except for that rare and precious wildflower.

In the tragic love story of Echo, Freud found a "compulsion to repeat" or "repetition complex." The compulsion to repeat is indeed, Freud believed, a conservative compulsion to restore the past in identical form. Children, Freud points out, cannot have their pleasurable experiences of stories and songs repeated often enough, and "they are inexorable in their insistence that the repetition shall be an identical one. This character trait disappears later on."[35] Thus, repetition, Freud claims, is both an infantile and a conservative compulsion, infantile in its demand for childish enjoyment, conservative in its desire to restore the past in identical form. "It seems then," Freud writes, "that an instinct is an urge inherent in organic life to restore an earlier state of things which the living entity has been obliged to abandon under the pressure of external disturbing forces."[36]

In the story of Narcissus, Freud believed he had found the origin of a set of instincts or drives that determine human personality: primary and secondary narcissism. Primary narcissism is that natural tendency in all human beings at the beginning of life, Freud believed, to love themselves: "We say that a human being has originally two sexual objects—himself and the woman who nurses him—and in doing so we are postulating a primary narcissism in everyone."[37] Primary narcissim as "self-love" is already a revolutionary concept in the Freudian metapsychology, for it postulates for the first time the notion of "ego-libido" as well as "object-libido." According to Freud's theory laid out in *The Interpretation of Dreams,* the ego drives are in no way erotic and the libidinal drives are not egoistic. Nevertheless, Freud remained committed to the revised account and seized upon it to postulate a form of "secondary narcissism," a kind of recurrence of narcissism in later adult life when the sexual instinct is cathected upon one's own ego.

Part of the charm of a child, Freud argues, lies precisely in narcissism, a kind of self-contentment, self-absorption, and inaccessibility to adults much like that of the charm of certain animals who do not concern themselves with us but remain aloof, such as cats and large beasts of prey. However, a recurrence and excess of auto-eroticism in adult life inevitably produces illness: "A strong egotism is a protection against falling ill, but in the last resort we must begin to love in order not to fall ill, and we are bound to fall ill if, in consequence of frustration, we are unable to love [an other or object]."[38] Freud's examples are controversial and even objectionable. There is the kind of woman, Freud says, for whom it is only ever themselves that they love with intensity, whose greatest need lies in the direction of being loved, not of loving an other. There are the kinds of parents who are "under a compulsion to ascribe every perfection to the child—which sober observation would find no occasion to do—and to conceal and forget all his shortcomings."[39] This, Freud says, is a revival and reproduction of their own narcissism. The child shall once more be the center and core of creation—"His Majesty the Baby"—just as we once fancied ourselves.[40] Thus, all cases of secondary narcissism are personality disturbances that are either neurotic or delusional illnesses embodying the "compulsion to repeat" or "repetition complex."

Merleau-Ponty carried on a dialogue with Freud throughout his entire intellectual life. Near the beginning, in "Cézanne's Doubt," he discussed Freud's oedipal reading of Leonardo's painting of *St. Anne with Virgin and Child* from Freud's *Introduction to the Method of Leonardo da Vinci,* in which Freud suggested that the Virgin's cloak appears as a vulture where it touches the face of the child, evidently repeating a childhood memory in which a vulture came to Leonardo's cradle and forced open his mouth with its tail. Whether a childhood memory or the fantasy of a grown man, "we are caught in a secret history, in a forest of symbols," Merleau-Ponty commented ("CD" 73; "DC" 38). To those who object that a doctrine which brings in sexuality everywhere cannot, by the rules of inductive logic, establish its effectiveness anywhere, Merleau-Ponty answered: "This is how one triumphs over psychoanalysis, but only on paper. For if the suggestions of the analyst can never be proven, neither can they be eliminated. . . . How can we deny that psychoanalysis has taught us to notice echoes, allusions, repetitions from one moment of life to another—a concatenation we would not dream of doubting if Freud had stated the theory correctly?" ("CD" 74; "DC" 42). Fascinated by the concrete analyses of dreams, of hysteria, of the repetitions from childhood to adulthood, Merleau-Ponty was yet looking for a theory that offered a more "hermeneutic musing" ("CD" 75; "DC" 43) upon these repetitions and echoes.

One of the last installments in Merleau-Ponty's dialogue with Freud was a preface Merleau-Ponty wrote for Hesnard's *The Work of Freud and Its Importance for the Modern World.* In 1960 Angelo Hesnard was president of the Société Française de Psychanalyse, and his book includes a chapter on phenomenology in which he discusses at length Merleau-Ponty's psychological studies in *The Structure of Behavior* and *Phenomenology of Perception.* That chapter concludes: "We think personally that the surest way toward a fruitful collaboration of Freudian psychoanalysis with phenomenology is that of the engaged consciousness of Merleau-Ponty."[41] Merleau-Ponty wrote in his preface: "Phenomenology and psychoanalysis are not parallel; much better, they are both aiming toward the same latency."[42] He added: "Since our philosophy has given us no better way to express that intemporal, that indestructible element in us which, says Freud, is the unconscious itself, perhaps we should continue calling it the unconscious—so long as we do not forget that the word is the index of an enigma."[43]

We need to reflect upon the enigma of the unconscious that is an "intemporal" in us, and we will come to that, but first it is imperative to distinguish as clearly as possible between what Merleau-Ponty means by referring to a "second or more profound sense of narcissism" and what Freud meant by "secondary narcissism." The second narcissism of which Merleau-Ponty speaks is really a reversal of vanity and self-absorption: not to see one's own reflection always and everywhere in others and all things, but always and everywhere to find others and all things in one's own growth. Rather than a movement inward into self-absorption, it is a movement outward toward others and the world. It is a movement that enlarges life rather than shrinking or impoverishing it. Throughout this study, we have stressed that in the experience of the beautiful we are being challenged and interrogated by the outside, and we also find and pursue the beauty of what is other, that is to say, new, strange, and different. In *The Being of the Phenomenon: Merleau-Ponty's Ontology,* Renaud Barbaras has written that in the thought of Merleau-Ponty, "desire is not the negation of the other," because the act of expression is just as much the "entrance into self" as it is the "leaving of self."[44] Barbaras stresses this point once again in the more recent *Desire and Distance:* "In desire the relationship to the self and the relationship to the other do not constitute an alternative. . . . Desire is what relates one to the other, the finite manifestation of an ultimate appearing that itself never appears."[45] Human self-awareness requires being questioned and challenged from the outside, even obstruction by the outside, and this is a gift of the beautiful, for thereby one gains an enlarged and enhanced version of life. The experience of the beautiful is the experience of a fundamental openness to Being.

"Eye and Mind" captures this essential thought in its reflections on mirrors and self-portraits. In the mirror, Merleau-Ponty says, "my externality becomes complete" ("EM" 129; *OE* 33). Or again, "the mirror phantom draws my flesh into the outer world. . . . Mirrors are instruments of a universal magic that converts things into spectacle, spectacle into things, myself into another, and another into myself" ("EM" 130; *OE* 33–34). Merleau-Ponty's interpretation of the mirror phenomenon may strike us as unusual, for we often associate the prolonged look at oneself in the mirror with the secondary, bad narcissism of adult vanity. However, Merleau-Ponty reverses that common association of mirrors with vanity and individualism, taking the mirror to be a technical object that discloses everything secret about us in plain view. The same "magic" of the mirror underlies the self-portrait, for on Merleau-Ponty's reading, self-portraits depend upon the painter looking at himself or herself in a mirror. Looking in one mirror reverses the face and body, left side becoming right side, and thus, painters have sometimes employed two mirrors to reverse the reversal, a doubling of the phantom.[46]

Merleau-Ponty's account could be strengthened by considering more recent self-portraits that do not flatter or stylize the subject, and are painted as if "seen by the outside," like a Modigliani portrait in which sitters did not recognize their image. Some of Cézanne's self-portraits, especially from the later years, had already moved in this direction, which was heightened even further in the ferocious self-portraits done by Picasso in the early 1970s in his waning years, or the portraits of herself painted by Frida Kahlo (1907–1953), the well-known Mexican painter, friend and wife of Diego Rivera, following her horrific bus accident that broke her spinal column and left her in a wheelchair. The insight could also be deepened by extension to self-portraits that do not depend upon mirrors at all. The African "passport masks" found in West African countries such as Ghana and Mali do not so much identify the individual person as mark out a tribal, social identity. The facial features are too exaggerated and often roughly fashioned to identify an individual, but the style of the mask, sometimes together with a predominant regional animal on the top, offers a social self-portrait of the individual as member of a tribal group. In the West, we have for a long time created portraits of individuals without mirrors, from the mundane driver's license snapshot that externalizes our face to the registry and police, to dental work, scars of healed injuries, fingerprinting, blood typing, and most recently, DNA. Handprints reveal the unique and delicate swirls at the fingertips and heel of the palm. They are the earliest and most common symbol of individual identity pressed onto cave walls over centuries in Europe and Australia.[47] In *Genetic Self-Portrait* (1999), Gary Schneider has created an exhibition of parts of his own body from the outside, as it were, by using contemporary scientific imaging techniques ranging from the simple X-ray to the most sophisticated instruments developed for the Human Genome Project. The exhibition includes images of the palm side of his open hands with their heat and sweat on film emulsions, his DNA sequence, images of forty-six chromosomes, a tumor-suppressor gene on chromosome 11, the irises of his eyes, the retinas of his eyes, a dried blood sample, a piece of his hair, his ears again pressed against film emulsion, a skin scraping from the inside of his cheek, and his sperm. This is a massive externalization of identity that completely mixes up intimate and public, inside and outside, individual and social. Schneider himself comments that he finds the image of the nucleus and mitochondria of his inner cheek cell "very beautiful," a surreal beauty to be sure, but one that Schneider compares to a heroic landscape portrayed in *The Riverbank* from AD 950, a Chinese screen by Dong Yuan in the collection of the Metropolitan Museum of Art in New York City. The image of the ears resembles constellations in the heavens, and Schneider says they remind him of the Lick Observatory publications such as volume 8, 1908, titled *Nebulae and Clusters.*[48] The image of the retinas showing the branching lines of the bright optic nerves surrounded by blood vessels resemble the moon in the sky seen through the branches of a tree on a bright night. Schneider's work offers us another opening onto the self and its relations with the "somethings" and the "someones." Certainly one of Freudian bent might bring against Schneider the charge of an exaggerated kind of self-absorption, but just as much, with Merleau-Ponty one might see in his work the kind of more "profound narcissism" that blends inside with outside and emigrates into the things, the world, and others.

To take up more directly the subject of "the enigma of the unconscious" and Merleau-Ponty's reinterpretation of the Freudian metapsychology, in the résumé of the course on passivity subtitled "Sleep, the Unconscious, Memory," we find this text: "The unconscious is a perceiving consciousness" and it operates "through a logic of implication or promiscuity, follows closer and closer a path whose slope it cannot see clearly, and envisages objects and creatures through the negative that it withholds, which suffices to regulate its steps without enabling it to name them 'by their names'" (*IPP* 118; *RC* 70–71). There are important points here. First, the unconscious, like the imaginary, is interwoven with perception, not separable from it as if it were a kind of "second awareness" in the basement of the psyche. The unconscious is not drives or instincts within us; rather, it is in front of us in our perceptions as in our dreams. Merleau-Ponty wrote: "This unconscious is to be sought not at the bottom of ourselves, behind the back of our 'consciousness,' but in front of us, as articulations of our field" (*VI* 180; *VIn* 231). Second, we find the notion that this kind of perceiving consciousness envisages and regulates through a withholding that is not able to name things "by their names." We might say, paradoxically, that the unconscious is a kind of knowing that is also a not knowing. This is exactly the very last formulation of the meaning of the unconscious that Merleau-Ponty gives us in the résumé of his last "Nature" course in 1959–60 titled "Nature and Logos: The Human Body" that we have cited previously: "The double formula of the unconscious ('I did not know' and 'I have always known it') corresponds to two aspects of the flesh, its poetic and its oneiric power" (*IPP* 198; *RC* 179). We recall what Rilke wrote in his letters about the art of Cézanne: "No thing can move you if you do not allow for it to surprise you with an unimaginable beauty. Beauty is always something we come to, but we don't know what this something is."[49]

Thus, the unconscious is that perceptual power of "sort of knowing" but not being able to say or name that which we know. We again find ourselves within the conceptual geography of the *Meno* paradox. Merleau-Ponty characterizes this "sort of knowing" as a "feeling" (*sentiment*) that we encountered earlier in our discussion of desire and beauty, like music, as sensible ideas given "behind the sensible, or in its heart" (*VI* 150; *VIn* 194), the heart that "has its reasons which reason does not know." "The unconscious," Merleau-Ponty writes, "is feeling itself [*le sentir lui-même*], since feeling is not the intellectual possession of 'what' is felt, but a dispossession of ourselves in favor of it, an opening toward that which *we do not have to think in order that we may recognize it* [my emphasis]" (*IPP* 198; *RC* 179). Then he adds that "the primordial unconsciousness would be a letting-be [*le laisser-être*], the initial yes, the undividedness of feeling" (*IPP* 199; *RC* 179). This is an affirmation of life and of our bond and engagement with the world in an undividedness of feeling that is again conveyed to us in the Heideggerian notion of care or "letting be."

Our desire and appreciation of beauty is, therefore, and ultimately, a kind of recognition that precedes any sort of exact or explicit knowledge that is based upon the "intemporal" element available to us in the fissures (*écarts*) or openings of the human body and its experiences. Our body "knows" more than we can say: "I do not know and have always known it." In this regard, Mauro Carbone has asked us to reconsider Merleau-Ponty's use of the term "clairvoyance."[50] The term appears in "Eye and Mind" in the second section on vision: "What would vision be without eye movement? And how could the movement of the eyes not blur things if movement were blind? If it were only a reflex? If it did not have its antennae, its clairvoyance? If vision were not prefigured in it?" ("EM" 124; *OE* 17). Clairvoyance means literally the capacity to see what is invisible, for example, to see the past or the future. That Merleau-Ponty believes this occurs through the "antennae" of vision itself is an indicator of his sustained theme that vision always requires a form of seeing that unites visible and invisible, presence and absence, activity and passivity, existence and essence, real and imaginary. We find another occurrence of the term explicitly in relation to love and desire in Merleau-Ponty's recently published notes for his course on "Institution in Personal and Public History." The context is Merleau-Ponty's reflection upon the narrator's love for Albertine in Proust's *Remembrance of Things Past.* "Instead of what you had imagined, life gives you something else, something which was secretly wanted, not fortuitous. Realization is not what was expected, but still that which was wanted: we move forward backwards, we do not choose directly, but in an oblique way, and yet we do what we want: love is a clairvoyance: it leads us just to what can tear us" (*IP* 75).[51] Though in love and desire we do not choose directly, but obliquely, yet we do get what we want, almost, as it were, in spite of ourselves, because love leads us to what can tear us (*à ce qui peut nous déchirer*).

There is one more text to consider, one discussing Freud near the end of the last "Nature" course, "Nature and Logos: The Human Body" (1959–60), in a section entitled "*Eros* and Consciousness" that again repeats Merleau-Ponty's phrase for the "double formula" of the unconscious. Merleau-Ponty asks:

> "What is thus this me that is not me, this weight, this surplus on this side of that which appears to me?" He answers: "It is sensing itself in that it is not the thinking of sensing (possession) but dispossession, *ek-stasis,* participation or identification, a blind, nondifferentiated recognition (of the touching and the touched, or me and my image over there), the zero degree of difference. The sensed = I don't know and I have always known it (Hyppolite). We do not need to know what it is that we see since we see it. To be at . . . fascination or deduction of the sensible. To see is to think without thinking." (*N* 283; *NN* 351)[52]

The phrase "blind, nondifferentiated recognition" would justify us in saying that love and desire are thus a kind of "blind clairvoyance," to use the phrase invented by Carbone.[53] This passage at the end of the third "Nature" course also seems implicitly to refer us back to the second course on animality, for there the notion of animal instinct that many suppose refers to a finality in the relation of animal and *Umwelt* is said to retain a blindness.

> The finality of the animal is blind, not regulated on a plan of the whole but on local conditions. . . . The instinct is an activity established from within but that possesses a blindness and does not know its object. . . . Instinct is before all else a theme, a style that meets up with that which evokes it in the milieu, but which does not have goals; it is an activity of pleasure. (*N* 182, 192, 193; *NN* 238, 250, 251)

Like instinct in the animal's relation with its milieu, love and desire are guided by an imaginary and an unconscious that are a *voyance* that is an uncanny *clairvoyance.*

Let us return to the story of Narcissus. The beginning of that story in Ovid's account is seldom told. It is about Tiresias, who, in spite of his blindness, had the power of clairvoyance, which for this blind prophet was the power of seeing the future. "Those who came to him for advice could not deny the power, his wit, in prophecy."[54] Liriope, a water-lady, in spite of being raped by Cephius and nearly drowned in a winding brook, nevertheless gave birth to a son so charming even as a baby that he inspired girls with thoughts of love. Liriope named the boy Narcissus and came to Tiresias to ask how long her child would live.

> To great old age? the prophet answered, "Only
> If never he comes to know himself." Then for
> A long time after this his prophecy
> Seemed vain, and yet what finally happened
> Proved it true: Narcissus' death, the way he died,
> And his odd love.[55]

In matters of the heart—love, desire, and beauty—Tiresias symbolizes the entire human condition. With Tiresias, we all share a blindness in beauty, love, and desire, but it is blindness that is not absolute, but rather a gift that is the power to have a "feel for" what we want even before we know it. Desire and Beauty are an intertwining in the Flesh that opens the self to another side of itself that it did not know and opens self to others and world in ways that we could not have conceptualized but yet have "always known." "Nature is at the first day. . . . It is a question of finding in the present, the flesh of the world, an 'ever new' and 'always the same'—a sort of time of sleep," Merleau-Ponty wrote (*VI* 267; *VIn* 320). As the "ever new" and "always the same," repetition and differences, theme and variations structure our experience of the beautiful. Our openness to others and the world is inevitably flawed and incomplete; nevertheless, in this very evident failing is also desire's success, for it establishes the fundamental relation to others and to the world as a "melody that sings itself in us." In desire's repetitions and in repetition's variations are moments of discovery, joy, and life. In this aspect alone Beauty fulfills its calling.

"A Radiant Image, a Particular Rhythm": Nietzsche

Beauty, repetition, and difference together mean rhythm. When Merleau-Ponty speaks of the primordial unconsciousness as a "letting-be, the initial yes, the undividedness of feeling" (*IPP* 199; *RC* 179), we hear the echo of what Nietzsche meant by the Dionysian element in art. When Merleau-Ponty speaks of "Nature at the first day" (*VI* 267; *VIn* 320) and gives us five "first times" ascending into the double forte crescendo of desire as the beginning of the paradox of expression (*VI* 143–44; *VIn* 189), this also directs our attention toward Nietzsche's thinking of life, beauty, and the sublime, for Zarathustra tells us that the name inscribed above the gateway of the eternal return of the same is "Moment."[56] We again quote Merleau-Ponty's text about beauty in cinematography from *The World of Perception* (*Causeries*): "Then, as now, the viewer will experience the unity and necessity of the temporal progression in a work of beauty without ever forming a clear idea of it. Then, as now, this viewer will be left not with a store of recipes but a radiant image, a particular rhythm" (*WP* 99; *C* 58). This passage is the text in which Merleau-Ponty speaks at greatest length on beauty, and it affirms what he wrote in the preface to *Phenomenology of Perception,* that beauty is an "experience without a concept" (*PP* xvii; *PhP* xii). It also tells us that he thought of beauty as a combination of the radiance of light together with rhythm.

We encounter the notion of beauty (*Schönheit*) as shining or radiance in Heidegger: "This is how self-concealing being is illuminated. Light of this kind joins its shining to and into the work. This shining, joined in the work, is the beautiful. *Beauty is one way in which truth occurs as unconcealedness.*"[57]

We know that Merleau-Ponty also thinks of the beautiful as radiance, colors, and light, for in discussing the "*logos* of color" in Klee, Merleau-Ponty was led back to Delauney's 1912 essay "Light," with its appropriation of the idea of a "voice of light" from the ancient hermeticist Hermes Trismegistus. Delaunay and Klee worked in paint toward a new idea of light as a "rhythmic simultaneity" that is vibration, pulse, and measure. Thus, in Merleau-Ponty's aesthetic and ontology, we are led from radiance to rhythm, and the notion of beauty as rhythm, I want to argue, offers us something truly unique in theorizing the aesthetic and art. Furthermore, the conjunction of rhythm with radiance as the meaning of the beautiful establishes a perhaps surprising resonance between Merleau-Ponty's aesthetics and that of Nietzsche, for it was Nietzsche who argued that the beauty of the artwork is the necessary "belonging together" of the Apollonian and the Dionysian. Rhythm is at the core of the Dionysian dithyramb as light is at the core of the Apollonian. Let us approach the questions of rhythm more patiently and work our way toward Nietzsche.

What is rhythm, and why did Merleau-Ponty accord it such importance with respect to beauty? We most commonly think of rhythm in a musical context as the pacing, pulse, and sometimes syncopation of the percussion played by the drumbeat or in the bass notes of the cello, string bass, bass guitar, the bass voices of the brass, or the piano's bass notes. In musical composition rhythm is denoted by the time signature in a musical score—4/4 time, 6/8 time, 3/4 time, and so on. This latter was the rhythm of the triptych that Paul Klee deployed in the aesthetic anatomy of *Rhythmical* (1930; *Rhythmisches*), which sets vibrating horizontal rows of alternating fields of black, then gray, then white, all painted on a background of brown, and of *Rhythmical, Stricter and Freer* (1930; *Rhythmisches strenger und freier*), presenting horizontal rows of alternating fields of purple, black, gray, and red, four colors, but each occurring in groupings of three. As we have seen, musically, both of these paintings express the rhythm of the three-beat bar in 3/4 time signature. Nevertheless, rhythm expands beyond its common musical context by leaps and bounds, for rhythm is vibration, rhythm is movement, rhythm is energy, rhythm is power, rhythm is Life. Rhythm is the beating of my heart that reaches all the way to the pulse I feel in my ears and in my forehead and in the other peripheries of my body: hands, fingers, feet, and toes. Already in *Phenomenology of Perception* Merleau-Ponty had connected life with rhythm: "My life is made up of rhythms which have not their *reason* in what I have chosen to be, but their *condition* in the humdrum setting which is mine. Thus there appears round our personal existence a margin of *almost* impersonal existence, which can be practically taken for granted, and which I rely on to keep me alive" (*PP* 84; *PhP* 99). This rhythm of life in a margin of "*almost* impersonal existence" is what Merleau-Ponty names our "anonymous" body or self that keeps us alive without and beyond our choosing; it is not our reason for living but our condition for being alive. Here is Merleau-Ponty's account of this anonymous body: "So it can be said that my organism, as a prepersonal cleaving to the general form of the world, as an anonymous and general existence, plays, beneath my personal life, the part of an *inborn complex*. It is not some kind of inert thing; it too has something of the momentum of existence" (*PP* 84; *PhP* 99). This phrase, "the momentum of existence," is the forward thrust of life that is rhythmically paced. In sum, therefore, mankind "taken as a concrete being is not a psyche joined to an organism, but the movement to and fro of existence . . . the movement of existence" (*PP* 88, 89; *PhP* 104, 105).

It is therefore to be expected that Merleau-Ponty's philosophy of painting and art would also highlight movement and rhythm, for in the well-known phrase Merleau-Ponty took over from Valéry, "the painter takes his body with him" ("EM" 123; *OE* 16). Already in "Cézanne's Doubt," Merleau-Ponty had written that the painter "recaptures and converts into visible objects . . . the vibration of appearances which is the cradle of things" ("CD" 68; "DC" 30). "Eye and Mind" describes the "latent line" of painting as "a movement by vibration or radiation" and says that Rodin's sculptures such as *The Walking Man* "bestride space" in a movement that is given through the "mutual confrontation of incompossibles" that "cause transition and duration to arise in bronze" ("EM" 144, 145; *OE* 77, 79). Nevertheless, when we investigate the etymological meaning of "rhythm," we find that its origin refers us, not to music and not to painting or sculpture, but to poetry, for "rhythm" is a derivation from the word "rhyme." The etymology of "rhythm" shows that it is a graphic variant of "rhyme" that occurred in the 1640s through the 1670s, and its meaning was originally the same as "rhyme," as in a rhyming or rhymed verse. Gradually, the meaning of "rhythm" expanded figuratively within verse or poetry to include a kind of metrical movement as determined by the relation of long and short, stressed and unstressed, syllables in a line.[58] Thus it happens that Merleau-Ponty's stress upon rhythm points us toward a greater emphasis upon language in relation to beauty, something of a corrective, perhaps, to the stress upon perception in relation to beauty proffered by radiance and light.

Through rhythm, it comes about that language, and metered language, take a central position in the philosophy of the beautiful. The voice of the poet is rhythm; the voice is form. The voice is also sound and, as relationships between and among sounds, voice is made melody. To return to the passage from *Phenomenology of Perception* on "singing the world" (*chanter le monde*), we recall that Merleau-Ponty makes poetry exemplary of this unique "singing." The problem under discussion in that text is the origin of language in the body, and Merleau-Ponty is defending the gestural theory of the meaning of speech (*la parole*). The verbal forms appear arbitrary—for example, "horse" in English, *cheval* in French, *equus* in Latin, *hippos* in Greek, *caballo* in Spanish, *Pferd* in German. However, these verbal forms would no longer appear so, he argues, if we took into account the word's "'gestural sense,' which is all-important in poetry. Then it would be found that the words, vowels and phonemes are so many ways of 'singing the world'" (*PP* 187; *PhP* 218). The various possibilities of vowels, consonants, and syntax in different natural languages are "several ways for the human body to sing the world's praises [*célébrer le monde*] and in the last resort to live it" (*PP* 187; *PhP* 218). *Chanter le monde, célébrer le monde:* these emotional melodies already present in everyday speech are raised to a higher power in the words, lines, and stanzas of poetry.

There is a beautiful text in the "Indirect Language" essay in which Merleau-Ponty speaks of language as a living being that gives us others and the world as living presences; language is not a mere utilitarian means to an end for something like the sharing of information. This text is worth citing at some length:

> Language is much more like a sort of being than a means, and that is why it can present something to us so well. A friend's speech over the telephone brings us the friend himself, as if he were wholly present in that manner of calling and saying goodbye to us, of beginning and ending his sentences, and of carrying on the conversation through things left unsaid. Because meaning is the total movement of speech, our thought crawls along in language. Yet for the same reason, our thought moves through language as a gesture goes beyond the individual points of its passage. At the very moment language fills our minds up to the top without leaving the smallest place for thought not taken into its vibration, and exactly to the extent that we abandon ourselves to it, it passes beyond the "signs" toward their meaning. And nothing separates us from that meaning any more. ("ILVS" 80; *S* 43; *Si* 54)

A friend calls us on the telephone, and from "hello" until "good-bye" we feel our friend's vital presence, for in his or her speech is a certain movement and rhythm, the cadence of the beginnings and endings of sentences, of things said and unsaid. In the movement of speech, thought "crawls along in language" and yet speech is a "vibration" that passes beyond signs toward their meaning.

Paul Valéry understands poetry as analogous to dancing. Walking is like prose, he thinks; both walking and prose have a definite aim, and when the walker or utilitarian writer reaches the goal, "this possession swallows up the entire action."[59] The dance goes nowhere in the sense of pursuing an object or end, but in dancing the dancer is "creating, maintaining, and exalting a certain *state*," which is a movement stimulated and regulated by auditory rhythms. Like the dance, "the poem does not die for having lived: it is expressly designed to be born again from its ashes and to become endlessly what it has just been."[60] Valéry's correlation of poetry with dancing and prose with walking returns us to the rhythms of our embodiment. As we have remembered the pulse of the heartbeat, we now remember as well the rhythms of copulation, pregnancy, and childbirth, and the very rhythms of breathing itself. Merleau-Ponty has connected the inspiration and expiration of breathing with childbirth in a very admirable text from "Eye and Mind." He writes first of the rhythm of breathing: "We speak of 'inspiration,' and the word should be taken literally. There really is inspiration and expiration of Being, respiration in Being, action and passion so slightly discernable that it becomes impossible to distinguish between who sees and who is seen, who paints and what is painted." Then comes the connection with birth, both the birth of a child and the birth of painting: "We say that a person is born the moment when something that was only virtually visible, inside the mother's body, becomes at one and the same time visible for us and for itself. The painter's vision is an ongoing birth" ("EM" 129; *OE* 31–32). Our heartbeat, our breathing, and our sexuality open onto space itself as diastole and systole, the world and field closing in, then opening up. Space participates in time and becomes rhythm, the measured pace of day and night, of the seasons, the tides, the moon, and planets.

On beauty, repetition, and difference, earlier in the chapter we have found much encouragement and augmentation of Merleau-Ponty's thought from that of Gilles Deleuze. In his book titled *Francis Bacon: The Logic of Sensations,* Deleuze has made the connection of repetition and difference to rhythm explicit in his study of the Irish-born painter Francis Bacon (1909–92). In this work, Deleuze argues that the painter seeks to make visible a kind of "original unity of the senses" in a multi-sensible Figure such as we find in Bacon's triptychs. This is possible, Deleuze argues, "only if the sensation of a particular domain (here, the visual) is in direct contact with a vital power that exceeds every domain and traverses them all. This power is Rhythm, which is more profound than vision, hearing, etc. Rhythm appears as music when it invests the auditory level, and as painting when it invests the visual level."[61] Deleuze continues to stress, in a way that accords very much with Merleau-Ponty, and especially Merleau-Ponty's studies of Cézanne and Klee, that "this is a 'logic of the senses,' as Cézanne said, which is neither rational nor cerebral. What is ultimate is thus the relation between sensation and rhythm, which places in each sensation the levels and domains through which it passes. This rhythm runs through a painting just as it runs through a piece of music." Deleuze, too, then extends rhythm in music and rhythm in painting into an ontological thesis about Life and Being: "It [rhythm] is diastole-systole: the world that seizes me by closing in around me, the self that opens to the world and opens the world itself. Cézanne, it is said, is the painter who put a vital rhythm into visual sensation."[62] In a moment contrary to Merleau-Ponty, Deleuze thinks that it is necessary to erase the phenomenological focus on the lived-body in order to uncover the more primordial and ontological notion of the rhythm of Life and Being. He calls the lived-body "a paltry thing in comparison with a more profound and almost unlivable Power [*Puissance*]."[63] We have already traced the movement in Merleau-Ponty's thought from the living body as flesh to the flesh of the world, within which we have found life, process, and power, so we need not enter into a dispute with Deleuze on the ontology of the lived-body. Rather, we are in a position to move together with his thought in finding three different rhythms in the triptychs of Bacon, as Deleuze analyzes the works: an "active" rhythm, which carries with it an increasing variation or amplification; a "passive" rhythm, with a decreasing variation or elimination; and an "attendant" rhythm that is something like the observer of the active and passive rhythms. Deleuze does not hesitate to extend his analysis of activity and passivity in the rhythms of painting and life beyond Bacon back in time toward a painter such as Rembrandt, invoking the same painting that also interested Merleau-Ponty, Rembrandt's *Night Watch* (1642). Whereas Merleau-Ponty was stressing depth when he discusses this painting in "Eye and Mind" ("EM" 128; *OE* 29) and Deleuze stresses rhythm, the two thinkers converge, for we know that the meaning of depth for Merleau-Ponty is about the voice of light that is a rhythmic simultaneity. Deleuze writes: "For in Rembrandt's still lifes or genre paintings, but also in his portraits, there is first of all a disturbance or vibration: the contour is in the service of vibration." This phrase, "in the service of vibration," reminds one immediately of Merleau-Ponty's apt phrase that the performer is "at the service of the sonata" (*VI* 151; *VIn* 199). Continuing to speak of Rembrandt, Deleuze writes:

> But there are also resonances that are derived from the layers of superimposed sensations. And even more, there is what Claudel described, this amplitude of light, an immense "stable and motionless background," that will have a strange effect, assuring the extreme division of Figures, their distribution into active, passive, and attendant Figures, as in Rembrandt's *Nightwatch*.[64]

When Deleuze describes rhythm as a Power (*Puissance*) and capitalizes that word, he describes that Power as "the unity of rhythm only at the point where rhythm itself plunges into chaos, into the night, at the point where the differences of level are perpetually and violently mixed."[65] This awakens the echo of Nietzsche's thought of Will and Power, which brings us to the Dionysian element in art, and in radiance and rhythm together, to the Apollonian-Dionysian pairing of Nietzsche's *The Birth of Tragedy Out of the Spirit of Music*. Merleau-Ponty's first published article, to our knowledge, appeared in 1935 in *La Vie Intellectuelle* on the subject of Scheler and Nietzsche's typology of *ressentiment* or rancor.[66] The article shows Merleau-Ponty's early awareness and study of Nietzsche's critique of Christianity as a slave morality that Nietzsche had argued turns against "the positive values of power, health, beauty, freedom, and independence" in favor of weakness, fear, anguish, and a slavish disposition.[67]

It also shows Merleau-Ponty's interest in Scheler's appropriation of Nietzsche's genealogy of morality together with Scheler's guarded, qualified critique: "According to Scheler, Nietzsche is not mistaken in his description of *ressentiment;* also, he is not mistaken when he believes that it can be recognized among certain Christians; but he is entirely mistaken when he believes that Christianity has been founded upon it."[68] Merleau-Ponty's expansion of the scope of his consideration of Nietzsche to include the Dionysian-Apollonian dyad is something we find in Merleau-Ponty's late lecture course, "Philosophy and Non-Philosophy Since Hegel," and in the fourth chapter of *The Visible and the Invisible* as well as several working notes.

If we did not know Merleau-Ponty had been reading Nietzsche, we might read right past Nietzsche's words without noticing them in chapter 4: "The Intertwining—The Chiasm." Here is Merleau-Ponty's text: "What there is then are . . . things we could not dream of seeing 'all naked' because the gaze itself envelops them, clothes them with its own flesh" (*VI* 131; *VIn* 173). Nietzsche's text referenced here is the preface to *The Gay Science* (also translated into English as *Joyful Wisdom*): "Today we consider it a matter of decency not to wish to see everything naked, or to be present at everything, or to understand and 'know' everything. One should have more respect for the bashfulness with which nature has hidden behind riddles and iridescent uncertainties."[69] We know that Merleau-Ponty had been studying *The Gay Science* because he quotes from sections 2, 3, and 4 of its preface in his course of 1960–61, "Philosophy and Non-Philosophy Since Hegel," and offers his commentary. This text is the source in which Merleau-Ponty agrees with Heidegger that Nietzsche's phrase, "God is dead," "means everything, except: there is no god" ("PNP" 13; *NC* 279). Nietzsche's text on nakedness and bashfulness ends with a praise of the Greeks that, in his commentary, Merleau-Ponty connected with Apollo and Dionysus. Nietzsche had written in *The Gay Science:* "Oh, those Greeks! They knew how to live. What is required for that is to stop courageously at the surface, the fold, the skin, to adore appearance, to believe in forms, tones, words, in the whole Olympus of appearance! These Greeks were superficial—*out of profundity.*"[70] This means, Merleau-Ponty's commentary states, that "when detached from life, philosophy is a panacea: a search for 'sunny places of thought.'" With regard to truth, Merleau-Ponty says that "truth is only a hidden truth. Do not seek to 'see' everything 'in its nakedness,' to 'know' all—be superficial through profundity (Apollo and Dionysus)" ("PNP" 12; *NC* 278).

When Merleau-Ponty links truth with appearances and invokes Nietzsche's analysis of the Dionysian and Apollonian elements in art, particularly ancient Greek tragedy, it is necessary to understand that appearance and truth—profundity—are not opposed in Nietzsche's thinking, or in Merleau-Ponty's. Plato was the philosopher who had established and authorized the opposition between truth and mere appearance in the Divided Line and the Allegory of the Cave in his *Republic,* and what we find in Nietzsche and Merleau-Ponty is the reversal of Platonism in favor of the wisdom of the Greek tragedians, especially Aeschylus and Sophocles. Nietzsche's *Birth of Tragedy* describes Apollo as "the luminous one" (*der Scheinende*), the god of light, the image-making god, the sculptor of images, dream-images, and "semblances."[71] The work of the Apollonian in Attic tragedy is creating the space and setting the scene for the action, characters, music, and poetry. The Apollonian is imperturbable calm, serenity, and repose, and it is also the "*principium individuationis,*" in Nietzsche's phrase, that principle which individuates and separates images and shapes.[72] Onto this serene setting strides the Dionysian impulse in art, which is its opposite but also its necessary counterpart: "Apollo could not live without Dionysos."[73] The Dionysian is body and nature, song and dance, it is a "tempestuous growth in music's other symbolic powers, in rhythm, dynamics, and harmony." The essence of nature expresses itself urgently in a "symbolism of the entire body, not just of the mouth, the face, the word, but the full gesture of dance with its rhythmical movement of every limb." The Dionysian is the chanting, singing, and drumbeat of the dithyramb, that urgent and unknown choral music of the cult of Dionysus, and thus the Dionysian challenges individuation in favor of "one-ness as the genius of humankind."[74] "Singing and dancing, man expresses his sense of belonging to a higher community; he has forgotten how to walk and talk and is on the brink of flying and dancing, up and away into the air above. His gestures speak of enchantment."[75]

Nietzsche has given us the pictorial image of the Apollonian-Dionysian pairing in *The Birth of Tragedy,* and it is the painting by Raphael titled *Transfiguration* (1516–20), Raphael's last painting, left unfinished upon his death in 1520. Indeed, it is an ironic gesture on Nietzsche's part to select this work as the monogram of his philosophy of art, a work that depicts the Christ transfigured in his glory of light and white raiment, talking with Moses and Elijah in the sky, and revealed to three of the apostles. Raphael's painting is divided into two halves, and in the lower half we see the demon-possessed boy, the boy's despairing father and companions, and the frightened disciples who are helpless to heal the boy—these are those who have been left behind while Jesus ascended the mountain with the chosen three disciples. This realm below in the bottom half of the picture is the realm of the Dionysian, and it shows us, Nietzsche says, "a reflection of the eternal, primal pain, the only ground of the world; here 'semblance' is a reflection of the eternal contradiction, the father of all things."[76] In the upper half of the picture, Raphael shows us the transfiguration scene: Moses and Elijah conversing with the Christ and all three figures hovering in the air above the ground, while the three chosen disciples, Peter, James, and John, lie on the ground apparently dazed and shading their eyes, with the whole scene bathed in a heavenly sky of blue and white. The transfiguration scene in the upper half of the picture is the realm of the Apollonian, Nietzsche says, and it is

> a luminous hovering in purest bliss and in wide-eyed contemplation, free of all pain. . . . With sublime gestures he [Apollo] shows us that the whole world of agony is needed in order to compel the individual to generate the releasing and redemptive vision and then, lost in contemplation of that vision, to sit calmly in his rocking boat in the midst of the sea.[77]

This painting taken in its entirety shows, Nietzsche believes, that Apollonian radiance with all its beauty rests on a hidden ground of suffering and sublimity. It is because of this hidden Dionysian ground that "Prometheus had to be torn apart by vultures on account of his Titanic love of mankind" and "Oedipus had to be plunged into a confusing maelstrom of atrocities because his unmeasured wisdom solved the riddle of the Sphinx."[78]

For the attentive reader of Merleau-Ponty, it should be clear that he does not want all of this as part of his philosophy of art when he introduces Apollo and Dionysus into his course on "Philosophy and Non-Philosophy Since Hegel." Our suspicion is that Merleau-Ponty would have agreed with Nietzsche's own self-criticism in finding his very early *Birth of Tragedy* overly imbued with the pessimism of Schopenhauer. "I now regret very much," Nietzsche wrote retrospectively in 1886, fourteen years after the publication of *The Birth of Tragedy* in 1872, "that I did not yet have the courage (or immodesty?) at that time to permit myself a *language of my own* for such personal views and acts of daring, laboring instead to express strange and new evaluations in Schopenhauerian and Kantian formulations."[79] For Merleau-Ponty's aesthetic, what we want from this Nietzschean trope, Apollo-Dionysus, is its pairing of radiance and rhythm, and its integration of these elements in the beautiful. In fact, one of the greatest weaknesses of Nietzsche's selection of Raphael's *Transfiguration* as monogram of the Dionysian and Apollonian is the separation of Dionysus and Apollo into two distinct halves of the painting rather than their mixture, their integration. The Dionysian appears below, the Apollonian above, and they exist in discrete sections of pictorial space. The disciples and those others below do not and cannot see or experience the transfigured vision that arises above them. Indeed, one of the greatest weaknesses of *The Birth of Tragedy* altogether is its increasing emphasis upon the Dionysian in isolation from the Apollonian, so much so that the Apollonian seems almost to drop out in some of the later sections of the book.

What Merleau-Ponty's aesthetic of the beautiful seeks is the movement through rhythm to the stillness of silence that is the fullness of calm, superabundant life. There is a distance between Merleau-Ponty and Nietzsche pertaining to silence and abyss. In a working note from February 1959 partially titled "History of Being," Merleau-Ponty reflects upon the circularity within his indirect ontology and indirect interrogation of thought and Being. He wrote: "This reversal itself—*circulus vitiosus deus*—is not hesitation, bad faith and bad dialectic, but return to *Sigè* the Abyss" (*VI* 179; *VIn* 233). The phrase "*circulus vitiosus deus*" is Nietzsche's from *Beyond Good and Evil.*[80] Its meaning may be "a vicious circle made god" or "God is a vicious circle," and it invokes once again Nietzsche's thought of God as a profound absence in the universe, an absence that threatens life with the wisdom of Silenus, that companion of Dionysus, whose wisdom is often cited in *The Birth of Tragedy:* "The very best thing is utterly beyond your reach, not to have been born, not to *be,* to be *nothing.* However, the second best thing for you is: to die soon."[81] All of Nietzsche's philosophy in *The Birth of Tragedy* seeks a justification for life in the face of the tragic wisdom of Silenus, and the conclusion of that work is that the existence of the world is justified only as an aesthetic phenomenon. "Yes, my friends, believe as I do in Dionysiac life and in the rebirth of tragedy. The time of Socratic man is past. Put on wreaths of ivy, take up the *thyrsus* and do not be surprised if tigers and panthers lie down, purring and curling round your legs. Now you must only dare to be tragic human beings, for you will be released and redeemed."[82]

In the working note of February 1959, Merleau-Ponty refuses the Nietzschean "*circulus vitiosus deus,*" erases it, and replaces it with another name, "*Sigè* the Abyss." *Sigē* = silence. This is the name Merleau-Ponty gives to the history of Being, and it is essential to remember that for Merleau-Ponty, an abyss is about depth, but it is not a nothingness (*S* 21; *Si* 29). "What will this silence be?" Merleau-Ponty asks (*VI* 179; *VIn* 233). After and through the intensity of rhythm and feeling—"the initial yes, the undividedness of feeling" (*IPP* 199; *RC* 179)—after the tumult of words and the turbulence of philosophy and myth well spoken, then there is the spent, meditative repose. In a tour de force, this kind of silence was named by Paul Claudel at the end of the first chapter of *Art poétique* titled

"Knowledge of Time" ("Connaissance du temps"): "Time is the means offered to all that which will be to be, in order to be no more. It is the *Invitation to Death* extended to each sentence, to decay in the explanatory and total harmony, to consummate the word of adoration, whispered in the ear of *Sigè,* the Abyss."[83] In the name *Sigē* that Merleau-Ponty appropriates from Claudel, Merleau-Ponty directs us away from the wisdom of Silenus and toward the word of adoration. And if it seems odd that this full and pregnant silence would yet be a word, this is not surprising, for this silence, the philosopher says, "will *not be the contrary* of language" (*VI* 179; *VIn* 233). This is a word that is "whispered," and in the whisper of this silence there endures "a radiant image and a particular rhythm."

8

Beauty and the Sublime

The eye accomplishes the prodigious work of opening the soul to what is not soul—the joyous realm of things and their god, the sun.

—Leonardo da Vinci, *Treatise on Painting*, quoted in Merleau-Ponty, "Eye and Mind"

Hence the feeling of the sublime is a feeling of displeasure that arises from the imagination's inadequacy, in an aesthetic estimation of magnitude . . . but is at the same time also a pleasure.

—Immanuel Kant, *Critique of Judgment*

As a philosopher of the beautiful, Merleau-Ponty is also a philosopher of the sublime, though he rarely used either of these words. The argument regarding the philosophy of Merleau-Ponty and the beautiful has already largely been made, though we now wish to measure our conclusions in comparison with the aesthetic of Kant. Above all, we now turn our attention fully to the question of the sublime. In the 1956–60 "Nature" course notes, we find Merleau-Ponty fully engaged with Kant's *Critique of Judgment,* this work that gives us analytics of both the beautiful and the sublime. When Merleau-Ponty cited the third *Critique* in the preface to *Phenomenology of Perception* from 1945 and agreed with Kant that "in experiencing the beautiful, I am aware of a harmony between sensation and concept, between myself and others, which is itself without any concept" (*PP* xvii; *PhP* xii), that passage had gone on to speak of imagination and aesthetic judgment as themselves conditions for the categorial activity of knowledge. "If [as Kant contends] the subject has a nature, then the hidden art of the imagination must condition the categorial activity. It is no longer merely the aesthetic judgment, but knowledge too which rests upon this art, an art which forms the basis of the unity of consciousness and of consciousnesses" (*PP* xvii; *PhP* xii). Since *Phenomenology of Perception* came near the beginning of Merleau-Ponty's career and the "Nature" lecture courses near the end, we may hazard the thought that Merleau-Ponty was engaged in a nearly lifelong project of coming to terms with Kant's "Transcendental Aesthetic" dealing with the intuitions of space and time and the faculties of the understanding, judgment, and imagination.[1] Thus, this chapter seeks an engagement of Merleau-Ponty's key aesthetic ideas with Kant's doctrines of the beautiful and sublime. This will lead us from Kant's humanist conception of beauty to a more ontological conception in which the beautiful is the depth, rhythm, and radiance of Being itself. Moreover, it will lead us toward thinking three aspects of the Merleau-Pontean sublime: phenomenological, historical, and ontological. The ontological sublime of the "event" will bring into play the philosophy of the sublime developed by Jean-François Lyotard, Merleau-Ponty's student and somewhat wayward "disciple."

Kant I: Contagion and the Beautiful

Intrinsic to the experience of aesthetic pleasure is something that we might call "contagion." Part and parcel of an experience of the beautiful is the desire to share the experience with others, to pass it on for the sake of mutual enjoyment and discussion, be it a beautiful painting, book, poem, film, dance, or musical work. We are even ready to discuss, debate, and defend our aesthetic views in the attempt to persuade others to share our enjoyment. Our efforts may or may not succeed, but the feeling of contagion witnesses against the complete subjectivity of aesthetic experience, that idea which claims that beauty is entirely in the eye of the beholder. A philosopher who held that view was George Santayana at the turn of the twentieth century in his famous definition from *The Sense of Beauty:* "Beauty is constituted by the objectification of pleasure. It is pleasure objectified."[2] Or, in a concluding formulation from the chapter on "The Nature of Beauty," Santayana says that there is no sharp line that separates beauty from the pleasures of sensation, just as the passage from sensation to perception is also gradual. "It depends upon the degree of objectivity my feeling has attained at the moment whether I say, 'It pleases me,' or 'It is beautiful.'"[3] This psychological "projection" theory of beauty subjectivizes beauty as the feeling of pleasure that one projects as if it were some quality in the thing enjoyed.

Yet the subjectivist view overlooks at least two things: the experience of the beautiful opens us up to a world beyond ourselves, and this is a world that is shared with those around us and whom we wish and expect to share in our experience. For example, if I am with friends in a forest setting and refer to a majestic oak as beautiful, I expect the others to "see what I mean," and if they do not, I expect of myself some ability to evoke their aesthetic sensitivity even though there is no concept, model, or formula to which we can appeal. I cannot say, for example, that this particular oak is a pin oak, a rare species seldom found in this region, for this simply classifies the oak cognitively as a member of a species and remains within the sphere of knowledge or information. Perhaps the quality of rarity might add a sense of "preciousness" that would influence aesthetic feeling, but not the mere species classification.[4] In general, the claim that something is beautiful is not a cognitive judgment, but at the same time it speaks in a voice that is plural and not merely personal. Therefore, one needs to speak about the features of the tree that evoke pleasure and delight—the shape of the tree and its sensuality, its vanilla-nutty aroma, the texture of its bark, the symmetry and asymmetry of its crossing branches, or the colors and patterns of its leaves. There is a paradox here inasmuch as the experience of the beautiful is a personal feeling, yet nevertheless results in a contagion that is the irresistible demand of sharing that experience.

This paradox—that aesthetic judgment is rooted in subjective feeling yet makes a claim to universality—is what Kant called the "remarkable feature" of aesthetic judgment. He wrote: "This special characteristic of an aesthetic judgment [of reflection], the universality to be found in judgments of taste, is a remarkable feature, not indeed for the logician but certainly for the transcendental philosopher" (*CJ* 8/57). Kant speaks of an imperative or "ought" with respect to aesthetic experience, but it is not the same "ought" of moral experience, which is governed by a rule. He writes: "Whoever declares something to be beautiful holds that everyone *ought* to give his approval to the object at hand and that he too should declare it beautiful" (*CJ* 19/86). The "*ought*" involved here is "solicitation" or invitation, and Kant makes it clear that this "*ought*" does not say that everyone will agree with our aesthetic judgment. Ultimately, he argues that there must be an a priori "common sense" as transcendental ground of the universality of aesthetic judgment, yet he concedes that this common aesthetic sense remains a "mere ideal standard" (*CJ* 22/89). Aesthetic judgments remain outside the domain of the faculty of the understanding and determinate concepts, therefore there is no concept to which one can appeal and be assured of universal agreement. With Kant's notion of the universality and necessity of taste, we have begun at an advanced point in the "Analytic of the Beautiful," in fact in the "Third Moment of Judgments of Taste," and we need to retreat somewhat and proceed more patiently in clarifying how Kant understands aesthetic judgment and the relation between aesthetic and cognitive judgments.

Kant delineates four moments of the beautiful falling under four headings derived from the *Critique of Pure Reason:* quantity, quality, relation, and modality. These have to do with the logical properties of judgments, including judgments of taste, even though judgments of taste are aesthetic judgments (*aisthesis* = "to sense") and not cognitive judgments. As the result of all four moments of the beautiful, Kant argues, in sum, that when we judge something to be beautiful we are making a genuine judgment of taste that has at least four components: it involves no empirical, theoretical, or practical interest; it is a singular judgment, rather than universal, which means it is about some one single instance of beauty, yet its content requires everyone else to agree with the judgment; it involves a feeling of pleasure or delight without any concept of the pleasure's purpose; and it bears a necessity that Kant calls "exemplary," meaning a "subjective universality" (*CJ* 22/89).[5] Thus, in a sense, Kant offers a hedonic theory of beauty grounded in our feeling of pleasure or delight, but the hedonic theory becomes increasingly qualified such that the pleasure involved is *contemplative* only and has to do with the disinterested contemplation of *form* (*CJ* 5/51). Each of these terms—pleasure, interest, and form—is at the center of controversy in explicating Kant's aesthetic of the beautiful, so let us move through them one at a time.

The pleasure involved in the experience of the beautiful is, for Kant, one of three different kinds of liking that must be distinguished carefully. Aesthetic judgment rests upon a special and distinctive kind of pleasure or "liking" different both from "agreeableness" and from "goodness" or "endorsement." Agreeableness is a kind of pleasantness that gratifies us, or as Kant says, "what the senses like in sensation" (*CJ* 3/47), and this kind of pleasantness or gratification is shared with nonhuman animals, for example, the pleasure of eating when hungry. Agreeableness in this sense is a subjective sensation linked with a particular organ of sense, the "taste" of food on the tongue in the case of eating, which is not what Kant means by "aesthetic taste." A liking for goodness is a moral liking that requires knowing the determinate concept of the thing or object and recognizing the object as an instance of the concept. Thus, the object comes under the judgment of practical reason and pure duty. Moral pleasure is a liking for the existence of the object, and thus is interested in Kant's sense. The distinctive pleasantness involved in the experience of beauty, therefore, is divorced both from the pleasure of sensation and that of a determinate concept that endorses the existence of something. Kant summarizes: "We call *agreeable* what GRATIFIES us, *beautiful* what we just

LIKE, *good* what we ESTEEM or *endorse* [*billigen*], i.e., that to which we attribute objective value" (*CJ* 5/52). The pure or disinterested form of liking peculiar to the beautiful does not arise from desires or needs and is, therefore, a judgment of "free beauty." It is "a non-conceptual awareness of a harmony," Kant says, "between imagination and understanding; in an aesthetic judgment of reflection we hold, for comparison, a *given* form up to the form of that harmony" (*CJ* 5/51, note 19).

Kant conceives the perceptual form of an object as the spatiotemporal relations among its elements or parts, and therefore the pleasure in the beautiful arises from the object's spatiotemporal structure. This form is to be differentiated from both charms, by which Kant understands what he regards as mere ornamental features of an object such as matter or color, and emotions: "Any taste remains barbaric if its liking requires that charms and emotions be mingled in, let alone if it makes these the standard of its approval" (*CJ* 13/69). Beautiful forms are those that the imagination would produce if at play under no constraint, that it would delight in producing for no other aim or purpose than to please itself, and certainly for no desire or need. Kant's concept of form means that the senses of smell, taste, and touch are too formless and amorphous to play a proper role in aesthetic judgment; only vision and hearing are properly formed. Thus, the smell of a rose, the taste of food or wine, and the texture of a fine wool, for example, are excluded from aesthetic experience. The visual arts and music are at the center of aesthetic experience, as are natural objects of vision and sound: a landscape or a sunset, birdsong or the rhythm of waves lapping the shore.

Before we begin with an analysis of Merleau-Ponty's response to all of this, we should pause to remember the historical context with which Merleau-Ponty was engaged, and that was the neo-Kantianism of Paris in the 1930s and 1940s, and particularly that of Léon Brunschvicg (1869–1944), the most influential professor at the Sorbonne while Merleau-Ponty was a student there from 1926 to 1930. Brunschvicg's presence, as well as that of Émile Bréhier, loomed very large while Merleau-Ponty did his postgraduate research on perception at the École Normale Supérieure from 1935 to 1939. Brunschvicg lectured on Plato, Descartes, Spinoza, Kant, and Pascal, but it was the mathematical Pascal he liked and not the existential Pascal of the famous wager.[6] Although Brunschvicg's book and lectures on the history of consciousness were influenced by Hegel's doctrine that thought and ideas occur in a historical development, there were no courses on Hegel and, of course, no courses on Marx, so that Merleau-Ponty attended Alexandre Kojève's lectures on Hegel at the École Pratique des Hautes Études.[7] Therefore, Merleau-Ponty no doubt developed something of an antipathy toward the neo-Kantianism that dominated his formal education. Kant was a persistent presence throughout Merleau-Ponty's *Phenomenology of Perception* and Brunschvicg a presence in the footnotes. In the first "Nature" course of 1956–57, Merleau-Ponty devotes an entire section to Brunschvicg's ideas of space and time and treats them as a transition from Kant to the Romanticism of Schelling. To paint with a very broad brush regarding *Phenomenology of Perception,* Merleau-Ponty's book moves from a rather sympathetic stance toward Kant in the preface, where he says that Kant had already discovered the notion of intentionality prior to Husserl and phenomenology, to a firm resistance against Kant as part of Cartesian intellectualism in the book's main dialectic between empiricism and intellectualism. Thus, though we are bringing Merleau-Ponty's aesthetic into a dialogue with Kant's, we should remember this context and these resistances.

Thus, to proceed: regarding Kant's account of the subjective universality of aesthetic judgment, we have already noted Merleau-Ponty's firm agreement with this position in the preface to *Phenomenology of Perception.* In experiencing the beautiful, we are aware of a harmony between sensation and concept, between myself and others, which is itself without any concept. Kant shows, Merleau-Ponty states in the first "Nature" course of 1956–57, that the understanding is at the service of the imagination in aesthetic judgment, which consists in the reconciliation of passivity and activity, "receptivity and spontaneity" (*N* 23; *NN* 43). The predominant role of the imagination over the understanding renders the experience of the beautiful a kind of pleasure that is without a concept, which Merleau-Ponty takes the opportunity to point out means the reconciliation of passivity and activity, a kind of dispossession or taking hold of the self by the outside. However, Merleau-Ponty argues against Kant's attempt to ground this "happy accident" of universal aesthetic judgment transcendentally. Kant's defense of a transcendental a priori "common sense" of aesthetic judgment, Merleau-Ponty says, turns into a humanist idea of nature that is implicitly supported in its background by theism or even polytheism. Merleau-Ponty says Kant's account is a "demonology" of supranatural forces or a "polytheism" (*N*26; *NN*46), because for Kant, the beauty found in nature renders beauty part of the ultimate aim or final goal of the natural order, an order, therefore, that cannot be limited to a purposeless mechanism. Kant's doctrine of an aesthetic common sense posits Nature as a system whose principle we do not find anywhere in the categories of the understanding, the principle of purposiveness. Kant wrote: "Under this principle, appearances must be judged as belonging not merely to nature as governed by its purposeless mechanism, but also to [nature considered by] analogy with art" (*CJ*23/99).

Merleau-Ponty's own philosophical account of the subjective universality of aesthetic experience breaks with transcendental philosophy. In *Phenomenology of Perception,* he states that phenomenology is involved with achieving a "new definition of the *a priori*" (*PP* 220; *PhP* 255) involving two aspects. The starting point of a new genealogy of the a priori is our affective experience, which means the lived structures of embodiment. In short, there is too little body in Kant's a priori. Kant's conclusion, Merleau-Ponty writes, "that I am a consciousness which embraces and constitutes the world . . . caused him to overlook the phenomenon of the body and that of the thing" (*PP* 303; *PhP* 349–50). Furthermore, the turn to embodied affection and auto-affection means that "the *a priori* is not knowable in advance of experience" and "there can be no question of distinguishing two elements of knowledge: one *a priori* and the other *a posteriori*" (*PP* 220; *PhP* 255). Merleau-Ponty argues that a priori truths are experience understood, reflected upon, made explicit. For example, it indeed would be contradictory to assert that the sense of touch is devoid of spatiality, and it is a priori impossible to touch without touching in space, but this is due to our bodily experience of a world. This does not represent any necessity external to touch, but comes about spontaneously in the experience of touching itself (*PP* 221; *PhP* 255–56). Thus, the a priori is a "historical *a priori*" and "history is neither a perpetual novelty, nor a perpetual repetition, but the *unique* movement which creates stable forms and breaks them up" (*PP* 88; *PhP* 104).

By the time of *The Visible and the Invisible,* Merleau-Ponty's new genealogy of the a priori had become the notion of the "sensible idea" that we have discussed in chapter 6 in relation to melody, color, and love. The meaning of the melody is inseparable from its expression, for melody is a sensible idea, in which essence and existence are intermingled. What is true of the musical idea is also true of the logic of color, namely that colors exist "without equivalents" intellectually, yet manifest "their logic, their coherence, their points of intersection, their concordances" (*VI* 149; *VIn* 194). We stress again that it is essential to these sensible ideas that they are known in and through the aesthesiological body and, in fact, would be entirely inaccessible if we were "pure mind," disembodied. Then they would truly be unknowable to us. In the sensible idea, body and mind, visible and invisible, are necessarily commingled, and sensibility and particularity are necessary to this kind of knowing. We remember the example that Merleau-Ponty adapted from Heidegger: the essence is in the red like the memory of the high school building is in its odor. Merleau-Ponty puts it this way: "They could not be given to us *as ideas* except in a carnal experience. . . . It is that they owe their authority, their fascinating, indestructible power, precisely to the fact that they are in transparency behind the sensible, or in its heart" (*VI* 150; *VIn* 194). This "knowing by sentiment [*connaissance par sentiment*]" (*VI* 249; *VIn* 297) that conjoins perception or sensibility with "feeling" led us previously to the expression, "having a feel for" something, rather than the mere state of pleasure or pain. We have a feel for a relationship or for a particular artist and style, which means a specially acquired sensitivity that has become sedimented in our bodily life. Speaking conceptually, this is pre-intellectual knowing, but nevertheless it is intelligent knowing. Sensible knowing is less precise conceptually than intellectual ideas of "pure ideality" and necessarily is somewhat "veiled with shadows" (*VI* 150; *VIn* 195). In *Ideas I,* Husserl himself had stated that for a genuinely descriptive phenomenology, in contrast with exact geometrical concepts, essences necessarily often retain a quality of vagueness or inexactness, and he gives as examples the meanings of the words "notches," "scalloped," "lens-shaped," and "umbelliform."[8]

Since Merleau-Ponty's account stresses melody together with color, his reworking of the a priori in terms of sensible ideas broadens Kant's limitation of aesthetic experience to form and includes color as something crucial within the beautiful, and much more central and worthy than mere ornamentation or "charm." The essence of a certain color of red, Merleau-Ponty writes, "is a *Wesen* that in principle is accessible only through the seeing, and is accessible as soon as the seeing is given, has then no more need to be *thought:* seeing is this sort of thought that has no need to think in order to possess the *Wesen*" (*VI* 247; *VIn* 295–96). Furthermore, the word "feeling" (*sentiment*), or having a "feel for" a musical idea or color juxtaposition, brings us to Kant's severance of beauty from the emotions. Kant requires that the appreciation of beauty not only pertain to form rather than charms, such as color, but also that beauty be dissociated from emotions: "Emotion," he wrote, "does not belong to beauty at all" (*CJ* 14/72). Yet, for Merleau-Ponty, beauty has many registers and intensities in different media from painting to music to poetry, and in different objects from artworks to human bodies to the things of nature. Some feelings awakened by beauty are very close to perception itself and seem almost purified of desire as Kant prescribed, as we enjoy the experience free of any longings or demands other than the simple "again" as we experience the serene pleasures of repetition and variation. Much less serene, much more intense feelings extend to joy and rapture. Rapture is "ascent beyond oneself" that risks the self, so that in reaching out toward the beautiful, Heidegger has written, we are "reaching out toward what we believe we can but barely overcome, barely survive."[9] Heidegger cites Rilke's "First Elegy" to describe the feeling of rapture that is quickened by the beautiful:

> For the beautiful is nothing
> but the beginning of the terrible, a beginning we but barely endure;
> and it amazes us so, since calmly it disdains
> to destroy us.[10]

Here it is resonant to recall our discussion of desire and love as clairvoyance that can tear us: "Realization is not what was expected, but still that which was wanted: we move forward backwards, we do not choose directly, but in an oblique way, and yet we do what we want: love is a clairvoyance: it leads us just to what can tear us [*ce qui peut nous déchirer*]" (*IP* 75).

Other experiences of the beautiful—these have to do with suffering and brokenness—arouse in us feelings of turbulence and sorrow that are linked to desires for succor and healing. Ralph Waldo Emerson has written that "even a corpse has its own beauty" inasmuch as "there is no object so foul that intense light will not make beautiful."[11] Dante's *Divine Comedy* captured Rodin's concentration and imagination as Rodin worked for more than twenty years to create *The Gates of Hell,* a work that he would never complete. In Dante's pages, Rodin saw the suffering bodies of another generation and learned that "there is a kind of weeping that encompasses the whole body, and that tears can come from all the pores."[12] Most agree that music, above all—with "its ebb and flow, its growth, its upheavals, its turbulence" ("EM" 123, *OE* 14), in Merleau-Ponty's phrase that we appropriated for interpreting the musical paintings of Paul Klee—music most powerfully creates an expanse of emotions that can scarcely be contained, and together with the sounds of poetry gives us the sonics, metrics, and rhythms that map the human soul.[13] "This, I believe, is the role of art," Rodin said. "The forms created should only provide a pretext for the emotion to expand indefinitely."[14]

Mikel Dufrenne argues in *The Phenomenology of Aesthetic Experience* that music above all discloses the meaning of reality and truth in the arts, for aesthetic meaning is not about representation, as in other arts such as painting, sculpture, and even literature that might mislead us, but presentation and discovery of reality: "The aesthetic object is thus an eminently real object, but it does not pretend to produce the real within itself or even to copy the real. The aesthetic object *says* the real and thus discovers it."[15] Therefore, what is produced and discovered musically is an entire world. "When we say that the joy expressed by a fugue opens Bach's world to us, the word 'world' indicates a relation to the real. There are neither images to populate this world nor concepts to catalogue it, yet it remains a true world."[16] In the music of Bach, we are given the whole sense of existence as a modality of joy. Suppose, Dufrenne says, that a captive in his prison, delivered over to hatred and unable to see the sky, hears a Bach fugue. "He knows clearly that the music is not meant for him. Someone has banned him from the world of Bach, or he may have banned himself."[17] There is also an Offenbachian sense of existence just as there is a Mozartian one.[18] The work of art is a light—a radiance—that illuminates aspects of the real, and its feelings deliver us over to a whole affective sense of the world. Reality itself is made in the revelations emerging from the creation and appreciation of the beautiful. We can lessen the tension in beauty's aesthetic paradox—subjective feeling is yet not merely private or personal but a contagious plural—by remembering as well that it is the beautiful that also gives us the feeling for the mystery of the world; it gives us the world as idea and feeling, but also as a question and interrogative power. We recall that Rodin has said: "Every masterpiece has this mysterious characteristic. One always finds in it a little bewilderment. Remember the question mark that hovers over all the paintings of Leonardo."[19] This mystery and interrogative power of the beautiful also draws us toward others with whom to puzzle, reflect, agree, and disagree.

The desire for the beautiful is thus more elemental and ontological than Kant's humanist conception could allow. The beautiful is the depth, repetition, variation, rhythm, and radiance of Being itself. In sum, Merleau-Ponty contests against Kant on the a priori, on form (color), and disinterestedness (emotion and desire). But Kant is to be praised for his conception of beauty as a subjective universality, for what follows from ontological, deep beauty is an imperative of "contagion": this beauty "ought" to be for all.

Kant II: The Natural Sublime

From the Kantian cleavage between disinterested contemplative pleasure on the one hand and emotion on the other, there opened up a split, a gap, between the beautiful and the sublime, for Kant thought of the sublime as a powerful emotion *in us*. That there is something artificial about this split and opposition between the beautiful and the sublime has been implicit in our studies of Merleau-Ponty's artists. We were led by an internal logic to use the term "sublime" in speaking of *The Burghers of Calais,* as did Rilke, and we also addressed that term to Rodin's *Balzac*.[20] It must be that there is a chiasm between the beautiful and sublime when beauty grows powerful, transcendent, and majestic, and that is the argument we seek to establish in our consideration of Kant's analytic of the sublime. Once again, we will attend to Kant's analysis before turning to the ideas of Merleau-Ponty.

The "Analytic of the Sublime" in the *Critique of Judgment* actually opens by noting the continuities between the beautiful and the sublime before Kant pushes them apart. These continuities are that we like both the beautiful and the sublime for their own sake; both presuppose that we make a judgment of reflection rather than a judgment of sense or of logic; in neither does our judgment depend upon mere agreeableness nor liking for the good; both are indeterminate with respect to concepts; both are connected with the power of exhibition in the imagination; and both kinds of judgment are singular ones that "nonetheless proclaim themselves universally valid for all subjects" (*CJ* 23/97). Kant's later *Anthropology from a Pragmatic Point of View* (1798) also noted the mixture of the sublime with the beautiful in a given artwork: "The *representation* of the sublime can and should nevertheless be beautiful in itself; otherwise it is coarse, barbaric, and contrary to good taste."[21] Nevertheless, that a representation of the sublime in a work of art is also beautiful, perhaps in a painting of a canyon or a waterfall by Thomas Cole or Frederic Church, by no means implies that these are identically the same in the Kantian aesthetic project, and indeed, Kant quickly sets forth their differences in the *Critique.* On my reading there are six such differences: the beautiful concerns the form of the object, and therefore is bounded, but the sublime consists in an unboundedness, even formlessness; the beautiful is connected with the presentation of quality, the sublime with quantity; the beautiful carries a feeling of life's being furthered, the sublime a momentary inhibition of vital forces; the sublime is an emotion of seriousness rather than play in the imagination, as is beauty; the beautiful is a positive pleasure, while the sublime is a negative pleasure that both attracts and repels the mind as admiration and respect; natural beauty carries purposiveness in its form (a "purposiveness without purpose," in Kant's phrase), whereas a feeling of the sublime may appear contra-purposive and even violent to our imagination.

These differences culminate in a final mark of differentiation: we may quite correctly call nature itself beautiful, but all we are entitled to say of a natural object is that "the object is suitable for exhibiting a sublimity that can be found in the mind" (*CJ* 23/99). Kant gives the image of the stormy ocean as his first instance: the ocean heaved up by storms cannot be called sublime since "the sight of it is horrible; and one must already have filled one's mind with all sorts of ideas if such an intuition is to attune it to a feeling that is itself sublime" (*CJ* 23/99). Thus, Kant concludes that for the beautiful in nature we must seek an explanation outside ourselves, but for the sublime a basis merely within ourselves "in the way of thinking that introduces sublimity into our presentation of nature" (*CJ* 23/100).

As is well known, Kant further divides the natural sublime into the mathematically and the dynamically sublime. In place of the restful contemplation found in the beautiful, the sublime carries with it a mental "agitation," the first kind of which is mathematical, the second a dynamic agitation or unrest. Lyotard has urged us not to construe this as meaning that there are two different kinds of sublime, mathematical and dynamical, but rather sublimity is an emotional "nexus" that may be viewed under the category of the mathematical and the category of the dynamical.[22] The mathematical sublime pertains to what is absolutely large, by which Kant means "what is large beyond all comparison." This is the feeling that the imagination is inadequate for comprehending the whole of an object, and this faltering before magnitude occurs in the apprehension, not of a work of art or of a natural thing such as an animal with a determinate concept, but rather in the apprehension of "crude nature." Kant gives the examples of mountain masses piled on one another in wild disarray with their pyramids of ice, or the gloomy raging sea. As well, he suggests that we consider the earth's diameter or the immense multitude of nebulous stars that comprise the Milky Way system. This is the place to draw the connection between the "Analytic of the Sublime" and the conclusion of Kant's second *Critique,* which speaks famously of the "increasing admiration and awe" inspired by "the starry heavens above."[23] An object is *colossal,* Kant tells us, if its concept is "too large for any exhibition." An object is *monstrous* "if by its magnitude it nullifies the purpose that constitutes its concept" (*CJ* 26/109). The colossal "borders on the relatively monstrous" (*CJ* 26/109). Kant does not explain further what he means by a "magnitude that nullifies the purpose that constitutes its concept" nor does he give any examples of the monstrous, but clearly he understands this term in relation to magnitude in nature and not deformity, ugliness, or cruelty that we might associate with someone like Frankenstein's unfortunate creature. For crude nature, the colossal, and the monstrous, the feeling or emotion evoked in us is a feeling of respect, Kant tells us, and the feeling is a displeasure, because it arises from the imagination's inadequacy, but it is at the same time a feeling of pleasure, for it is in harmony with the rational idea of striving to estimate the magnitude of any sense object. We find a similar torsion that combines pleasure and displeasure also at work in the dynamical sublime, which pertains to nature as a *might* and as arousing fear, including instances such as threatening rocks, thunderclouds accompanied by lightning and thunderclaps, volcanoes, hurricanes, the high waterfall of a mighty river, and more. The sight of such natural forces carries the oddly paradoxical feelings of both attraction and repulsion. Provided we are in a safe place, we take a strange pleasure in these inasmuch as they allow us to discover in ourselves an ability to resist "which gives us the courage to believe that we could be a match for nature's seeming omnipotence" (*CJ* 28/120).

The agitation of soul that occurs in both kinds of sublime, magnitude and might, may be compared, Kant tells us, with a vibration that is a rapid alternation of repulsion from, and attraction to, one and the same object. Kant's text on this emotional tension, or emotional dissonance, is highly engaging:

> If a thing is excessive for the imagination and the imagination is driven to such excess as it apprehends the thing in intuition, then the thing is, as it were, an abyss in which the imagination is afraid to lose itself. Yet, at the same time, for reason's idea of the supersensible this same thing is not excessive but conforms to reason's law to give rise to such striving by the imagination. Hence the thing is now attractive to the same degree to which formerly it was repulsive to mere sensibility. (*CJ* 27/115)

Respect, admiration, and awe, on the one hand, in tandem with fear on the other, even fear of an abyss—these are the emotions of the Kantian natural sublime, both pleasant and unpleasant, discordant yet held in a simultaneous unity.

Clearly, there are ways in which we must distance the philosophy of Merleau-Ponty from the Kantian sublime, before we seek to bring out threads of relation between them. For one thing, Kant's account locates the sublime as an emotion experienced in inner consciousness. The sublime feeling occurs "within" me and does not pertain to a natural object or thing "outside" me. This separation fails to take cognizance of the way in which emotions themselves exhibit intentionality with objective reference in at least part of their structure. One does not experience anger without that anger being directed toward someone, just as one does not experience fear without that fear being directed outward toward some specific object, and just as one does not love without loving someone in particular. This is not to forget both the behavioral component and the subjective "feel" of an emotion, the former having to do with what we mean when we say an emotion moves us toward some action, the latter having to do with the physiological changes we undergo when experiencing an emotion, such as heightened or lowered blood pressure, changes in breathing rate, and inner pressures and flows such as when, in fear, the blood drains from our face or when, with the blush of embarrassment, it rushes there. In their cognitive or appraisal feature, emotions are value judgments about the world: anger is the judgment that someone has wronged us unjustly and the wrong needs to be repaired; fear is the judgment that some object, event, or person might be harmful to us; love is the judgment that someone is worthy of our affection and devotion, or in the words of the *Symposium,* that the beloved is beautiful. Love involves double reference both to the one who loves and the beloved who is lovely. Merleau-Ponty writes in *Phenomenology of Perception* that love may actually be "in" a bouquet of flowers, perhaps in a way that remains ambiguous to an outside observer, though the meaning of the flowers is clear enough to the recipient:

> Love *is* in the flowers prepared by Félix de Vandenesse for Madame de Mortsauf, just as unmistakeably as in a caress . . . The flowers are self-evidently a love-bouquet, and yet it is impossible to say what in them signifies love, and that is even the reason why Mme. de Mortsauf can accept them without breaking her vows. There is no way of understanding them other than by looking at them, but to the beholder they say what they mean. (*PP* 321; *PhP* 371)

For the case of the natural sublime, therefore, the emotions of awe and terror that natural wildness inspires reflect our appraisal of the natural order as magnificent, yet dangerous and beyond comprehension. There is no reason to subjectivize and compartmentalize the sublime as "inner" and nature as "outer." Just as for the beautiful, the experience is between the world and us, so it is also for the experience of the natural sublime. The experience is two-sided, fully relational between perceiver and world, just as perceiving the Grand Canyon or the Milky Way as sublime is fully relational: awe, wonder, and fear are about magnitude and might in the natural order.

Another problematic feature of Kant's account of the natural sublime is its restriction of the sublime feeling to nature rather than artworks, for the purposiveness of an artwork is too determinate, Kant would say. Here it seems clear that Kant was imprisoned by eighteenth-century art, as is most evident by his limitation of the sublime to nature, even on the cusp of the coming of Beethoven and Goethe, whose music and poetry vindicated the sublime as an artistic reality long before the appropriation of the sublime by Barnett Newman, Mark Rothko, and Jackson Pollock. Already in the late nineteenth and early twentieth centuries, Rodin's *Balzac* was a work of abstract art that was criticized precisely for its formlessness. We recall that critics accused Rodin of having depicted Balzac as a penguin, a snowman, a sack of coal, and a shapeless larva, of presenting him as if he had just gotten out of bed to confront a creditor. The work was said to possess "too much philosophy and not enough modeling."[24] Moreover, Rodin was but a precursor to the more fully developed abstractions that would follow in Cézanne and Klee. The story grows even worse for Kant's bifurcation of the artwork from nature in the realm of the sublime with the appearance of the earthscapes of artists such as Andy Goldsworthy with his nests, piles of rocks, leaf paintings, and snow paintings. Equally to the point are earthworks such as Robert Smithson's *Spiral Jetty* (1970) created at Rozel Point in the Great Salt Lake, Utah, the *Spiral Hill* (1971) at Emmen, Holland, and many others. *Spiral Jetty* is as sublime a work of art as one can ever imagine, as sublime as *Balzac,* as sublime as the vast red and white streaked desert that surrounds it, as sublime as the sunsets and nighttime moonlight that bathe it in warm, varied, and luminous colors. It is impossible to imagine, faced with such artistic wonders, that Kant would deny these earthscapes and earthworks the standing of proper artworks. This is not to suggest a crude historicism, that if only Kant had experienced more contemporary artworks he would have changed his aesthetic philosophy. Rather, it is to stress once again Merleau-Ponty's contention for the importance of modern art, and that if not Kant, then certainly we ourselves ought to draw out a philosophy of the beautiful and sublime in close concert with the experiments of modern artists.

Another point of contention with Kant's account of the natural sublime is that it remains caught in a humanist or anthropological framework that seems to bring with it a self-congratulatory, rationalist atmosphere; on the one hand, the sublime is an evocation of respect for the might and magnitude of nature, yet, on the other hand, Kant turns this into a contention for the superiority of humans over nonhuman nature due to the human rational faculty. He ends section 28, "On Nature as a Might," by remarking that "we can become conscious of our superiority to nature within us, and thereby also to nature outside us . . . by the ability, with which we have been endowed, to judge nature without fear and to think of our vocation as being sublimely above nature" (*CJ* 28/123). This Enlightenment bent leads on to a final caution. The rational faculty that calms our fear of nature's might is also continuous, in Kant's text, with a surprising linkage of the sublime emotion with a technological sublime. What is it, he asks, that is of highest admiration? He answers: "It is a person who is not terrified, not afraid, and hence does not yield to danger but promptly sets to work with vigor and full deliberation." This, Kant continues, explains our "superior esteem for the warrior" whose mind cannot be subdued by danger. "Even war has something sublime about it if it is carried on in an orderly way and with respect for the sanctity of the citizens' rights" (*CJ* 28/121–22).[25] In this instance, for Kant, the natural sublime is continuous with the technological sublime.[26]

The beautiful and the sublime have different emotional intensities to be sure, yet rather than a sharp separation, they also intermingle in a way that we might think of as what Merleau-Ponty designates as "lace-works." In a lovely text from Merleau-Ponty's working notes discussing both perception and emotion, he introduced this metaphor:

> The whole architecture of the notions of psycho-logy (perception, idea—affection, pleasure, desire, love, Eros) all that, all this bric-a-brac, is suddenly clarified when one ceases to think all these terms as *positive* (the more or less dense "spiritual") in order to think them not as negatives or negentities (for that brings back the same difficulties), but as *differentiations* of one sole and *massive* adhesion to Being which is the flesh (eventually as "lace-works"). (*VI* 270; *VIn* 318)

"Laceworks" (*les dentelles*) give us the image of stitching or crossing that ties threads together without closing off airiness; in fact, incorporating airiness within the work itself. The image translates much of the interrelationship we are seeking: touches between the beautiful and sublime, yet gaps. It strikes us as too easy to say that the sublime is beauty heightened or beauties in the extreme, for there are differences to be mapped, as Kant has delineated. The emotional registers are different, as are the cognitive features and pleasures. Yet a bifurcation such as two separated fabrics does not capture the continuities between the beautiful and sublime, as the image of lacework does: continuities with gaps. In the same note, Merleau-Ponty adds that intentionality and affectivity are not "transversal" to one another as Scheler had set forth the problematic; rather, each is a dimension of one and the same Being, Flesh, and thus each is internal to the other. Edward Casey has made the point this way: "We can say that the sublime arises from the interaction of earth and world—and of sky and sea—with the mind (or better, *psyche*) in the creation of a work of art. Nature is not sublime in itself—with this much of Kant's theory we can agree—but it *becomes* sublime by a process of psychical internalization that leads in turn to re-exteriorization."[27] Therefore, it seems to me critical, with these cautions clearly in view, that Merleau-Ponty's aesthetic of the beautiful be given its other side as an aesthetic of the sublime. There is in Merleau-Ponty the "happy Spring and generous beauty," as Bernard Sichère has said, but there is also the inhuman, wild meaning, and silence.[28] As we discussed previously in relation to "glimpses of beauty" in our second chapter on "Eye and Mind," Merleau-

Ponty himself spoke of the sublime in his defense of Sartre against the charges that Sartre was a "scandalous author." Sartre was not interested in a cult or "religion of the beautiful" wherein lies "the beauty of the Greek god," Merleau-Ponty says, but rather Sartre wrote "the violence of the sublime." This is a "minor sublimity, a sublimity without eloquence or illusions which is, I believe, an invention of our time" (*SNS* 43; *SeNS* 76). There are, we believe, three aspects of this philosophical figure of the Merleau-Pontean sublime: phenomenological, historical, and ontological. The phenomenological has to do with Merleau-Ponty's philosophy of perception, the historical with his late engagement with Husserl and the philosophy of wild being (*l'être sauvage*) and brute mind (*l'esprit brut*), and the ontological with the primordial source, the *il y a,* the origin and non-origin of the event.

Merleau-Ponty's account of an inhuman element in perception and the paintings of Cézanne is our first point of embarkation. Already in *The Structure of Behavior,* Merleau-Ponty had said that it was certain painters, especially Cézanne, who "have taught us . . . to regard faces as stones" (*SB* 167; *SC* 181). "Cezanne's Doubt" extended this thought: "Cézanne's people," Merleau-Ponty wrote, "are strange, as if viewed by a creature of another species. Nature itself is stripped . . . there is no wind in the landscape, no movement on the Lac d'Annecy; the frozen objects hesitate as at the beginning of the world" ("CD" 66; "DC" 28). So there is a primordial perception that has to do with thingliness, indestructibility, and sheer monumentality. The chapter of *Phenomenology of Perception* on "The Thing and the Natural World" says that ordinarily we do not notice the "nonhuman element" in things because our perception in the context of our everyday concerns "alights on things" only "sufficiently attentively to discover their familiar presence." Primary perception exports us out of everyday secondary perception into a world beyond the safety of personal history and subjectivity, into a world that is a stranger, "alien, no longer an interlocutor, but a resolutely silent Other." This is why the paintings of Cézanne are "those of a pre-world in which as yet no men existed" (*PP* 322; *PhP* 372). This vision "penetrates right to the root of things beneath the imposed order of humanity" ("CD" 67; "DC" 28). I contend that this is a perceptual sublime that bears many features of the Kantian sublime: the inhuman, awe and respect, yet risk and threat to personal safety and everyday preoccupations.

This leads on to a second point of contact centering on wildness and wild being. We find in Kant that the sublime is associated with "crude nature" and with wildness, which principally means a kind of immense formlessness. In Merleau-Ponty's last writings and *inédits,* he too speaks of wild being (*l'être sauvage*) and brute mind (*l'esprit brut*). In

"The Philosopher and His Shadow," Merleau-Ponty wrote with regard to Schelling: ""What resists phenomenology within us—natural being, the 'barbarous' source Schelling spoke of—cannot remain outside phenomenology and should have its place within it" (*S* 178; *Si* 225). And from the "Nature" courses, Merleau-Ponty speaks of Schelling regarding "this barbaric principle, the source of all grandeur and all beauty" (*N* 38; *NN* 62). Merleau-Ponty strove throughout his writings, especially his later works, to find a language of philosophy capable of expressing this wild being (*l'être sauvage*) and wild spirit within Being. At the end of *The Visible and the Invisible,* Merleau-Ponty wrote that "the whole of philosophy, as Husserl says, consists in restoring a power to signify, a birth of meaning, or a wild meaning [*un sens sauvage*]," and, following Valéry, calls this "the voice of no one . . . the very voice of the things, the waves, and the forests" (*VI* 155; *VIn* 203–4). The philosopher lives in between the polarity of an empty silence that would leave Being as we find it and striving to create a subtle and supple language that bears witness to the birthplace of the world from within the depths of Being itself.

While there is here a point of contact in Merleau-Ponty with the Kantian natural sublime, we also find a profound divergence. For Merleau-Ponty, this wild Being and wild meaning must be interpreted within the frame of history, multiples, and instituting. From the time of the "Institution" course in 1954–55 and forward, Merleau-Ponty's confrontations with the problems of historical time had taught him that speaking in such an unqualified way about primordial perception as giving us a genuine "thing-in-itself" or wild Being had to be qualified. The body's birth into a symbolic world of culture introduces an order of relations "that pure physiology and biology do not have the slightest idea of" (*N* 69; *NN* 86). We cited the text in our previous chapter regarding the material imaginary: seeing, touching, hearing, even disease itself now have a history: seeing is a crossing—a "strabism" (*N* 72; *NN* 103), i.e., "crossed eyes"—between nature and culture. This is what, in the context of the sublime, we should call Merleau-Ponty's discovery of a historical sublime within culture that seeks the renewal of culture. Thus, a historically sublime moment stands within a heritage but opens it up to a kind of "budding [*bourgeonnement*]" (*IP* 87) which designates "that fecundity of the products of a culture which continue to have value after their appearance and which open a field of investigations" in which they come to life again. Here there is some notion of rebirth, resurrection, or repetition that Husserl calls "the power to forget origins" in giving those origins new life, "which is the noble form of memory" ("ILVS" 96; *S* 59; *Si* 74). Advent is a "transfiguration" ("ILVS" 97; *S* 60; *Si* 75) of events that institutes meaning in history through its power in its own time to draw together an "elective affinity" of the ideas current at the time. Advent has "suggestive power in its inheritors" because there is in it an "excess" over and above the artist's own intentions and achievements. Within culture itself, there remains an unconquered and untamed excess or surplus that is capable of renewing culture, and the philosopher and the artist together seek an openness to this surplus. We find many lines of contact here with the experience, thinking, and writing of Henry David Thoreau, who not only argued that in nature and wilderness there is a Wildness that is "the preservation of the world," but this Wildness also has historical, cultural shape. There is Wildness in the forests, in the animals, and in us, but there is also a preserve of Wildness in "wild thinking" and "wild literature" that is particularly the domain of mythology and poetry.[29] There are many questions yet to be raised and discussed about this historical sublime: where exactly to situate it in history, if in the participants or the observers; whether it can be experienced in prospect or only in retrospect; and how strongly the analogies between the aesthetic sublime and historical sublime ought to be pursued. I think that such questions carry us somewhat beyond Merleau-Ponty toward Lyotard, but for our purposes we want to leave those questions in play and move to the third thread of a Merleau-Pontean sublime, namely that of the ontological sublime and the event.[30] This, in fact, brings into play Lyotard's "postmodern sublime."

Lyotard: The Sublime of the Event

To come to the point of the "postmodern sublime," with Jean-François Lyotard we may refer once again to Newman's breakthrough painting *Onement I* (1948) that we featured in our very opening chapter for its repudiation of "beauty." It is actually an unfinished work, for as Newman was at work, he suddenly was overwhelmed by it, stopped painting, and meditated about it for almost a year trying to understand it.[31] He found an emptiness in the work that was the emptiness, not of nothing, but of an original and sublime *il y a,* "there is something," that which we call oneness, origin, genesis, and creation. The title, *Onement,* suggests the conjunction of oneness with wonder and with moment. Harold Rosenberg expresses Newman's meaning this way:

> The commonsense response to Newman's paintings that there is "nothing" in them ought not to be dismissed—Newman's meaning lies in how this nothing is received. . . . His goal was to induce emptiness to

> exclaim its secrets. Aiming at the sublime, he knew that the sublime was neither yellow nor blue . . . His creations had to be black or red because they had to be something, so that they might function as part of a totality.[32]

Lyotard argues that Newman is emblematic of today's experimental arts that express the desire for the *event,* the desire, simply, *that something happen.* Can anything happen anymore? In this light, it is easy to see why the most contemporary experimental arts have evolved toward film, installation, and performance in the pursuit of this "happening." The modernist natural sublime is still about the thing and our feelings in the presence of the thing; the contemporary postmodern sublime is about the event, the moment of something happening—what Heidegger called an *Ereignis.* It is well known that Merleau-Ponty's philosophy of time in *Phenomenology of Perception* remained closely attached to Husserl's philosophy of internal time-consciousness, exemplified paradigmatically in the auditory retentions that remain present in something like hearing a melody. Though Merleau-Ponty did succeed in replacing the inner experience of the consciousness of time with the operative experience of time in our embodiment, his early philosophy of time remained largely within the Husserlian frame of temporal continuity. Lyotard emphasizes this point and even goes so far as to claim that the philosophy of time as continuity extends right on into Merleau-Ponty's later philosophy of Flesh. Lyotard argues that the "greatest of pitfalls" (*le point de leurre par excellence*) for Merleau-Ponty is the category of continuity.[33] It is both with and against Lyotard and other critics that we now argue for a philosophy of the event in Merleau-Ponty as an ontological meaning of the sublime.

Lyotard's early *Discours, figure,* a work that takes much of its inspiration directly from Merleau-Ponty, gives a "tamed" reading of the difference, desire, dispossession, and passivity that are at the heart of "Eye and Mind" and *The Visible and the Invisible.* Lyotard's reading of Merleau-Ponty "keeps the lid on" these ground-shaking topics, we might say, and we have taken the lid off in our own reading of Merleau-Ponty. Thus, if it is plausible to cast Merleau-Ponty as a philosopher of the beautiful, it would, for Lyotard, be impossible to find any notion of the sublime in the thought of Merleau-Ponty. To Lyotard, Merleau-Ponty remained a phenomenological philosopher caught up in the philosophic endeavor of unity and continuity. Lyotard agrees with us that Merleau-Ponty's "ultimate concept, his most delicate concept for the apprehension of the event-like quality of the datum, is surely not intentionality: it is passivity." But then he immediately offers this critique: "This concept can only function in the field set up by phenomenology, as the opposite or correlate of intentional activity, as its underlying support. . . . What Cézanne desires was Mount Sainte-Victoire to cease being a visual object and become an event in the visual field; and that is what the phenomenologist hopes to—and in my opinion cannot—understand."[34] Merleau-Ponty moved from the "I" to the anonymity of the "One" who speaks and thinks through us, Lyotard admits, but "consider the distance remaining between 'One' and 'That' [*entre On et Ça*]."[35] By this "That," Lyotard means the unconscious and unconscious desire. Yet this is a strange criticism, for we have just considered Merleau-Ponty's extensive reinterpretation of the meaning of the unconscious in our previous chapter. One final passage from Lyotard critical of Merleau-Ponty is illuminating:

> It is not the search for the conditions, anonymous or otherwise, of the data that immobilized Cézanne before his mountain; it was the search for the donation. Phenomenology cannot reach the donation because, faithful to the philosophical tradition of the West, it remains a reflection on knowledge, and the function of such a reflection is to reabsorb the event, to retrieve the Other in the Same.[36]

Perhaps it would be fair to say that we have offered throughout a reading of Merleau-Ponty that was already educated by Lyotard's criticisms, for everything has revolved around the reformed notion of the paradox of expression as a desire in between a Sartrean negativity and Freudian positivity that is the movement—not of need—but of life itself toward others and the world, a notion of divergence (*écart*) found in the repetitions and differences, themes and variations of the beautiful, and love as a bodily clairvoyance that both "does not know yet always has known" what it desires, which was Merleau-Ponty's double formula of the true meaning of the unconscious. Lyotard humbly states that "it may be arrogant to declare that what I am seeking here is, in the same direction as that indicated by Merleau-Ponty's last writing, why and how poetry and dreams are related to hyperreflection." Yet he shortly adds that though he is on the same path as Merleau-Ponty, he goes "in the other direction, our back turned to him."[37]

Yet, in Lyotard's reading, insufficient attention has been given to Merleau-Ponty's movement from Cézanne to Paul Klee, and from Husserl to Heidegger, not that Cézanne and Husserl are ever left behind. This intellectual movement brings Merleau-Ponty's aesthetic and ontology close to what Lyotard himself thinks: the aesthetic field, both as the field of perception and the field of artistic production, becomes the field of desire and loss, desire and distance, desire and dispossession. This is precisely the desire for the experience of Being itself, the *il y a* or "there is something." The opening section of "Eye and Mind" criticizes modern science for abandoning the "there is" in favor of techniques and manipulations of nature and puts forward the artist as the one who works that field: "Scientific thinking, a thinking which looks on from above, and thinks of the object-in-general, must return to the 'there is' which precedes it [*un 'il y a' prélable*]; to the site, the soil of the sensible and humanly modified world such as it is for our lives and for our bodies" ("EM" 122; *OE* 12). *The Visible and the Invisible* criticizes Cartesian philosophy in the same vein: "To reduce perception to the thought of perceiving," Merleau-Ponty argues, as Descartes posited in his "Optics"—"it is the mind which sees, not the eye"—"is to forego comprehending the effective world and move to a type of certitude that will never restore to us the 'there is' [*il y a*] of the world" (*VI* 36; *VIn* 57, 58). Merleau-Ponty's name for Being, Flesh, gives us a sensible feel for time. This is why Merleau-Ponty did not want an abstract concept such as Substance or even Life to carry the greatest philosophical weight.[38] He gave us a rich and long list of temporal metaphors for Flesh as a genesis: emergence, transcendence, coming of itself to itself, coiling up, reversal, doubling back, divergence from inside to outside. Flesh is the explosion of seedpods, the dehiscence of the colors of fire, the labor of pregnancy, the joy and pain of new life and separation, the work of mourning and grieving. "I call the world Flesh," Merleau-Ponty wrote, "in order to say that it is a *pregnancy* of possibles" (*VI* 250; *VIn* 298). Flesh is not a stranglehold of univocal Being-Knowing, for the Flesh that is flesh-and-blood time is as inscrutable, strange, foreign, and other as it is colorful, creative, and promiscuous. Something about world time, deep time, is at the heart of the last sentence of "Eye and Mind": "If creations are not permanent acquisitions, it is not just that, like all things, they pass away; it is also that they have almost their entire lives before them" ("EM" 149; *OE* 92–93).

Merleau-Ponty's later thought makes clear that the artwork participates in an order of time other than serial time, and this other order is about "event" and advent. We find in *The Visible and the Invisible* the thought of multiple historical times that encroach upon one another, multiple cultures and individuals that do not exist in a single serial space and time but in many spaces and times that pile up, proliferate, and encroach upon one another in differing ways that have to do with differing acts of genesis, production, and reproduction (*VI* 115; *VIn* 154–55). Within history, there is another sense of "event" than "mere events" that occupies a proximity and spacing of resonance with what Heidegger has meant by *Ereignis* and that brings into view an ontological sublime. Merleau-Ponty argues that the philosopher can participate in the return to the wonder of the "there is." This is the perceptual faith, that there is a world, that there is wildness, and that the world maintains a generosity that will speak to a spirit of wonder and openness. These experiences are connected with all that Merleau-Ponty has to say about the fecundity and fullness of silence, like Lyotard's notion of the event bordering on a silent and loving expectancy. The silence of things, like the silence of painting, is not mute, but pregnant and teeming with the figurations that call to be seen and to be expressed. We recall Merleau-Ponty's reference to the "mute radiance" (*le rayonnement muet*) of painting ("ILVS" 115; *S* 78; *Si* 97), which in this context we can also extend to nature. This mute radiance means that silence and vacuity are not defects, but the occasion for solitude and contemplation, a sense of fullness rather than emptiness. Again, we find a crossing between Merleau-Ponty and Heidegger on stillness and silence right down to the shared use of the Greek term *sigē*. Moreover, this is the reason we connect Merleau-Ponty on event and advent with Heidegger's *Ereignis*. "How does be-ing hold sway," Heidegger asks in *Contributions to Philosophy*. He answers: "Reticence in silence means mindful lawfulness of being reticent and silent (*sigē*). Reticence in silence is the 'logic' of philosophy."[39] From our discussion of the Dionysian and rhythm at the end of our previous chapter, we recall Merleau-Ponty's appropriation from Paul Claudel: "Time is the means offered to all that which will be to be, in order to be no more. It is the *Invitation to Death* extended to each sentence, to decay in the explanatory and total harmony, to consummate the word of adoration, whispered in the ear of *Sigè*, the Abyss" (*VI* 179; *VIn* 233).[40] Now here, and this is far from ordinary, joining Lyotard, Merleau-Ponty speaks of silence as abyssal. Thus, there is a contemplative aspect of sublimity in our confrontation with the immensities and grandeur of nature, and this contemplative aspect is indeed found as well in the zips of Newman and the bands of Rothko, wherein the beautiful has expanded in magnificence and transcendence, and thus mingles itself with the sublime.

Merleau-Ponty writes that nature, as well as Klee's touches (*taches*) of color, are "simultaneously older than everything and 'of the first day'" (*VI* 211 and 267; *VIn* 264 and 320). This paradoxical newness found in the repetitions of art, nature, and life puts the flow of time out of joint, introduces an exteriority that splits past from future, and, thereby, establishes time as dislocation. This is the radical irruption of the "event" that is both "once and for all" and also ever new. A poignant case of such an event would be death, though our own death is a stoppage of time; thus death as event is especially the death of others whom we love and without whom life must somehow go on after the mourning, but it is life transformed as irreversibly and immemorially out of joint. The first such great event of life, and the event par excellence for Merleau-Ponty, is the event of birth. As Françoise Dastur has written, "We are not at the origin of our own existence. To be born means that we are conditioned by a past that was never present to us."[41] In each new event that is to come there is a repetition of the "proto-event" of birth; in the new, there is repetition of the origin, which is a non-origin, and this is why activity is always conditioned by passivity. Merleau-Ponty wrote that "philosophy has never spoken . . . of the passivity of our activity, as Valéry spoke of a *body of the spirit:* new as our initiatives may be, they come to birth at the heart of being" (*VI* 221; *VIn* 274). And a few lines later he added those words that we recall: "I am not even the author of that hollow [*ce creux*] that forms within me by the passage from the present to the retention, it is not I who makes myself think any more than it is I who makes my heart beat" (*VI* 221; *VIn* 275). This signifies: of the event of birth, what is most our own is a past we never possess; of the event of death, what is most our own is a future that we have lost already; of the event of love, we love in part what is not known to us. The event is the invisibility of time as the birth and non-origin, but an invisibility that does not transcend the visible, but is the genesis of the visible itself. The invisibilities of the event—birth, death, and love—are not invisibilities of another world, they are invisibilities of this world, for the dimension of invisibility is implied in the visible itself. This is the irruption or dehiscence of time that Merleau-Ponty designated as "vertical time," which is the repetition of deep time in the new. Openness to the event as repetition and birth marks the contingency of existence; it bestows both destiny and expectancy as that paradox, the "impossible possible," the "expected unexpected."[42]

We left Cézanne on his mountain at the folding over of time and memory, equally at Aix before his mountain as at the caves of Lascaux in "a beyond of color, without any previous memories."[43] His touches of color, as well as Klee's, are "simultaneously older than everything and 'of the first day'" (*VI* 211 and 267; *VIn* 264 and 320). Lyotard has written that Newman's "now" in the phrase "the sublime is now" cannot be merely the present instant in between past and future in conscious experience. A work by Newman does not refer. It is an annunciation, a presentation. Thus, in Newman's paintings, the nature of time changes; there is a forgetting or dismantling of time. Newman's "*now*" is a stranger to consciousness. "It is what dismantles consciousness, what deposes consciousness, it is what consciousness cannot formulate, and even what consciousness forgets in order to constitute itself."[44] As it is in Lyotard's philosophy of the annunciation of time in Newman's paintings, so it is in Merleau-Ponty's philosophy of the event in Cézanne, Rodin, and Klee—touches older than everything, yet still "of the first day." This philosophy of Being and time opens us to the pleasures and joys of the beautiful, but also to the confrontations of the perceptual and historical multiples of the sublime and the desire for the event in the contemporary sublime. We have come full circle from where we began. In the arc of that circle, we have learned that Barnett Newman's declaration, "the sublime is now," does not require the death of beauty but its celebration. For, in the philosophy of Merleau-Ponty, the beautiful and the sublime are hinged together in a lacework that is a monogram of the generosity of birth, genesis, and event.

Notes

Preface

1. Barnett Newman, "Interview with Emile de Antonio," in *Barnett Newman: Selected Writings and Interviews,* ed. John P. O'Neill (New York: Alfred A. Knopf, 1990), 302–3.

2. I owe to an exchange with Heidegger scholar Theodore Kisiel the phrase "repeat, review, revise" as the summary of the Heideggerian "past-present-future" authentic relationship with tradition.

3. Rainer Maria Rilke, *Auguste Rodin,* trans. Daniel Slager (New York: Archipelago Books, 2004), 67–69.

4. We will discuss the significance of Merleau-Ponty's rendition of the epitaph on Klee's tomb in chapter 5.

Chapter 1

The first epigraph for this chapter is from Barnett Newman, "The New Sense of Fate," in *Barnett Newman: Selected Writings and Interviews,* ed. John P. O'Neill (New York: Alfred A. Knopf, 1990), 167. The second epigraph is from Martin Heidegger, "Rapture as Form-Engendering Force," in *Nietzsche,* vol. 1, *The Will to Power as Art,* trans. David Farrell Krell (San Francisco: Harper Collins, 1991), 123.

1. Hagi Kenaan, *The Present Personal: The Hidden Face of Language* (New York: Columbia University Press, 2005), 136.

2. Heidegger, *Will to Power as Art,* 123.

3. See Véronique M. Fóti, "The Evidences of Painting: Merleau-Ponty and Contemporary Abstraction," in *Merleau-Ponty: Difference, Materiality, Painting,* ed. Véronique M. Fóti (New Jersey: Humanities, 1996), 137–68. See also my article "The Invisible and the Unpresentable: Barnett Newman's Abstract Expressionism and the Aesthetics of Merleau-Ponty," *Analecta Husserliana* 75 (2002): 179–89.

4. Both essays may be found in *The Lyotard Reader,* ed. Andrew Benjamin (Cambridge, Eng.: Blackwell, 1989).

5. Barnett Newman, "Interview with Emile de Antonio," in *Barnett Newman: Selected Writings and Interviews,* 302–3.

6. See Harold Rosenberg, *Barnett Newman* (New York: Harry N. Abrams, 1994, repr. ed.), 244–45.

7. Laurie Fendrich argues that Duchamp made it abundantly manifest in both his art of found, factory-produced objects and his ironic comments that he "had nothing but contempt for beauty." See Laurie Fendrich, "Sleeping Beauty," *Common Review* 3, no. 3 (Winter 2004). Arthur Danto offers a more charitable view, that Duchamp's ready-mades deflect the meaning of art to a mode of celebration at a time when plumbing itself was not something taken for granted as it is today. See Arthur C. Danto, "Beauty and Morality," in *Uncontrollable Beauty: Toward a New Aesthetics,* ed. Bill Beckley and David Shapiro (New York: Allworth, 1998), 32.

8. R. G. Collingwood, *The Principles of Art* (Oxford: Oxford University Press, 1938), 38.

9. John Dewey, *Art as Experience* (New York: Capricorn Books, 1934), 129–30.

10. Mikel Dufrenne, *The Phenomenology of Aesthetic Experience,* trans. Edward S. Casey (Evanston, Ill.: Northwestern University Press, 1973), lvii, lx.

11. Naomi Wolf, *The Beauty Myth: How Images of Beauty Are Used Against Women* (New York: Doubleday Anchor Books, 1991).

12. Paul C. Taylor, "Malcolm's Conk and Danto's Colors; or, Four Logical Petitions Concerning Race, Beauty, and Aesthetics," in *Beauty Matters,* ed. Peg Zeglin Brand (Bloomington: Indiana University Press, 2000), 57–64.

13. Michel Foucault, "Friendship as a Way of Life," in *Ethics: Subjectivity and Truth,* ed. Paul Rabinow, vol. 1 of *The Essential Works of Michel Foucault: 1954–1984* (New York: New Press, 1997), 136. This work was originally published in French as *Dits et écrits: 1954–1988* (Paris: Éditions Gallimard, 1994).

14. See Dave Hickey, "Enter the Dragon: On the Vernacular of Beauty," in Beckley and Shapiro, *Uncontrollable Beauty,* 17–19.

15. See Mary Mothersill, *Beauty Restored* (Oxford: Clarendon, 1984); Arthur C. Danto, *The Abuse of Beauty: Aesthetics and the Concept of Art* (Chicago: Open Court, 2003); Elaine Scarry, *On Beauty and Being Just* (Princeton, N.J.: Princeton University Press, 1999). See also Crispin Sartwell, *Six Names of Beauty* (New York: Routledge, 2004); Beckley and Shapiro, *Uncontrollable Beauty;* and Brand, *Beauty Matters.*

16. See Hans-George Gadamer, "The Relevance of the Beautiful," in *The Relevance of the Beautiful and Other Essays,* ed. Robert Bernasconi, trans. Nicolas Walker (Cambridge, Eng.: Cambridge University Press, 1986), 3–53; Stephen Watson, "On the Withdrawal of the Beautiful: Adorno and Merleau-Ponty's Readings of Paul Klee," *Chiasmi International* 5 (2003): 201–20; and Umberto Eco, ed., *The History of Beauty,* trans. Alastair McEwen (New York: Rizzoli International, 2004). Eco has also now edited a volume titled *On Ugliness,* trans. Alastair McEwan (New York: Rizzoli, 2007).

17. "Regarding Beauty: A View of the Late 20th Century," Cantz/Hirshhorn Museum and Sculpture Garden, Washington, D.C., 1999.

18. See Watson, "Withdrawal of the Beautiful," 204.

19. Martin Heidegger, *Being and Time,* trans. John Macquarrie and Edward Robinson (New York: Harper and Row, 1962), section 6, p. 41.

Chapter 2

The first epigraph for this chapter is from Merleau-Ponty, "EM" 121; *OE* title facing page. The second epigraph is from "EM" 146; *OE* 82.

1. These are now available for study in the Bibliothèque Nationale in Paris, site Richelieu, as volume 7 of the Merleau-Ponty archive in the *salle des manuscrits*.

2. Jacques Derrida, *On Touching—Jean-Luc Nancy*, trans. Christine Irizarry (Stanford, Calif.: Stanford University Press, 2005), 215.

3. These drafts are now available as volume 5 of the Merleau-Ponty archive in the *salle des manuscrits* in the Bibliothèque Nationale in Paris, site Richelieu.

4. Jean-François Lyotard, "Philosophy and Painting in the Age of Their Experimentation: Contribution to an Idea of Postmodernity," in *The Merleau-Ponty Aesthetics Reader: Philosophy and Painting*, ed. Galen A. Johnson (Evanston, Ill.: Northwestern University Press, 1993, 1998), 329.

5. For a rich analysis of the concept of expression in Merleau-Ponty, see Lawrence Hass, *Merleau-Ponty's Philosophy* (Bloomington: Indiana University Press, 2008), chaps. 6 and 7.

6. Edmund Husserl, author's preface to the English edition of *Ideas Pertaining to a Pure Phenomenology and to a Phenomenological Philosophy*, book 1, trans. F. Kersten (Dordrecht, Neth.: Kluwer Academic, 1982), 20–21.

7. French original: "Le peintre est aussi loin du désespoir que de la suffisance, et l'on doit souhaiter à l'humanité beaucoup d'hommes qui comme lui solidairement contemplent le monde et le transforment" (my transcription; translation by Michael B. Smith).

8. Merleau-Ponty's "La philosophie aujourd'hui," "L'ontologie cartésienne et l'ontologie d'aujourd'hui," and "Philosophie et non-philosophie depuis Hegel" are all found in *NC*.

9. See Leonard Lawlor, "*Un Écart Infime (Part II):* Merleau-Ponty's Mixturism," chap. 6 of *The Implications of Immanence: Toward a New Concept of Life* (New York: Fordham University Press, 2006).

10. Margaret Atherton, "How to Write the History of Vision: Understanding the Relationship Between Berkeley and Descartes," in *Sites of Vision: The Discursive Construction of Sight in the History of Philosophy*, ed. David Michael Levin (Cambridge, Mass.: MIT Press, 1997), 139.

11. Ibid., 144.

12. Ibid., 148.

13. René Descartes, "Optics," in *Discourse on Method, Optics, Geometry, and Meteorology*, trans. Paul J. Olscamp (Indianapolis, Ind.: Bobbs Merrill, Library of Liberal Arts, 1965), 108.

14. Ibid., 66.

15. Ibid.

16. Ibid., 67.

17. Ibid., 101.

18. Ibid.

19. Ibid.

20. René Descartes, *The Passions of the Soul,* in *The Philosophical Writings of Descartes,* vol. 1, trans. John Cottingham, Robert Stoothoff, and Dugald Murdoch (Cambridge, Eng.: Cambridge University Press, 1985), section 85, p. 358.

21. Descartes, "Optics," 90.

22. Ibid.

23. See Emmanuel de Saint Aubert, "La 'promiscuité': Merleau-Ponty à la recherche d'une psychanalyse ontologique," *Archives de Philosophie* 69 (2006): 11–35.

24. "[Discourse] of Hermes Trismegistus: Poimandres," in *Hermetica: The Greek "Corpus Hermeticum" and the Latin "Aslepius,"* ed. and trans. Brian P. Copenhaver (Cambridge, Eng.: Cambridge University Press, 1992), 1.

25. Friedrich Nietzsche, *The Genealogy of Morals,* first esssay, section 13, in *The Birth of Tragedy and The Genealogy of Morals,* trans. Francis Golffing (New York: Doubleday, 1956), 178–79.

26. Aristotle's analysis of the eight senses of the word "in" is found in the *Physics,* book 4, 3. The analysis occurs in the context of Aristotle's discussion of the category of place. The *Oxford English Dictionary* lists forty definitions of "in" as a preposition and twenty-one definitions of "in" as an adverb of motion or direction, e.g., "he went in."

27. I owe the suggestion of these terms to Emmanuel de Saint Aubert. See his essay "Le mystère de la chair: Merleau-Ponty et Gabriel Marcel," *Studia Phaenomenologica* 3 (2003): 73–106.

28. See Derrida, *On Touching—Jean-Luc Nancy,* 203–15.

29. For further discussion of Baumgarten's introduction of this term, see Jean-François Lyotard, "The Sublime and the Avant-Garde," in Benjamin, *The Lyotard Reader,* 203ff. See also the entry "Origin of Aesthetics," and particularly the first section titled "Historical and Conceptual Overview" by Paul Oskar Kristeller, in the *Encyclopedia of Aesthetics,* vol. 3, ed. Michael Kelly (Oxford: Oxford University Press, 1998), especially 425ff.

30. The term "aesthetics" occurs only twice in "Eye and Mind," as a reference to the "cyberneticians 'aesthetic information'" ("EM" 149; *OE* 91) and in "Cézanne's Doubt" in discussing the "Impressionist aesthetic" ("CD" 62; "DC" 21).

31. The notion of supervenience to account for the relation between sense qualities and aesthetic qualities was stated by Frank Sibley and has given rise to analysis and controversy over whether the supervenience relation is a logical truth-conditional one or a causal one. See *Aesthetic Concepts: Essays After Sibley,* ed. Emily Brady and Jerrold Levinson (Oxford: Clarendon, 2001).

32. Rilke, *Auguste Rodin,* 70.

33. Ibid.

34. J. Hoberman, "Pop and Circumstance," review of *Guernica: The Biography of a Twentieth-Century Icon* by Gijs van Hensbergen, *The Nation,* December 13, 2004, p. 22.

35. Sartwell, *Six Names of Beauty,* 17–18.

36. Cited in J. Hoberman, "Pop and Circumstance," 25.

37. With regard to the "third realm" as worthy of aesthetic consideration, see Arthur Danto, "Beauty and Beautification," in Brand, *Beauty Matters,* 65–83, as well as his "Furniture as Art" in *Embodied Meanings: Critical Essays and Aesthetic Meditations* (New York: Farrar, Straus and Giroux, 1994), 74–81.

Chapter 3

The first epigraph for this chapter is from Merleau-Ponty, "EM" 129; *OE* 32. The second epigraph is from Émile Bernard, "Paul Cézanne, from *L'Occident,*" in *Conversations with Cézanne,* ed. Michael Doran, trans. Julie Lawrence Cochran (Berkeley: University of California Press, 2001), 39. "Word of Cambronne" refers to Napolean's famous reply when asked to surrender at Cambronne, "merde." See Doran, *Conversations with Cézanne,* 234, note 21. The third epigraph is from Rainer Maria Rilke, *Letters on Cézanne,* ed. Clara Rilke, trans. Joel Agee (New York: Fromm International, 1985), 49.

1. Émile Bernard, "Memories of Paul Cézanne," from *Mercure de France,* in Doran, *Conversations with Cézanne,* 59.

2. Paul Cézanne, "Letters to Bernard," in Doran, *Conversations with Cézanne,* 48.

3. Kurt Badt, *The Art of Cézanne,* trans. Sheila Ann Ogilvie (London: Faber and Faber, 1965), 265.

4. Ibid.

5. These terms are from D. H. Lawrence, "Introduction to These Paintings," in *Cézanne in Perspective,* ed. Judith Wechsler (Englewood Cliffs, N.J.: Prentice-Hall, 1975), 91.

6. These are now available as volume 5 of the Merleau-Ponty inventory of manuscripts in the Bibliothèque Nationale in Paris, site Richelieu, *salle des manuscrits.*

7. The other two references are in parts 4 and 5. In part 4 of "Eye and Mind," in his famous commentary on "freeing the line" or "letting a line muse"—"to go line" (*aller ligne*)—Merleau-Ponty referred to Bergson's idea of "'the visible lines of the figure,' that it is 'no more here than there,' and yet gives the key to the whole" ("EM" 143; *OE* 72–73). The reference from part 5 states that "the figurations of literature and philosophy are no more settled than those of painting" ("EM" 149; *OE* 91).

8. Henri Bergson, *The Creative Mind,* trans. Mabelle L. Andison (New York: Greenwood, 1968), 274.

9. Ibid.

10. See Jenny Slatman, *L'Expression au-delà de la représentation: Sur l'aesthesis et l'esthétique chez Merleau-Ponty* (Paris: Peeters Vrin, 2003), 227 (my translation).

11. Henri Rochefort, "The Love of Ugliness" (1903), in Wechsler, *Cézanne in Perspective,* 37–38.

12. Richard Shiff, *Cézanne and the End of Impressionism: A Study of the Theory,*

Technique, and Critical Evaluation of Modern Art (Chicago: University of Chicago Press, 1984), 196.

13. Bernard, "Memories of Cézanne," 63.

14. Bernard, "Paul Cézanne, from *L'Occident*," 36, 41, 43.

15. Ibid., 42.

16. Ibid.

17. Ibid.

18. Ibid., 43.

19. G. W. F. Hegel, *Introductory Lectures on Aesthetics*, trans. Bernard Bosanquet (New York: Penguin Books, 1993), 41 [LVI, αα].

20. Gustave Geffroy, "Paul Cézanne" (1895), in *La vie artistique*, 8 vols. (Paris, 1992–1903), 6:218. Cited in Shiff, *Cézanne and the End of Impressionism*, 190.

21. Thadée Natanson, "Paul Cézanne," *La Revue Blanche* 9 (December 1, 1895): 500. Cited in Doran, *Conversations with Cézanne*, xix.

22. Cézanne, "Letters to Bernard," 47.

23. Paul Cézanne, "My Confidences," in Doran, *Conversations with Cézanne*, 101.

24. Bernard, "Memories of Cézanne," 62.

25. See Jean Clair, "Adventures of the Optic Nerve," in *Bonnard: The Late Paintings*, ed. Sasha M. Newman (London: Thames and Hudson, 1984), 41.

26. Bernard, "Memories of Paul Cézanne," 64.

27. Ibid.

28. Rilke, *Letters on Cézanne*, 35.

29. Émile Bernard, "A Conversation with Cézanne" (*Mercure de France*, 1921), in Doran, *Conversations with Cézanne*, 163–64.

30. Rilke, *Letters on Cézanne*, 29.

31. Ibid., 33.

32. Ibid., 40.

33. Ibid., 64.

34. Rilke, *Auguste Rodin*, 69.

35. Rilke, *Letters on Cézanne*, 75.

36. Ibid., 61.

37. Ibid., 47.

38. Cited in Bernard, "Memories of Cézanne," 57–58.

39. Rilke, *Letters on Cézanne*, 33.

40. Lawrence, "Introduction to These Paintings": "It is the appleyness of the portrait of Cézanne's wife that makes it so permanently interesting" (91).

41. See Susan Sidlauskas, "Emotion, Color, Cézanne (The Portraits of Hortense)," *Nineteenth-Century Art Worldwide: A Journal of Nineteenth-Century Visual Culture* 3, no. 2 (Autumn 2004): 2. Sidlauskas offers a convincing reinterpretation of the portraits of Mme. Cézanne, originating from the one portrait of Mme. Cézanne with her hair down (1890–92), which she finds full of expression and emotion. Of all the portraits together she writes: "Fiquet Cézanne's lack of fixedness is, in part, the *subject* of the series; an expression of the instability inherent in

any human contact, of the unpredictability of being mirrored, resisted, complemented, and challenged, all at once, by another individual" (4). I thank my student, Michaela McCaughey, for bringing the work of Sidlauskas to my attention.

42. Merleau-Ponty is not discussing Cézanne's portraits of his wife in this text, but the account seems remarkably apt.

43. John Rewald, *Paul Cézanne: The Watercolors—A Catalog Raisonné* (Boston: Little, Brown, 1983), 135; Ruth Butler, *Hidden in the Shadow of the Master: The Model-Wives of Cézanne, Monet, and Rodin* (New Haven, Conn.: Yale University Press, 2008), 53–54.

44. Meyer Shapiro, *Paul Cézanne* (New York: Harry N. Abrams, 1988), 126.

45. Rilke, *Letters on Cézanne,* 68.

46. Ibid., 65.

47. Rilke, *Auguste Rodin,* 67.

48. I owe to my student, Michaela McCaughey, this association between cooler aesthetic desire and the cool temperature of the color blue.

49. Edmund Burke, *A Philosophical Enquiry into the Origin of Our Ideas of the Sublime and Beautiful* (Oxford: Oxford University Press, 1990), 105.

50. Ibid., 106.

51. Jeremy Gilbert-Rolfe, "Beauty and the Contemporary Sublime," in Beckley and Shapiro, *Uncontrollable Beauty,* 48.

52. Cézanne, "Letters to Bernard," 48. For an extended commentary on the meanings of the statement by Cézanne in French, see Jacques Derrida, "Passe-Partout," in *The Truth in Painting,* trans. Geoff Bennington and Ian McLeod (Chicago: University of Chicago Press, 1987), 1–13; originally published as *La verité en peinture* (Paris: Flammarion, 1978).

53. Lawrence Hass has laid out Merleau-Ponty's critique and rejection of the Cartesian representational model of the mind and truth quite emphatically and clearly in "Prelude: Scenes from the Cartesian Theater," in his *Merleau-Ponty's Philosophy* (Bloomington: Indiana University Press, 2008), 11–25.

54. Martin Heidegger, "The Origin of the Work of Art," in *Poetry, Language, Thought,* trans. Alfred Hofstadter (New York: Harper and Row, 1971), 39.

55. Ibid., 56.

56. Ibid., 72.

57. Ibid., 75.

58. Ibid., 34.

59. Derrida, "Restitutions of the Truth in Pointing [*Pointure*]," chap. 4 of *The Truth in Painting,* 255ff.

60. Indeed, in the early versions of "The Origin" from Heidegger's Freiburg and Zurich lectures, Heidegger does not discuss Van Gogh's shoes painting. See Hugh Silverman, "The Autobiographical Textuality of Heidegger's Shoes," chap. 13 of *Textualities: Between Hermeneutics and Deconstruction* (London: Routledge, 1994), 250, note 5.

61. Heidegger, *Being and Time,* 104–5 (marginal numbering 74–75).

62. Heidegger, "Origin of the Work of Art," 42.

63. Ibid., 47.

64. See Jacques Taminiaux, "Philosophical Heritage in Heidegger's Conception of Art," the third section of "Heidegger, Martin," in Kelly, *Encyclopedia of Aesthetics:* "When Heidegger confirms that truth irrupts in the work of art in the form of combat between the World and the Earth, and emphasizes that what is at stake is not only between concealment and unconcealment, but also between measure and excess, one cannot refrain from suspecting here an echo of Nietzsche's meditation about Apollo and Dionysus" (2:383).

65. Heidegger, *Will to Power as Art,* 103–4.

66. Heidegger, "Origin of the Work of Art," 37.

67. See Gilles Deleuze and Félix Guattari, "The Plane of Immanence," chap. 2 of *What Is Philosophy?* trans. Hugh Tomlinson and Graham Burchell (New York: Columbia University Press, 1994), 35–60.

68. Heidegger, "Origin of the Work of Art," 63.

69. See Julian Young, *Heidegger's Philosophy of Art* (Cambridge, Eng.: Cambridge University Press, 2001), 62–64.

70. Heidegger refers explicitly to Heraclitus, fragment 53, to mark the conjunction of dualities that "earth" conveys as contradictory tendencies: "what is holy and unholy, what great and what small, what brave and what cowardly, what lofty and what flighty, what master and what slave" ("Origin of the Work of Art," 43).

71. See Young, *Heidegger's Philosophy of Art,* 150.

72. Ibid., 150–51. The statement is confirmed in Heinrich Wiegand Petzet, *Encounters and Dialogues with Martin Heidegger, 1929–1976,* trans. Parvis Emad and Kenneth Maly (Chicago: University of Chicago Press, 1993), 143.

73. Petzet, *Encounters and Dialogues with Heidegger,* 144.

74. Cited in Young, *Heidegger's Philosophy of Art,* 152.

Chapter 4

The first epigraph for this chapter is from Auguste Rodin, *Art: Conversations with Paul Gsell,* trans. Jacques de Caso and Patricia B. Sanders (Berkeley: University of California Press, 1984), 18; originally published as *L'Art: Entretiens reúnis par Paul Gsell* (1911; Paris: Éditions Gallimard, 1953). The second epigraph is from Charles Baudelaire, *The Painter of Modern Life and Other Essays,* trans. Jonathan Mayne (London: Phaidon, 1964), 3. The third epigraph is from Merleau-Ponty, *PP* 147; *PhP* 172.

1. Michel Foucault wrote a chapter titled "Man and His Doubles" in *The Order of Things: An Archeology of the Human Sciences* (New York: Vintage, 1966, 1970) that contains a critique of phenomenology, and Merleau-Ponty is not named but seems implicated. In Foucault's famous phrase, this mixture of the empirical and the transcendental in phenomenology, and modern philosophy in general, creates for the first time in Western history the idea of "man" as a "strange empirico-transcendental doublet," for he becomes both the object of knowledge and the subject whose mind includes the transcendental conditions

that render all knowledge possible. Foucault intends the image and concept of the doublet as a critique of phenomenology and the whole nineteenth-century introduction of the sciences of "man." For a discussion that places Foucault and Merleau-Ponty closer together than Foucault's critique would suggest, see Lawlor, "*Un Écart Infime.*"

2. *The Kiss* shocked the authorities when it was brought to the Chicago World's Fair in 1893, and it was put away as unfit for public viewing, with admission upon personal application only. Rodin himself later diminished *The Kiss* as "pretty" but conventional, a work in which he had made "no discovery." See William Harlan Hale, *The World of Rodin: 1840–1917* (New York: Time-Life Books, 1969), 14–15.

3. Charles Baudelaire, "Beauty (La Beauté)," number 17 of *The Flowers of Evil,* in *The Flowers of Evil and Paris Spleen,* trans. William H. Crosby (Brockport, N.Y.: BOA Editions, 1991), 46, 47.

4. See Hale, *World of Rodin,* 70.

5. Ruth Butler, *Rodin: The Shape of Genius* (New Haven, Conn.: Yale University Press, 1993), 187, 189.

6. The model was Adèle Abruzzezzi, sister of Anna, both of whom worked in Rodin's studio in the early 1880s. See Butler, *Rodin: The Shape of Genius,* 188. Butler comments that Rodin recognized his models as artistic collaborators, and Adèle and Anna were an integral part of his studio. The posture of *The Crouching Woman* depends upon an "exceptional rapport" between artist and model.

7. Albert E. Elsen, *Rodin* (New York: Museum of Modern Art, 1963), 59.

8. The addition of the arms and head in the making of *St. John the Baptist Preaching* actually has the effect of diminishing the powerful feeling of walking. However, the addition of the arms, head, and a mandatory fig leaf enabled the sculpture to win a third prize before the Salon of 1880. See Hale, *World of Rodin,* 80.

9. Rodin, *Art: Conversations with Paul Gsell,* 29.

10. Ibid., 10.

11. Ibid., 23, 24.

12. See Ernst-Gerhard Güse, *Auguste Rodin: Drawings and Watercolors,* trans. John Gabriel and Michael Taylor (New York: Rizzoli International, 1984), 171–72, and illustration 142.

13. Amelia Jones, "Beauty Discourse," http://strikingdistance.com/xtra/XTra100/v2n3/ajones1.html, p. 3. See also Lynda Nead, *The Female Nude: Art, Obscenity, and Sexuality* (London: Routledge, 1992).

14. Burke, *Philosophical Inquiry into the Sublime and Beautiful,* 105.

15. Immanuel Kant, *Observations on the Feeling of the Beautiful and Sublime,* trans. John T. Goldthwait (Berkeley: University of California Press, 1960), 78.

16. Ibid., 79.

17. Ibid., 81.

18. John T. Goldthwait, "Translator's Introduction" to Kant, *Observations on the Feeling of the Beautiful and Sublime,* 11.

19. Rodin married Rose Beuret at the end of January 1917, and she died

fifteen days later. Rodin contracted pneumonia and died on November 17, 1917. See Elsen, *Rodin,* 213.

20. See Reine-Marie Paris, *Camille: The Life of Camille Claudel, Rodin's Muse and Mistress,* trans. Liliane Emery Tuck (New York: Henry Holt, 1984, 1988); and Odile Ayral-Clause, *Camille Claudel: A Life* (New York: Harry N. Abrams, 2002).

21. Paul Claudel, "Camille Claudel Statuary" (1905), in Paris, *The Life of Camille Claudel,* xvii, xviii.

22. Lisa Lyon was the first World Women's Bodybuilding Champion. See Arthur C. Danto, *Playing with the Edge: The Photographic Achievement of Robert Mapplethorpe* (Berkeley: University of California Press, 1996), 121.

23. Rilke, *Auguste Rodin,* 48.

24. Rodin, *Art: Conversations with Paul Gsell,* 49, 50.

25. Elsen, *Rodin,* 63.

26. Rodin, *Art: Conversations with Paul Gsell,* 45.

27. Kant, *Observations on the Beautiful and Sublime,* 92.

28. Rilke, *Auguste Rodin,* 55.

29. Ibid., 18–19.

30. Ibid., 19.

31. See Aristotle, *The Poetics,* in *Aristotle on Poetry and Style,* trans. G. M. A. Grube (Indianapolis, Ind.: Hackett, 1989), 1454b11, 1452a10–12, 1451a4–15. See also the article on "Beauty," and particularly its second section regarding "Classical Concepts" by Nickolas Pappas, in Kelly, *Encyclopedia of Aesthetics,* 1:246.

32. Aristotle, *Poetics,* 1449b25–28.

33. The canons of Charles Blanc are outlined by Elsen, *Rodin,* 16–17.

34. Ibid., 17.

35. So strong were the classical elements in his works that Rodin's celebrity, which had reached such heights during his lifetime, went into eclipse in the decades immediately following his death. The influence of the modernist elements in his work has only more recently begun to be properly appreciated, beginning with an exhibition at the National Gallery, Washington, D.C. (June 1981–January 1982), titled "Rodin Rediscovered." See the review by John Hunisak, "Rodin Rediscovered," *Art Journal* (Winter 1981): 370–75.

36. Rilke, *Auguste Rodin,* 41.

37. Rodin, *Art: Conversations with Paul Gsell,* 19.

38. Theodor Adorno, "The Ugly, the Beautiful, and Technique," in *Aesthetic Theory,* ed. Gretel Adorno and Rolf Tiedemann, trans. Robert Hullot-Kentor (Minneapolis: University of Minnesota Press, 1997), 45–61.

39. Rodin, *Art: Conversations with Paul Gsell,* 4–5.

40. Ibid., 59–60.

41. Rilke, *Auguste Rodin,* 56.

42. Cited in Rodin, *Art: Conversations with Paul Gsell,* 18. See Baudelaire, *Flowers of Evil,* 68–69.

43. Cézanne, too, talked of Baudelaire and recited "Une Charogne" without mistakes. He wrote his own verse inspired by Baudelaire. See Bernard, "Memories of Cézanne," in 71–72.

44. See my essay "The Colors of Fire: Depth and Desire in Merleau-Ponty's 'Eye and Mind,'" *Journal of the British Society for Phenomenology* 25, no. 1 (1994): 60.

45. Merleau-Ponty's courses at University of Lyon are detailed by Hugh J. Silverman in the "Translator's Preface" to his translation of *Consciousness and the Acquisition of Language* (Evanston, Ill.: Northwestern University Press, 1973), xxxviii. The 1947–48 Lyon course was on aesthetics, and particularly modern poetry, focusing on the symbolists: Baudelaire, Rimbaud, and Mallarmé.

46. Charles Baudelaire, "The Desire to Paint," from *Prose Poems,* translated in *Baudelaire, Rimbaud, Verlaine: Selected Verse and Poems,* ed. Joseph M. Bernstein (New York: Citadel), 147.

47. Hale, *World of Rodin,* 94.

48. William Gass, "Rilke's Rodin," introduction to Rilke, *Auguste Rodin,* 18.

49. Baudelaire, *Painter of Modern Life,* 3.

50. See Michel Brix, "Modern Beauty versus Platonist Beauty," trans. Tony Campbell, in *Baudelaire and the Poetics of Modernity,* ed. Patricia A. Ward (Nashville, Tenn.: Vanderbilt University Press, 2001), 1–14.

51. Elsen, *Rodin,* 76.

52. Rilke, *Auguste Rodin,* 59–60.

53. See Rilke, *Auguste Rodin,* 60. "Originally," Rodin says, "I thought of the Burghers leaving the market place. In the confusion of the good-byes, only Saint Pierre has begun to walk in order to cut short the painful scene. . . . They are tied voluntarily by the same sacrifice, but each one responds individually according to his age and situation." See Elsen, *Rodin,* 74.

54. Elsen, *Rodin,* 78.

55. Rilke, *Auguste Rodin,* 60–61.

56. Ibid., 62.

57. Elsen, *Rodin,* 74.

58. Rodin lost this fight with the town, and his sculpture of *The Burghers* was placed in front of a public garden and not moved to the town square until several years after Rodin's death. See Elsen, *Rodin,* 72.

59. See Brix, "Modern Beauty versus Platonist Beauty," 8.

60. Charles Baudelaire, "Horreur Sympathique," number 81 of *The Flowers of Evil,* in *The Flowers of Evil and Paris Spleen,* 144–45. For further comment, see Michel Brix, "Modern Beauty versus Platonist Beauty," 9–10.

61. For a discussion that does situate Baudelaire within the nineteenth-century context of pessimistic nihilism, see A. E. Carter, *Charles Baudelaire* (Boston: Twayne, 1977), 61.

62. Rodin, *Art: Conversations with Paul Gsell,* 66-67.

63. Ibid., 25.

64. Jules Boréley, "Cézanne at Aix," in Doran, *Conversations with Cézanne,* 20.

65. Monet and Rodin had exhibited together in 1889 and were also close friends. See Félix Jeantet, "Review of the Monet/Rodin Exhibition at Georges Petit and Rodin's Work at the Exposition Universelle (1889)," in *Rodin in Perspective,* ed. Ruth Butler (Englewood Cliffs, N.J.: Prentice-Hall, 1980), 74–77.

66. Gustave Geffroy, "Excerpt from *Claude Monet, His Life, His Times, His Works* (1894)," in Doran, *Conversations with Cézanne,* 4.

67. Joachim Gasquet, "What He Told Me. . . . Excerpt from *Cézanne,*" in Doran, *Conversations with Cézanne,* 109.

68. *The Age of Bronze* was accused of being cast from life: "I am rejected; they say that I have put a corpse on its feet (what nonsense)." Ruth Butler, "Introduction" to *Rodin in Perspective,* 2–3.

69. Ruth Butler attributes Cézanne's kneeling before Rodin to his decoration with the "Cross of the Chevalier of the Legion of Honor." See Butler, *Rodin in Perspective,* 7. Regarding Rodin's "mixed emotions" about receiving the Cross of the Legion of Honor, see Butler, *Rodin: The Shape of Genius,* 210–11. Regarding Rodin's promotion to the second-highest rank of *grand officier,* see Frederic V. Grunfeld, *Rodin: A Biography* (New York: Henry Holt, 1987), 592.

70. The five orders of the Legion of Honor (from highest to lowest) are grand cross, grand officer, commander, officer, and chevalier (knight). Merleau-Ponty was offered membership at the rank of chevalier.

71. Here is the complete text of Merleau-Ponty's letter:

> Paris, 30 April 1957: Dear Sir, You have informed me that on the strength of your proposal the President of the Republic has bestowed upon me the title Chevalier of the Legion of Honor. I am most appreciative of the intention of those who have desired to honor my teaching and writings, and I would like to express to you, Sir, my thanks for the proposal you made in my favor. But, as your letter points out, this distinction also attests to the goodwill of the government. Now, I am convinced as a citizen that the government has avoided doing its job, and compromised as never before the very idea of government. Its goodwill toward me is misdirected, and it would be wrong of me to accept it. I therefore do not intend, in the present state of affairs, to act upon the letter you inform me of from the Grand Chancellor, nor to be received into the Order [of the Legion of Honor]. I have not forgotten, in writing you, the numerous members of my family who have borne that decoration. The fact that they were able to do so is attributable to the circumstance that the government that granted those decorations, whether or not they agreed with it, had in their eyes its moral authority intact. I will not make this letter public, as I do not wish to implicate the institution to which I belong in my political opinions. But I did at least want to let you know what the views of one of your present-day honorees might be. Yours truly, Maurice Merleau-Ponty

The French original reads as follows:

> Paris, le 30 avril 1957: Monsieur le Ministre, Vous avez bien voulu me faire savoir que, sur votre proposition, M. le Président de la République m'a nommé chevalier de la Légion d'Honneur. Je suis très sensible à la pensée de ceux qui ont voulu honorer mon enseignment et mes travaux, et j'aimerais, Monsieur le Ministre, vous exprimer mes remerciements pour la proposition que vous avez faite en ma faveur. Mais, comme votre le rappelle, cette distinction est aussi témoignage de la bienveillance du Gouvernement. Or je suis convaincu comme citoyen qu'il a éludé les tâches qui étaient les siennes, et compromis,

comme jamais on ne l'avait fait, l'idée même du gouvernement. Sa bienveillance s'égarerait en se portant sur moi, et il serait de ma part abusif d'en recevoir le témoignage. Je n'ai donc pas l'intention, dans l'état présent des choses, de donner suite à la lettre du Grand Chancelier que vous m'annoncez, ni de me faire recevoir dans l'Ordre. Je n'oublie pas, en vous écrivant, ceux nombreux dans ma famille, qui ont porté cette décoration: s'ils ont pu le faire, c'est que le gouvernement qui la leur décernait, qu'ils fûssent ou non d'accord avec lui, avait à leurs yeux son autorité morale entière. Je ne rendrai pas publique cette lettre, ne voulant pas impliquer, dans mes jugements politiques, l'institution à laquelle j'appartiens. Du moins voulais-je vous faire connaître ce que peuvent être, aujourd'hui, les sentiments d'un de ceux que vous décorez. Veuillez agréer, je vous prie, Monsieur le Ministre, l'assurance de ma haute consideration. Maurice Merleau-Ponty

This text is my transcription from the Archives, Collège de France, Paris; translation by Michael B. Smith.

72. See Elsen, *Rodin,* 102.

73. In March 1952, on the first vote for the Chair of Philosophy by the professors of the Collège de France, Merleau-Ponty received 17 votes, Etienne Souriau 7, Gaston Berger 4, and Stephane Lupasco 2, with 6 abstentions, rendering Merleau-Ponty short of an absolute majority. On the second vote, Merleau-Ponty received 23 votes, Souriau 5, Berger 3, and Lupasco 0, rendering Merleau-Ponty "en première ligne." On a third vote, Souriau was placed "en deuxième ligne" (Souriau 20, Lupasco 5, Berger 4). The administrator of the Collège de France forwarded the vote to the Academy of Moral and Political Sciences, and on March 20, 1952, the academy announced Gaston Berger in first place, with Etienne Souriau in second place. Merleau-Ponty wrote a strongly worded letter of protest to the academy in which he referred to the actions of the academy as unprecedented, upon which he was announced for the Chair of Philosophy commencing April 1, 1952. At age 44, he was the youngest professor elected to the chair. He gave his inaugural lecture on January 15, 1953.

74. My translation of the French: "Institution d'une oeuvre, comme d'un amour [veut dire] sens comme signification ouverte, se développant par bourgeonnement, virage, décentration et recentration, zig-zg, passage ambigu" (*IP* 87).

75. Some years after Rodin's death, *Balzac* was installed in Paris at the intersection of Boulevard Raspail and Boulevard Montparnasse. Today it resides in the garden of the Musée Rodin at Hotel Biron.

76. Elsen, *Rodin,* 103.

77. Ibid.

78. Rodin, *Art: Conversations with Paul Gsell,* 32. Merleau-Ponty cites this remark in "Eye and Mind" ("EM" 145; *OE* 80).

79. Indeed, in one of the nude studies for *Balzac,* the hands are placed over the crotch.

80. Ralph Waldo Emerson, "The Poet," in *Essays: Second Series,* collected in *Emerson: Essays and Lectures,* ed. Joel Porte (New York: Library of America, 1983), 450.

81. Rodin, *Art: Conversations with Paul Gsell,* 81.

82. Gasquet, "What He Told Me. . . . Excerpt from *Cézanne,*" 128–29.

83. Ibid., 129.

84. Ibid.

85. Edward Steichen's introduction to Rodin in 1900 and his subsequent Rodin portraits are discussed in Butler, *Rodin: The Shape of Genius,* 405–6. Steichen went on to become one of Rodin's biggest American promoters and organized the first American exhibition of Rodin's watercolor drawings of female nudes in 1908 at Steichen's 291 Gallery in New York City. See Butler, *Rodin: The Shape of Genius,* 436. See also Grunfeld, *Rodin: A Biography,* 401, 445.

86. "The figures are sublime in their simplicity." Rilke, *Rodin,* 61.

87. Rodin, *Art: Conversations with Paul Gsell,* 81, 83.

88. Rilke, *Rodin,* 88.

Chapter 5

The first epigraph for this chapter is from Klee, *DPK* 49–50/142. The second epigraph is from Klee, *DPK* 26/67; 52/152. The third epigraph is from Merleau-Ponty, *WP* 99; *C* 58.

1. Paul Klee, "Creative Credo," in *Notebooks, Volume 1: The Thinking Eye,* trans. Ralph Mannheim (New York: George Wittenborn, 1961), 76.

2. Ibid., 78.

3. Ibid.

4. Klee writes that the telegram announcing Franz Marc's death "struck me like lightning. . . . The bell rang, shrill and long, the way it rings at night when an urgent telegram is delivered. With a sense of impending disaster, I went—I don't remember how—to the garden gate, and the catastrophe occurred" (*DPK* 323–24/965).

5. Klee's experiences in the army are detailed in the final section of his *Diaries* ("Diary IV"), including the letter requesting discharge in the final entry (*DPK* 410–11/1134).

6. See Robert Delaunay, "Light" (1912), in *The New Art of Color: The Writings of Robert and Sonia Delaunay,* ed. Arthur A. Cohen, trans. David Shapiro and Arthur A. Cohen (New York: Viking, 1978), 81. Klee's translation was published in *Der Sturm,* no. 144–45 (February 1913).

7. Delaunay, "Light," 80, 84.

8. Ibid., 81.

9. Ibid., 83.

10. Ibid., 86.

11. Ibid., 87.

12. On the one hand, for example, Saint Augustine, himself Egyptian, rejected hermeticism, yet on the other hand, when a Greek manuscript of the *Corpus Hermetica* reached Florence in the early Renaissance around 1460, Cosimo de Medici ordered Ficino to translate it into Latin even before the works of Plato. See Anthony Preus, "Hemetica," in *Encyclopedia of Classical Philosophy,* ed. Don-

ald J. Zeyl (Westport, Conn.: Greenwood, 1997), 263–65. See also Frances A. Yates, "Hermeticism," in *The Encyclopedia of Philosophy,* ed. Paul Edwards (New York: Macmillan, 1967), 3:489–90; and *Gnosis and Hermeticism: From Antiquity to Modern Times,* ed. Roelof van den Broek and Wouter J. Hanegraaff (Albany: State University of New York Press, 1998), chap. 1.

13. "[Discourse] of Hermes Trismegistus: Poimandres," 1.

14. Mauro Carbone has made a study of this question in "La lumière de la chair: Instances antiplatoniciennes et traces néoplatoniciennes dans la pensée du dernier Merleau-Ponty." This text by Carbone has, to date, been published only in Italian as a chapter in his *Sullo schermo dell'estetica: La pittura, il cinema e la filosofia da fare* (Milan: Mimesis, 2008).

15. For example, see Susanna Partsch, "The Trip to Tunisia," in *Paul Klee: 1879–1940* (London: Taschen, 2003), 30–46.

16. Will Grohmann, *Paul Klee* (New York: Harry N. Abrams, 1954), 144.

17. Klee's pedagogical notebooks were edited and published in German in 1956 under the title *Das bildnerische Denken* (Basel: Benno Schwabe) and appeared in French translation in 1959. The first English publication edited from the pedagogical notebooks of Klee during his Bauhaus period (1921–30) appeared under the title of *Paul Klee: The Thinking Eye,* trans. Ralph Mannheim (New York: George Wittenborn, 1961).

18. See Klee, *Notebooks, Volume 1: The Thinking Eye,* 467–511.

19. Ibid., 489.

20. Andrew Kagan, *Paul Klee/Art and Music* (Ithaca, N.Y.: Cornell University Press, 1983); Hajo Düchting, *Paul Klee: Painting Music* (Munich: Prestel Verlag, 1997).

21. For an interesting review of both the Stuttgart and Paris exhibitions, see Richard Verdi, "Art and Music in the Twentieth Century: Stuttgart and Paris," *Burlington Magazine* 127, no. 993 (December 1985): 923–26.

22. Gunther Schuller, *Seven Studies on Themes of Paul Klee* (London: Universal Edition, 1962).

23. Maurice Merleau-Ponty, "Two Unpublished Notes on Music," trans. Leonard Lawlor, *Chiasmi International* 3 (2001): 17–18.

24. By the time young Paul Klee was eleven years old, he was a good enough violinist to play as an extra with the Bern symphony, and he eventually became a second violinist with the City of Bern Orchestra. The woman he married, Lily Stumpf, was a pianist who supported the family by giving piano lessons while Paul struggled to master painting in their early years together. See Kagan, *Paul Klee/Art and Music,* 20–21.

25. "The celebrated musicality of Klee's art is one of the qualities that has most captured the imagination of the public." Kagan, *Paul Klee/Art and Music,* 21.

26. Wassily Kandinsky, *Concerning the Spiritual in Art,* trans. M. T. H. Sadler (New York: Dover, 1911, 1977), 25.

27. Ibid., 38–41.

28. Klee, *Notebooks, Volume 1: The Thinking Eye,* 422ff.

29. Mayer-Gross and Stein, *Über einige Abänderungen der Sinnestätigkeit im Meskalinrausch* (1926). The 1920s marked the height of synesthetic psychological research, but there is similar research today regarding perception altered by LSD. See Amy Ione and Christopher Tyler, "Synesthesia: Is F-Sharp Colored Violet?" *Journal of the History of the Neurosciences* 13, no. 1 (2004): 58–65.

30. See Amy Ione, "Klee and Kandinsky: Polyphonic Painting, Chromatic Chords, and Synaesthesia," *Journal of Consciousness Studies* 11, no. 3–4 (2004): 154.

31. Synesthetic experiences have been reported by a long list of famous artists, including Baudelaire, Rimbaud, Rimsky-Korsakov, Scriabin, and Nabokov, as well as Kandinsky. See Ione and Taylor, "Is F-Sharp Colored Violet?" 58.

32. Ibid.

33. These are noted on the back of a watercolor study for his *Orchestras* series. See Jean-Louis Ferrier, *Paul Klee* (Paris: Finest SA/Pierre Terrail Editions, 2001), 20.

34. Klee, "Creative Credo," 79.

35. Klee, *Notebooks, Volume 1: The Thinking Eye,* 69.

36. Ibid., 490.

37. Jean-Louis Ferrier reports that it is painted as homage to Klee's friend, the great violinist Adolf Busch. See Ferrier, *Paul Klee,* 40.

38. Klee, *Notebooks, Volume 1: The Thinking Eye,* 285–87.

39. See my essay "The Colors of Fire," 62.

40. See David Burnett, "Paul Klee: The Romantic Landscape," *Art Journal* 36, no. 4 (Summer 1977): 326.

41. Klee wrote these words in 1900 at age 22.

42. Petzet, *Encounters and Dialogues with Heidegger,* 148.

43. Ibid., 151.

44. Kagan, *Paul Klee/Art and Music,* 140.

45. In the last two years of his life, Klee increased his angel production and created twenty-eight of the fifty angel drawings that he produced. Grohmann, *Paul Klee,* 350.

46. Walter Benjamin, *Illuminations,* trans. Harry Zohn (New York: Schocken Books, 1968), 257. Benjamin purchased *Angelus Novus* in 1921.

47. Gert Schiff, "Klee's Array of Angels," *Artforum* 25, no. 9 (May 1982): 129.

48. Grohmann, *Paul Klee,* 357.

49. See Marcel Franciscono, "Klee's Relationship to Kandinsky and Marc," in *Paul Klee: His Work and Thought* (Chicago: University of Chicago Press, 1991), 165–75.

50. Klee, *Notebooks, Volume 1: The Thinking Eye,* 407. See the excellent commentary on these matters by Stephen H. Watson, "Gadamer, Aesthetic Modernism, and the Rehabilitation of Allegory: The Relevance of Paul Klee," *Research in Phenomenology* 34 (2004): 45–68, especially 51–53, 66–68.

51. It is a eulogy to the virtuoso tympanist Knauer, whom Klee had heard and admired at the Dresden Opera. See Kagan, *Paul Klee/Art and Music,* 137.

52. Ibid., 137–38.

53. This is the German original: "Diesseitig bin ich gar nicht fassbar, denn ich wohne grad so gut bei den Toten wie bei den Ungeborenen." This is the

French translation by Klossowski: "Ici-bas je ne suis guère saisissable, car j'habite tout aussi bien chez les morts que chez ceux qui ne sont pas nés encore." Paul Klee, *Journal,* trans. Pierre Klossowski (Paris: Bernard Grasset, 1959), 354.

54. For further recent work on Merleau-Ponty in relation to incarnation and sacramentality, see Saint Aubert, "Le mystère et la chair"; and Emmanuel de Saint Aubert, "L'Incarnation change tout: Merleau-Ponty critique de la 'théologie explicative,'" *Archives de Philosophie* 71, no. 3 (Autumn 2008): 371–405. See also my article "Desire and Invisibility in *Eye and Mind:* Some Remarks on Merleau-Ponty's Spirituality," in *Merleau-Ponty in Contemporary Perspective,* ed. Patrick Burke and Jan Van der Veken (Dordrecht, Neth.: Kluwer Academic, 1993), 85–96.

55. Maurice Merleau-Ponty, "Phenomenology and Analytic Philosophy" (1960), in *Texts and Dialogues: On Philosophy, Politics, and Culture,* ed. Hugh J. Silverman and James Barry (Atlantic Highlands, N.J.: Humanities, 1991), 66. This item originally appeared in French as "Phénoménologie contre 'The Concept of Mind,'" in *La philosophie analytique* (Paris: Minuit, 1960).

56. Sophocles, *Oedipus at Colonus,* in *The Oedipus Cycle,* trans. Robert Fitzgerald (New York: Harcourt, 1977), 166–67.

57. Paul Valéry, "La cimetière marin," in *Poems,* trans. David Paul, vol. 1 of *The Collected Works of Paul Valéry* (Princeton, N.J.: Princeton University Press, 1971), 216, 217.

58. See Peter Hadreas, *In Place of the Flawed Diamond: An Investigation of Merleau-Ponty's Philosophy* (New York: Peter Lang, 1986), chap. 2.

59. Valéry, "La cimetière marin," 212, 213.

60. Grohmann, *Paul Klee,* 360. In one of the rare errors in Grohman's classic study, he misidentifies the angel drawing in *Last Still Life* as *Jacob Wrestling with the Angel.* It has given me much pause about the source of this error.

61. This latter is the interpretation adopted by Gert Schiff in "Klee's Array of Angels": "In the [original] drawing, it stood for the female sex. Its new shape [in *Last Still Life*] helps us to realize that the angel, in the drawing still earthly, carnal, caught in the process of change, has now become thoroughly spiritual" (132).

62. See Mauro Carbone, "The Time of Half-Sleep: Merleau-Ponty Between Husserl and Proust," chap. 1 of *The Thinking of the Sensible: Merleau-Ponty's A-Philosophy* (Evanston, Ill.: Northwestern University Press, 2004), especially 112–13. See also Mauro Carbone, "The Mythical Time of the Ideas: Merleau-Ponty and Deleuze as Readers of Proust," *Journal of the British Society for Phenomenology,* special issue: "Merleau-Ponty 1908–2008," vol. 39, no. 1 (January 2008): 12–26.

63. Klee, "Creative Credo," 79.

64. See Watson, "Gadamer, Aesthetic Modernism," 49.

65. Paul Klee, Jena Lecture "On Modern Art" (1924), in *Notebooks, Volume 1: The Thinking Eye,* 92.

66. Ibid., 93. Since Merleau-Ponty's citation of Klee's 1924 lecture is drawn from Grohmann's *Paul Klee,* I am citing from the English translation of Grohmann, *Paul Klee,* 367.

67. Emmanuel de Saint Aubert, *Vers une ontologie indirecte: Sources et enjeux*

critiques de l'appel à l'ontologie chez Merleau-Ponty (Paris: Librairie Philosophique J. Vrin, 2006), 167: "Le mouvement merleau-pontienne est celui d'une recherche et d'une endurance de la profondeur de plus en plus synonymes d'un desire du désir, essentiel â sa conception de l'être" (my translation).

68. See Felix Klee, *Paul Klee: His Life and Work in Documents,* trans. Richard Winston and Clara Winston (New York: George Braziller, 1962), 62–63.

69. Grohmann, *Paul Klee,* 273–74.

70. Ibid., 275.

71. Ibid., 276.

72. I owe this musical reference and suggestion of Bach's *Art of the Fugue* to Elizabeth A. Behnke, director of the Study Project in Phenomenology of the Body, profound scholar of Husserl and Merleau-Ponty, and accomplished violinist and musician. See Elizabeth A. Behnke, "At the Service of the Sonata: Music Lessons with Merleau-Ponty," in *Merleau-Ponty: Critical Essays,* ed. Henry Pietersma (Washington, D.C.: Center for Advanced Research in Phenomenology, University Press of America, 1989), 23–29.

73. *Signs* also references the Sphinx, speaking of the "happy centuries" in which philosophers "thought to tame the Sphinx" and of the future of philosophy in which "they will keep on giving answers to the many riddles she puts to them" (*S* 158; *Si* 200). As well as the weight of monumentality, the Sphinx is also inscrutability and the interrogative.

74. Klee, *Notebooks, Volume 1: The Thinking Eye,* 113.

Chapter 6

The first epigraph for this chapter is from Merleau-Ponty, *VI* 144; *VIn* 189. The second epigraph is from Heidegger, *Will to Power as Art,* 110.

1. Hegel, *Introductory Lectures on Aesthetics,* 41 [LVI, αα].

2. Eco, "Introduction" to *History of Beauty,* 8.

3. Rilke, *Letters on Cézanne,* 61.

4. Ibid., 47.

5. Jean-Paul Sartre, *Being and Nothingness: A Phenomenological Essay on Ontology,* trans. Hazel E. Barnes (New York: Simon and Schuster Pocket Books, 1956), 342; originally published as *L'Être et le néant: Essai d'ontologie phénoménologique* (Paris: Gallimard, 1943), 301–2.

6. Sartre, *Being and Nothingness,* 479; Sartre, *L'Être et le néant,* 416.

7. Scarry, *On Beauty and Being Just,* 57.

8. Ibid., 58.

9. G. W. F. Hegel, *Phenomenology of Spirit,* trans. A. V. Miller (Oxford: Oxford University Press, 1977), paragraph 167, p. 105. See also the following paragraph 168: "Self-consciousness which is simply *for itself* and directly characterizes its object as *a negative element* [my emphasis], or is primarily *desire,* will therefore, on the contrary, learn through experience that the object is independent."

10. Jean Hyppolite, *Genesis and Structure of Hegel's "Phenomenology of Spirit,"*

trans. Samuel Cherniak and John Heckman (Evanston, Ill.: Northwestern University Press, 1974), 160. See also Judith Butler, *Subjects of Desire: Hegelian Reflections in Twentieth-Century France* (New York: Columbia University Press, 1987), 35: "Desire can thus be said to reveal negation as constitutive of experience itself."

11. See Alexandre Kojève, *Introduction to the Reading of Hegel: Lectures on the Phenomenology of Spirit,* trans. James H. Nichols, Jr. (New York: Basic Books, 1969); originally published as *Introduction à la lecture de Hegel* (Paris: Éditions Gallimard, 1947). Kojève gave his famous lectures at the École Practique des Hautes Études from 1933 to 1939, and they were attended by Merleau-Ponty as well as by Sartre and other emerging leading French intellectuals of the 1930s and '40s.

12. Hegel, *Introductory Lectures on Aesthetics,* 41 [LVI, αα].

13. Ibid., 43 [LVIII, γγ].

14. Ibid., 44 [LVIII, γγ].

15. Renaud Barbaras, *Desire and Distance: An Introduction to a Phenomenology of Perception,* trans. Paul B. Milan (Stanford, Calif.: Stanford University Press, 2006), 111.

16. Ibid., 112. Barbaras cites Levinas's exposition of Husserl for support of this interpretation. See Emmanuel Levinas, *Otherwise Than Being, or Beyond Essence* (Boston: Martinus Nijhoff, 1981), 66.

17. Barbaras, *Desire and Distance,* 113, 114.

18. Ibid., 116.

19. Ibid., 121.

20. See the commentary on this passage by Gary B. Madison, "Flesh as Otherness," in *Ontology and Alterity in Merleau-Ponty,* ed. Galen A. Johnson and Michael B. Smith (Evanston, Ill.: Northwestern University Press, 1990), 33–34.

21. The French word *pointillé* means a stipple drawing or engraving, or a dotted line.

22. Hegel, *Introductory Lectures on Aesthetics,* 43 [LVIII, γγ].

23. Plato, *Symposium,* trans. Alexander Nehamas and Paul Woodruff (Indianapolis, Ind.: Hackett, 1989), 211e–212a, pp. 59–60.

24. Ibid., 200e, pp. 42–43.

25. Plato, *Republic,* trans. G. M. A. Grube (Indianapolis, Ind.: Hackett, 1974), 440c, p. 104.

26. Plato, *Symposium,* 192c-d, p. 28.

27. Heidegger, *Will to Power as Art,* 108.

28. Ibid., 109.

29. Martin Heidegger, "On the Essence of Truth," in *Martin Heidegger: Basic Writings,* ed. David Ferrell Krell (San Francisco: Harper San Francisco, 1977, 1933), 125.

30. Ibid., 129.

31. Heidegger, *Will to Power as Art,* 110.

32. Mauro Carbone, "Letting-Be According to Heidegger and Merleau-Ponty," in *Thinking of the Sensible,* 42, 43.

33. Blaise Pascal, *Pensées,* in *The Essential Pascal,* ed. Robert W. Gleason,

trans. G. F. Pullen (New York: New American Library, 1966), *pensée* number 626, p. 195.

34. Martin Heidegger, *Introduction to Metaphysics,* trans. Ralph Manheim (Garden City, N.Y.: Doubleday, 1961), 27–28.

35. See Bernard Waldenfels, "The Paradox of Expression," in *Chiasms: Merleau-Ponty's Notion of Flesh,* ed. Fred Evans and Leonard Lawlor (Albany: State University of New York Press, 2000), 90.

36. Ibid., 95–97. Waldenfels delineates four aspects of Merleau-Ponty's paradox of expression: divergence, translation, delayed effect (*après coup*), and excess.

37. See David Michael Kleinberg-Levin, "The Remembrance of Nature in the Voice of the Subject," chap. 1 of *Before the Voice of Reason: Echoes of Responsibility in Merleau-Ponty's Ecology and Levinas's Ethics* (Albany: State University of New York Press, 2008).

38. It would be speculation on our part to attempt to fill in which philosophies Merleau-Ponty had in mind as these "semantic philosophies." We know, for example, that he had an exchange with Gilbert Ryle, W. V. O. Quine, and A. J. Ayer in 1960, even though Merleau-Ponty had selected Ryle to write the chapter on Hume in *Les philosophes célèbres.* See Merleau-Ponty, "Phenomenology and Analytic Philosophy," esp. 65–72.

39. Carbone, *Thinking of the Sensible,* xv.

40. See the similar conclusion at which Mauro Carbone has arrived: "Merleau-Ponty's approach seems to extend, to the entire sensible domain, Kant's characterizaton of the limited domain of the beautiful, at least according to the interpretation that Heidegger proposes, in his Nietzsche courses, on the first moment of the judgment of taste." *Thinking of the Sensible,* 42.

Chapter 7

The first epigraph for this chapter is from Søren Kierkegaard, *Repetition: A Venture in Experimenting Psychology* [Report by Constantin Constantius], ed. and trans. Howard V. Hong and Edna H. Hong (Princeton, N.J.: Princeton University Press, 1983), 132. The second epigraph is from Merleau-Ponty, *PP* 242; *PhP* 280. The third epigraph is from Gilles Deleuze, *Difference and Repetition,* trans. Paul Patton (New York: Columbia University Press, 1994), 76. The French original, *Différence et repetition,* appeared in 1968 from the Athlone Press.

1. Vesela Sretenovic, "InVisible Silence," David Winton Bell Gallery, Brown University, Providence, R.I., September 11–October 26, 2004. As curator of Brown University's Bell Gallery, in introducing the exhibit, Sretenovic writes: "The exhibition *InVisible Silence* pays homage to Merleau-Ponty's ontology of the visible and the invisible, especially his notions of *silence* (indirect, implicit, latent meaning that operates via sensuousness and affectivity) and *reversibility* (recursive intertwining of the self and world, and visible perception and invisible meaning)."

2. *Echo* was one of the three-part exhibition called "Air-Conditioned (E:R Conditionée)," which represented the Luxemborg Pavilion at the Venice Biennale in 2003, and which received a Golden Lion for the best National Pavilion.

3. Plato, *Symposium,* 206d, p. 53.

4. Kierkegaard, *Repetition: A Venture in Experimenting Psychology,* 131.

5. Ibid.

6. Ibid., 136.

7. Ibid., 132.

8. Deleuze, *Difference and Repetition,* 90.

9. Ibid.

10. Plato, *Meno,* in *Plato: Five Dialogues,* trans. by G. M. A. Grube, ed. Donald J. Zeyl (Indianapolis, Ind.: Hackett, 1981), 80e, p. 69.

11. See David Wood's discussion of this Nietzschean dilemma in "Nietzsche's Transvaluation of Time," in *Exceedingly Nietzsche: Aspects of Contemporary Nietzsche Interpretation,* ed. David Farrell Krell and David Wood (New York: Routledge, 1988), 51–54.

12. Deleuze, *Difference and Repetition,* 201–2.

13. Warhol multiplied seemingly endless repetitions of icons of erotic sensuality like Elvis Presley and Marilyn Monroe, as well as iconic images of cultural history such as *Mona Lisa.* Other examples of repetitions were included in the 1999–2000 exhibition titled "Regarding Beauty" at the Hirshhorn Museum in Washington, D. C., which included Warhol's *Marilyn Monroe's Lips.* Variation is doubled and tripled in Yasumasa Morimura's 1988 *Portrait* (*Futago*), in which Morimura himself assumes the role of the subject of Édouard Manet's famous *Olympia* (1863), except that Morimura wears a blonde wig, junk jewelry, pink nail polish, and metallic slippers, and the artist reclines on a bed covered with a kimono. Morimura also poses as the black servant from Manet's original, although holding a basket of plastic rather than fresh flowers. The curator, Olga M. Viso, comments in the catalog for the exhibition that "the brilliance of Morimura's seeming pastiche is the manner in which he draws on Manet's own iconoclasm for his purposes." "Regarding Beauty: A View of the Late Twentieth Century," 95.

14. In "The Originality of the Avant-Garde," Rosalind Krauss argues that the necessary "other" to originality is repetition. See *The Originality of the Avant-Garde and Other Modernist Myths* (Cambridge, Mass.: MIT Press, 1985), 151–70.

15. See Barnett Newman, "Remarks at Artists' Sessions at Studio 35," in *Barnett Newman: Selected Writings and Interviews,* 240.

16. Cited in Ann Temkin, "Barnett Newman on Exhibition," in *Barnett Newman,* catalog of the exhibition "Barnett Newman," Philadelphia Museum of Art, March 24–July 7, 2002, and Tate Modern, London, September 19, 2002–January 5, 2003 (Philadelphia: Philadelphia Museum of Art, 2002), 40.

17. These were the proportions displayed in Da Vinci's famous drawing of a male nude, *Vitruvian Man.* The number PHI, derived from the Fibonacci sequence, is so ubiquitous in nature that it was thought to be the Divine Proportion: 1.68, sometimes also called the Golden Section. Leonardo named his draw-

ing for Marcus Vitruvius, the brilliant Roman architect who praised the Divine Proportion in his text *De Architectura.*

18. On Merleau-Ponty's use of music and melody for explicating nature, particularly the relationship of animal to milieu, see Ted Toadvine, "Gestalts and Refrains: On the Musical Structure of Nature," *Environmental Philosophy* 2, no. 2 (Fall 2005): 61–71; as well as his "The Melody of Life and the Motif of Philosophy," *Chiasmi International* 7 (2005): 263–79. These themes recur in Toadvine's book *Merleau-Ponty's Philosophy of Nature* (Evanston, Ill.: Northwestern University Press, 2009).

19. Carbone, *Thinking of the Sensible,* 37.

20. I have corrected the English translation based upon the French original: "'je ne savais pas' et 'je l'ai toujours su.'"

21. I appropriate this term, which means crossed eyes, from Merleau-Ponty's account of Husserl's phenomenology, which "denounces the natural attitude and at the same time does more than any other philosophy to rehabilitate it" as the *Lebenswelt.*

22. M. C. Dillon, "The Unconscious: Language and World," in Burke and Van der Veken, *Merleau-Ponty in Contemporary Perspective,* 72–73.

23. Leonard Lawlor, *Thinking Through French Philosophy: The Being of the Question* (Bloomington: Indiana University Press, 2003), 90. Bernard Waldenfels argues that "this withdrawal of the origin" recalls much of what Derrida and Levinas come to speak of as "*après coup*" and "trace." See Waldenfels, "Paradox of Expression," 96.

24. For an excellent account of the concept of the imagination in Merleau-Ponty, and discussion of its difference from the Sartrean account, see Glen Mazis, "*La Chair et L'Imaginaire:* The Developing Role of Imagination in Merleau-Ponty's Philosophy," *Philosophy Today* 32, no. 4 (Spring 1988): 30–42.

25. Deleuze, *Difference and Repetition,* 76.

26. Gaston Bachelard, *On Poetic Imagination and Reverie: Selections from the Works of Gaston Bachelard,* trans. Colette Gaudin (Indianapolis, Ind.: Bobbs-Merrill, 1971), 10, 12; originally published as Gaston Bachelard, *L'Eau et les rêves: Essai sur l'imagination de la matière* (Paris: Librairie José Corti, 1942), 1–3.

27. Rilke, *Auguste Rodin,* 67–69.

28. George Santayana, *The Sense of Beauty: Being the Outlines of Aesthetic Theory* (Cambridge, Mass.: MIT Press, 1988; orig. pub. New York: Charles Scribner's Sons, 1896), 8.

29. Lucien Herr was a professor at the École Normale Supérieure in the early part of the twentieth century and was part of the French Hegel renaissance in France, along with Alexandre Kojéve and Jean Hyppolite. The phrase "Nature is at the first day" is found in Lucien Herr, *Choix d'écrits, II: Philosophie, histoire, philologie* (Paris: Éditions Redier, 1932): "Cette évolution de la nature est une reconstruction logique, mais non pas une histoire de la nature: pour Hegel comme pour Aristote, la nature est au premier jour, est, depuis qu'elle est, ce qu'elle est aujourd'hui" (127–28). This Hegelian account also brings to mind what Emerson and the transcendentalists called "the Newness."

30. Edith Hamilton, *Mythology* (New York: Mentor Book, New American Library, 1942), 87.

31. Ovid, *The Metamorphoses,* trans. Horace Gregory (New York: Mentor Book, New American Library, 1960), book 3, p. 97.

32. Ibid.

33. Ibid., book 3, p. 98.

34. Ibid., book 3, p. 100.

35. Sigmund Freud, "Beyond the Pleasure Principle," in *The Freud Reader,* ed. Peter Gay (New York: W. W. Norton, 1989), 611.

36. Ibid., 612.

37. Sigmund Freud, "On Narcissism: An Introduction," in *The Freud Reader,* 554.

38. Ibid., 553.

39. Ibid., 556.

40. In secondary narcissism, too, Freud believes he finds the explanation of the homosexual personality. Homosexuals are "plainly seeking themselves as a love-object, and exhibiting a type of object-choice which must be termed 'narcissistic'" (ibid., 554). This surely remains one of the most facile overextensions of a theory available in the Freudian literature.

41. Angelo Hesnard, *L'Oeuvre de Freud et son importance pour le monde moderne* (Paris: Payot, 1960), 327 (my translation).

42. Maurice Merleau-Ponty, "Phenomenology and Psychoanalysis: Preface to Hesnard's *L'Oeuvre de Freud,*" trans. Alden Fisher, *Review of Existential Psychology and Psychiatry* 18, nos. 1, 2, and 3 (1982–83): 71.

43. Ibid.

44. Renaud Barbaras, *The Being of the Phenomenon: Merleau-Ponty's Ontology,* trans. Ted Toadvine and Leonard Lawlor (Bloomington: Indiana University Press, 2004), 269. See also the full discussion on 266–72.

45. Barbaras, *Desire and Distance,* 121, 125.

46. For detailed analysis of the history of self-portraits and the use of mirrors, see Hugh Silverman, "Cézanne's Mirror Stage," in Johnson, *Merleau-Ponty Aesthetics Reader,* 262–77.

47. See Bettyann Holtzmann Kevles, "Portrait Without the Camera Face," in Gary Schneider, *Genetic Self-Portrait* (Syracuse, N.Y.: Light, Work, 1999), pages not numbered.

48. See the artist's commentary on the individual works in Schneider, *Genetic Self-Portrait.*

49. Rilke, *Auguste Rodin,* 69.

50. Mauro Carbone, "Voyance," in *Thinking of the Sensible,* 31–35.

51. This is the French: "En échange de ce qu'on avait imaginé, la vie vous donne autre chose, et autre chose qui était secrètement voulu, non fortuit. Réalisation n'est pas ce qui était prévu, mais tout de même ce qui était voulu: on avance à reculons, on ne choisit pas directement, mais obliquement, mais on fait tout de même ce qu'on veut: l'amour est clairvoyant, il nous addresse justment à ce qui peut nous déchirer" (*IP* 75).

52. Merleau-Ponty's reference is to Jean Hyppolite's article "Commentaire parlé sur la '*Verneinung*' de Freud," now published in Hyppolite, *Figures de la pensée philosophique,* vol. 1 (Paris: Presses Universitaires de France, 1971), 385–96.

53. I owe this phrase entirely to Mauro Carbone's paper "Love and Music: Theme and Variations," *Chiasmi International* 11 (2009), forthcoming; French translation available as "Amour et musique: Thème et variations," *Alter* 15 (2007): 103–21. Carbone explores similar themes in his yet-unpublished paper "How Can One Recognize What One Did Not Know? *Mnemosyne* and the Art of the Twentieth Century," in *Phenomenology and Literature,* ed. P. Vandevelde (Würzburg, Ger.: Koenigshausen und Neumann, forthcoming).

54. Ovid, *Metamorphoses,* book 3, p. 95.

55. Ibid., book 3, pp. 95–96.

56. Friedrich Nietzsche, *Thus Spoke Zarathustra,* trans. Walter Kaufmann, in *The Portable Nietzsche* (New York: Viking, 1968), part 3, section 2, pp. 269–70.

57. Heidegger, "Origin of the Work of Art," 56.

58. See *The Compact Edition of the Oxford English Dictionary, Complete Text Reproduced Micrographically,* vol. 2: P-Z (Oxford: Oxford University Press, 1971), 636.

59. Paul Valéry, "Poetry and Abstract Thought," in *The Art of Poetry,* trans. Denise Folliot (New York: Pantheon Books, 1958), 71.

60. Ibid., 72.

61. Gilles Deleuze, *Francis Bacon: The Logic of Sensation,* trans. Daniel W. Smith (Minneapolis: University of Minnesota Press, 2003), 37.

62. Ibid.

63. Ibid., 39.

64. Ibid., 61.

65. Ibid., 39.

66. Merleau-Ponty, "Christianisme et ressentiment," *La Vie Intellectuelle,* new series, vol. 36 (1935): 278–308. This article first appeared in English translation in the *Review of Existential Psychology and Psychiatry* 9 (1968–69). It has now been anthologized under the title "Christianity and *Ressentiment*" in *Texts and Dialogues,* 85–100.

67. Merleau-Ponty, "Christianity and *Ressentiment,*" 86.

68. Ibid., 97. Moreover, Merleau-Ponty agrees that all of Nietzsche's enemies—Schopenhauer, Wagner, Socrates, Saint Paul—were "internal enemies," by which he means that they were "nothing but phantoms conjured in his own mind." Therefore, for Nietzsche, the "Christianity which he tramples underfoot is none other than an aspect of himself" (97).

69. Friedrich Nietzsche, *The Gay Science,* 2nd ed., trans. Walter Kaufmann (New York: Random House, 1974), preface, p. 38.

70. Ibid., 38.

71. Friedrich Nietzsche, *The Birth of Tragedy and Other Writings,* ed. Raymond Geuss and Ronald Spiers, trans. Ronald Spiers (Cambridge, Eng.: Cambridge University Press, 1999), 16.

72. Ibid., 26.

73. Ibid., 27.

74. Ibid., 21.

75. Ibid., 18.

76. Ibid., 26.

77. Ibid.

78. Ibid., 27. For another commentary on Raphael's *Transfiguration* in relation to Nietzsche's *The Birth of Tragedy,* see Günter Figal, "Aesthetically Limited Reason: On Nietzsche's *The Birth of Tragedy,*" in *Philosophy and Tragedy,* ed. Miguel de Beistegui and Simon Sparks (London: Routledge, 2000), 145–46.

79. Friedrich Nietzsche, "An Attempt at Self-Criticism," in *The Birth of Tragedy and Other Writings,* 10.

80. See Friedrich Nietzsche, *Beyond Good and Evil,* trans. Walter Kaufmann (New York: Vintage Books, 1966), section 56, p. 68.

81. Nietzsche, *The Birth of Tragedy and Other Writings,* 23.

82. Ibid., 98.

83. Paul Claudel, "Knowledge of Time," in *Poetic Art,* trans. Renee Spodheim (New York: Philosophical Library, 1948), 35; originally published as "Connaissance du temps," in *Art Poétique* (Paris: Mercure de France, 1929), 57.

Chapter 8

The first epigraph for this chapter is from Merleau-Ponty, "EM" 146; *OE* 83. The second epigraph is from Kant, *CJ* 27/115.

1. Stephen Watson has similarly written that "surely Kant's retrieval of the symbolics of the beautiful always hovers nearby *The Phenomenology of Perception*'s attempts to articulate a new transcendental aesthetic." See Watson, "Withdrawal of the Beautiful," 203.

2. Santayana, *Sense of Beauty,* 35.

3. Ibid., 34.

4. We are aware that in the contemporary aesthetics of nature there is a literature discussing and debating this point, namely whether scientific knowledge and information regarding a forest or other landscape or seascape enhances or detracts from our aesthetic experience. See Holmes Rolston III, "The Aesthetic Experience of Forests," and Cheryl Foster, "The Narrative and the Ambient in Environmental Aesthetics," both in *The Aesthetics of Natural Environments,* ed. Allen Carlson and Arnold Berleant (Toronto: Broadview, 2004), 182–96, 197–213, respectively. See also Salim Kemal and Ivan Gaskell, eds., *Landscape, Natural Beauty, and the Arts* (Cambridge, Eng.: Cambridge University Press, 1993).

5. In enumerating these four constituents of a judgment of taste, I am following the analysis of Jean-François Lyotard, *Peregrinations: Law, Form, Event* (New York: Columbia University Press, 1988), 29–30. See also Jean-François Lyotard, *Lessons on the Analytic of the Sublime,* trans. Elizabeth Rottenberg (Stanford, Calif.: Stanford University Press, 1994).

6. See Alan D. Schrift, *Twentieth-Century French Philosophy: Key Themes and*

Thinkers (Oxford: Blackwell, 2006), 166–69; 107–8. See also *The Columbia History of Twentieth-Century French Thought,* ed. Lawrence D. Kritzman (New York: Columbia University Press, 2006), 459–60.

7. See Léon Brunschvicg, *Le progrès de la conscience dans la philosophie occidentale* (Paris: Alcan, 1927). This is one of two books cited by Merleau-Ponty throughout *Phenomenology of Perception,* the other being *L'Experience humaine et la causalité physique* (Paris: Alcan, 1922).

8. Edmund Husserl, *Ideas Pertaining to a Pure Phenomenology and to Phenomenological Philosophy,* First Book: "General Introduction to Pure Phenomenology," trans. F. Kersten (Dordrecht, Neth.: Kluwer Academic, 1982), section 74, p. 166. See also sections 67–69, pp. 153–57. (Note: "Umbelliform" is a botanical term referring to a number of short flower stalks called pedicels that are equal in length and spread from a common point, somewhat like umbrella ribs. Umbels are a characteristic of plants such as carrot, parsley, dill, and fennel.)

9. Heidegger, *Will to Power in Art,* 116.

10. Ibid. See Rainer Maria Rilke, *Duino Elegies,* trans. Stephen Cohn (Evanston, Ill.: Northwestern University Press, 1989): "For Beauty is only the infant of scarcely endurable Terror, and we are amazed when it casually spares us" (21).

11. Ralph Waldo Emerson, "Beauty," chap. 3 of *Nature,* in *Ralph Waldo Emerson: Essays and Lectures* (New York: Library of America, 1983), 14.

12. Rilke, *Auguste Rodin,* 38.

13. Dufrenne, *Phenomenology of Aesthetic Experience,* 516ff. On the intelligence of music, see also Martha Nussbaum, "Music and Emotion," chap. 5 of *Upheavals of Thought: The Intelligence of the Emotions* (Cambridge, Eng.: Cambridge University Press, 2001).

14. Rodin, *Art: Conversations with Paul Gsell,* 74.

15. Dufrenne, *Phenomenology of Aesthetic Experience,* 516.

16. Ibid., 518.

17. Ibid., 519.

18. Ibid., 516–28.

19. Rodin, *Art: Conversations with Paul Gsell,* 83.

20. "The figures are sublime in their simplicity." Rilke, *Auguste Rodin,* 61.

21. Immanuel Kant, *Anthropology from a Pragmatic Point of View,* trans. Robert B. Louden (Cambridge, Eng.: Cambridge University Press, 2006), 138.

22. Lyotard, *Lessons on the Analytic of the Sublime,* 90–93.

23. Immanuel Kant, *Critique of Practical Reason,* trans. Thomas Kingsmill Abbott (Mineola, N.Y.: Dover, 2004), 170.

24. Elsen, *Rodin,* 103.

25. It is puzzling how to square this view of the possibility of war as part of the sublime with Kant's 1795 project of perpetual peace, federalism, and a league of peace among nations. See Immanuel Kant, "To Perpetual Peace: A Philosophical Sketch," in *Perpetual Peace and Other Essays,* trans. Ted Humphrey (Indianapolis, Ind.: Hackett, 1983), esp. "Second Article," 115–18.

26. Some have recently extended the Kantian sublime toward a particularly "American" version of the technological sublime. See David E. Nye, *American*

Technological Sublime (Cambridge, Mass.: MIT Press, 1994), chaps. 1 and 2. Be that as it may, this aspect of Kant's philosophy of the sublime seems unaware of the alienation in the modern sublime feeling discussed later in Walter Benjamin's analysis of fascism and Marinetti's futurist manifesto declaring that "war is beautiful." "The logical result of Fascism," Benjamin wrote, "is the introduction of aesthetics into politics." "Mankind has reached such a degree of self-alienation that it can experience its own destruction as an aesthetic pleasure of the first order." See Walter Benjamin, "The Work of Art in the Age of Mechanical Reproduction," in *Illuminations,* trans. Harry Zohn (New York: Schocken Books, 1968), 241–42. Lyotard, too, has written of a particular aesthetics of the political linked with the sublime: "The aesthetics of the sublime, thus neutralized and converted into a politics of myth," he writes, "was able to come and build its architectures of human 'formations' on the Zeppelin Feld in Nürnberg," the party rally grounds for the military maneuvers and parades of the Nazi Party designed by Alfred Speer. See Lyotard, "Sublime and the Avant-Garde," 209.

27. Edward S. Casey, *Representing Place: Landscape Painting and Maps* (Minneapolis: University of Minnesota Press, 2002), 90.

28. Bernard Sichère, unpublished manuscript of a talk at the University of Essex, England, "Merleau-Ponty: On Painting," April 26, 1991, manuscript page 8. Sichère asked and replied: "Is this world beautiful? Merleau-Ponty seems to think so, he seems to think that painting is made to unveil or disclose this generous beauty, this happy spring of primary things. But he has also mentioned in one early writing, 'Cézanne's Doubt,' that Cézanne's painting shows to us the 'depth of inhuman nature.'"

29. Henry David Thoreau, "Walking," in *Civil Disobedience and Other Essays* (New York: Dover, 1993), 61, 64–65. This essay was first published posthumously in the June 1862 issue of *The Atlantic Monthly,* only one month after Thoreau's death on May 6, 1862. He had submitted the essay on March 11, 1862. See Robert D. Richardson, *Henry Thoreau: A Life of the Mind* (Berkeley: University of California Press, 1986), 387–88. Richardson argues: "As *Walden* was Thoreau's central book, so 'Walking' is his central essay" (224). Indeed, "The Wild" was a favorite lecture for Thoreau to give beginning from April 1851, given many times.

30. See my article "The Beautiful and the Sublime in Merleau-Ponty and Lyotard," *Chiasmi International,* 10th anniversary edition for Maurice Merleau-Ponty, 1908–2008, vol. 10, new series (2008): 207–26.

31. Rosenberg, *Barnett Newman,* 47.

32. Ibid., 62.

33. Jean-François Lyotard, *Discours, figure* (Paris: Klincksieck, 1971; 5th printing, 2002), 20; "Excerpts from *Discours, figure,*" trans. Michael B. Smith, in Johnson, *Merleau-Ponty Aesthetics Reader,* 311. The complete volume of *Discours, figure* has not yet been translated into English.

34. Lyotard, "Excerpts from *Discours, figure,*" 312.

35. Ibid., 313.

36. Ibid.

37. Ibid., 317, 318.

38. Renaud Barbaras has argued for the substitution of the term "Life" for Merleau-Ponty's notion of Flesh, and that is what I am objecting to here. Barbaras argues that Flesh is a univocal concept constructed on the basis of the human body, but the body itself has to be understood more primordially in terms of life and movement, following Aristotle. Our whole endeavor has been to show the multiplicities in the meaning of "Flesh" and to emphasize the element of time as genesis. See Barbaras, *Desire and Distance,* 83–87.

39. Martin Heidegger, *Contributions to Philosophy (From Enowning),* trans. Parvis Emad and Kenneth Maly (Bloomington: Indiana University Press, 1999), 54. See also Walter Brogan, "Da-Sein and the Leap of Being," in *Companion to Heidegger's "Contributions to Philosophy,"* ed. Charles E. Scott and others (Bloomington: Indiana University Press, 2001), 173.

40. Claudel, "Knowledge of Time," 35; Claudel, "Connaissance du temps," 57.

41. Françoise Dastur, "Phenomenology of the Event: Waiting and Surprise," *Hypatia* 15, no. 4 (Autumn 2000): 186. The thinking of "event" in this chapter is very much indebted to this work by Professor Dastur, and I express my thanks.

42. Ibid., 183.

43. Rilke, *Letters on Cézanne,* 65.

44. Lyotard, "Sublime and the Avant-Garde," 197.

Bibliography

Adorno, Theodor. *Aesthetic Theory,* ed. Gretel Adorno and Rolf Tiedemann, trans. Robert Hullot-Kentor. Minneapolis: University of Minnesota Press, 1997.

Aichele, K. Porter. *Paul Klee, Poet/Painter.* New York: Camden House, 2006.

———. *Paul Klee's Pictorial Writing.* Cambridge, Eng.: Cambridge University Press, 2002.

Aristotle. *The Poetics,* in *Aristotle on Poetry and Style,* trans. G. M. A. Grube. Indianapolis, Ind.: Hackett, 1989.

Atherton, Margaret. "How to Write the History of Vision: Understanding the Relationship Between Berkeley and Descartes." In *Sites of Vision: The Discursive Construction of Sight in the History of Philosophy,* ed. David Michael Levin, 139–65. Cambridge, Mass.: MIT Press, 1997.

Ayral-Clause, Odile. *Camille Claudel: A Life.* New York: Harry N. Abrams, 2002.

Bachelard, Gaston. *On Poetic Imagination and Reverie: Selections from the Works of Gaston Bachelard,* trans. Colette Gaudin. Indianapolis, Ind.: Bobbs-Merrill, 1971. Originally published as *L'Eau et les rêves: Essai sur l'imagination de la matière.* Paris: Librairie José Corti, 1942.

Badt, Kurt. *The Art of Cézanne,* trans. Sheila Ann Ogilvie. London: Faber and Faber, 1965.

Barbaras, Renaud. *The Being of the Phenomenon: Merleau-Ponty's Ontology,* trans. Ted Toadvine and Leonard Lawlor. Bloomington: Indiana University Press, 2004.

———. *Desire and Distance: An Introduction to a Phenomenology of Perception,* trans. Paul B. Milan. Stanford, Calif.: Stanford University Press, 2006.

Baudelaire, Charles. *The Flowers of Evil and Paris Spleen,* trans. William H. Crosby. Brockport, N.Y.: BOA Editions, 1991.

———. *The Painter of Modern Life and Other Essays,* trans. Jonathan Mayne. London: Phaidon, 1964.

———. *Prose Poems.* In *Baudelaire, Rimbaud, Verlaine: Selected Verse and Poems,* ed. Joseph M. Bernstein. New York: Citadel, 1991.

Beckley, Bill, and David Shapiro, eds. *Uncontrollable Beauty: Toward a New Aesthetics.* New York: Allworth, 1998.

Behnke, Elizabeth A. "At the Service of the Sonata: Music Lessons with Merleau-Ponty." In *Merleau-Ponty: Critical Essays,* ed. Henry Pietersma, 23–29. Washington, D.C.: Center for Advanced Research in Phenomenology, University Press of America, 1989.

Beistegui, Miguel de. *The New Heidegger.* London: Continuum, 2005.

———. *Thinking with Heidegger: Displacements.* Bloomington: Indiana University Press, 2003.

Beistegui, Miguel de, and Simon Sparks, eds. *Philosophy and Tragedy.* London: Routledge, 2000.

Benjamin, Walter. *Illuminations,* trans. Harry Zohn. New York: Schocken Books, 1968.

Bergson, Henri. *The Creative Mind,* trans. Mabelle L. Andison. New York: Greenwood, 1968.

Bernard, Émile. *Souvenirs sur Paul Cézanne.* Paris: Société de Trente Albert Messein, 1912.

Bonan, Ronald. *Premières leçons sur l'esthétique de Merleau-Ponty.* Paris: Presses Universitaires de France, 1997.

Brady, Emily, and Jerrold Levinson, eds. *Aesthetic Concepts: Essays After Sibley.* Oxford: Clarendon, 2001.

Brand, Peg Zeglin, ed. *Beauty Matters.* Bloomington: Indiana University Press, 2000.

Brix, Michael. "Modern Beauty versus Platonist Beauty," trans. Tony Campbell. In *Baudelaire and the Poetics of Modernity,* ed. Patricia A. Ward, 1–14. Nashville, Tenn.: Vanderbilt University Press, 2001.

Brown, Charles S., and Ted Toadvine, eds. *Nature's Edge: Boundary Explorations in Ecological Theory and Practice.* Albany: State University of New York Press, 2007.

Brubaker, David. "Painting from the Heart: Beauty, Moore, and Merleau-Ponty's Wholes of Visibility." *Analecta Husserliana* 92 (2006): 103–11.

Burke, Edmund. *A Philosophical Enquiry into the Origin of Our Ideas of the Sublime and Beautiful.* Oxford: Oxford University Press, 1990.

Butler, Judith. "Sexual Difference as a Question of Ethics: Alterities of the Flesh in Irigaray and Merleau-Ponty." *Chiasmi International,* 10th anniversary edition for Maurice Merleau-Ponty, 1908–2008, vol. 10, new series (2008): 321–47.

———. *Subjects of Desire: Hegelian Reflections in Twentieth-Century France.* New York: Columbia University Press, 1987.

Butler, Ruth. *Hidden in the Shadow of the Master: The Model-Wives of Cézanne, Monet, and Rodin.* New Haven, Conn.: Yale University Press, 2008.

———, ed. *Rodin in Perspective.* Englewood Cliffs, N.J.: Prentice-Hall, 1980.

———. *Rodin: The Shape of Genius.* New Haven, Conn.: Yale University Press, 1993.

Carbone, Mauro. "Amour et musique: Thème et variations." *Alter* 15 (2007): 103–21. Translated into English as "Love and Music: Theme and Variations," *Chiasmi International* 11 (2009): forthcoming.

———. "The Mythical Time of the Ideas: Merleau-Ponty and Deleuze as Readers of Proust." *Journal of the British Society for Phenomenology,* special issue, Merleau-Ponty 1908–2008, vol. 39, no. 1 (January 2008): 12–26.

———. *The Thinking of the Sensible: Merleau-Ponty's A-Philosophy.* Evanston, Ill.: Northwestern University Press, 2004.

Carlson, Allen, and Arnold Berleant, eds. *The Aesthetics of Natural Environments.* Toronto: Broadview, 2004.

Carter, A. E. *Charles Baudelaire.* Boston: Twayne, 1977.

Casey, Edward S. *Representing Place: Landscape Painting and Maps.* Minneapolis: University of Minnesota Press, 2002.

Cataldi, Suzanne, and William Hamrick, eds. *Merleau-Ponty and Environmental Philosophy: Dwelling on the Landscapes of Thought.* Albany: State University of New York Press, 2007.

Chapman, Emmanuel. *Saint Augustine's Philosophy of Beauty.* New York: Sheed and Ward, 1939.

Cohen, Jeffrey Jerome, and Gail Weiss, eds. *Thinking the Limits of the Body.* Albany: State University of New York Press, 2003.

Collingwood, R. G. *The Principles of Art.* Oxford: Oxford University Press, 1938.

Copenhaver, Brian, ed. *Hermetica: The Greek "Corpus Hermeticum" and the Latin "Asclepius,"* trans. Brian Copenhaver. Cambridge, Eng.: Cambridge University Press, 1992.

Danto, Arthur C. *The Abuse of Beauty: Aesthetics and the Concept of Art.* Chicago: Open Court, 2003.

———. "Beauty and Morality." In *Uncontrollable Beauty: Toward a New Aesthetics,* ed. Bill Beckley and David Shapiro, 25–38. New York: Allworth, 1998.

———. *Embodied Meanings: Critical Essays and Aesthetic Meditations.* New York: Farrar, Straus and Giroux, 1994.

———. "Rothko and Beauty." In *The Madonna of the Future: Essays in a Pluralistic Art World,* 335–42. New York: Farrar, Straus and Giroux, 2000.

Delaunay, Robert. "Light" (1912). In *The New Art of Color: The Writings of Robert and Sonia Delaunay,* ed. Arthur A. Cohen, trans. David Shapiro and Arthur A. Cohen, 80–86. New York: Viking, 1978. Originally published as "La lumière," in *Du cubisme à l'art abstrait.* Paris: SEVPEN, 1957.

Delcò, Alessandro. *Merleau-Ponty et l'expérience de la création: Du paradigme au scheme.* Paris: Presses Universitaires de France, 2005.

———. "Phénoménologie et peinture: Merleau-Ponty à la école de Klee." *Archives de philosophie* 65 (2002): 609–15.

Deleuze, Gilles. *Difference and Repetition,* trans. Paul Patton. New York: Columbia University Press, 1994. Originally published as *Différence et repetition.* Paris: Athlone, 1968.

———. *Francis Bacon: The Logic of Sensation,* trans. Daniel W. Smith. Minneapolis: University of Minnesota Press, 2003. Originally published as *Francis Bacon: Logique de la sensation.* Éditions de la Différence, 1981; Éditions du Seuil, 2002.

Deleuze, Gilles, and Félix Guattari. *What Is Philosophy?* trans. Hugh Tomlinson and Graham Burchell. New York: Columbia University Press, 1994. Originally published as *Qu'est-que la philosophie?* Paris: Les Éditions de Minuet, 1991.

Derrida, Jacques. *Memoirs of the Blind: The Self-Portrait and Other Ruins,* trans. Pascale-Anne Brault and Michael Naas. Chicago: University of Chicago

Press, 1993. Originally published as *Mémoires d'aveugle: L'Autoportrait et autres ruines*. Paris: Éditions de la Réunion des musées nationaux, 1990.

———. *On Touching—Jean-Luc Nancy*, trans. Christine Irizarry. Stanford, Calif.: Stanford University Press, 2005. Originally published as *Le toucher, Jean-Luc Nancy*. Paris: Éditions Galilée, 2000.

———. *The Truth in Painting*, trans. Geoff Bennington and Ian McLeod. Chicago: University of Chicago Press, 1987. Originally published as *La vérité en peinture*. Paris: Flammarion, 1978.

Descartes, René. "Optics." In *Discourse on Method, Optics, Geometry, and Meteorology*, trans. Paul J. Olscamp. Indianapolis, Ind.: Bobbs-Merrill, Library of Liberal Arts, 1965.

———. *The Passions of the Soul*. In *The Philosophical Writings of Descartes*, vol. 1, trans. John Cottingham, Robert Stoothoff, and Dugald Murdoch. Cambridge, Eng.: Cambridge University Press, 1985.

Dewey, John. *Art as Experience*. New York: Capricorn Books, 1934.

Dillon, M. C. "*A Priority* in Kant and Merleau-Ponty." *Kant-Studien* 17, no. 3: 403–23.

———, ed. *Écart and Difference: Merleau-Ponty and Derrida on Seeing and Writing*. New Jersey: Humanities, 1997.

———. *Merleau-Ponty's Ontology*. Bloomington: Indiana University Press, 1988.

———. "The Unconscious: Language and World." In *Merleau-Ponty in Contemporary Perspective*, ed. Patrick Burke and Jan Van der Veken, 69–83. Dordrecht, Neth.: Kluwer Academic.

Doran, Michael, ed. *Conversations with Cézanne*, trans. Julie Lawrence Cochran. Berkeley: University of California Press, 2001.

Düchting, Hajo. *Paul Klee: Painting Music*. Munich: Prestel Verlag, 1997.

Dufrenne, Mikel. *The Phenomenology of Aesthetic Experience*, trans. Edward S. Casey. Evanston, Ill.: Northwestern University Press, 1973.

Eco, Umberto. *Art and Beauty in the Middle Ages*, trans. Hugh Bredin. New Haven, Conn.: Yale University Press, 1986.

———. *The History of Beauty*, trans. Alastair McEwen. New York: Rizzoli International, 2004.

———. *On Ugliness*, trans. Alastair McEwen. New York: Rizzoli International, 2007.

Elsen, Albert E. *Rodin*. New York: Museum of Modern Art, 1963.

Emerson, Ralph Waldo. *Nature*, chapter 3: "Beauty." In *Ralph Waldo Emerson: Essays and Lectures*, ed. Joel Porte, 14–19. New York: Library of America, 1983.

Evans, Fred, and Leonard Lawlor, eds. *Chiasms: Merleau-Ponty's Notion of Flesh*. Albany: State University of New York Press, 2000.

Fendrich, Laurie. "Sleeping Beauty." *Common Review* 3, no. 3 (Winter 2004).

———. *Why Painting Still Matters*. Bloomington, Ind.: Phi Delta Kappa Educational Foundation, 2000.

Ferrier, Jean-Louis. *Paul Klee*. Paris: Finest SA/Pierre Terrail Editions, 2001.

Figal, Günter. "Aesthetically Limited Reason: On Nietzsche's *The Birth of Tragedy*." In *Philosophy and Tragedy*, ed. Miguel de Beistegui and Simon Sparks, 139–51. London: Routledge, 2000.

Foster, Cheryl. "The Narrative and the Ambient in Environmental Aesthetics." In *The Aesthetics of Natural Environments*, ed. Allen Carlson and Arnold Berleant. Toronto: Broadview, 2004.

Foster, Hal. *Compulsive Beauty*. Cambridge, Mass.: MIT Press, 1993.

Fóti, Véronique M. *Heidegger and the Poets: Poiesis/Sophia/Techne*. New Jersey: Humanities, 1992.

———, ed. *Merleau-Ponty: Difference, Materiality, Painting*. New Jersey: Humanities, 1996.

Foucault, Michel. "Friendship as a Way of Life." In *Ethics: Subjectivity and Truth*, ed. Paul Rabinow. Vol. 1 of *The Essential Works of Michel Foucault: 1954–1984*. New York: New Press, 1997. Originally published as *Dits et écrits: 1954–1988*. Paris: Éditions Gallimard, 1994.

———. *The Order of Things: An Archaeology of the Human Sciences*. New York: Vintage Books, 1973. Originally published as *Les mots et les choses*. Paris: Éditions Gallimard, 1966.

———. *This Is Not a Pipe*, trans. James Harkness. Berkeley: University of California Press, 1983. Originally published as *Ceci n'est pas une pipe*. Montpellier, Fr.: Éditions Fata Morgana, 1973.

Franciscono, Marcel. *Paul Klee: His Work and Thought*. Chicago: University of Chicago Press, 1991.

Freud, Sigmund. *The Freud Reader*, ed. Peter Gay. New York: W. W. Norton, 1989.

Fry, Roger. *Cézanne: A Study of His Development*. New York: Farrar, Straus and Giroux, 1970.

Gadamer, Hans-Georg. *The Relevance of the Beautiful and Other Essays*, ed. Robert Bernasconi, trans. Nicolas Walker. Cambridge, Eng.: Cambridge University Press, 1986.

Gasquet, Joachim. *Joachim Gasquet's Cézanne: A Memoir with Conversations*, trans. Christopher Pemberton. London: Thames and Hudson, 1991.

Grohmann, Will. *Paul Klee*. New York: Harry N. Abrams, 1954.

Güse, Ernst-Gerhard. *Auguste Rodin: Drawings and Watercolors*, trans. John Gabriel and Michael Taylor. New York: Rizzoli International, 1984.

Hadreas, Peter. *In Place of the Flawed Diamond: An Investigation of Merleau-Ponty's Philosophy*. New York: Peter Lang, 1986.

Hamrick, William S. *Kindness and the Good Society*. Albany: State University of New York Press, 2002.

Hass, Lawrence. *Merleau-Ponty's Philosophy*. Bloomington: Indiana University Press, 2008.

Hass, Lawrence, and Dorothea Olkowski, eds. *Rereading Merleau-Ponty: Essays Beyond the Continental-Analytic Divide*. New York: Humanity Books, Prometheus, 2000.

Hegel, G. W. F. *Introductory Lectures on Aesthetics*, trans. Bernard Bosanquet. New York: Penguin Books, 1993.

———. *Phenomenology of Spirit,* trans. A. V. Miller. Oxford: Oxford University Press, 1977.

Heidegger, Martin. *Being and Time,* trans. John Macquarrie and Edward Robinson. New York: Harper and Row, 1962.

———. *Introduction to Metaphysics,* trans. Ralph Manheim. Garden City, N.Y.: Doubleday, 1961.

———. *Nietzsche.* Vol. 1, *The Will to Power as Art,* trans. David Farrell Krell. San Francisco: Harper Collins, 1991.

———. "On the Essence of Truth." In *Martin Heidegger: Basic Writings,* ed. David Ferrell Krell, 115–38. San Francisco: Harper San Francisco, 1977.

———. "The Origin of the Work of Art." In *Poetry, Language, Thought,* trans. Albert Hofstadter, 15–86. New York: Harper and Row, 1971. Also in *Martin Heidegger: Basic Writings,* ed. David Farrell Krell, 143–206. San Francisco: Harper San Francisco, 1977.

Herr, Lucien. *Choix d'écrits, II: Philosophie, histoire, philologie.* Paris: Éditions Redier, 1932.

Hesnard, Angelo. *L'Oeuvre de Freud et son importance pour le monde moderne.* Paris: Payot, 1960.

Hess, Thomas B. *Barnett Newman.* New York: Museum of Modern Art, 1971.

Hickey, Dave. "Enter the Dragon: On the Vernacular of Beauty." In *Uncontrollable Beauty: Toward a New Aesthetics,* ed. Bill Beckley and David Shapiro, 15–24. New York: Allworth, 1998.

Husserl, Edmund. *Cartesian Meditations: An Introduction to Phenomenology,* trans. Dorion Cairns. The Hague, Neth.: Martinus Nijhoff, 1969.

———. *The Crisis of European Sciences and Transcendental Phenomenology,* trans. David Carr. Evanston, Ill.: Northwestern University Press, 1970.

———. *Ideas Pertaining to a Pure Phenomenology and to a Phenomenological Philosophy,* First Book: "General Introduction to Pure Phenomenology," trans. F. Kersten. Dordrecht, Neth.: Kluwer Academic, 1982.

Hyppolite, Jean. *Genesis and Structure of Hegel's "Phenomenology of Spirit,"* trans. Samuel Cherniak and John Heckman. Evanston, Ill.: Northwestern University Press, 1974.

Ione, Amy. "Klee and Kandinsky: Polyphonic Painting, Chromatic Chords, and Synaesthesia." *Journal of Consciousness Studies* 11, no. 3–4 (2004).

Ione, Amy, and Christopher Tyler. "Synesthesia: Is F-Sharp Colored Violet?" *Journal of the History of Consciousness* 13, no. 1 (2004): 58–65.

Irigaray, Luce. *An Ethics of Sexual Difference,* trans. Carolyn Burke and Gillian C. Gill. Ithaca, N.Y.: Cornell University Press, 1993. Originally published as *Ethique de la difference sexuelle.* Paris: Les Éditions de Minuit, 1984.

Johnson, Galen A. "The Beautiful and the Sublime in Merleau-Ponty and Lyotard." *Chiasmi International,* 10th anniversary edition for Maurice Merleau-Ponty, 1908–2008, vol. 10, new series (2008): 207–26.

———. "The Colors of Fire: Depth and Desire in Merleau-Ponty's 'Eye and Mind.'" *Journal of the British Society for Phenomenology* 25, no. 1 (1994): 53–63.

———. "Desire and Invisibility in 'Eye and Mind': Some Remarks on Merleau-

Ponty's Spirituality." In *Merleau-Ponty in Contemporary Perspectives,* ed. Patrick Burke and Jan Van der Veken, 85–96. Dordrecht, Neth.: Kluwer Academic, 1993.

———. *Earth and Sky, History and Philosophy.* New York: Peter Lang, 1989.

———. "From Aristotle's *Poetics* to Newman's *Vir Heroicus Sublimis:* The Contest over Origins." *Epoche: A Journal for the History of Philosophy* 10, no. 1 (Fall 2005): 65–79.

———. "Inside and Outside: Ontological Considerations." In *Merleau-Ponty: Interiority and Exteriority, Psychic Life and the World,* ed. Dorothea Olkowski and James Morley, 25–34. Albany: State University of New York Press, 1999.

———. "The Invisible and the Unpresentable: Barnett Newman's Abstract Expressionism and the Aesthetics of Merleau-Ponty." *Analecta Husserliana* 75 (2002): 179–89.

———, ed. *The Merleau-Ponty Aesthetics Reader: Philosophy and Painting.* Evanston, Ill.: Northwestern University Press, 1998.

Johnson, Galen, and Michael B. Smith, eds. *Ontology and Alterity in Merleau-Ponty.* Evanston, Ill.: Northwestern University Press, 1990.

Johnson, Randall. "Skin-of-Body-Flesh-of-World: Merleau-Ponty, Pataocka, Barbaras." Unpublished manuscript.

Kagan, Andrew. *Paul Klee/Art and Music.* Ithaca, N.Y.: Cornell University Press, 1983.

Kandinsky, Wassily. *Concerning the Spiritual in Art,* trans. M. T. H. Sadler. New York: Dover, 1977.

Kant, Immanuel. *Anthropology from a Pragmatic Point of View,* trans. Robert B. Louden. Cambridge, Eng.: Cambridge University Press, 2006.

———. *Critique of Judgment,* trans. Werner S. Pluhar. Indianapolis, Ind.: Hackett, 1987.

———. *Critique of Practical Reason,* trans. Thomas Kinsmill Abbott. Meneola, N.Y.: Dover, 2004.

———. *Observations on the Feeling of the Beautiful and Sublime,* trans. John T. Goldthwait. Berkeley: University of California Press, 1960.

Kelly, Michael, ed. *Encyclopedia of Aesthetics.* 4 vols. Oxford: Oxford University Press, 1998.

Kemal, Salim, and Ivan Gaskell, eds. *Landscape, Natural Beauty, and the Arts.* Cambridge, Eng.: Cambridge University Press, 1993.

Kenaan, Hagi. *The Present Personal: The Hidden Face of Language.* New York: Columbia University Press, 2005.

Kierkegaard, Søren. *Repetition: A Venture in Experimenting Psychology* [Report by Constantin Constantius], trans. Howard V. Hong and Edna H. Hong. Princeton, N.J.: Princeton University Press, 1983.

Klee, Felix. *Paul Klee: His Life and Work in Documents,* trans. Richard Winston and Clara Winston. New York: George Braziller, 1962.

Klee, Paul. *The Diaries of Paul Klee, 1898–1918,* ed. Felix Klee, trans. from the German authorized by Felix Klee. Berkeley: University of California Press, 1964.

———. *Notebooks, Volume 1: The Thinking Eye,* trans. Ralph Mannheim. New York: George Wittenborn, 1961. Originally published as *Das Bildnerische Denken.* Basel: Benno Schwabe, 1956.

———. *Notebooks, Volume 2: The Nature of Nature.* New York: George Wittenborn, 1973. Originally published as *Unendliche Naturgeschichte.* Basel: Schwabe, Verlag, 1970.

Kleinberg-Levin, David Michael. *Before the Voice of Reason: Echoes of Responsibility in Merleau-Ponty's Ecology and Levinas's Ethics.* Albany: State University of New York Press, 2008.

———, ed. *Sites of Vision: The Discursive Construction of Sight in the History of Philosophy.* Cambridge, Mass.: MIT Press, 1997.

Krauss, Rosalind. *The Originality of the Avant-Garde and Other Modernist Myths.* Cambridge, Mass.: MIT Press, 1985.

Krell, David Ferrell, and David Wood. *Exceedingly Nietzsche: Aspects of Contemporary Nietzsche Interpretation.* New York: Routledge, 1988.

Kundera, Milan. *The Art of the Novel,* trans. Linda Asher. New York: Grove, 1988.

Lawlor, Leonard. *Challenge of Bergsonism: Phenomenology, Ontology, Ethics.* London: Continuum International, 2003.

———. *Derrida and Husserl: The Basic Problem of Phenomenology.* Bloomington: Indiana University Press, 2002.

———. "Eliminating Some Confusion: The Relation of Being and Writing in Merleau-Ponty and Derrida." In *Écart and Difference: Merleau-Ponty and Derrida on Seeing and Writing,* ed. M. C. Dillon, 71–93. New Jersey: Humanities, 1997.

———. *The Implications of Immanence: Toward a New Concept of Life.* Bronx, N.Y.: Fordham University Press, 2006.

———. *Thinking Through French Philosophy: The Being of the Question.* Bloomington: Indiana University Press, 2003.

Levinas, Emmanuel. *Otherwise Than Being, or Beyond Essence.* Boston: Martinus Nijhoff, 1981.

Lyotard, Jean-François. *Discours, figure.* Éditions Klincksiek, 1971.

———. *Lessons on the Analytic of the Sublime,* trans. Elizabeth Rottenberg. Stanford, Calif.: Stanford University Press, 1994.

———. "Newman: The Instant." In *The Lyotard Reader,* ed. Andrew Benjamin, 240–49. Cambridge, Eng.: Blackwell, 1989.

———. *Peregrinations: Law, Form, Event.* New York: Columbia University Press, 1988.

———. "Philosophy and Painting in the Age of Their Experimentation: Contribution to an Idea of Postmodernity." In *The Merleau-Ponty Aesthetics Reader: Philosophy and Painting,* ed. Galen Johnson, 323–35. Evanston, Ill.: Northwestern University Press, 1998.

———. "The Sublime and the Avant-Garde." In *The Lyotard Reader,* ed. Andrew Benjamin, 196–211. Cambridge, Eng.: Blackwell, 1989.

Marie, David. *Expérience quotidienne et expérience esthétique chez Heidegger et Merleau-Ponty: L'Inattendu.* Paris: L'Harmattan, 2002.

Maso, Carole. *Beauty Is Convulsive: The Passion of Frida Kahlo.* Washington, D.C., 2002.

Mazis, Glen A. *Earthbodies: Rediscovering Our Planetary Senses.* Albany: State University of New York Press, 2002.

———. *Emotion and Embodiment: Fragile Ontology.* New York: Peter Lang, 1993.

———. "*La Chair et L'Imaginaire:* The Developing Role of Imagination in Merleau-Ponty's Philosophy." *Philosophy Today* 32, no. 4 (Spring 1988): 30–42.

McGinn, Colin. *Ethics, Evil, and Fiction.* Oxford: Clarendon, 1997.

Ménasé, Stéphanie. *Passivité et création: Merleau-Ponty et l'art moderne.* Paris: Presses Universitaires de France, 2003.

Mercury, Jean-Yves. *La chair du visible: Paul Cézanne et Maurice Merleau-Ponty.* Paris: L'Harmattan, 2005.

Merleau-Ponty, Maurice. *Consciousness and the Acquisition of Language,* trans. Hugh J. Silverman. Evanston, Ill.: Northwestern University Press, 1973.

———. *Texts and Dialogues: On Philosophy, Politics, and Culture,* ed. Hugh J. Silverman and James Barry, Jr. New Jersey: Humanities, 1992.

Morley, James. "The Sleeping Subject: Merleau-Ponty on Dreaming." *Theory and Psychology* 9, no. 1 (1999): 89–101.

———. "The Texture of the Real: Merleau-Ponty, Imagination, and Psychopathology." In *Imagination and Its Pathologies,* ed. James Phillips and James Morley, 87–102. Cambridge, Mass.: MIT Press, 2008.

Mothersill, Mary. *Beauty Restored.* Oxford: Clarendon, 1984.

Nead, Lynda. *The Female Nude: Art, Obscenity, and Sexuality.* London: Routledge, 1992.

Newman, Barnett. "Interview with Emile de Antonio." In *Barnett Newman: Selected Writings and Interviews,* ed. John P. O'Neill, 302–8. New York: Alfred A. Knopf, 1990.

———. "The New Sense of Fate." In *Barnett Newman: Selected Writings and Interviews,* ed. John P. O'Neill. New York: Alfred A. Knopf, 1990.

———. "Remarks at the Fourth Annual Woodstock Art Conference." In *Barnett Newman: Selected Writings and Interviews,* ed. John P. O'Neill, 242–47. New York: Alfred A. Knopf, 1990.

———. "The Sublime Is Now." In *Barnett Newman: Selected Writings and Interviews,* ed. John P. O'Neill, 170–73. New York: Alfred A. Knopf, 1990.

Newman, Sasha M., ed. *Bonnard: The Late Paintings.* London: Thames and Hudson, in association with the Phillips Collection, Washington, D.C., and the Dallas Museum of Art, 1984.

Nietzsche, Friedrich. *Beyond Good and Evil,* trans. Walter Kaufmann. New York: Vintage Books, 1966.

———. *The Gay Science, with a Prelude in Rhymes and an Appendix of Songs,* trans. Walter Kaufmann. New York: Vintage Books, 1974.

———. *The Genealogy of Morals.* In *The Birth of Tragedy and The Genealogy of Morals,* trans. Francis Golffing. New York: Doubleday, 1956.

———. *Thus Spoke Zarathustra.* In *The Portable Nietzsche,* ed. Walter Kaufmann. New York: Penguin Books, 1954.

———. *Twilight of the Idols.* In *The Portable Nietzsche,* ed. Walter Kaufmann. New York: Penguin Books, 1954.

Norton, Robert E. *The Beautiful Soul: Aesthetic Morality in the Eighteenth Century.* Ithaca, N.Y.: Cornell University Press, 1995.

Nussbaum, Martha C. *The Fragility of Goodness: Luck and Ethics in Greek Tragedy and Philosophy.* Cambridge, Eng.: Cambridge University Press, 1986.

———. *Poetic Justice: The Literary Imagination and Public Life.* Boston: Beacon, 1995.

———. *Upheavals of Thought: The Intelligence of the Emotions.* Cambridge, Eng.: Cambridge University Press, 2001.

Nye, David E. *American Technological Sublime.* Cambridge, Mass.: MIT Press, 1994.

Olkowski, Dorothea. *Gilles Deleuze and the Ruin of Representation.* Berkeley: University of California Press, 1999.

———. *The Universal (In the Realm of the Sensible): Beyond Continental Philosophy.* New York: Columbia University Press, 2007.

Olkowski, Dorothea, and James Morley, eds. *Merleau-Ponty: Interiority and Exteriority, Psychic Life and the World.* Albany: State University of New York Press, 1999.

Olkowski, Dorothea, and Gail Weiss, eds. *Feminist Interpretations of Maurice Merleau-Ponty.* State College: Pennsylvania State University Press, 2006.

Paris, Reine-Marie. *Camille: The Life of Camille Claudel, Rodin's Muse and Mistress,* trans. Liliane Emery Tuck. New York: Henry Holt, 1988.

Partsch, Susanna. *Paul Klee: 1879–1940.* London: Taschen, 2003.

Petzet, Heinrich Wiegand. *Encounters and Dialogues with Martin Heidegger, 1929–1976,* trans. Parvis Emad and Kenneth Maly. Chicago: University of Chicago Press, 1993.

Pietersma, Henry. *Phenomenological Epistemology.* Oxford: Oxford University Press, 2000.

Plant, Margaret. *Paul Klee: Figures and Faces.* London: Thames and Hudson, 1978.

Plato. *Meno,* trans. G. M. A. Grube. In *Five Dialogues: Euthyphro, Apology, Crito, Meno, Phaedo,* ed. Donald J. Zeyl. Indianapolis, Ind.: Hackett, 1981.

———. *Plato's Republic,* trans. G. M. A. Grube. Indianapolis, Ind.: Hackett, 1974.

———. *Symposium,* trans. Alexander Nehamas and Paul Woodruff. Indianapolis, Ind.: Hackett, 1989.

Ragland-Sullivan, Ellie. *Jacques Lacan and the Philosophy of Psychoanalysis.* Urbana: University of Illinois Press, 1986.

"Regarding Beauty: A View of the Late 20th Century." Cantz/Hirshhorn Museum and Sculpture Garden, Washington, D.C., 1999.

Rewald, John. *Paul Cézanne,* trans. Margaret H. Liebman. London: Spring Books, 1959.

———, ed. *Paul Cézanne Letters,* trans. Seymour Hacker. New York: Hacker Art Books, 1984.

———. *Paul Cézanne: The Watercolors—A Catalog Raisonné.* Boston: Little, Brown, 1983.

Ricoeur, Paul. *History and Truth,* trans. Charles A. Kelbley. Evanston, Ill.: Northwestern University Press, 1965. Originally published as *Histoire et vérité.* Paris: Éditions Seuil, 1955.

Rilke, Rainer Maria. *Auguste Rodin,* trans. Daniel Slager. New York: Archipelago Books, 2004.

———. *Duino Elegies,* trans. Stephen Cohn. Evanston, Ill.: Northwestern University Press, 1989.

———. *Letters on Cézanne,* ed. Clara Rilke, trans. Joel Agee. New York: Fromm International, 1985.

Robinson, Jenefer. *Deeper Than Reason: Emotion and Its Role in Literature, Music, and Art.* Oxford: Clarendon, 2005.

Rodin, Auguste. *Art: Conversations with Paul Gsell,* trans. Jacques de Caso and Patricia B. Sanders. Berkeley: University of California Press, 1984. Originally published as *L'Art: Entretiens reúnis par Paul Gsell.* 1911. Paris: Éditions Gallimard, 1953.

Rosenberg, Harold. *Barnett Newman.* New York: Harry N. Abrams, 1994.

Saint Aubert, Emmanuel de. "Conscience et expression chez Merleau-Ponty: L'Apport du cours inédit sur le monde sensible et le monde de l'expression." *Chiasmi International,* 10th anniversary edition for Maurice Merleau-Ponty, 1908–2008, vol. 10, new series (2008): 85–106.

———. *Du lien des êtres aux éléments de l'être: Merleau-Ponty au tournant des années 1945–1951.* Paris: Librairie Philosophique J. Vrin, 2004.

———. "La 'promiscuité': Merleau-Ponty à la recherche d'une psychanalyse ontologique." *Archives de Philosophie* 69 (2006): 11–35.

———. "Le mystère de la chair: Merleau-Ponty et Gabriel Marcel." *Studia Phaenomenologica* 3 (2003): 73–106.

———. *Le scénario cartésian: Recherches sur la formation et la cohérence de l'intention philosophique de Merleau-Ponty.* Paris: Librairie Philosophique J. Vrin, 2005.

———. "L'Incarnation change tout: Merleau-Ponty critique de la 'théologie explicative.'" *Archives de Philosophie* 71, no. 3 (Autumn 2008): 371–405.

———. *Vers une ontologie indirecte: Sources et enjeux critiques de l'appel à l'ontologie chez Merleau-Ponty.* Paris: Librairie Philosophique J. Vrin, 2006.

Santayana, George. *The Sense of Beauty: Being the Outlines of Aesthetic Theory.* 1896; Cambridge, Mass.: MIT Press, 1988.

Sartre, Jean-Paul. *Being and Nothingness: A Phenomenological Essay on Ontology,* trans. Hazel E. Barnes. New York: Simon and Schuster Pocket Books, 1956. Originally published as *L'Être et le néant: Essai d'ontologie phénoménologique.* Paris: Éditions Gallimard, 1943.

Sartwell, Crispin. *Six Names of Beauty.* New York: Routledge, 2004.

Scarry, Elaine. *On Beauty and Being Just.* Princeton, N.J.: Princeton University Press, 1999.

Schelling, F. W. J. *The Abyss of Freedom/Ages of the World,* trans. Judith Norman. Ann Arbor: University of Michigan Press, 1997.

———. *The Philosophy of Art,* ed. and trans. Douglas W. Stott. Minneapolis: University of Minnesota Press, 1989.

Schiff, Gert. "Klee's Array of Angels." *Artforum* 25, no. 9 (May 1982): 126–33.

Schneider, Gary. *Genetic Self-Portrait.* Syracuse, N.Y.: Light, Work, 1999.

Schuller, Gunther. *Seven Studies on Themes of Paul Klee.* London: Universal Edition, 1962.

Shapiro, Gary. *Archeologies of Vision: Foucault and Nietzsche on Seeing and Saying.* Chicago: University of Chicago Press, 2003.

———. *Earthwards: Robert Smithson and Art After Babel.* Berkeley: University of California Press, 1997.

Shapiro, Meyer. *Paul Cézanne.* New York: Harry N. Abrams, 1988.

Shiff, Richard. *Cézanne and the End of Impressionism: A Study of the Theory, Technique, and Critical Evaluation of Modern Art.* Chicago: University of Chicago Press, 1984.

Sidlauskas, Susan. "Emotion, Color, Cézanne (The Portraits of Hortense)." *Nineteenth-Century Art Worldwide: A Journal of Nineteenth-Century Visual Culture* 3, no. 2 (Autumn 2004).

Silverman, Hugh J. "Cézanne's Mirror Stage." In *The Merleau-Ponty Aesthetics Reader: Philosophy and Painting,* ed. Galen Johnson, 262–77. Evanston, Ill.: Northwestern University Press, 1998.

———, ed. *Lyotard: Philosophy, Politics, and the Sublime.* New York: Routledge, 2002.

———, ed. *Philosophy and Desire.* London: Routledge, 2000.

———. *Textualities: Between Hermeneutics and Deconstruction.* London: Routledge, 1994.

Silverman, Hugh J., and Gary E. Aylesworth, eds. *The Textual Sublime: Deconstruction and Its Difference.* Albany: State University of New York Press, 1990.

Stack, George. *Nietzsche and Emerson: An Elective Affinity.* Athens: Ohio University Press, 1992.

Temkin, Ann. "Barnett Newman on Exhibition." In *Barnett Newman,* catalog of the exhibition "Barnett Newman," Philadelphia Museum of Art, March 24–July 7, 2002, and Tate Modern, London, September 19, 2002–January 5, 2003. Philadelphia: Philadelphia Museum of Art, 2002.

Toadvine, Ted. "Gestalts and Refrains: On the Musical Structure of Nature." *Environmental Philosophy* 2, no. 2 (Fall 2005): 61–71.

———. "The Melody of Life and the Motif of Philosophy." *Chiasmi International* 7 (2005): 263–79.

———. *Merleau-Ponty's Philosophy of Nature.* Evanston, Ill.: Northwestern University Press, 2009.

Toadvine, Ted, and Charles S. Brown, eds. *Eco-Phenomenology: Back to the Earth Itself.* Albany: State University of New York Press, 2003.

Treier, Daniel J., Mark Husbands, and Roger Lundin. *The Beauty of God: Theology and the Arts.* Downers Grove, Ill.: IVP Academic, 2007.

Verdi, Richard. *Klee and Nature.* New York: Rizzoli International, 1985.

Waldenfels, Bernard. "The Paradox of Expression." In *Chiasms: Merleau-Ponty's Notion of Flesh,* ed. Fred Evans and Leonard Lawlor. Albany: State University of New York Press, 2000.

Ward, Patricia, ed. *Baudelaire and the Poetics of Modernity.* Nashville, Tenn.: Vanderbilt University Press, 2001.

Watson, Stephen H. *Crescent Moon over the Rational: Philosophical Interpretations of Paul Klee.* Palo Alto, Calif.: Stanford University Press, 2009.

———. "Gadamer, Aesthetic Modernism, and the Rehabilitation of Allegory: The Relevance of Paul Klee." *Research in Phenomenology* 34 (2004): 45–68.

———. "Heidegger, Paul Klee, and the Origin of the Work of Art." *Review of Metaphysics* 60, no. 2 (December 2006): 327–58.

———. *In the Shadow of Phenomenology: Writings After Merleau-Ponty I.* London: Continuum International, 2009.

———. "On the Withdrawal of the Beautiful: Adorno and Merleau-Ponty's Readings of Paul Klee." *Chiasmi International* 5 (2003): 201–20.

———. *Tradition(s) II: Hermeneutics, Ethics, and the Dispensation of the Good.* Bloomington: Indiana University Press, 2001.

Wechsler, Judith. *Cézanne in Perspective.* Englewood Cliffs, N.J.: Prentice-Hall, 1975.

Weiss, Gail, ed. *Body Images: Embodiment as Intercorporeality.* London: Routledge, 1998.

———. *Refiguring the Ordinary.* Bloomington: Indiana University Press, 2008.

Whitehead, Alfred North. Chapter 17, "Beauty," and chapter 18, "Truth and Beauty." In *Adventures of Ideas.* New York: Free Press, 1933.

Wolf, Naomi. *The Beauty Myth: How Images of Beauty Are Used Against Women.* New York: Doubleday Anchor Books, 1991.

Young, Julian. *Heidegger's Philosophy of Art.* Cambridge, Eng.: Cambridge University Press, 2001.

Index

About the Author

Galen A. Johnson is an honors professor of philosophy at the University of Rhode Island, director of the University of Rhode Island Center for the Humanities, and general secretary of the International Merleau-Ponty Circle.